LIBRARY C

MW01137327

Edited by Mark A. Noll and Heath W. Carter

The LIBRARY OF RELIGIOUS BIOGRAPHY is a series of original biographies on important religious figures throughout American and British history.

The authors are well-known historians, each a recognized authority in the period of religious history in which his or her subject lived and worked. Grounded in solid research of both published and archival sources, these volumes link the lives of their subjects — not always thought of as "religious" persons — to the broader cultural contexts and religious issues that surrounded them. Each volume includes a bibliographical essay and an index to serve the needs of students, teachers, and researchers.

Marked by careful scholarship yet free of footnotes and academic jargon, the books in this series are well-written narratives meant to be *read* and *enjoyed* as well as studied.

LIBRARY OF RELIGIOUS BIOGRAPHY

The Religious Life of Robert E. Lee

R. David Cox

*For Jack,
with warm wishes
from President [...]
college and last home
town.

Roland Cox
Lexington
Baccalaureate Day.
May 24, 2017*

WILLIAM B. EERDMANS PUBLISHING COMPANY

GRAND RAPIDS, MICHIGAN

Wm. B. Eerdmans Publishing Co.
2140 Oak Industrial Drive NE, Grand Rapids, Michigan 49505
www.eerdmans.com

23 22 21 20 19 18 17   1 2 3 4 5 6 7

ISBN 978-0-8028-7482-5

Library of Congress Cataloging-in-Publication Data

Names: Cox, R. David, author.
Title: The religious life of Robert E. Lee / R. David Cox.
Description: Grand Rapids : Eerdmans Publishing Co., 2017. |
    Series: Library of religious biography |
    Includes bibliographical references and index.
Identifiers: LCCN 2016050798 | ISBN 9780802874825 (pbk. : alk. paper)
Subjects: LCSH: Lee, Robert E. (Robert Edward), 1807–1870—Religion. |
    Generals—Confederate States of America—Biography. |
    United States—History—Civil War, 1861–1865—Biography.
Classification: LCC E467.1.L4 C77 2017 | DDC 973.7/3092 [B] —dc23
    LC record available at https://lccn.loc.gov/2016050798

In thanksgiving for Don and Billie

Contents

Contents

Contents

Foreword

In his new biography, *American Ulysses: A Life of Ulysses S. Grant* (Random House, 2016), Ronald White supplies telling details about a scene very well known to anyone with even basic knowledge of American history. The details flesh out the conversation between Grant and Robert E. Lee that took place as the commanding generals of the Union and the Confederacy met to arrange the surrender of Lee's Army of Northern Virginia, which effectively ended the Civil War. It was Palm Sunday, April 9, 1865, at the home of Wilmer McLean who had moved to out-of-the-way Appomattox Court House, Virginia, after his earlier residence near Manassas, Virginia, had been destroyed four years earlier during the First Battle of Bull Run. The visuals of that momentous scene have been reproduced many times—Grant in a dusty private's blouse with muddy boots and no sword, Lee in a new uniform with full dress regalia complemented by a jeweled sword. Also well fixed in American lore is Grant's magnanimity toward the defeated Confederates—granting a full parole to all officers and men, and allowing the Confederates to leave with their horses so as to assist with spring plowing.

A particularly illuminating detail added by biographer White concerns the conversation that took place before the business of surrender got under way. After shaking hands, Grant and Lee reminisced about their service in the Mexican War where Grant remembered having met Lee once, but also told the Confederate general that he, no doubt, did not remember, since Grant was much younger and in a junior position of responsibility. Then comes the telling detail. Grant seemed eager to continue reminiscing about their joint service in that earlier war, but Lee brought the conversation up short by reminding the Union general about the purpose of their meeting. In a flash we glimpse the humanity of two individuals who so easily appear as only stock iconic figures.

Good biographers of well-known figures must of course present well-known factual information. But they also push their research into little-used or neglected sources in order to reveal fresh information, and therefore provide fresh insight about their subjects. White's excellent biography performs that service for many aspects of Grant's life, including the religious beliefs and practices that very few earlier biographers had noticed. As it happens, Grant was a life-long Methodist who enjoyed a warm relationship with the minister of the Methodist church in Galena, Illinois, that he attended with his wife before the Civil War began. Although he did not go to church regularly during his years as president in Washington D.C., Grant did faithfully serve a Methodist congregation there as a trustee and he did give special privileges to Quakers who took the lead in humane programs for Native Americans. According to White, Grant's sensitivity to Christian values, which few historians have noted, may explain as much about his even-tempered, sagacious character as his supposed battle with alcoholism, which has been the subject of endless historical speculation.

R. David Cox performs a similar service for another well-known figure in his outstanding book on the religious life of Grant's most capable military foe, Robert E. Lee. Historians have often noted Lee's general Christian convictions and his deference to traditional Christian practices. But until the appearance of this deeply researched and carefully nuanced study, no one has so capably explored the length, depth, and breadth of Robert E. Lee's Christian faith. Cox's portrait does pause to flesh out what others have sketched before—Lee's solicitous religious concern for his wife and children, his deep trust in Providence, and his remarkable humanity as he turned from waging war to acts of reconciliation. Those acts included sacrificial service as a college president, humility as an honored war hero, and especially a willingness to accept Confederate defeat. Cox also skillfully illuminates Lee's complicated stance on slavery and race. As a Virginia patrician and someone committed paternalistically to the welfare of his slaves and then former slaves, Lee on many occasions responded to the basic humanity of African Americans. Yet as a man of his time and place, he also accepted the racist stereotypes that pervaded white American culture of his day.

On all of these matters, Cox's deep research provides an unusually full portrait. The greatest merit of the book, however, is to take the measure of Lee's life as an Episcopalian. What it meant for Lee to embrace Virginia Episcopalianism cannot be equated with anything modern, whether in the Episcopal Church in the United States of America or in contemporary Anglican alternatives--or even with the Anglican culture of his parent's colonial America. It was, instead, a religion situated between popular appeal and elite privilege, the Bible and the Prayer Book, respect for bishops and empowerment of laity. As few other historical accounts, this book explains how that tradition had developed in the early decades of the new republic and—uniquely—why it holds the key to "The Religious Life of Robert E. Lee."

A last reward for readers of this well written, accessible biography comes right at the end, where the author unpacks yet another revealing detail about what happened at Appomattox Court House when Lee met Grant at the end of the nation's great civil war.

MARK A. NOLL

Preface

Picking their way around the hulks of burned-out buildings one late spring Sunday in 1865, members of St. Paul's Episcopal Church in Richmond, Virginia, headed to worship. Their city lay in ruins, the result of a conflagration set by retreating Confederate troops trying to prevent supplies from falling into the hands of the hated Yankee invaders. Like so much of the war, the fire spread out of control, and accomplished nothing except destruction; the Army of Northern Virginia surrendered just days later at Appomattox. Soon after, the Yankees nabbed Confederate President Jefferson Davis, who had last been seen in public rushing out of that very church before Union troops reached the city. Dreams of Southern independence lay in ashes. The Civil War, the War between the States, was effectively over.

Still, the spire atop their Greek Revival building rose dramatically over the devastation, as did, just across Ninth Street, Thomas Jefferson's pillared state capitol that for four years had served as the seat of the Confederacy.

That day was a Communion Sunday, the occasional celebration of the Lord's Supper now more commonly called the Holy Eucharist. Their rector, or pastor, the Reverend Dr. Charles Minnigerode, had concluded his sermon, said the prayers that consecrated the bread and wine, and beckoned the congregation forward to receive the sacrament. From the back of the church strode an African American, who knelt down at the communion rail. Everyone froze. For as long as anyone could remember, black "servants" had shared in the Lord's Supper. They, too, were brothers and sisters in Christ even if they were, in this life, slaves: the bishop of Virginia, William Meade, had declared as much. He even remembered the day when a slave belonging to George Washington's nephew came forward, and his master knelt down with him, "feeling no doubt that one God made them and one God redeemed them."[1] But that was long before, in another church, in a less tumultuous era; and slaves would not have had the effrontery of going first. Mr. Minnigerode stood stock-still, the story went, as members of the congregation remained fixed in their pews.

From the left side of the church, a tall, bewhiskered man strode forward, his worn gray coat testifying that he had been a Confederate soldier. Though shorn of its insignia, the coat needed no stars to identify its wearer to the congregation. General Robert Edward Lee dropped to his knees at the altar rail, near the black communicant, and bade the rector to proceed. With the hard ice of racism and resentment broken, the congregation walked forward to receive the sacrament that unites humans in fellowship with God and with each other.

That is one possible interpretation of the event—if the incident happened at all. It may not have. The story first appeared in print forty long years after the event supposedly occurred, and from only one source, an unreconstructed Confederate officer from West Virginia. He did not hail Lee for promoting harmony and unity following the most divisive struggle in American history. On the contrary, he praised Lee for reasserting white supremacy against Federal authorities who, he claimed, had persuaded the African American to exploit the new regime that they were imposing.[2]

From the moment Lee decided to side with the South, he became a polarizing figure. So he remains today. To some, admirers and detractors alike, he symbolizes the Old South either at its best or at its worst, and its attitudes on secession and slavery (which Lee largely opposed) and states' rights (which he largely supported). To others, he became an American hero who in his latter years worked for peace and reconciliation. The stories of Lee provide each side with material to vindicate its position. Sometimes the same story can be used to justify totally opposite conclusions, such as the alleged incident at St. Paul's has done.

Myths, as a literary form, are not stories that are necessarily false. Rather, they convey, at their heart, an embedded understanding of the past or its patterns. Legends, those tales of history, may be embellished by repeated tellings, but they frequently hold at their core a kernel of fact. The myths and legends that portray Lee as a person of faith hold more than a morsel of accuracy. Nearly everyone who has written about

Lee recognizes that he was a person of religious devotion. But no author has systematically considered the substance of his faith. On one side are historians who recognize that he was a religious person but do not plumb the depths of that characterization and often rely on inaccuracies that accrue in myths and legends. On the other side are those who use his religious life to burnish the halo of "Saint Bob." Theirs is an exercise not so much in history or theology as in hagiography, an endeavor that Lee surely would have repudiated.[3]

This book strives to understand what Lee believed, what were the roots of his belief, how his faith developed from those roots, how he expressed it in the context of his family and the churches he attended, and perhaps most significantly, why he made some of his most crucial decisions. It also seeks to trace Lee's religious growth, the process of transformation central to his church's understanding of the spiritual life.

Lee was not a religious thinker. He never formally studied theology, much less attended seminary. He was not a preacher, though he heard many a sermon and often commented on them and those who preached them. He was not a theologian but a soldier. His beliefs were far more practical than speculative. He was neither original in his thinking nor unusual in his convictions. He was an evangelical Protestant Virginia Episcopalian of the first half of the nineteenth century, a description that defines a particular religious type. Understanding that type, and even more, comprehending its meaning for Lee's life, helps to explain the motivations that define his character and actions. If one must not make too much of Lee as a student of faith, neither must one make too little of him as a person of faith, for faith was central to his character—so central that it redirected his life, especially in defeat.

Lee commanded tremendous respect in his day, from many in the South and some in the North. He was an accomplished soldier who served his cause well, whatever one may think of that cause. But his cause lost. Accomplishment alone cannot account for the standing that Lee attained. Accomplishment earns respect; character wins admiration.

Indeed, Lee came to be venerated soon after his death. The trustees of the college where he died in office as president immediately renamed it Washington and Lee University. The church in Lexington, Virginia, where he worshiped, and where he spent his last public afternoon in a difficult meeting, honored him with a new edifice and eventually came to be known as R. E. Lee Memorial Episcopal Church.

At one point Lee was considered the paramount saint of the South. But in the biblical sense, what makes a saint is not miraculous acts or a heroic death. Rather, a saint is one of God's faithful people, consecrated to God and joined to Christ. A "saint" is, most simply, a Christian.[4]

Robert E. Lee was many things: soldier, engineer, college president, husband, father, gentleman, Virginia aristocrat, a member by birth and marriage into the commonwealth's most prominent families. He was also a person of deep Christian convictions.

These convictions permeated Lee's life and actions, but he articulated them most clearly in personal letters, especially letters to his family and, above all, to his wife. Always a private man—some thought him aloof or remote, the "marble man"—he never bared his soul to anyone. Still, his letters reveal the development of a theology that was at once his own yet also broadly characteristic of Virginia Episcopalians and of American Protestants of that era.

And how the Lees wrote letters! The Virginia Historical Society (VHS) holds thousands of them—original manuscripts, copies, or letter books—with hundreds more at Washington and Lee University and the Library of Congress, with many at the Library of Virginia. More continue to appear. The Lee Family Digital Archive (LFDA) is also making correspondence available online. This work has benefited from recent discoveries, notably of two trunks full of some four thousand papers held by Mary Custis Lee, the general's oldest daughter, found in an Alexandria bank in 2002 and now at VHS, and of recent acquisitions by Washington and Lee.

Fortunately for readers of these manuscripts, Robert E. Lee retained the beautiful penmanship he developed as a child. Not so his wife, whose hand, never as graceful as Lee's, shows over the decades the increasing effects of arthritis. As for spelling, Lee retained a lifelong preference for the British style that utilized the letter *u* in words like "favour," which Noah Webster taught Americans to delete, and kept a superfluous *l* in naming his famous horse, Traveller. While his children favored Webster's style, they varied in their punctuation. To give a flavor of the era, direct quotations in this book generally reproduce their authors' use, and have retained the original spelling, punctuation, and underlining for emphasis. Unless otherwise indicated, all emphasis exists in the original documents.

Lee's faith evolved over the six decades of his life. It had its foundation in his family, which brought their religion from England even as it had already been established in Virginia. For that reason, the nature of the Anglican tradition becomes a vital component of his story. Lee's beliefs continued to grow from that basis as years went by. He exhibited the broader influences of American Protestantism, particularly of evangelicalism, while his own denomination assimilated at least some of them as well: These, too, are part of the story. So while Lee's convictions were in one sense uniquely his, and uniquely lived, they developed within the wider context of nineteenth-century American religion. The spiritual life of Robert E. Lee, then, fits within the vast mosaic of American religion, even as it shaped his contribution to American history.

A Note about the Chapter Titles

Chapter titles are taken from the Book of Common Prayer (BCP). The first American BCP of 1879, which Lee used, did not initially have page numbers, so citations will give the section number and its title. Spelling, capitalization, and punctuation as in original.

1. **"All Our Doings Being Ordered by Thy Governance"**
   The chapter title comes from "A Collect for Grace," BCP 1789.

2. **"A Goodly Heritage"**
   The chapter title comes from Ps. 16:7, BCP 1789, §29, the Psalter.

3. **"A House Divided"**
   The chapter title comes from Luke 11:17 KJV, Gospel for the Third Sunday in Lent, BCP 1789, §12.

4. **"Who Setteth the Solitary in Families"**
   The chapter title comes from Ps. 68:6 KJV.

5. **"To Illuminate All Bishops"**
   The chapter title comes from BCP 1789, the Great Litany, appended to §10, Evening Prayer.

6. **"With the Sign of the Cross"**
   The chapter title comes from BCP 1789, §14, the Ministration of Public Baptism of Infants.

7. **"To Have and to Hold"**
The chapter title comes from BCP 1789, §19, the Form of Solemnization of Matrimony.

8. **"Christ's Faithful Soldier and Servant"**
The chapter title comes from the prayer said over a newly baptized child, BCP 1789, §15, Public Baptism.

9. **"This Our Bounden Duty and Service"**
The chapter title comes from BCP 1789, §14, Holy Communion.

10. **"That, as We Grow in Age, We May Grow in Grace"**
The chapter title comes from BCP 1789, §28, Forms of Prayers to Be Used in Families (Morning Prayer).

11. **"That He May Continue Thine Forever"**
The chapter title comes from BCP 1789, §19, the Order for Confirmation, from the prayer said by the bishop: "Defend, O Lord, this thy child [or, *this thy Servant*] with thy heavenly grace; that *he* may continue thine for ever; and daily increase in thy Holy Spirit more and more, until *he* come unto thy everlasting kingdom. Amen."

12. **"Of the Traditions of the Church"**
The chapter title comes from Articles of Religion 34, BCP 1789.

13. **"Whose Never-Failing Providence Ordereth All Things"**
The chapter title comes from the Collect for the Eighth Sunday after Trinity, BCP 1789, §13.

14. **"Under the Protection of Thy Good Providence"**
The chapter title comes from the Collect for the Second Sunday after Trinity, BCP 1789, §13.

15. **"Help Thy Servants, Whom Thou Hast Redeemed"**
The chapter title comes from *Te Deum Laudamus*, BCP 1789, §9, Morning Prayer.

16. **"Scatter Thou the Peoples That Delight in War"**
The chapter title comes from Ps. 68:30, BCP 1789, §30, the Psalter.

17. **"Who Teacheth My Hands to War"**
    The chapter title comes from Ps. 144:1, BCP 1789, §30, the Psalter (KJV). Freeman alleges that this page was the most thumbed in Lee's "field Testament" (which he identifies in a footnote as Lee's Book of Common Prayer) that he said he had seen: Stuart W. Smith, ed., *Douglas Southall Freeman on Leadership* (Shippensburg, PA: White Mane Publishing, 1990), pp. 132 and 133n6. The whereabouts of Lee's volume are unknown.

18. **"In the Bond of Peace, and in Righteousness of Life"**
    The chapter title comes from BCP 1789, §9, Morning Prayer, "A Prayer for All Conditions of Men."

19. **"To Put Away the Leaven of Malice"**
    The chapter title comes from BCP 1789, Collect for the First Sunday after Easter, §12.

20. **"The Mouth of the Deceitful Is Opened upon Me"**
    The chapter title comes from Ps. 109:2; BCP 1789, §29.

21. **"Do Now Rest from Their Labors"**
    The chapter title comes from BCP 1789, §23, the Order for the Burial of the Dead.

Family Names and Relationships

Parents: Henry Lee III ("Light-Horse Harry") (1756–1818)
Ann* Hill Carter Lee (1773–1829)

Siblings: Henry Lee IV ("Black-Horse Harry") (1787–1837)
Anne Kinloch Lee Marshall (1800–1864)
Charles Carter Lee (1798–1871)
Sidney Smith Lee (1802–1869)
Mildred Lee Childe (1811–1856)
    Son: Edward Lee Childe

Wife: Mary Anna Randolph Custis Lee (1808–1873)

Children: George Washington Custis Lee (Boo) (1832–1913)
Mary Custis Lee (Daughter) (1835–1918)
William Henry Fitzhugh Lee (Rooney) (1837–91)
Anne Carter Lee (Annie) (1839–1862)
Eleanor Agnes Lee (Agnes) (1841–1873)
Robert Edward Lee Jr. (Rob) (1843–1914)
Mildred Childe Lee (Precious Life) (1846–1905)

Parents-in-law: George Washington Parke Custis (1781–1857)
Mary Lee Fitzhugh Custis (Molly) (1788–1853)

---

* Robert's mother's name is variously spelled with and without an *e*. This book will use "Ann," as she is identified on her niche at Lee Chapel at Washington and Lee University.

CHAPTER 1

"All Our Doings Being Ordered by Thy Governance"

~

September 18, 1865: A gray-suited gentleman in a brown hat, gray bearded and erect atop his steel-gray horse, rode quietly along the valley road through the fields of Rockbridge County, Virginia. Ever since leaving his temporary home in Powhatan County, he had journeyed through towns and countryside badly damaged in the brutal civil war that had ended only five months before. None was as bleak as what he saw on the outskirts of the little town of Lexington, his destination. To his right, he passed the scorched hulk of the Virginia Military Institute (VMI), burned by Federal troops under General David Hunter in retribution for the young VMI cadets whipping the Yankees in the Battle of New Market. A short distance farther, he could see the charred remains of the home of John Letcher, who, as governor of Virginia, oversaw the state's secession from the Union not five years earlier. On the hill above it, Washington College stood, forlornly, its statue of the nation's first president still atop its main hall, presiding over a dismal scene of broken glass and shattered buildings. The town fared hardly better. Though the area had been largely unionist before secession, it had seized the frenzy of Southern independence and sent its men into battle, not least of which was the VMI instructor Thomas Jonathan Jackson, soon to be known as "Stonewall." For its change of loyalty, the region paid dearly. Bodies of Jackson; his aide "Sandie" Pendleton, son of the local Episcopal priest who became a Confederate general; and dozens of others lay beneath tombstones in the local cemetery.

As horse and rider climbed the hill on Main Street toward the town center, a Confederate veteran realized who they were. He let out a shout: Robert E. Lee, his former commanding general, had come to town.

Word quickly spread. Allan McDonald, a young teenager who with his mother and six siblings had vainly fled to Lexington for shelter, ran to tell his brother, who immediately raced to the window and, years later, vividly recalled the scene. The former general had removed all military insignia from his old uniform, the three stars on each collar, the Confederate buttons. "Slowly he passed, raising his brown slouch hat to those on the pavement who recognized him and not appearing conscious that he more than anybody else was the object of attention." Allan, having made himself presentable to the famous newcomer, dashed to the Lexington Hotel to watch him dismount from his horse, Traveller. He returned home with a souvenir plucked from Traveller's tail that, he announced, he would preserve so his wife could wear it in her breastpin. He was but the first of many to rob Traveller of his hair.[1] Robert E. Lee had arrived at his final post, on an assignment he believed had been ordered by God.

*   *   *

How different his ride to Lexington was from the one he made to Alexandria, on a balmy April 21, 1861, when Lee and his daughter, Mary Custis, went to church. Enslaved drivers had brought their carriage to the door of Arlington House, the mansion his father-in-law had built high on a hill on the Virginia side of the Potomac River, overlooking Washington, DC, for the nine-mile trip to Christ Church. As a family, they observed the Sabbath, sometimes at the little chapel on the estate, at other times in their parlor, but often at the old family parish. None was more regular in worship than Colonel Lee himself. At whatever post the army assigned him or wherever he traveled on temporary duty, unless prevented by military or family obligation, Lee found his way to church.

Lee held his faith dear. By 1861 he had gleaned considerable experience of American religion in general, and of his own Episcopal Church in particular. He knew his Bible and his church's Book of Common Prayer. He followed developments through church publications. He remained on familiar terms with bishops and other clergy. He developed an understanding, a theology, that may not have been broad—he never showed any interest in the mysteries of the Trinity, for example—but was definitely deep. It was also practical, for his theological perspective helped him cope with challenges and tribulations and shaped his perspective on events of the day, including those besetting his nation at the very moment it was dissolving.

Lee's religious life essentially began at the church to which they were driving. Though probably baptized where he was born, at the old Lee estate of Stratford Hall on Virginia's Northern Neck, he had spent but three years there when his family had to move to Alexandria. They lived first within a block of Christ Church, then some five blocks away on Oronoco Street. Sunday by Sunday, the family could walk to the old brick edifice. During the long services, Lee as a boy could glance at the pew once owned by George Washington, on whose staff Lee's father had served during the Revolution, and whom the elder Lee had eulogized as "first in war, first in peace, first in the hearts of his countrymen." On some Sundays, young Lee might see members of Washington's family, including, seated in the gallery, the man who was at once the general's step-grandson, adopted son, and namesake: George Washington Parke Custis. Perhaps he spotted, too, Custis's only child, a girl about his own age, Mary Anna Randolph Custis, never dreaming—or did he?—that she would become his wife.

As a youngster, Lee came to know the man in the pulpit. William Meade became Christ Church's new rector (as Episcopalians call their pastor) at the same time the Lees moved into the neighborhood. The dynamic young cleric began immediately to challenge the worldly temper he found in his new congregation. He also established a direct connection with Robert Lee, and all the children of his parish, who recited to him their catechism, their church's basic teachings about the Christian faith. Meade never forgot that experience. Nor did Lee.

That fine April day, the two Lees, father and daughter, rode to church along the Potomac River road. The gentle temperatures and gloriously blooming trees of the Virginia springtime belied the foul mood of the nation. It had been a disconcerting week. Even the weather had been odd. The previous Wednesday, temperatures in Washington never varied from a precise but chilly 42 degrees, morning, afternoon, and night.[2] Now the weather seemed to right itself.

But dark clouds of a different sort enshrouded them. The previous Sunday, as they left Christ Church, the Lees had learned that Fort Sumter had fallen. The US Army outpost in Charleston, South Carolina, had surrendered after several days of ferocious bombardment by the seceded state's troops. "Poor General Anderson!" Lee remarked of the commander, Robert Anderson, whom he knew through the close circles of the army. "He was a determined man, & I know he held out to the last."[3]

Then, on Thursday, Lee was summoned from Arlington to Washington to meet Francis Preston Blair, a seasoned power broker, at the home of Blair's son, Montgomery, who was Abraham Lincoln's postmaster general. At the president's behest, the senior Blair exhorted Lee to accept command of the military forces of the United States of America. Lee declined, then walked across the street to the War Department. There he discussed the offer with his, and the military's, commanding officer, General Winfield Scott, "Old Fuss 'n Feathers," who first earned his fame in the War of 1812. Colonel Lee, who had distinguished himself on Scott's staff in the war with Mexico, reiterated his refusal. A special convention in Richmond was at that moment considering Virginia's secession from the Union, and if it left, Lee was determined not to raise his sword against his native state. Only when Lee arrived back at Arlington did he learn that the convention in Richmond had indeed voted, the day before, to secede.

On Friday, Virginia troops began seizing Federal military complexes in Harpers Ferry and Norfolk. In Baltimore, a mob of Southern sympathizers attacked Massachusetts soldiers traveling toward Washington to defend the capital. A friend of Lee's wife had died in the riot. On Saturday morning, as soon as Lee heard the news, he summoned his family to his study and read a letter he had already sent to Scott: his resignation from the army he had served for more than three decades. "I mention this to show you that I was not at all influenced by the exciting news from 'Baltimore.'" Family members, most of them Unionist in sympathy, were stunned.[4]

At last the carriage pulled up to the familiar churchyard. The Lees strode through the doors and walked to the pew they had bought just a few years before, knelt for silent devotions, and, opening their Prayer Books, joined the congregation in the familiar rite of Morning Prayer. As Lee sat at the end of his pew, his cousin Cassius's daughter, Harriotte, noticed that his hair had grayed since she last saw him, before she had gone away to school and he to Texas. He seemed much older to her than did her father, who was but a year younger.

That Sunday fell midway through the church's season of Eastertide. The biblical lessons proclaimed resurrection and new life, even as the old life of the parishioners' state and nation was ebbing. Might Lee have noted how the prayer of the day addressed the Divine? "Almighty

God, who showest to them that are in error the light of thy truth, to the intent that they may return into the way of righteousness." If that were not enough, the Epistle assigned for the day, if it was read, contained a pertinent passage: "Submit yourself to every ordinance of man for the Lord's sake; whether it be to the king, as supreme; or unto governors, as unto them that are sent by him."[5] Did Lee make anything of these words in light of his decision?

On the surface, everything seemed so ordinary. They said the psalms, sang the hymns, and heard the Reverend Cornelius Walker preach from the lofty pulpit. The liturgy proceeded as usual to its appointed end, the rector bidding "the grace of our Lord Jesus Christ, and the love of God, and the fellowship of the Holy Ghost" upon the congregation. As the two left church, they found "that really quiet little town in another great state of fermentation," as Mary Custis described it a decade later. Townspeople joined parishioners swirling around Colonel Lee. Though he ranked lower than other officers in Uncle Sam's army, few matched his renown: a hero of the Mexican War, a former superintendent of the Military Academy at West Point, esteemed within the service and beyond. Rumors about him had already spread—that he had resigned his commission (true); that he had been arrested (clearly false); that he would side—well, with whom? Crowds surrounded him, Mary Custis noted, "as if their faith was pinned to him alone."[6]

Following their normal pattern, the Lees walked to a relative's nearby home for lunch. Cousin Harriotte also stopped in, hoping to share with Mary Custis that she had seen her brother Fitzhugh (or Rooney, as the family called him) on the train from Richmond. Before she could say a word, Mary Custis told her of Lee's resignation. Of all the family, she alone was "Secesh," and as such was first to approve. Still, Harriotte found Daughter standing apart from the crowd in a sober mood. "It is no gratification to us," Mary Custis told her cousin, "it is like a death in the house. Since my father went to West Point, the army had been his home and his life, he expected to live and die belonging to it, and only his sense of duty made him leave it."[7]

By some accounts, Lee had found a moment to huddle privately in the churchyard with John Robertson, a former congressman, a current judge, and a member of the "peace convention" that two months before had sought vainly to broker a deal between North and South to avert secession. Robertson had tried, and failed, to see Lee the previous day. Mary Custis recorded that "two gentlemen" brought to Arlington a

5

message from "a gentleman"—Robertson?—asking Lee to meet with Governor Letcher in Richmond the next day. Accordingly, on Monday, Lee returned to Alexandria, boarded a train with Robertson, met with Letcher, and accepted command of the military forces of the now-seceded state.[8] In a week's time, he became the only person in history to be offered the command of two opposing armies.

Lee's decision changed his life, on the grand scale and also in its mundane patterns: he and his family never again made their Sunday trip to Christ Church.

✳   ✳   ✳

Just a few days shy of four years later, Lee took another ride, a long, slow, mournful trek from Appomattox to Richmond, following the hardest week of his life. On Sunday, April 2, 1865, a message from Lee interrupted Confederate President Jefferson Davis's worship at St. Paul's with news that the Army of Northern Virginia had to evacuate Petersburg, leaving Richmond to its fate. Lee led his troops westward in a vain search for supplies. Confronted by Federal forces, frustrated in all attempts to escape, Lee began to accept the inevitable. On Sunday, April 9, he surrendered his army to General Ulysses S. Grant.

On April 12, having obtained paroles for himself and his soldiers, and having duly reported his actions to President Davis, Lee headed toward a rented house in Richmond, the nearest thing he had to a home. Along the way, having been joined by a few remaining members of his staff, he pitched his tent outside his brother Carter's house in Powhatan County, there being no room inside, on April 14. The next day, joined by Rooney, he entered Richmond amidst a downpour. It was Good Friday. That night in Washington, John Wilkes Booth assassinated Abraham Lincoln.

No one knows his thoughts during that hundred-mile ride. Lee never recorded them. Others, however, did record their thoughts, and they often thought of God. Lee, like many Southerners, believed that if God were on their side, they would have won the war. They lost. "Oh it is bitter! bitter!!" one young soldier wrote to his mother. "If any ones whole soul was wrapped up in the cause it was mine and I always felt and frequently said when fellow officers would get disheartened that I did not believe God would allow us to be crushed."[9] Lee, like many Southerners, had some spiritual accounting to do.

*   *   *

Four months later, in August 1865, Lee took another ride. He wanted to chat with a friend. No carriage this time, no slaves, no family with him, nor any military staff: only his horse Traveller. Though his fame had spread around the globe as a brilliant general, he was a defeated one. He had no home, no funds, no job. His wife had become physically debilitated. Six of his children had survived the war, but sickness had claimed his daughter Annie, his daughter-in-law Charlotte, and two grandchildren. Union forces had occupied his wife's family estate, Arlington, then with purposeful vengeance turned it into a cemetery. The Lees held no hope of ever living there again.

They were better off than many. The South, and especially his native state, lay in ruins. A quarter of its men had died. A third or more of its net worth had vanished, some from war, much because of emancipation of the slaves. Hunger, poverty, homelessness pervaded the region.

In the summer of 1865, Lee, his wife, Mary, and two daughters left their temporary house in Richmond for a borrowed farmhouse forty miles to the west, on the edge of Powhatan County. Undisturbed there by inquisitive crowds like those that had plagued him in Richmond, he pondered taking up farming for a living, for lack of anything else he could accept. Daughter Mary Custis was heard to say that while Southerners would give Lee everything he might need, no one ever offered him a job to support his family.[10]

Then one materialized from a most unpromising source. The trustees of a small school in the isolated little town of Lexington in the Valley of Virginia asked Lee to become its president. The war had been no kinder to Washington College than to anything else in the state. It was impoverished, devastated, and struggling for its very existence. As many Southerners did during the war, the trustees in its wake looked to Lee almost as a savior. They delegated Judge John Brockenbrough to make the case to Lee. When he visited Lee, he tried his best.

Pondering Brockenbrough's plea, Lee rode forty miles to Albemarle County to visit a friend, an Episcopal priest named Joseph Pere Bell Wilmer. Lee poured out his quandary. Given the threat of being tried for treason, his own future remained uncertain. The college stood on the brink of extinction. But it bore the admired name of George Washington, with whom Robert and Mary Lee had unparalleled connections. Robert's father had guided President Washington to direct a munificent

7

gift he had received from the commonwealth to the tiny Liberty Hall Academy, which in gratitude adopted its donor's name as its own. Its past held an allure. But Lee looked also to its future. Young men could receive educations aimed at rebuilding the South and renewing the bonds of the entire nation. He could help them. Should he go?

When Wilmer suggested that other, "more conspicuous" schools would welcome Lee, he quickly "discovered that his mind towered above these earthly distinctions" and that "the *cause* gave dignity to the institution." Lee argued that "this door and not another was opened to him by Providence." The more they spoke about the position's potential "to make his few remaining years a comfort and a blessing to his suffering country," Wilmer reported, the more that Lee's "whole countenance glowed with animation."[11]

Tenderly, tentatively, Lee responded to the trustees' offer. He could not teach classes as all the college's previous presidents had done. He worried that a person of his notoriety in that position "might draw upon the College a feeling of hostility; & I should therefore cause injury to an Institution which it would be my highest desire to advance." So, not wanting "to be the cause of animadversion," Lee thought it best to decline.

Then he returned the decision to the trustees: "Should you however take a different view & think that my services in the position tendered me by the Board will be advantageous to the College & Country, I will yield to your judgment & accept it." The board most certainly did, and quickly ratified his election on August 31.[12]

Two weeks later, Lee left Powhatan County to take the leadership of the struggling Washington College. He rode into town on what he perceived to be a mission given him by God, confirmed through the trustees. In so doing, he became one of the only generals in history, vanquished in a bitter civil war, to devote himself fully to promoting peace and reconciliation.

Lee acted on a faith that had grown from his childhood. Like his father, Lee looked to a God whose providential care guides nations and peoples, especially through qualities such as virtue and duty. Like his mother, he also believed in a God whose providential hand not only guides nations but also shepherds souls toward personal salvation and individual service. Lee came to combine the two, with his concept of divine providence binding them together.

Lee's own words at the time help to explain the two great decisions of his life. The decision to side with the South emanated more from his father's style of faith. His analysis of virtue, honor, and loyalty led him to support his native state. His commitment to go to Lexington, however, clearly reflected his evangelical convictions. Those convictions kept him from leaving the country, as some leading ex-Confederates were doing and as he was invited to do. They inspired him instead to remain and rebuild, choosing Washington College as the place to do it. This was his mission from God.

It also became the final chapter in a long process of transformation. Most immediately, his life transformed from that of defeated military general to that of college president. Dramatic as that change was, his motivations for making it point to a deeper, even spiritual, process that continued for virtually his entire lifetime. The arc of that process conformed to a pattern that was classic for his church.

From baptism to death, Lee lived his life in the Episcopal Church. Anglican worship, tradition, and ways profoundly influenced his personal life, conduct, and decisions. Yet the historic church into which Lee was baptized evolved during his lifetime, and Lee along with it. Understanding Lee's faith, then, requires some grasp of the history and nature of the Anglican[13] heritage of which he was always a part.

CHAPTER 2

"A Goodly Heritage"

~

Anglicanism in Lee's Virginia

On Sunday afternoons in 1812, a five-year-old boy strode the four blocks from his home on Oronoco Street to Christ Church in Alexandria, to fulfill his solemn duty of reciting the catechism of his church to the formidable young rector, William Meade. His mother had taught him these basics of the Christian faith as outlined in the questions and answers in the Episcopal Book of Common Prayer. "What is your name?" Meade would ask. "Robert Edward," the boy would respond. "Who gave you this name?" "My sponsors in baptism; wherein I was made a member of Christ, the child of God, and an inheritor of the kingdom of heaven."[1]

No record survives of Robert's baptism, nor of who spoke for him as his godparents. If Virginia custom held true, it occurred within a week or so of his birth on January 19, 1807. Just as surely, it took place at the family home or, in their case, plantation. For his was no ordinary home, no ordinary family: Robert Edward bore the surname Lee; and the family home was the Northern Neck estate of Stratford Hall.

On the walls of the mansion were portraits of Lee forebears: Richard, who brought the family to Virginia in the 1640s; his son, another Richard; and Richard's son Thomas, who created Stratford Hall. Robert's father, Henry Lee III, won the name "Light-Horse Harry" for his dashing exploits as a Revolutionary cavalry officer. He later served on the staff of the great Washington himself and was elected governor of Virginia. No less distinguished were the ancestors on Robert's mother's side, starting with Robert "King" Carter, one of Virginia's richest colonials. His son married into the Hill family of Shirley Plantation, cultivated since 1613 and owned by the Hills since 1638. His mother's very name, Ann Hill Carter, conveyed her family's history.

Until the Revolution and beyond, to be a Lee was to be an Anglican. The only exception was Light-Horse Harry's widowed cousin Hannah Lee Corbin, and whether she scandalized the family more by becoming a Baptist, and a zealous one at that, or by cohabitating with a man not her husband and bearing his child, is hard to say.[2] By every Lee standard—social, ecclesial, and familial—Robert, the youngest twig in the big old family tree, would be baptized into the family faith, and taught it as he grew. Their tradition became his tradition. It influenced his entire life.

The Lees were a household of faith in more ways than one. William Meade and the young Lee were intertwined within the tangle of faith, families, and friendships of Virginians. Robert's uncle, Edmund Jennings Lee, was a close associate of Meade. The parson himself was a younger cousin of Mary Lee Fitzhugh Custis, the wife of George Washington Parke Custis, a scion of Mount Vernon. Meade became godfather to their daughter, who married Robert E. Lee. Virginia's Episcopal Church was in many ways, some literally, an extended family, and, as priest and later bishop, Meade led their prayers.

During Lee's youth, it was also a family in crisis. Storms of change buffeted the church in ways that affected its status and its very faith. Even as a boy, Robert had reason to sense that blustering gales would shake the religious tradition that shaped his life and grounded his beliefs.

Adapting the Faith of England

By birth, Robert Lee entered a family that had been in Virginia for 163 years. By baptism, he assumed a faith that the earliest settlers brought with them exactly 200 years before. As soon as John Smith and his companions stepped off the *Goodspeed* in 1607 at the place they named Jamestown, their chaplain, the Reverend Robert Hunt, opened the Book of Common Prayer to lead their thanksgivings. Each day, as the new colonists built their settlement, Hunt led Morning and Evening prayer, reading from the Bible in English. Each Sunday he preached two sermons, just as he had in England. Following their Anglican customs gave a modicum of structure to the life of their colony, then and thereafter.

These settlers were all children of the English Reformation, ongoing at the time. As Anglicans, Virginia's colonists brought with them a very definite but very mixed set of ideas that the leaders of the Church of England had developed. Some concepts arose directly from Protestantism. They read the Bible and prayed in English, not Latin. Their clergy could marry, if women were around to have them. They shared a perception of human sinfulness, remedied by God through justification by one's faith in Christ, and they scorned "Romish doctrines" such as purgatory, relics, and the supremacy of the pope. Unlike in Catholic churches, laity could receive both bread and cup at the Eucharist, a sign of their more equitable relationship with clergy.

Yet these Anglicans differed from other Protestants by retaining, albeit reforming, elements of their Catholic heritage. Bishops led the church, ordaining clergy such as Hunt. Anglicans did not invoke saints, but they did remember them on days set forth in their Prayer Book. They used a prescribed liturgy in worship, though in English and in the Prayer Book authorized by Crown and Parliament, which outlined what they should believe. Indeed, the Church of England was the official church of the land and of its new colony of Virginia.[3]

Religion was a central reality in the lives of early Virginians. In contrast to the Pilgrims and Puritans, who settled New England in the 1620s and 1630s for spiritual purposes, gold may have motivated their migration more than God. Still, they were religious. Their convictions and practices reflected the moderate Anglicanism of England's church and court. But they were not doctrinaire. They never worried much about the controversies that beset their far-off mother country. More immediate concerns shaped their settlement and, thus, their religion. Soon discovering that tobacco grew well here, they scattered across the land to plant what quickly became a tremendously profitable crop. As a result, colonial life differed from that in England, where people gathered in towns and villages, close to one another and to their church. Being dispersed on widespread farms limited Virginians' ability to attend Sunday services, much less daily ones.

Three elements helped hold them together and guided their religious life: their books, their clergy, and the laity who oversaw both church and colony. Each played a key role in developing Virginia Episcopalianism.

First were their books. In Virginia, as in England, the two volumes most often found in any Anglican home that could afford them were the Bible and the Book of Common Prayer. These two tomes provided a thorough and portable means of worship. The appointed services for the day and week fostered a sense of order, and also of unity for Virginians. Whether in log cabins or plantation mansions, dutiful colonial Anglicans joined in the same prayers and readings wherever they were, which also provided a link with the mother church in England.[4]

Clergy arriving from England, before the colony started producing its own, encountered a vastly unfamiliar setting. Whereas an English parish priest generally served one church with his parishioners nearby, the average priest in Virginia had to ride long distances to reach multiple congregations and visit parishioners. Geography had another effect: the nearest bishop resided an ocean away. Colonial America had none. That meant that any Virginian wanting to be confirmed or to be ordained to sacred ministry, which duties could be performed only by bishops, had to journey across the Atlantic for the rite. Few did, so Virginians accommodated by offering Communion to the unconfirmed and allowing them to serve on vestries, as did George Washington and Robert Lee.[5]

With no bishop and few clergy, laypeople took on far more responsibility for their church than did the laity of England. Virginia's Crown-appointed governor and the elected House of Burgesses, all layfolk, supervised the colony's spiritual as well as physical welfare. On local levels, governing bodies of laity, usually composed of the leading land-owners, oversaw parish life. These "vestries" provided the buildings, furnishings, and books, and procured clergy as pastors, preachers, and teachers.[6] They oversaw care for the sick and poor, licensed marriages, regulated moral behavior, punished vice, and required parishioners—who, as in England, technically included every person regardless of individual conviction—to attend services and to pay for church expenses in the obligatory tithes. As a result, the church held a central place in the lives of Virginians, Anglican or otherwise, for spiritual, social, and even civic aims.[7]

Religion in the Home

Though the House of Burgesses required all Virginians to worship God each week in church, weather and distance often overruled even the strictest of laws. But the Anglican way made worship in homes a viable alternative. In Virginia, as in England, families gathered in prayer once and even twice a day. Colonial religion centered on the home.

Between the Bible and the Book of Common Prayer, a household had everything it needed to conduct the offices of Morning and Evening prayer. The Prayer Book set forth the structure, provided the prayers, and indicated the scriptural passages to read, day by day. Virginians who could afford to buy books of prayers, meditations, and sermons incorporated these into family devotions. Religious works far outnumbered books on all other topics on their shelves.[8]

Thus equipped, family members gathered for prayers, morning and night, every day of the week. Lees and Custises did just that, well into the nineteenth century. Individuals used these same resources for private meditations, an additional and more personal element of the customary devotional regimen.[9]

Virginians also integrated religious observances into daily life. The church's yearly cycle of feasts and fasts punctuated domestic routines, often at the table. Foods varied with liturgical seasons: luscious cakes at Christmas, pointedly simpler fare during Lent. Though rites of passage such as baptisms and marriages were supposed to occur at church, they more often took place in homes, which intensified their place as religious centers. Tellingly, Robert E. Lee was baptized (presumably), said daily prayers, and was married in a family home.[10]

With Sunday schools far in the future, colonial homes became the primary schoolrooms for religious and secular learning. Each child was expected to learn the catechism from parents and godparents.[11] Daily prayers helped in teaching, especially as they included sermons and devotional works; and many children learned to read from religious materials (such as the famous New England primer that began "In Adam's fall we sinn'd all"). What children learned from these, they held on to for life. As a result, young Virginians reared in homes that took their religious duties seriously found themselves well instructed in their faith.

A Faith of the Church

When they managed to overcome "occasions"—heat, cold, rain, snow, distance, impassable roads—Virginia's Anglicans spent Sundays in church. If religious motivation were not enough, the requirements of law and the lure of social gatherings made churchgoing such a priority that, until the Revolution, Anglicans often filled their churches to capacity.[12]

Once they arrived, the day was as full as the pews. At 11 a.m., after greeting friends, worshipers would take their places not on benches or chairs, a later innovation, but rather in box pews somewhat like modern office cubicles. Often a family would purchase a box for its own use, even decorating it to its taste, as George Washington did at Christ Church, Alexandria.

Colonial Anglican churches tended to be plain, and were often built with the floor plan of a cross. Clear glass allowed natural light to reflect off of whitewashed walls; stained glass did not appear until the 1830s. A pulpit dominated the space, rising as much as a floor above the congregation, perhaps topped by a "sounding board" to improve acoustics, often incorporating a lectern for a lay reader or "clerk" to help lead the service. A small table could be brought to the front on the few Sundays when Communion was celebrated, but it would never be adorned with flowers, candles, or a cross. By an old order of Queen Anne, some churches displayed the Ten Commandments, the Apostles' Creed, and the Lord's Prayer, all learned in catechism, all reminders of faith and duty.[13]

Typically, worship began with the Order for Morning Prayer, which included one or more psalms, two biblical lessons (sometimes a full chapter each) followed by canticles (songs from the Bible, sometimes set to music), the Apostles' Creed, and prayers. Then came the Litany, a series of petitions for nearly everything under God. Ante-Communion, the first portion of the eucharistic rite, followed to the point of the consecration of elements, even on Sundays when Communion was not offered; the sacrament itself was rarely administered more than four times a year.[14]

That done, the minister would climb to the lofty pulpit and deliver his sermon, which lasted as long as an hour. Many clergy of the era read what amounted to lectures. Often they quoted, if not recited in full, writings of English prelates that tended to instruct more than inspire. They promoted an ethical, responsible, useful, and above all reasonable faith in sermons that emphasized virtue, morality, and duty in ordinary life. As the Reverend James Blair preached, "Good morality is good Christianity." In the absence of clergy, which was often, a lay reader led the service and read a sermon of one of those Englishmen. Laity often concluded that they might as well read it in the comfort of their own homes.[15]

Afterward, more socializing followed, in the churchyard and beyond. Adjourning to their own house or that of a relative, the family might discuss the sermon. Virginians appreciated sermons they could contemplate all week long. Through them, the clergy helped shape the spirituality of Virginia.

The Faith of the Colonial Church

Since most of Virginia's colonists emigrated to increase fortunes rather than escape persecution, their religion tended not to be contentious, nor did the colony attract many who wanted to be. Most accepted the norms of the Church of England of their day. They said their prayers and largely avoided the divisiveness that produced the English Civil War and Puritan dominance, and cost a king his head. When Charles II, son of the executed king, restored monarchy and Anglicanism to Britain in 1660, Virginians, always more interested in crops than contretemps, easily adapted to the more relaxed mood then in force. This spirit prevailed virtually to the time of Robert E. Lee's birth.

Virginians derived that spirit from English theologians, preachers, and bishops who emphasized the practice rather than the precepts of faith, through books and sermons that found their way to America. They aimed in part to transcend theological controversy, in part to address depravities they perceived in society at large and, in particular, in the randy royal court prior to the Glorious Revolution of 1688. They stressed themes such as personal virtue and private duty, urging not so much correctness of doctrine as the effective exercise of Christianity.[16]

These down-to-earth attitudes rested upon the more abstract work of speculative theologians who underscored the importance of "reason" and "virtue." They sought a moderate way between the "enthusiasm"—by which they meant "fanaticism"—of the Puritans and the growing influence of rationalism. Reacting to the wrathful God depicted by Puritans in England and Massachusetts, these scholars saw the Almighty as both creator and friend, "most affectionate and kind, most faithful and sure, most able and willing, and ever most ready to perform all friendly offices, to yield advice on all our doubts, succor in all our needs, comfort in all our troubles." Theirs being a God of reason, they welcomed the advances in scientific knowledge then being dramatically produced by the likes of Isaac Newton. These groups, notably the well-named "latitudinarians" like John Tillotson, an archbishop of Canterbury (1691–1694), promoted greater toleration as a welcome relief to the sectarian persecutions and religious wars that had spilled so much blood onto English and European soil. Instead of doctrinal conformity, they stressed personal striving toward the likeness of God. Against skeptics who set science against religion, they sought to integrate reason with Scripture, prizing such human qualities as common sense. Admitting the reality of evil and the individual's responsibility, and thus the need—and ability—to repent of sin, they conveyed a sense of optimism in a purposefully plainspoken way that strove to promote the soul's relationship with God.[17]

By the early eighteenth century, the Enlightenment held sway over the Church of England in Britain and Virginia alike. Newton's work in science and John Locke's in philosophy joined with theology to promote an intellectual and rational view of God and faith. "Enlightened" Christianity upheld a human role in redemption that cherished human freedom and goodness and rejected predestination; this became known as "Arminianism." It stressed the simplicity of Christianity. It advocated ethical behavior as the chief end of faith, underscoring the importance of virtue and morality. It downplayed the sacraments and accentuated the role of clergy as pastors and moral instructors. It distrusted tradition as a source of authority, thus seeking to free humanity from history while optimistically lauding progress in human destiny. But mind alone was insufficient unless it led to virtuous living. One colonial Virginian advised his son that a "good faith is a good life."[18] It was, in brief, a practical, useful faith to live by.

Some Anglicans took this approach to an extreme. Matthew Tindal (1657–1733), an Oxford don, in 1730 published *Christianity as Old as the Creation*. In it he presented God as creator whose aim for humanity is happiness, which is best attained in virtuously performing one's duty. Nature reveals God, and nature's God is reasonable. Jesus served primarily as moral example. Biblical truths were true as far as they conformed to God's gift of human reason. This "deism" viewed God as an impersonal being removed from everyday life.[19] Such was the faith of Thomas Jefferson, and of Robert's father, Henry Lee.

Far removed from deistic Oxford, the saintly bishop Thomas Wilson (1663–1755) composed prayers and manuals promoting devotion to God. These were collected, published, and treasured by some Americans, including Martha Washington, and then the Custises, who inherited her copy. Wilson's son presented President Washington with yet another copy. It passed to Mr. Custis, who gave it to William Meade, who quoted it copiously in his book of devotions for Virginians.[20]

By 1776 these principles of the Enlightenment religion, from latitudinarian to deistic, permeated at least the upper reaches of Virginian society. Within its genial spirit, the College of William and Mary was founded in 1693 in the colony's capital of Williamsburg to provide "a seminary of ministers of the Gospel, to the schools provided for poor children."[21] By 1775 about half of all Anglican clergy in Virginia had studied there. Nearly all of them promulgated Tillotson's ideas from their pulpits, and when they were absent, lay readers often relied on one of his sermons. Countless publications echoed his perspective, so that "the pursuit of virtuous happiness was clearly among the preeminent lessons of the church." Duty, forged in the humility of repentance and aspiring to the happiness of virtue, encouraged Virginians to show forth in their lives what they professed by their faith.[22]

All these elements—the Bible read regularly, the Prayer Book used daily in homes and weekly at church together with its rites that marked the passages of life, the pragmatically themed preaching, the books of devotion—sought to promote a life of Christian transformation. Conversion was, above all, an ongoing process of becoming ever closer to God, ever more holy. This faith was practical rather than doctrinal, pastoral rather than dogmatic.[23]

That was the Anglican way. It was the way that many colonial Virginians faithfully followed, adapting it to the particular realities they faced. For generations, what one scholar has called "a cheerful and comfortable faith" infused the lives of colonial Anglicans, who, officially at least, constituted the vast majority of the population. Although the enthusiasm and evangelicalism of the Great Awakening in the eighteenth century posed a challenge to Anglicans, their church survived and even flourished. Even when as a result of the Revolution it was formally disestablished, abandoned by many of its clergy, and shorn of much of its property, it continued to influence Episcopal Virginians generally, and the elite in particular. It helped sustain Anglican faith through tumultuous decades.

George Washington was typical of many well-to-do Virginia Anglicans. He perceived the deity as a distant, impersonal force. He talked of "Providence" and "Destiny" rather than "God," and did not discuss topics such as eternal life that he deemed beyond human knowing.

Duty toward others was a primary concern. In a childhood exercise, he copied down the 110 rules in *Rules of Civility and Decent Behaviour in Company and Conversation*. These precepts ranged from "Every action done in company ought to be done with some sign of respect to those that are present" to "Kill no vermin, or fleas, lice, ticks, etc. in the sight of others." He rarely if ever took Communion but did serve on parish vestries. No clergyman attended him at his deathbed; no prayers accompanied his passing. His faith, like that of many in the Virginia aristocracy, was formal, intellectual, and reserved, as impersonal as the God they perceived.[24]

Enlightenment Christianity advocated a faith lodged primarily in the mind and leading to the practice of virtue. But what of the heart and indeed of the soul, an emotional element in faith or even a mystical one? Challenges to rationalistic belief came in two stages. The first was "evangelical," the next a "catholic revival" that reacted in an immediate sense to evangelicalism but also to rationalism. As Robert Lee strode manfully to say his catechism, little did the five-year-old realize how each of these two nineteenth-century religious movements would shake his church, and affect his life and the faith he was learning.

CHAPTER 3

"A House Divided"

~

Faith in the Lee Household

Robert Edward Lee entered as religious a world, and as religious a household, as any. Henry and Ann Carter Lee practiced their faith in ways befitting their status, heritage, and church. They sought conscientiously to uphold their duties to God and neighbor. Yet their fourth child arrived amid change and discord in home and church. As admonished by Scripture, both of Lee's parents wanted to bring up their children in "the way they should go."[1] The question became, then, which way was that? Each was Christian. Each was Episcopalian. But the Lees were two people divided by a common faith. Robert was caught in the middle.

Outwardly, unity prevailed. The Lees, like the Custises and nearly all their circle, shared bonds of social prestige, large estates, and seeming wealth. By their marriage, Ann and Henry Lee had united two of Virginia's most distinguished families. Of course, such prominent Virginians would also be, officially at least, Episcopalian. They passed its practices—the cycle of daily prayers at home and of attending church on Sundays—from generation to generation.

But events beyond the home altered their church and then fractured it in ways that bisected the Lee household. One force was the very independence that Henry helped win. Being part of a church praying for, and nominally governed by, the British monarch no longer made sense. Americans forged their own entity, which they called the Protestant Episcopal Church in the United States of America. Bishops were elected by each diocese to oversee and lead the diocese's clergy and congregations. A bicameral legislature, the General Convention, governed the church body, bishops in one house and duly elected clergy and lay "deputies" in the other. Virginia formed one of those dioceses.

The same democratic spirit that led Episcopalians to choose bishops and deputies by election also inspired state governments to disestablish their official churches. In Virginia, the Statute of Religious Liberty provided for toleration of all faiths and removed tax support for any. Soon the legislature ended altogether the Anglicans' official, legal role in society.

With independence, too, many "loyalist" clergy who had opposed the Revolution fled Virginia. A depleted rank of priests proved itself less able and sometimes less virtuous: Carter Lee, no prude, testified to the moral laxity of Alexandria's clergy, as did the very prudish Meade. One priest preached the old moralism but overly savored "good company and the pleasures of the table." The next "was of an unhappy temper and too much given to the intoxicating cup." Meade's predecessor had married a local woman despite having a wife in the West Indies. While Virginia had a bishop in James Madison, cousin to the fourth US president, he took more interest in his day job heading the College of William and Mary than in overseeing a vast, declining, problematic diocese.[2]

Independent or not, Episcopalians still looked across the ocean to the ecclesiastical mother country. In style, services, and theology, England still ruled by example. Far from departing "from the Church of England in any essential point of doctrine, discipline, or worship" any "further than local circumstances require," Episcopalians officially professed that its doctrines "are preserved entire" in the daughter church "as being judged perfectly agreeable to the gospel."[3]

Yet the Americans were separate. They published their own Book of Common Prayer in 1789. Interceding for the king was out, using a Scottish prayer for Communion was in (a nod to the Scots, who consecrated the first American as bishop when English prelates snubbed the Yankee priest elected for the job). Some rites were shortened.[4]

Nevertheless, the young Robert Lee's worship mirrored that of his parents' childhoods, at church and also in homes. Family worship even grew in popularity in the early 1800s, a practice encouraged by the new American Prayer Book's addition of special forms of worship for family use. Carter and Robert Lee each reminisced fondly of mealtime prayers and hearth-side devotions. Meanwhile at Arlington House, Mrs. Custis led the twice-daily prayers that gathered family, visitors, and the enslaved "servants" of the household.[5]

Despite its effects on church and clergy, independence hardly changed the daily religious habits of parishioners. Then came a second major influence on the newly independent Episcopal Church: an evangelical revival.

The Great Awakening and the Episcopal Church

When the Beatles, Rolling Stones, and other pop bands took America by storm in the 1960s, drawing huge crowds of fans who shrieked and even fainted in ecstasy, the "British Invasion" created a cultural phenomenon like one other, more than two centuries before. In the 1730s, two English clergymen, George Whitefield and John Wesley, started a spiritual renewal that soon spread to America, rousing the colonists into a similar if more spiritual frenzy. The preaching of Whitefield, reinforced by sermons of the likes of Jonathan Edwards of New England, sparked the Great Awakening, a religious revival that rapidly swept through the thirteen colonies. They preached an antithesis to the dry, reasoned intellectualism of the latitudinarians. Whitefield vehemently attacked Tillotson's notions of virtuous happiness. Edwards, though better known for comparing congregants' sinful souls to spiders dangling above hellfire held by a thread in the hands of an angry God, more often penned theological tomes upholding Calvinist orthodoxy against the incursions of deists like Tindal.[6]

Less touched than other groups by the revival, colonial Anglicans clung to their church and their "reasonable" faith as the fervor faded. Then, after the Revolution, the revival took on new life. Methodist circuit riders inspired by Wesley traveled throughout the new country commending not so much the edification of the mind as the warming of the heart, and a "method" of spiritual growth. Baptist and Methodist churches grew once again. But this Second Great Awakening also had a stronger effect than its predecessor on the newly renamed Episcopalians, reviving the staid, old, but no longer established church.

One sign of change could literally be heard in services. Previously, congregations had sung only psalms and biblical canticles, set to tunes imported from England a century before. Newfangled hymns, at first deemed "Methodistical," were as unsuitable for Episcopalians as crosses (even simple ones were damned as popish). Nonetheless, many Episcopalians started singing them in church and learning them at home.[7] During Lee's lifetime, hymn singing became a thoroughly accepted part of Episcopal worship.

A new spiritual fuel fired formerly stolid preaching. In place of lectures that appealed to the mind, sermons spoke to the heart and the soul. Pastors started expecting more from their parishioners, commending a lively faith that would bear fruit in their lives, and urging a spiritual transformation even more immediate and direct than the classical Anglican tradition had advocated.

Increasingly, parishioners responded by incorporating revivalist themes and traits into their daily devotions. Some underwent genuine religious conversions. Among them were William Meade, then a student at the College of New Jersey (by then casually called "Princeton"), and republican aristocrats such as Mary Custis and Ann Lee.[8]

What appealed to upper-class Virginians? Evangelicalism had already won over many a British blue blood. The Countess of Huntingdon promoted it. A prominent member of Parliament, William Wilberforce, composed a long opus entitled *A Practical View of Christianity*.[9] What was good for England's elite must be good for Virginia's.

Furthermore, a faith of the heart provided greater religious sustenance, especially to women. Washington, Jefferson, and Madison all preferred a reasoned religion of the mind, but "founding mothers" such as Martha Washington took comfort in a Christianity more personal than the latitudinarian, more orthodox than the deist, and more emotional than the rationality of the "Age of Reason." A faith of the heart better addressed genuine personal suffering in an era when afflictions knew no social status: Mary Custis's sister-in-law Nelly Lewis, Martha Washington's granddaughter, endured labor for a week before her first child was born. Four of her children died before reaching age three. As well, while men dominated the clerical and lay leadership of parishes, evangelical religion was open to women, who avidly promoted the myriad societies and missionary causes that sprang from pious incentives to transform the world.[10]

This faith of the heart spread among many Episcopalians, along with Baptists, Methodists, and some Presbyterians and Congregationalists. But the spiritual energy of the new evangelicalism also brought conflict. It divided households, congregations, and denominations, including the Episcopal Church.

"Enlightened" Christianity still retained strength among many Episcopalians, Presbyterians, and some Congregationalists while providing the theological basis for Unitarians and deists. For them, God created the universe and guided it through an overall "providence" that pervaded the world. Nature provided a way to know God; science thus stood alongside the Bible, expanding it, justifying it, on some points replacing it. Lives marked by morality, virtue, and duty remained the goal. Episcopalians of this inclination prized the church itself, its sacraments, liturgy, forms, and uniqueness, but scorned the "enthusiasm" and super-righteousness they perceived in revivalism.

Evangelicals scorned them back. "Formalists," one priestly colleague of Meade called those of the "enlightened" school. Charles McIlvaine, then chaplain to the US Senate and later to West Point when Lee was a cadet, promoted a conversion of the soul that marked a spiritual rebirth from which a "saving religion of the heart" could grow.[11] To evangelicals, God not only created the world but was also directly and intimately involved with what happened in it. God's providence directed the lives of individuals as well as nations. Given human depravity and personal sin, only in repentance and conversion could one gain a proper relationship with God. Jesus Christ, by his death on the cross (the atonement) and resurrection, was the unquestionable savior. The Bible, not nature, was their chief and often sole source for faith. Reason took at best a secondary place.[12]

The two sides differed most directly on the nature of salvation: How could one know he or she was saved by God? The "formalists" said one was saved through faithfully receiving the sacrament of baptism; the "enthusiasts" said, through the renewal of the converted heart. Bishop William White of Pennsylvania, the Episcopal Church's first and long-tenured presiding bishop who strongly influenced its theology, pronounced the legitimacy of both sources of "blessed assurance." By accepting each, he blessed both.[13]

White's theological *via media* allowed Virginia Episcopalians to unite—eventually. This was their natural inclination. From the first settlers onward, they generally avoided disputations over theological complexities and appreciated instead what one called a "practical godliness." Thanks to White's centrist position, latitudinarians could take comfort in the knowledge of their baptism, and evangelicals like Meade, in their conversions. The very idea of "latitude" implied a broad acceptance of divergent views, and Meade, McIlvaine, and others all read Tillotson and Butler before they read Wilberforce. Crucially, too, each side perceived the Christian life as a process of transformation. Both inherited the Anglican idea of steady growth. They disagreed over precisely when that process began: one said at baptism; the other, at personal conversion. But both cherished the Prayer Book and its traditional formularies for nurturing spiritual growth.

For evangelicals, the various Prayer Book rites promoted a life of conversion, redemption, new birth, and new life. When the catechism defined "sacrament" as an "outward and visible sign" signifying an "inward and spiritual grace," McIlvaine seized upon that latter aspect as central to "the life and being of all genuine piety before God." While disagreeing with others on the nature of baptism, clergy like Meade stressed its pragmatic importance by insisting on higher standards for administering it, and for living it in practice.

Evangelical Episcopalians differed with latitudinarians and deists, who took a more rationalist approach toward the personal experience of faith as the ultimate guarantee of salvation. Their disagreement marked one divide between what became known as the "low church" and "high church" parties. At the same time, the evangelical understanding of salvation brought Episcopal evangelicals closer to their counterparts in other denominations who shared a similar emphasis on conversion. On that basis, Meade and his school perceived a unity in what they considered true Christianity.[14] They were early ecumenists. Yet this very attempt to transcend denominations further separated the "low church" evangelicals from "high church" "formalists" who, in cherishing Anglican uniqueness, often disparaged the validity of Christians of other persuasions.

The Episcopal Church as a whole tried to bridge a fault line between two tectonic plates that threatened not just its own unity, but also that of one Protestant church after another. Evangelicalism was rapidly becoming the paramount religious force in America. The rumblings extended from the highest levels of denominations to local congregations, to households. The Lee home on Oronoco Street in Alexandria felt its tremors, and may have caused some.

The War of 1812

For all the storied hopes that surrounded the day of their marriage, life at the pinnacle of Virginia society quickly soured for Henry and Ann Lee, Robert's parents. Great in war, successful in politics, Henry failed in business. Every foolproof scheme to reverse financial disaster proved him the fool. Apparently this was nothing new. His first wife, whose maiden name, Matilda Ludwell Lee, signifies a familial relationship—she was Henry's second cousin—was the person who inherited Stratford Hall. She carefully bequeathed the estate not to her husband, but to their son, Henry IV, thereby keeping it out of Light-Horse Harry's untrustworthy hands. Nonetheless, he sold off what he could of Stratford Hall's property and mortgaged the rest.

Yet Ann relied on him heavily. When her father died, leaving his large estate to her brothers and providing no ongoing support for her, she pleaded with her husband as an "afflicted Fatherless wife" who "can now, only look to you, to smooth her rugged path through life, and soften her bed of death!"[15]

Ann truly needed help. With Robert's birth in 1807, she had four children to rear; one more would follow. Her pleadings for Henry to behave responsibly availed nothing. By 1810, Henry Lee IV had come of age and could take possession of Stratford Hall so that summer, after Light-Horse Harry was released from debtors' prison, Ann moved the family to a borrowed house in Alexandria. Robert was only three. Before leaving Stratford, according to family lore, he knelt down in the nursery room where he was born to say farewell to two angels displayed on the iron at the back of the fireplace.[16] The fire iron with angels remains in the house to this day.

In his later years, Robert remembered his father's moving the family to Alexandria "for purposes of educating his children." He also retained a fondness for Stratford. Not so his mother, who by 1809 informed her brother that Stratford was not "the part of the world I wished to fix in." She decided, while Light-Horse Harry was still in jail, on "reserving to myself the right of choosing my place of residence afterwards."[17] If so, despite Robert's memory of his childhood, she and not Henry determined where the family would live.

Matters soon grew even worse. As a Federalist, Henry Lee opposed Jefferson, Madison, and the War of 1812. So did a friend in Baltimore who published a newspaper bitterly critical of the war. On July 27, 1812, Henry was visiting the friend when a pro-war mob attacked the house. The Revolutionary War hero organized a defense. Maryland's militia arrived and took Henry and his cohorts into protective custody in jail. But the next night the jingoists returned. The militia vanished, whereupon the rioters burst into the prison, smashed open the cells, and mauled Lee and his friends. After slashing his face and pouring hot candle wax on his eyes, they left Lee for dead, a fate only slightly better than that of some of his companions.[18] To recover his devastated health—or was it to escape his creditors?—Lee fled to Barbados in 1813. He never saw his family again. Robert was six.

In 1814, after sacking Washington, DC, the British occupied Alexandria. Ann Lee and family may have fled, but young Robert might have seen the flames from the White House and Capitol across the river, and then His Majesty's troops plundering the town's warehouses.[19]

The war not only subverted national pride; it also strained the economy for years. When Carter, then at Harvard, posted a typical collegian's plea for money, Ann firmly denied him. The postwar depression had eroded her investment earnings, forcing her to cut back on all expenses. She complained that "scarcely a [chicken] back falls to Smith & Robert's share, so that they rather not be tantalized with the sight of them."[20] And Henry was no help.

Marital iciness reached into the Caribbean. From various isles, Henry wrote of his ills and his hopes of returning home. They were as vain as his hopes for letters from Ann. In one letter he scribbled: "Altho I never hear from you nor any of my children, my dear wife, I write whenever I can." In another he declared, "I do not know, why I never hear from my dear wife. It is a grace[?] I ought not to be denied. . . . My children I wish much to hear about, especially Ann's hand." Then, chillingly, in a letter written just after Christmas: "Kiss our dear children for me & do make Smith write to me. Make Ann write to me, as you will not."[21]

Along with all their other troubles, the couple disagreed over religion. He favored the Enlightenment style, she the evangelical.

Having grown up in the context of Anglican Enlightenment, Henry had studied at Princeton. There he overlapped as a student with James Madison, the future president. Both were influenced by the Scottish Presbyterian minister John Witherspoon, still new to the college presidency. Taking a required course in moral philosophy in his final year, Lee heard Witherspoon expound ideas from the Scottish Enlightenment, particularly notions of "commonsense realism." In stark contrast with an earlier Princeton president, Jonathan Edwards, of Great Awakening fame, Witherspoon understood the fundamental concepts of ethics and moral guidelines arising not primarily from the Bible but from human nature itself. God's providence had endowed each person with a moral sense. Thus, ethics, for him, constituted a science comparable to natural sciences, revealing truths that were self-evident. Witherspoon's philosophy influenced American revolutionary thinking from Thomas Paine's *Common Sense* to Jefferson's Declaration of Independence and Madison's *Federalist Papers*. Its pragmatic realism also ensured a bias in Henry Lee against all things evangelical.[22]

George Washington served as Henry Lee's model. Both had absorbed from youth the lessons of an Anglican culture that esteemed virtue, duty, and reason. Henry sought to inculcate these values in his children. "I remember my father's telling me," Carter wrote, "that 'the Great Washington' (that was his expression) had often told him, that he never could have discharged the duties devolved by Providence upon his life, had it not been for his habit of early rising."[23]

Henry knew his wife was devoutly religious. "Your dearest mother," he wrote Carter, "is singularly pious from love to Almighty God and love of virtue, which are synonymous; not from fear of hell—a low base influence." He never used the term "evangelical," but that is what she was. Some of her surviving letters hint at her convictions. She consoled a Carter kinswoman on the death of her daughter, assuring her that "time, and the influence of divine mercy can alone restore your tranquillity!" When her sister died, she wrote the widower, Carter Berkeley, "We know that our dear friend is for ever removed from pain and distress, and we hope and believe that her pure and virtuous life has insured her endless ages of unfading felicity!"[24] In 1809, while Henry was in debtors' prison, Berkeley had offered to let Ann stay at his home. She politely declined. By then, along with marital and financial ills, she was not healthy. To her ailing brother Robert, Ann promised that, "having been so often an invalid" herself, she would "implore my Heavenly Father, that I may find you, my best beloved Brother daily progressing in health!"[25]

To Henry, evangelicals' excited passions dangerously overran reason. One night in Alexandria, Carter came home late. Henry wanted to know where his son had been. Carter and friends had visited a Methodist service. "The Methodist Meeting House!" his father declared. "I had as soon you should go to a cock fight!" Whether his objection was to Methodist religion or to the boys' mocking of Methodist practice is unclear, "for the purposes for which we attended it, as my father knew," Carter related, were "to laugh at the funny exhibitions & exclamations of the peculiarly illumed, these being such of all classes & colours in their Church."[26]

From Barbados in 1813, Henry assured Ann of his prayers for his family but feared that his children would soon "loose their father." Two days later he wrote Carter, "If God almighty should bless my endeavors to recover my health I shall return directly afterwards to my family."[27] A month later, in a veritable valedictory—to whom he was writing seems to vary within the letter—he confirmed his own deistic faith. For him, religion was a means, in good Enlightenment thinking, to achieve "virtue." "Learning only becomes most valuable & is by me only wished for my children to open to their views the charms of virtue & to bind them ste[a]dfastly to its practice in word & deed. To be virtuous, reason & experience tell us we must be religious. Hold fast yourself (& inculcate on your brother to do like) this sheet anchor of happiness, this cititadel in the perils & tempests of life. Cherish it fondly."

Virtue, then, arose from religion, but only certain kinds of religion. Henry exhorted Carter to "abhor its two great enemys superstition & enthusiasm." These were the two bugaboos of Enlightenment faith: superstition, the opposite of knowledge and learning, epitomized in Roman Catholicism, and "enthusiasm," a euphemism for the evangelicalism that the Great Awakening—and his wife—embraced. "What I understand to be pure religion is a heart void of offence to God & man & a belief or faith in one God who delights in right & reproves wrong," he wrote; "the forms & ceremonys of religion differ, but in essence they all worship the almighty Creator & rest on his providence & protection here & hereafter."

To breed that virtue, Henry advised Carter to read classical writers like Cicero and Plato, and "among the moderns the history of jesus Christ commonly called the new testament, especially its first four books." Lee prized Jesus's teaching even as he doubted Jesus's divine nature. "Whether Christ was an inspired man as some beleive, or the son of God as Christians assert & some of them beleive, all must acknowledge the excellence of the morality he taught & wish its spread for the good of mankind."

Moving from theology to liturgy, Henry had a clear preference. "I cannot help thinking the quaker mode of worship most impressive of man's humility & therefore to be preferred," he declared. "In silence they adore God, to whom the tongue of man cannot utter appropriate ideas & therefore rightly does the quaker apply silence as best expressing our inferiority & God's superiority—best comporting with our nothingness & his supremacy. But the form of religion is unimportant & may be left with the individual—not so as to its obligations & duties."

Indeed, Christianity was not the only source of virtue. He quoted Seneca: "I have always admired the fulness & revered the truth so well expressed by a roman, Ingratum qui dixerit, omnia dixit: no man can be good without being grateful in heart & to whom ought man to be most grateful but to his highest benefactor, his prop, his stay, his comforter, & his protector. Religion commands man to love [and] adore in the warmest feelings of gratitude the great God—Virtue inculcated the same obligations & nourishes in mind & in act under the benign mantle of religion." By correlating virtue and religion, he reiterated the deistic ethic. "Enjoin my dear Carter to hold[?] his heart void of offence to God & man & to wrath in the path of virtue."[28]

Henry's letter reveals him as a child of the Enlightenment. In alluding to Roman writers, in equating "love to Almighty God and love of virtue," and in distrusting "superstition" and "enthusiasm," he evinces a faith common among Revolutionary leaders, like his hero Washington, who went to church, honored the Divine, but also drew inspiration from classical writers. Henry's uncertainty over the personhood of Jesus matched that of Thomas Jefferson.[29]

General Lee's letter also shows him thoroughly at odds with his wife. In its emphasis upon the mind and rationality, Enlightenment Christianity considered "superstition" and "enthusiasm" antithetical to true religion. For him to use the pejorative code word "enthusiasm" insulted the faith of his wife, to whom he was ostensibly writing. If that were not enough, by praising Quakerism, Henry also belittled Ann's Episcopalianism. The worship of the Religious Society of Friends was as far from that of the Episcopal Church as any denomination could be. In their "meetings," Quakers have no set order of service, but instead await the inspiration of the Holy Spirit; only then does anyone speak. By contrast, the liturgy of the Book of Common Prayer orders the service, provides the prayers, sets forth the biblical lessons to be read, and prescribes who says what, including the congregation—all of which Episcopal evangelicals assiduously followed. Henry Lee was about as distant from his wife liturgically and theologically as he was geographically. Not surprisingly, she ignored him.

For Henry was gone forever from Oronoco Street. Ann's influence abided, and when her children left, she sought to extend it to where they were. When, from Harvard, Carter begged for funds, she denied him, then added a postscript: "My dear Carter, I am at times very unhappy lest you should become a sosinion—If you should, I shall have aided in making you so, as I permitted you to go to a College, where the principles of that sect were disseminated—Oh! pray fervently for faith in Jesus Christ. He is the only rock of your salvation; and the only security for your resurrection from the grave!"[30] Socinians rejected the divinity of Christ and the doctrine of the Trinity in favor of the oneness and unipersonality of God. As "enthusiast" became an epithet for "evangelical," so too "Socinian" became an epithet for the religion of the Enlightenment typified especially by Unitarians. Rational, open to scientific methods and the possibility of truth in non-Christian religions, critical of evangelical tenets like the unique personhood of Christ, the Fall, atonement, and eternal punishment, Unitarians were everything that Ann Carter Lee was not—and nearly everything that her absent husband praised. And they were thriving at Harvard.[31]

Carter, seeing the division in his family, conceded his father's weaknesses. "The rock on which I am in the greatest danger of splitting is a disposition to aim too high, or at too much," he confessed to his mother. "It was this, which ruined my great father, in dispersing his mighty powers. I hope, however to profit by his example."[32] In the end, he followed in his father's religious footsteps. "Aunt Lewis," Mr. Custis's sister, trenchantly noted in 1821, "I am sorry to hear that Carter is travelling about with his vile Brother [Henry], they are both *Deists*." She added, "May the Almighty change Carters heart for the sake of his amiable Mother & Sister."[33]

In time, Robert followed a different path. He eventually combined the two religious strands that Henry and Ann Lee exemplified: the one from his father that prized reason, virtue, and duty; the other from his mother that emphasized personal faith. In so doing, he reflected a broader trend in American Protestantism. But society at large did not influence Lee nearly as much as the members of his family, starting with his mother in particular but extending to the innumerable aunts, uncles, and cousins. Among those cousins was the family into which he married in 1831 and which had a principal role in molding his faith. It too was divided along the same lines, though not nearly as intensely as his own. Encompassing them all was the family that was the Diocese of Virginia, joined by faith and often by blood. Presiding over it was its right reverend father in God, William Meade, Lee's childhood pastor and, to the degree that anyone filled that role, his lifelong spiritual father.

CHAPTER 4

"Who Setteth the Solitary in Families"

~

Lee's Extended Clan

R obert Edward grew up surrounded by Lees. Even if he wanted to, he could not escape them, either in history and heritage, or in proximity. They were everywhere.

Lees infused the new nation's history. Two great-great-uncles sat in the Continental Congress that declared American independence. Richard Henry Lee made the formal motion to separate from Britain, then together with his brother, Francis Lightfoot, signed the declaration that Thomas Jefferson composed. Jefferson, too, was a distant kinsman, but most Lees, being Federalists, welcomed the distance: Henry III, Robert's father, disliked him so much that, as a lame-duck member of Congress, he voted for Aaron Burr in the controversial presidential election of 1800. Thirty years later, Robert's half brother, Henry IV, wrote a diatribe attacking the Sage of Monticello.[1]

Robert's father was the oldest of his generation. Next in line came Charles, who served as US attorney general under Washington and Adams and represented the plaintiff in the groundbreaking Supreme Court case, *Marbury v. Madison*, that established the principle of judicial review of the constitutionality of Congressional actions. The third son, Richard Bland, represented Virginia in the first three sessions of the US House of Representatives. In 1811 he sold his plantation, Sully (near what is now Dulles Airport), in part because of losses arising from overinvolvement in Henry's financial woes, in part because of his own share in the family habit of mismanaging money. He and his wife moved to Alexandria for a time during Robert's childhood. Edmund Jennings, the youngest, who also endangered his finances by assuming some responsibility for Henry's debts after Richard Bland's fortune collapsed, became prominent in Alexandria.[2]

The Lees were also closely connected through marriage. Among Henry's siblings, Charles and Edmund married daughters of their great-uncle Richard Henry Lee. When their sister Mary, known as Mollie, married Philip Fendall, her new husband became Henry's, Charles's, and Edmund's cousin, brother-in-law, and stepfather-in-law.

The family even lived together in what Alexandrians came to call Lee Corner. The first Richard Lee had obtained substantial property along that section of the Potomac. Several generations later, descendants started moving there, in abundance. Edmund and Charles lived next door to each other on Washington Street, then as now the main north-south route through town. Adjacent to them stood what is now known as the Lee-Fendall House, on the corner of Washington and Oronoco, the home of Mollie Lee Fendall. She, in turn, helped arrange for Ann Carter Lee to use the house at 607 Oronoco owned by their kinsman William Fitzhugh, which stood immediately next door to the home of still another distant Lee cousin, Cornelia Lee Hopkins.[3] Robert truly did grow up surrounded by Lees.

Edmund and his family became especially close to Robert. While his older brothers were serving the nation, Edmund dedicated himself to local efforts. A lawyer, he was elected to the Alexandria common council before Robert's family arrived, and then served as mayor from 1815 to 1818. He then became clerk of the court, a post he held for the rest of his life. He and his family ardently supported Christ Church and the Diocese of Virginia. Staunchly evangelical, undoubtedly to his oldest brother's disgust, Edmund helped to elect the equally zealous Richard Channing Moore as the second bishop of Virginia. Trying to apply his religion to daily practice, he refused to let his servants travel on Sunday lest they, and by extension he, violate the fourth commandment by breaking the Sabbath. As mayor, he crusaded against gambling. William Meade called him "a man of great decision and perseverance in what he deemed right," who could be "obstinate . . . even to a fault." There "was no compromise at all in him, with any thing which he thought wrong."[4]

His sons followed similar paths: William Fitzhugh Lee was ordained and served parishes around Richmond until ill health led him to a less taxing role as first editor of the diocesan newspaper, the *Southern Churchman*. Cassius maintained an especially close and lifelong tie with

Robert. Separated in age by only a year, the two cousins often played together, went to school together, and worshiped together. In time, Cassius became a leading layman of Christ Church and spent much of his life as treasurer of Virginia Theological Seminary (VTS), which, like the *Southern Churchman*, resulted from the evangelical revival so actively promoted by their father, Edmund.[5]

Farther afield lived hosts of Lees. Not all were as religiously active as Edmund and his family, but some held their own convictions with as much fervor. Several of Robert's cousins detested slavery, including one who freed all his slaves, and another who fled slaveholding Virginia for the free soil of Pennsylvania.[6]

The extended family widened the arc all the more. William Henry Fitzhugh, whom Robert affectionately called "uncle," was actually the son of his grandfather's nephew. He lived on the twenty-thousand-acre estate of Ravensworth, about ten miles away in what is now Annandale. He had inherited the house on Oronoco Street where, by his generosity, Ann Carter Lee lived.[7] Robert and his family often visited Ravensworth, where his mother died in 1829.

Through Fitzhugh came another connection of increasing importance to Robert Lee. Fitzhugh's sister, christened Mary Lee and known as Molly, in 1804 married George Washington Parke Custis of the Arlington estate. Custis was the grandson of Martha Washington, a widow whose son, Custis's father, had also died. After marrying Martha, George Washington adopted the young boy, so that Custis became at once the namesake, step-grandson, and son of the "father of his country."

Born in 1781, shortly before his father died of illness at Yorktown, Custis grew up at Mount Vernon and in the presidential residences in New York and Philadelphia. The first First Family doted on the chubby child they nicknamed Washtub, or more simply Tub. Lazy and unruly in youth, he flunked out of Princeton and then St. John's College in Annapolis, then served long enough in the military to justify his military title of major. When he inherited the Custis fortune, he built the magnificent house that still offers one of the finest views of Washington, DC, from across the Potomac River. He used his house, leisure, and wealth to perpetuate the legacy of George Washington. He observed July 4 and February 22 as virtual civic feasts: the birthdays of the nation and of its first president. Attired in the general's uniform, Custis welcomed hordes of admirers eager to see Washington's tent and other heirlooms of the War for Independence. He regaled them with firsthand accounts of his adoptive father's generation. As a self-taught and not very accomplished artist, he painted scenes of the glory days of the Revolution. He himself was a veritable if useless relic of the era.[8]

Custis's religious upbringing varied from the standard for Virginia Episcopalians in that family prayers were not part of it. Reminiscing to his deeply religious niece, Markie Williams, Custis said his grandmother, Martha, retired each day to her room for an hour "where she read & literally held communion with her God." At Arlington House, Markie had seen Martha's large, worn Prayer Book, where family births were recorded; her expensive edition of the Bible with engravings of scenes copied from Old Masters; and the portrait of the Countess of Huntingdon, keen supporter of Wesley and Whitefield, which had hung in her room at Mount Vernon. Whether the general habitually read his Bible, Custis did not know, but as president he "always attended Christ's Church in Philadelphia." At Mount Vernon, they went either to Pohick, seven miles away, or Christ Church, Alexandria, nine miles off, where Washington owned a pew and served on the vestry.[9]

At Arlington House, Custis let his wife lead the prayers. A young visitor in the 1840s recalled an evening "when the prayers were longer than usual we all got up from our knees but Mr. C., who was asleep with Toem [i.e., Tom, his favorite cat] on his back, also asleep. Our laugh awakened the sleepers." A decade later, Markie found him drifting off in front of the fire while she, at his request, read chapters of the Bible or a sermon by some divine.[10] Although essentially deistic in understanding God and in his habits of attending church and family prayers, Custis—unlike Henry Lee—inched toward the evangelicalism into which he married, and, wisely enough, tolerated it.

For his wife, Mary Lee Fitzhugh Custis, was a thoroughgoing product of the evangelical revival. The Fitzhugh family had generously supported the established church for generations.[11] Mrs. Custis followed, then intensified, the family tradition. A friend called her "one of the happiest Christians I ever knew"—then, as many did, asked her spiritual advice.[12]

As mistress of Arlington, she usually led the prayers of the household, consciously including the enslaved servants who worked in the mansion. She was on warm terms with her parish clergy and could knowledgeably discuss current theological controversies. During one visit on a winter day in 1839, her rector, Charles Dana, and she discussed the Socinian view of the authenticity of the epistle to the Hebrews. She wrote to Mary of having read with "shock" the sermons of William Ellery Channing, a leading Massachusetts Unitarian, and described hearing from friends of a Methodist preacher in Alexandria who seemed to question human depravity and Christ's atonement. "There was doubtless many a silent prayer in our little company that he might be guided into all truth."[13]

Mrs. Custis's influence extended well beyond Arlington. At the time of her daughter Mary's birth, she urged her young cousin and spiritual protégé, William Meade, to seek ordination, found him a mentor to prepare him for sacred ministry,[14] and made him Mary's godfather. She then supported his efforts to revive Virginia's Episcopal Church and to resolve the issue of race in America by sending freed slaves to Africa.

From a young age, the children of Ann and Henry Lee visited Arlington. Carter recalled his first visit to the estate, on a Christmas Day, "carried there from Church by Mr. Custis & cousin Molly, as I always called his wife."[15] As a young boy, Robert visited Arlington too, becoming acquainted with his distant kinfolk whose daughter—his second cousin once removed—he would marry.

One more person who stood on the fringes of the huge family circle would also play a major role in Lee's life. That was William Meade, the young boy's pastor, who became an evangelical leader and then the third bishop of Virginia. By force of personality and of theological conviction, he became the paramount religious figure in the Diocese of Virginia, and for Robert E. Lee.

CHAPTER 5

"To Illuminate All Bishops"

~

William Meade and His Influence

General Robert E. Lee, military adviser to Confederate President Jefferson Davis, was working at his desk in Richmond on Thursday evening, March 13, 1862, when he received an urgent summons. His childhood pastor who had become his longtime bishop was dying. An ailing William Meade had dragged himself from Clark County in northern Virginia to Richmond to consecrate the son of his long-ago colleague William Wilmer as bishop of Alabama; his presence was needed to meet the minimum of three bishops required by Anglican tradition to confer episcopal authority upon another. Though historic for being the only such ordination in the short life of the Episcopal Church in the Confederacy, the effort proved more than the frail seventy-two-year-old man could endure. Writing to his wife, Mary, Lee described what happened: "The good & noble Bishop Meade died last night. He was very anxious to see you. Sent you his love and kindest remembrances. . . . Between 6 & 7 P.M. yesterday he sent for me. Said he wished to bid me good bye & to give me his blessing, which he did in the most affecting manner. Called me Robert and reverted to the time I used to say the catechism to him, invoked the blessing of God upon me & the Country. He spoke with difficulty & pain, but perfectly calm & clear. His hand was then cold & pulseless, yet he shook mine warmly."[1]

Meade had become the predominant figure of the Episcopal Church in Virginia, leading it out of its post-Revolutionary torpor into a vigorously evangelical fellowship. The Lees knew him more intimately. Officially, he was Mary's godfather. Unofficially, he became Robert's, too. Lee told Mary on the day after Meade died, "I ne'er shall look upon his like again."[2]

Christ Church was not a happy place when the Lees moved to Alexandria. Old-fashioned ways persisted: rationalist latitudinarianism, moralistic sermons, and long, dull services. Clergy repeatedly scandalized the congregation. Its leaders, savoring the perquisites of office, held their vestry meetings over delectable dinners featuring fine wines, warm conviviality, and a trifling bit of business. Then Meade came to town.

Meade had grown up in a family of ardent Episcopalians who were kin to Mary Fitzhugh Custis of Arlington. Attending Princeton, he led a multifarious student life, studying Scottish rationalism, sharing in a student rebellion, and sensing a spiritual stirring that his cousin Mrs. Custis was only too happy to foster. When he pondered a call to ordained ministry, she helped apprentice him to a priest across the Potomac in Georgetown, Walter Addison. At Addison's direction, Meade read the classics of enlightened Anglicanism, such as Butler's works and William Paley's *Evidences of Christianity*, which sought to undergird Christian faith on the basis of nature. But Addison also modeled an evangelical mind-set and ministry befitting the evangelical way that Meade was only too eager to pursue.[3]

Meade vowed to change Christ Church into a model evangelical parish. He ended the vestry's fancy dinner meetings. He insisted that baptisms occur in the sanctity of church rather than amid the often-riotous parties in homes.[4] That was just the start.

Meade tried to infuse worship at Christ Church with energy and participation. He included more hymns. He shortened services. Reforming the old practice of responses made only by a "clerk, who, in a loud voice, sung or drawled them out," Meade involved the whole congregation, as the Prayer Book expected. He enlisted children from his catechism class to speak those parts so their parents would too. Robert Lee may have figured in Meade's plan.[5]

It all worked. Alleging that "the Gospel . . . had not been clearly preached in times past," Meade preached it, and "God's blessing was granted." Attendance soared. Congressmen came from Washington to hear Meade preach.[6]

Meade aimed even higher. He sought to elevate the Christian behavior of his people. He required sponsors at baptisms to be worthy of their role and set good examples. So should those being confirmed and admitted to Communion, he insisted, for they constituted the church on display to the world. On laity, no less than clergy, rested the credibility of the entire evangelical enterprise.

That enterprise spread from a single congregation to a region. Before returning to his home area of Winchester in 1813, seventeen months after arriving in Arlington, Meade recruited William Holland Wilmer (father of the bishop he helped consecrate in 1862) for the rectorship of nearby St. Paul's Church, and Oliver Norris as his successor at Christ Church. This trio led what came to be known as the Washington School. They aspired to bring "those views of the Gospel and the Church which the evangelical clergy and laity of England were then so zealously and successfully propagating there." Joining them were clergy such as Charles McIlvaine and John Johns—both future bishops—and laity including Francis Scott Key and Lee's uncle Edmund.

Then revival spread even further. This band of like-minded brothers set out to achieve what many, including the US Supreme Court Chief Justice John Marshall, thought impossible: resurrecting the Episcopal Church in Virginia. They succeeded because they developed a structured, wide-ranging plan of reform and drew wide support from Marshall,[7] the Custises, the Lees, and countless others.

The Evangelical Program: Renewing the Virginia Diocese

Like evangelicals generally, Meade and his group promoted three priorities: a deep awareness of personal sin, the need to be born again, and the mission of transforming the world in the name of God.[8] By framing these objectives in the context of the Prayer Book and Episcopal tradition, they gave new meaning to the church's rites while opening the door to renewed vigor within the institution.

Clear in their convictions, the reformers began implementing a cohesive plan that started with new leadership at the top. Bishop Madison died in 1812. Virginians were unable to organize themselves sufficiently to call a new bishop until 1814, giving Meade, Edmund Lee, and their allies the opening to pursue Richard Channing Moore of New York. Influenced by the Second Great Awakening, a promoter of religious societies and of hymns in the liturgy, and a powerful preacher, Moore was a kindred spirit whom they duly elected as bishop.[9]

With a bishop at last on their side, the evangelical allies developed vehicles for communication. No serious Episcopal journal then existed south of New York. In 1819 the group created the *Washington Theological Repertory* to set forth principles "of the Bible, as illustrated in the

Articles, Liturgy, and Homilies of the Protestant Episcopal Church," "catholic principles" that supported "the Apostolical character of her institution, the pious tendency of her rites and ceremonies, and the evangelical nature of her doctrines." It aimed "to humble the sinner, and to exalt the Saviour, to show him the utmost depth of his depravity, as the best and the only means of inducing him to fly for refuge to the Lord Jesus Christ." With Wilmer as editor and McIlvaine a major contributor, the journal published sermons, articles, news, and views from the wider church, including from England, all promoting the importance of the Reformation, of conversion, and of a devout and holy life.[10] To communicate with a broader audience, the diocese created the *Southern Churchman* fifteen years later. From 1835, with Robert's cousin William Fitzhugh Lee as editor and with a motto of "Catholic for every truth of God. Protestant for every error of man," this weekly newspaper brought reports and commentary to the homes of Episcopalians. The Custis and Lee families subscribed to it and read it.[11]

An "Education Society" began promoting learning among clergy. The old apprentice system had proven haphazard, so this society envisioned a seminary to train prospective clergy employing evangelical principles. In 1823 Virginia Theological Seminary (VTS) opened in Alexandria. Cassius Lee devoted much of his life to it.[12]

Once educated and ordained, new clergy required nurturing. "Clerical associations" formed to meet the need. Clergy met by regions for fellowship, prayer, preaching, services, and collecting funds for mission work in the diocese's western frontiers. Annual diocesan conventions, gathering clergy and lay delegates for business, grew into veritable revivals and virtual family reunions—not least of all for Meade: a clergyman visiting a convention some years later noticed that half the delegates referred to their bishop as "Cousin William."[13]

By the time Robert E. Lee was a teenager, the diocese was beginning to convert the commonwealth. Congregations multiplied across the state. New church buildings sprouted to meet the needs of expanding populations. Demands on Moore became so great that in 1829 the diocese elected Meade as a bishop to assist him. Under these two, the reach and scope of the Episcopal Church expanded all the more.

They attracted clergy whose fervor was equal to their own. One was a West Point graduate named William Nelson Pendleton. Born in Caroline County into an old Virginia family—his mother was among the first people Bishop Madison confirmed—he served army posts, then taught mathematics at a Pennsylvania college where he discerned a call to ordained ministry. Bishop Meade, a cousin by marriage, ordained Pendleton deacon in 1837. The next year, Pendleton's sister-in-law married Meade's oldest son. The year after that, Meade coaxed Pendleton to found Episcopal High School, next door to VTS, to provide a first-rate education and strict discipline to sons of church families, including those of modest means.[14]

Clergy alone could not grow the church. Laity often organized new congregations. In the far-off town of Lexington, home of the Presbyterian-dominated Washington College, Francis Henney Smith led in founding the Virginia Military Institute in 1839. Months later, he and other Episcopal faculty members created Grace Church to minister, as their first rector stated, to "the number of youths of Episcopal families collected at the different [academic] institutions, chiefly at the Military Institute," to Episcopalians in the area (few though they were), and to the "hundreds of unconverted," especially among the young. By 1842, at Meade's urging, they had erected a simple brick edifice. Clergy came and went until 1853 when Pendleton, then serving a parish in Maryland, became Grace Church's first full-time rector.[15]

The Evangelical Life: Transforming Individuals

Growing the church was one major goal. Nurturing Christian lives was another. Evangelicals devoutly believed that the outward and visible reflected the inward and spiritual. A transformed heart will show forth in transformed behavior. The idea was not new. The Prayer Book, reflecting Titus 1:16 ("They profess to know God, but they deny him by their deeds"), included a prayer for "all who are admitted into the Fellowship of Christ's religion, that they may avoid those things that are contrary to their profession." In that spirit, latitudinarians frowned on "worldly amusements." Bishop White opposed them, as did Richard Henry Lee, who proposed in 1778 that the Continental Congress limit them. Evangelicals went still further. Though they enshrined morality in canon and even civil law, what truly mattered for them was the state of the heart: the truly converted person will in all things act like one.[16]

So, for them, Christian conviction dictated such everyday details as food, entertainment, and apparel. Here they found a tension, as did New England Puritans before them. A fine line existed between appreciating God's gifts of food, clothing, and song and condemning the abuse of them, especially taking them to excess.[17]

Meade tried to set a standard. As bishop, he fought snow and cold to visit on horseback a flock dispersed across what are now two states. He furnished his home austerely. He served "neither wine, nor strong drink, nor the Virginia weed"—tobacco—though he tolerated alcohol for medicinal use and at times sipped a mixture of currant wine and water, but only at home.[18]

While pursuing a positive approach of exemplifying a Christian way of life, Meade also assailed negative behaviors and "worldly entertainments." He set about reforming society in broader ways, starting with members of his own diocese. He began with the clergy. The diocesan convention of 1815 considered rules, borrowed from the Diocese of Maryland, condemning drunkenness, gaming, extortion, and similar vices among the ordained. Initially deemed radical, the rules were approved two years later.[19]

What then of laity? Should not delegates to diocesan conventions who make such demands of others conform their own lives to the gospel? "The strange anomaly of persons legislating for others and not being themselves subject to such legislation was allowed in the Church." By raising the bar for its lay leaders, the convention urged the godly life for all, especially godparents and communicants, those entitled to receive Holy Communion.[20]

Francis Scott Key tried to spread that message to the entire Episcopal Church. As a deputy at the 1817 General Convention, he proposed enjoining the clergy to "recommend sobriety of life and conversion" and for all to forswear the "vain amusements of the world" (like "playing at cards") as "inconsistent with Christian sobriety, dangerous to the morals of the members of the Church, and peculiarly unbecoming the character of communicants." The proposal failed. Virginia Episcopalians took their time instituting disciplinary measures as well, only in 1850 passing by a slim margin a measure to discipline members who pursued evil ways, which included "gaming, attendance on horse racing, and theatrical amusements, witnessing immodest and licentious exhibitions or shows, attending public balls."[21]

Paradoxically, many of Meade's people were those who most loved such pleasures. The Virginia elite were Meade's kith, kin, and friends, but he seemed to hold a loving aversion to them. He was repelled by their excesses; he condemned their "amusements";

and he lived in austere contrast with his family on a lean farm he worked himself. Over the decades of Meade's preaching, teaching, and downright hectoring, he eventually won these people to his views to a surprising degree. He shamed some of them into it, like his early parishioners at Christ Church; some he outlasted; and some, like many in the Custis and Lee families, he inspired by his evangelical vision of a godly life.

Of course, Arlington House was never "simple," nor its way of life "austere." Mrs. Custis, along with her daughter and son-in-law, remained always close to Meade, and yet Robert never forsook his love for dance. Southern—and Episcopal—life retained its contradictions.

The Evangelical Life: The Contradiction of Slavery

As the evangelical revival spread across denominations and through the nation, it did not confine itself to the conversion of parishes or individual lives. The greater goal remained to transform society itself. Countless efforts emerged to reform education and prisons, to reduce alcohol abuse, and to ensure safety in food, health, and sanitation. The Diocese of Virginia itself promoted a host of voluntary organizations, many for women, to advance missionary work, schools, the Bible, the Prayer Book, and tracts. It supported education to such an extent that by 1832 Virginia had more Sunday schools affiliated with a national association than any other Southern state.[22] Yet one overriding concern increasingly dominated them all, a basic paradox that Virginia's clergy saw each time they looked at their own pews populated with white faces and at least a few black ones: slavery.

Meade felt the contradiction personally. During his youth, when the revolutionary spirit persisted, American Christians developed ambivalent attitudes toward slavery. In the North, the Episcopal presiding bishop, John Henry Hopkins of Vermont, justified the institution as late as 1861. In the South, Meade's family owned slaves, as did the priest for whom he worked in Winchester, as did Meade himself. Yet he admired his sister Ann Meade Page and his mentor Walter Addison, who considered slavery an inherited evil, as did his evangelical hero, Wilberforce, whose labors to end slavery led to its abolition in the British Empire in 1833. Meade tended to agree. He also proclaimed that Christ died for all, regardless of race. Therefore, he argued, "servants" needed to be instructed in the gospel as much as anyone else. He exhorted his diocese to do just that.[23]

His theology appears in a testy letter to Jefferson Davis. In 1862 a new book, dedicated to the Confederate president, oddly combined "creationism" and "evolution." It alleged that whites were descended from Adam and Eve, and blacks from apes. Meade took offense on two counts. Dismissing God's creation of *all* races through Adam struck Meade as a "positive denial of the divine inspiration & truth of the Bible" and its teaching that all humankind is related, thus implying that Christ died only for some, namely, whites. Then, the "disgusting vilification of the whole African race" by "placing it next to the Ape, monkey, or gorilla" undercut his efforts to get "masters & mistresses . . . to Xtianize this race." He urged Davis to disavow the work.[24]

For many years Meade pursued a popular though ultimately unrealistic plan to resolve the issue of slavery. In December 1816, he, Key, Wilmer, Edmund Jennings Lee, Richard Bland Lee, and Mary Custis's brother, William Fitzhugh, gathered in Washington with others to charter the Society for Colonizing the Free People of Color of America. It proposed to free slaves, send them to western Africa, sponsor missionaries to support them, and thereby create a Christian state in what they came to call Liberia, next to the British counterpart in Sierra Leone.

"Colonization" became a Meade family passion. Ann Page freed twenty-three slaves and sent them to Liberia between 1832 and 1838. Her son-in-law became an agent of the society. With his usual vigor, Meade helped to organize the effort, arouse support, raise funds, and select its first colonists.[25] He shared with Mrs. Custis the progress of the society and his frustrations on its shortcomings, and convinced her husband to participate. After founding local societies throughout Virginia and Maryland, Meade ventured to other states, North as well as South, trying to raise support. He presided over the African Education Society of the United States, which provided potential colonists with practical training in agriculture and mechanics. His efforts inspired one Custis cousin to raise poultry and knit socks to glean funds for the project; Mary and Robert joked about eating her chickens.[26]

Still, slavery deeply worried the bishop. In 1833, he wrote Mrs. Custis, "We must make the since [sins] of our Fathers our own" and remove "an evil which grows with our growth & strengthens with our strength, and will soon outgrow us & heave us to the ground." He resolved to free his own slaves "as soon as I possibly can without injury to themselves & prejudice to the general cause." He complained, "I am heartily sick of the thousand drawbacks they continually present to my souls welfare" and to the "cause which I have undertaken." When he did free them, though, their freedom did not fulfill his hopes for them, and most freed slaves, many whose families had been in America for generations, chose not to go to Africa.[27]

Meade drew some fine lines. His sister deemed slavery inherently evil. He did not. But in 1854 he wrote to his fellow bishop, Leonidas Polk, who owned more than three hundred slaves, that it "is in a certain sense a divine institution." Given myriad biblical references to masters and servants, he argued, owning slaves "certainly is permitted & sanctioned by God." *Taking* slaves, however, he intensely opposed, also on scriptural grounds. "The many passages forbi[d]ding man stealing & speaking compassionately of captives, & those in bondage, commending them to our prayers & relief shew that it is our duty to discourage & condemn the practice of making slaves of our fellow beings, who are in the enjoyment of liberty, especially when great cruelty attends the same, as certainly is the case with the African slave trade." Countering Polk, he called "the African slave trade a great sin. By encouraging it at all we promote a great evil among that unhappy race."

But *holding* slaves could be a positive good. "I think it probable that the free negroes in the North wld be generally happier & better, if they were slaves in the South," he admitted to Polk. But, he insisted, that did not justify enslaving free blacks in the North and bringing them south "for the sake of the good that might result to them & their posterity from the change."[28]

Meade echoed an increasingly common if hopelessly contorted justification of slavery posed by Southern Christians: God, who made all people, condoned slavery especially for blacks, who, the argument went, were inherently inferior. Slaves in the South were better off than free blacks in the North. Meade differed from the broader consensus only in believing that slaves needed to be taught Christianity. Their souls needed to be saved too.[29]

With secession, Meade faced a bitter internal struggle. He hated the thought of disunion, both for itself and for the damage that a "fratricidal war" would do to "the establishment of Christ's kingdom in all the earth," for which "our country [could] be one of the most effective and honored instruments." In a letter to his diocese in 1861, he asked, "Is there not enough room for us all to dwell together in peace in this widely-extended country . . . ?"[30]

Evidently not. In the 1840s, Methodists, Baptists, and some Presbyterians divided along North-South lines, which to Meade revealed and reinforced divisiveness. In late 1860 he wrote McIlvaine that "the Churches sympathize with and sustain the politicians of the South. To a certain, and, I fear, a large extent, the union of both Church and country is no more." For churches to split was signally tragic. If "Christian ministers . . . cannot continue together to consult about the Kingdom of the Prince of Peace, even while the civil rulers have preserved their union, can we expect the selfish politicians to do it? . . . You see that I am almost in despair."[31]

As it happened, the two old evangelical allies were themselves diverging. Having rejected colonization, McIlvaine slowly accepted the antislavery position and, in 1860, even supported Lincoln for the presidency.[32] Meade veered in the opposite direction. In May 1861 he told McIlvaine, "I have slowly and reluctantly come to the conclusion, that we must separate." When Virginia seceded and Federal troops threatened, Meade became a Southern patriot convinced that success in secession "is undoubted." He asked his 1861 convention, "Who can desire to retain a Union which has become so hateful," and by its use of armed force would become "ten times more hateful"?[33]

Separation engendered intense personal sorrow. Meade lamented to the wealthy Richmond Episcopal layman John Stewart (who owned the Franklin Street home that the Lees later rented), "The thought is painful that during the remainder of my life I am probably separated allmost entirely from all those who have been so dear to me." Ecclesial division was institutionalized when Southern dioceses formed the Protestant Episcopal Church of the Confederate States of America.[34]

As he predicted, war wrought a terrible personal toll. "One of my grandsons was injured—he is losing his right arm," he wrote Stewart. Another grandson survived a battle that claimed men on each side of him. "God has been most gracious to mine," he wrote; but cherished sites fell to the foe. "The federal troops took possession of our Seminary buildings. . . . All our beautiful groves are doubtless prostrated as have those around & back of Arlington House!" Along the nine-mile range of hills "lay the camps of our foes & the soil of which is destined, in all human probability, to be covered with blood & bones of the slain." In time he related that his injured grandson had worsened, and "our poor boy" grasped life by a "slender thread."[35]

Still, somewhere, somehow, God's hand guided great battles and private mercies. Meade's doctrine of providence dictated that he believe no less. How could God not have been acting when Union generals had planned "most admirably" their strategies near Winchester (where his "boys" were engaged), and Southerners won almost despite themselves? "How clear had God determined to take them & their own [Northern] craftiness & make their very movement the very means of displaying his power to make the few conquer the many. . . . But God had directed it all. . . . It is impossible that the victory could have been more compleat if our whole army had been engaged and advantageous circumstances, while the disparity of numbers must make it evident to all that our men will not be conquered . . . tho we also believe that God makes use of these in order to giving [*sic*] us the victory."[36]

Even when the news turned bad, Meade drew consolation from the idea of providence. God surely willed "a gracious design in all the sufferings he permits & may permit to fall upon us, & we I trust will submit as Christians. Our enemies are opening an impassable gulph between us & our descendants & them & theirs, & doubtless God sees that this is for good."[37] On his deathbed, he assured his suffragan and successor Bishop Johns, "I trust the South will persevere in separation."

In 1862, his life ebbing, Meade reaffirmed his "hope . . . in Christ, 'the Rock of Ages.'" He asserted, "I am at peace with God through Jesus Christ, my Lord, and in charity with all men, even our bitterest enemies." Then he added, Protestant to the end, "All that has ever been said in commendation of me I loathe and abhor, as utterly inconsistent with my consciousness of sin."[38]

Meade died on March 13, 1862, by his own confession a humble evangelical Episcopal Christian. Robert E. Lee was profoundly moved. His life, and his family's, had intersected with Meade's repeatedly over the course of a half century. "He was very anxious to see you," Robert wrote his wife of his last conversation with the bishop. "Sent you his love and kindest remembrances, & had I known in time yesterday I would have sent expressly for you to come up." He wrote to Carter, "Our good Bishop died last night. May our end be like his!"[39]

Meade's professions of humility aside, efforts to memorialize him began almost as soon as the war ended. Bishop Johns began a biography of his longtime superior. Lee encouraged that project and, two years later, the idea of building a monument to Meade. He considered the proposed design "chaste & handsome," though—despite the bishop's disclaimers of "commendations" of himself—Lee "should have preferred a structure grander & more massive in its form, & something commensurate with the estimation in which our late good Bishop was held by the people of VA."[40] It was never built, but a decade after Meade's death, Meade Memorial Church was founded as a mission to African Americans in Alexandria. It survives today as a parish church.

Lee cherished the place of "our good and beloved Bishop Meade" in his life. After the war, he recalled the "affection and interest, begun at that time," with which Meade heard him say his catechism, that continued "to the present." "Of all the men I have ever known," he wrote Johns, "I considered him the purest."[41] Lee himself may have been Meade's greatest personal legacy.

CHAPTER 6

"With the Sign of the Cross"

~

The Young Officer

If Robert Lee had any idea of the theological battles swirling about him as a boy, he left no clear sign of it: no recollections of any other tensions between his parents, no record of memories of the church of his youth beyond saying his catechism to William Meade.

When Lee was baptized, presumably at Stratford Hall,[1] his parents and godparents vowed to bring him up in the Christian faith and life. Of course, not everyone took such vows seriously, which (together with holding baptisms at home rather than at church) explains why Meade and his companions complained so vociferously about baptismal practices.

When Henry fled the country in 1813, Ann became a sole parent, a role she had functionally filled for some time. That, together with the power of her own convictions, made her the most immediate influence on her son's religious life. Though his father tried to intervene in the religious training of their children, his absence made his efforts entirely ineffective. Lee, in his forties, voiced a comment that probably reflected his personal experience: "A child learns all that it has of good from its mother."[2]

If Lee learned anything from his mother's situation, and from his father's words if not always his example, it was the need for duty. While his father stressed duty as a classic virtue, Ann Lee's evangelicalism made Christian responsibility just as ethically imperative. Her precarious health made it practically necessary. Robert was six when his father left, eleven when he died. His sister Ann was chronically ill and sometimes required treatment in Philadelphia. His mother was becoming the invalid she would remain for the rest of her life. With Carter at

Harvard and then starting a law practice, and with Smith joining the navy in 1820, Robert remained virtually alone to oversee the household and care for its members. "He kept house under his mother's direction," his cousin Sarah, Edmund Jennings's daughter, recalled after his death. "She was one of the most methodical, and beautiful managers, always cheerful, and dignified. I think dear Robert's disposition was very like his mother's." All the while, he kept up his studies at the Alexandria Academy, a free school he attended along with Sarah's brother, Cassius.[3] Like Sarah, Cassius reminisced to Mary about their cousin's youth. "I recollect his uniform correct deportment at school and elsewhere, and his attention to his studies. What impressed me most in my youthful days, was his devotion to his mother, who as you know was for many years an invalid. She used to say he was son & daughter to her. He was her housekeeper & relieved her of all domestic cares, looked after the horses, rode out in the carriage with her, did the marketing for the family."[4]

Dutifully, the Lees attended church and paid close attention to what was going on in the service. They said family prayers, which had a lasting effect. When the nine-year-old Carter Lee walked into a new boarding school in 1807, he spotted a Bible, a Book of Common Prayer, and Blair's sermons, all like those he had seen at Stratford Hall (where the family was still living).[5] Ann Lee made sure, too, that her children knew their catechism. Robert remembered her teaching it to him "before I could read." That was prudent on her part, for Lee would have recited it to Meade, whose expectations were exceptionally high for the entire process of Christian education, including the catechism that parents were supposed to teach.[6]

Meade's expectations arose from the entire evangelical program. For that reason Meade and his colleagues elevated the standards for confirmation, as they had for baptism. In confirmation, an individual, normally baptized as an infant, affirmed for himself or herself the fundamental vows of a Christian in the presence of a bishop. Episcopal evangelicals considered the renewal of these vows in confirmation to be a vital moment in the Christian life, a veritable outward and visible sign of inward conversion. They gave an Episcopal twist to the evangelical doctrine of personal apprehension of Christ. Receiving this rite in turn qualified the confirmand to receive Holy Communion and thus become a communicant. Such a spiritual status demanded a high level not only of belief but also of behavior, as canons of the diocese eventually insisted. These standards also applied to those aspiring to become communicants. Meade expected "a candidate for confirmation coming with that true penitence and lively faith promised at his baptism, to thank God for the renovation of his heart, and the forgiveness of all his sins, and to be admitted by the rite of confirmation to full communion with the people of God at the Lord's supper."[7] Communion, hence confirmation, hence catechism—all became vital stages in the life of spiritual transformation that began at baptism, with standards of behavior to match.

Meade so highly esteemed the catechism as a means of preparing the young for faithful life that he published several books about it.[8] The catechism instructed the individual on the nature of Christian faith and provided a means by which a person might grow into that faith. Far from being an intellectual enterprise alone, the catechetical process was to be profoundly spiritual.

Meade's rigorous approach elevated the spiritual bar for confirmation and Communion alike. He urged confirmands to rise to it by pondering how well they were living out their baptismal promises. He pressed confirmands to understand the dangers of those worldly pleasures he so heartily discouraged. He also asked how they had been influenced by God, in belief itself but also in the practice that arises from belief.

These were high standards of conviction as well as behavior. Though theoretically imbued with God's grace, they offered little latitude for candidates who did not measure up to what was expected of the communicant. It was also much to demand of a boy dealing with a fractured household and an ailing mother along with schoolwork and an uncertain future. Becoming a confirmed communicant may well have been a step he considered beyond his ability to take. For whatever reasons, Robert Lee waited until middle age to receive the rite in 1853.

The Cadet and Young Officer

By the time he reached seventeen, Lee faced the prospect of leaving home for school or a job or both. Lee had to focus on his future. The United States Military Academy beckoned. It offered a free education and the promise of a military career. Cassius gleaned the impression that the army "was his choice as a profession—tho' it is very probable a desire to relieve his mother [of paying for his schooling] may have had something to do in influencing his choice."[9] She had already struggled to meet Carter's bills at Harvard.

Obtaining an appointment, even for the son of a Revolutionary War hero, was not easy, so the extended family pulled out all stops. Mr. Custis's sister, "Aunt Lewis," introduced Lee to Andrew Jackson. Testimonial letters to Secretary of War John C. Calhoun described Lee's habits and deportment as "correct and gentlemanly," his disposition as "amiable & his morals irreproachable." Calhoun bestowed an appointment, but for the class matriculating in 1825. Lee had a year to fill. So he set about improving his mathematics under a Quaker named Benjamin Hallowell, who had just opened a school next door to the Lees, in yet another house owned by William Fitzhugh. Hallowell later recalled that the young man "was a most exemplary pupil in every respect. He was never behind time at his studies; never failed in a single recitation; was perfectly observant of the rules and regulations of the institution; was gentlemanly, unobtrusive, and respectful in all his deportment to teacher and his fellow-students. His specialty was finishing up. He imparted a finish and a neatness, as he proceeded, to everything he undertook."[10]

The year's delay did provide one big consolation. In the fall of 1824, the Marquis de Lafayette, the French hero of the American Revolution, made a triumphal tour of the United States. Lee had a role in the festivities. In a gala parade to welcome Lafayette's return to Washington's home turf, Lee, son of one of Lafayette's colleagues on Washington's staff, served as an honorary marshal. A day or two after the parade, he and his brothers chatted with the marquis at Arlington House.[11]

As the summer of 1825 dawned, Lee faced the difficult task of leaving Alexandria, and a mother who increasingly depended on him. Parting was inevitable—and he would do it many more times in his life. He left for New York to begin what quickly became a distinguished career at West Point.

He found an institution dominated, as the Episcopal Church in Virginia came to be, by one person. Sylvanus Thayer had been superintendent since 1817. Like Bishop Meade, Thayer knew his institution. Also like Meade, he cut an austere figure who brooked no frivolity. Lee wrote home that cadets suspected him of spying on them because he knew everything that happened. That included the distinctly unofficial lesson on "the mysteries of eggnog" planned for Christmas Eve, 1826.

At that time, once cadets arrived at West Point, they rarely left (unless permanently), not even for Christmas holidays. A group of Southerners led by the Mississippian Jefferson Davis decided to celebrate the Yule in a manner befitting their region, a manner that included a certain libation, even though one of its most crucial ingredients was strictly forbidden. Thayer caught wind of their plan, put his staff and cadet officers on alert, and warned the corps against undue revelry. Undeterred, the plotters procured the necessary spirits from Benny Havens's nearby tavern, smuggled them into the north barracks, and lay low until midnight, when they assumed the guard would be less guarded. As Christmas Eve turned to Christmas Day, the lesson in eggnog commenced. Predictable results ensued. Noise from the party reached the ears of Captain Ethan Allen Hitchcock, who, on finding its source, ordered cadets, by name, to their rooms, under arrest. Davis had fortuitously stepped away in time to miss the mutinous riot.[12]

With order restored and investigations completed, nineteen cadets were dismissed. Davis barely avoided being among them.[13] Two other Southerners—and future generals—skipped the merrymaking altogether: Robert Lee and Joseph Johnston.

Nor did Lee figure in a phenomenon most unlike the Yuletide frolic. Religious life at West Point was perfunctory at best. Thayer, as head of a national institution, insisted that strict denominational neutrality be maintained. At the first academic institution in the country in which sciences rather than liberal arts dominated the curriculum, and when conflicts between science and religion were just emerging, very few at West Point held much interest in spiritual matters. Of all those at the academy, only three, all wives of faculty, were known to be communicants. Cadets had to attend religious services on Sunday, but they were not required to listen. The departing Presbyterian chaplain's long, boring sermons gave them little incentive to do so.[14]

That changed. In 1825, not only did Lee arrive as a cadet, but so did the Reverend Dr. Charles McIlvaine as professor of geography, history, and ethics. He also served as chaplain. Only twenty-six years old, this Episcopal priest had already been chaplain to the United States Senate, and a partner with Meade in revivalism. With a passion akin to Meade's, McIlvaine set about invigorating the dismal scene he found. Tall, eloquent, and earnest, he advanced the same evangelical outlook, spirituality, and style that he had helped foster in Washington. Even sermons of two hours' length did not dissuade at least some of his young listeners.[15] Still, the ingrained habits of the cadets, the hostility of the faculty, and the propensity of teenagers to sleep, especially after a hard week's work, made progress slow. Then one Sunday in McIlvaine's second year, a cadet knelt for prayer in the chapel. This was unheard of: a cadet actually taking religion seriously. Leonidas Polk was two years Lee's senior. Under McIlvaine's spiritual guidance, Polk and a few cadets read the Bible together. More and more of them met with him for worship, instruction, and prayer, once, twice, even three times a week.[16]

The minirevival lasted only briefly. "High church" proclivities in the Diocese of New York, fears of the faculty, and charges that he was "aiming to make young men soldiers in the Church militant" forced McIlvaine to leave in late 1827 for St. Ann's Church in Brooklyn.[17]

No evidence connects Lee with either the revival or the revelries, though in the small world of West Point he surely knew of both. His class had only forty-six members by the time it graduated. Lee climbed to the top of it. He ranked second academically, compiling a record unsullied by a single demerit. His success led to his remaining another year as assistant professor of mathematics.[18] That extra year of preparation proved to serve him well.

Motherless Child, Future Husband

Lee's father died in 1818 when Robert was eleven. No record exists of how Henry's death affected his son. Robert's mother began her final decline as Robert was concluding his cadetship. Ann had moved to Georgetown after Robert left for the academy. She seemed to rally in the spring of 1829, but by June the Fitzhughs, who had sustained her for so long, insisted that they care for her at Ravensworth. There, just after graduation, Robert joined her. His cousin Sarah noted that his mother watched every move her son made as he mixed her medicines and tried to comfort her.[19]

Ann Lee died in midsummer (scholars disagree over the date). Robert inconsolably paced her room, so stricken with grief that he could not bear to attend her funeral. She was buried at Ravensworth.[20]

Even for an orphan, life goes on. Responsibilities quickly demanded his attention. General Charles Gratiot, the army's chief of engineers, ordered Lee to report to Cockspur Island in the Savannah River in Georgia. Slowly moving beyond the sadness of July, Lee seemed to regain his earlier composure and cheerfulness. A cousin described him "as full of life, fun and particularly of teasing as any of us."[21]

The newly commissioned Brevet Second Lieutenant Lee needed all the cheerfulness he could muster, once he confronted the realities of a junior officer's life in the Corps of Engineers. Ominously named for a hawthorn plant with long, sharp thorns, the island consisted mostly of marshland subject to flooding and was infested with sand fleas and "moschetoes." The army assigned him to build a fort on the site to guard the entrance to Savannah, some twelve miles upriver.[22]

Constructing what became Fort Pulaski constituted hard labor. If Lee was not standing knee deep in mud, he was enduring water up to his armpits, which at least may have provided relief from air so turgid that work in summer lulled to a stop. His commanding officer, a largely absentee major, possessed little understanding of the task, faced acute personal problems, and often was simply absent. Lee took charge by default: duty called.

Savannah became for Lee a haven both worldly and spiritual. In the family home of his West Point friend Jack Mackay, assigned to an artillery post in the city, Lee found a ready welcome. Jack's widowed mother virtually adopted the young Virginian. That she had four unwed daughters made her home even more appealing. That they introduced him to the city's society gave him still more reason to travel to Savannah as often as possible. As well, Savannah had the closest houses of worship. Lee attended Christ Church whenever possible.

However mixed his motives in venturing to Savannah, Lee took on the traits of a good churchman. Observing the liturgical year, he attended the Christmas service in Savannah. He listened to clergy, hoping for worthwhile words from the pulpit, as often as not in vain. For him, this was not an irreligious time, but it was not especially spiritual either. He mentioned God in letters to family, but only as an idiom; after his commander's wife suddenly departed, he wrote Carter that "Madame had separated from him, and had carried off her youngest child, and that neither the Maj. or her friends knew what had become of her. This may be mere report or slander, God knows for I don't."[23]

As he faced his twenty-fourth birthday, death, duty, and the realities of the human condition had descended upon Robert Edward Lee. He had also taken on such religious responsibilities as attending church for himself. Not coincidentally, he had turned considerable attention to Arlington, where dwelt a certain young lady. He had come of age.

CHAPTER 7

"To Have and to Hold"

~

Struggling to Unite Two as One

Lights blazed from the parlor of Arlington House on Thursday evening, June 30, 1831. Outside, rainstorms soaked the Custis estate. Inside, all was joy. The daughter of Arlington, Mary Anna Randolph Custis, and the handsome young army lieutenant Robert Edward Lee were being joined in holy matrimony. The Reverend Ruell Keith, a teacher at Virginia Seminary that the couple knew from Christ Church, officiated in the words of the Episcopal rite. The groom reported feeling that "he dwelt upon them as if he had been reading my Death warrant." Lee sensed in his bride as well a "tremulousness in the hand I held that made me anxious for him to end." As Lee confessed to his good friend Andrew Talcott a fortnight later, "I am told I looked 'pale & interesting' which might have been the fact. I felt as 'bold as a sheep' & was surprised at my want of Romance in so great a degree as not to feel more excitement than at the Black Board at West Point."[1]

The wedding had been a hard time coming. Even weeks before, the ceremony remained uncertain. The religion they shared had come close to tearing them apart.

From childhood, Robert had lifted up admiring eyes unto the hills of Arlington. He once called Tub Custis's home "a House any one might see with half an eye." There lived Mary Anna Randolph, the Custises' only surviving child, a year younger than Lee.[2]

By 1830 Mary Custis ranked among the most desirable young ladies in Virginia. Though not considered beautiful, she possessed a pedigree and a potential inheritance virtually without equal. For young women of her day, she was uncommonly well read. Her sparkling eyes and spirit caught the attention of many a potential beau, among them Tennessee

Congressman Sam Houston, born in Rockbridge County, Virginia, who eventually became president of the Republic of Texas. All the Lee boys took an interest in her: Carter, Smith, and, not to be left out, Robert.[3]

Robert and Mary were entangled within the intricate web of Virginia family kinships. Sharing a great-great-grandfather made their mothers second cousins. As children, they had played together, perhaps even planted trees at Arlington. Lee recalled her father as a man "whose affection I experienced in boyhood." By the time Mary and Robert were about seventeen, they viewed each other as more than playmates. "Do you recollect that [Christmas] of 1824," Lee cryptically asked Mary after they were engaged, "& the cake in the storeroom?"[4]

Robert was not nearly as desirable a marital prospect as Mary. While his pedigree almost matched hers, the estate he shared with his brothers consisted of twenty thousand remote acres in southwestern Virginia, considered worthless and encumbered with debt. Along with land, his mother left her three sons thirty slaves, most of whom were sold at her death. His father, Light-Horse Harry, had died in debt and disgrace. Worse yet, his half brother had earned the nickname "Black-Horse Harry" for an adulterous affair with his sister-in-law ten years earlier. The scandal resurfaced in March 1830, just as Robert was wooing Mary, when the US Senate unanimously rejected Henry Lee IV's appointment as consul to Algiers. Dirty Lee linen became known to all.[5]

Still, Robert was dashing, handsome, and spirited. At some time, most likely in the late summer of 1830, Mary agreed to become his wife.[6] But the engagement proved to be easier to attain than the wedding. Not only did her father hesitate to give his consent, but Mary discerned the love of another. Her discovery called into question every aspect of her life, including whether she should marry the young Lieutenant Lee. For her other love was God.

Growing Up Custis

By any worldly reckoning, Mary Anna Randolph Custis lived a charmed life. Born at the pinnacle of Virginia's elite and wealth, she had been doted on by relatives in her large and loving extended family and pampered by servants (as the family always termed their slaves).[7]

Like Robert, Mary grew up a practicing Episcopalian of the Virginia style. She regularly made the long trip to Christ Church, Alexandria. She knew the clergy and they knew her. The family marked the church's cycle of observances, including Christmas, Good Friday, and Easter. Led by her mother, the Arlington household gathered each day to pray and to ponder new religious works, such as a new biography of Edward Payson, a popular Congregational preacher in Maine, in July 1830. Mrs. Custis often discussed sermons, theological controversies, and personalities—the gossip of the church. She also used those occasions to teach the enslaved children to read the Bible and Prayer Book, to benefit their souls as well as to prepare them for Liberia, where Mrs. Custis dreamed of sending them through the Colonization Society.[8]

By letter and visit, Meade kept in touch with the Custises and involved them in his efforts to revitalize the diocese and improve the world. His sister, Ann Randolph Page, invited the Custises to a religious assembly in April 1830, which may have been the diocesan convention. Not sharing his wife's religious ardor, Mr. Custis would have shown no interest in so evangelical an event. He did, though, join her in supporting Meade's colonization project as a way to resolve what he considered America's racial predicament. In his 1831 play extolling Pocahontas's marriage to a white settler, he saw "no footing for the colored man" in America. "They have no right to a homestead in the white man's country. Let this fair land, which the white man won by his chivalry . . . be kept sacred for his descendants."[9]

Like Mount Vernon, Arlington was a busy place. Innumerable visitors, from the great to the ordinary, regularly came and went. Presidents dropped in, as Franklin Pierce did one June day in 1853.[10] But no event matched the Fourth of July, when Custis annually opened the estate to all comers, who could view Washington's tent and tableware and hear his adopted son laud at length the nation's first president. Whether anyone listened remains a mystery.

Mary's Great Awakening

On that feast of feasts of American independence in 1830, the daughter of Arlington began a diary. Nary a mention of the day's celebrations appears. Something even greater consumed her heart, soul, and mind: the love of God. "O my Father, let me thank thee for thy mercies to me, that thou has drawn me to thee by the cords of love." She continued, "What shall I render to the Lord for all his goodness. . . . I would live

58

with a simple eye to his service—yet—Oh my Saviour thou who hast borne our human nature knowest how weak we are, how utterly unable to do any thing of ourselves[,] thou wilt pity me & support me—oh my Father in Heaven enable me daily to offer up fervent supplications to that throne of mercy. . . . Enable me to feel that what thou hast promised. . . ."[11] Mary had undergone a spiritual conversion.

What produced this great personal awakening? During that spring, Mary related, "The world seemed as bright and alluring as ever." Then sorrow intruded. On May 21, her thirty-eight-year-old uncle, William Henry Fitzhugh, full of life and promise—that winter at a state constitutional convention he had urged greater democracy by reducing restrictions on who could vote—suddenly died. At first Mary resented the personal inconvenience of his death because "my mourning days would prevent my entering gay society." Her mother, though, "endeavoured to impress me with . . . the awful judgements of my God." Mrs. Custis asked, "If this blow does not turn your thoughts to Heaven what will do it?" Then Mary, "still thirsting after the world & its honours," visited Ravensworth, "where I had spent my happiest hours. There," her uncle gone and his widow deeply grieving, "all was desolation & woe. There first I prayed to my God to change my heart & make me his true & faithful servant."[12] By July 4, her heart had indeed changed.

On a rainy July 8, after private prayers and breakfast, Mary shared "the tale of my feelings" with her mother. "She wept & thanked God for this great blessing. Oh then I was so overwhelmed with a sense of my unworthiness that my heart felt as if it would burst."[13]

The diary Mary began on July 4 developed into a record of her spiritual progress. She maintained it nearly daily at first, then weekly on Sundays for just over a year, then sporadically for the rest of her life. It is unlikely she shared it with anyone, even her mother.

It reveals two struggles of the soul. One concerns the ebb and flow of feeling, from a confidence that warmed her whole being to ambivalence, sloth, even despair. Only a day after her conversion, she complained, "how cold how languid is my love today. Doubts & fears come over me. I am ready to exclaim Am I indeed a child of God? Oh my Saviour intercede for me that I faint not. Warm my heart." Two days later she wrote, "I have been troubled about many things but now I feel as if I could cast all my cares upon my Father. O God strengthen my faith & make me perfect in love to thee."[14] This contrast between faith and doubt became a constant inner wrangle.

The other struggle pits heavenly yearnings against earthly desires. Her uncle's death may have intensified the lures of this world, for she knew she would inherit his sizable estate. "I have years of worldly thoughts and indifference to contend with yet I wish to thank him whenever I feel the burden of my sins & my base ingratitude. When I examine my heart & my motives they are so weak so sinful, selfishness pervades even my prayers. . . . May He who has begun this good work in me. . . finish it." A week later, she faced her struggle directly. She partied on the evening of July 16 "in the company of worldly young gentlemen who flattered my vanity & pleased me in spite of myself." At that precise moment of temptation, she "received a delightful letter" from a friend of her mother that turned her back to God. "Whenever I think of the kindness of my friends, my mother's compassionate love & then how infinitely more tender is the love of my God . . . I can only pray to my Father to shed abroad more of his spirit in me."[15]

In this tension between heaven and earth, could worldly love find a place? Mary's conversion coincided with her growing attachment to Robert. Never, though, during the course of the year did she record his name, and she alluded to him only rarely. What, then, was his place? What was she to do? Could she love both God and Robert E. Lee?

On July 10, she confronted the problem. She had given herself to God. He "alone canst preserve me from the temptations which daily beset me[.] I feel no desires now for the fain pleasures of the world[.] I feel as if I could give them up from love to my God." That produced the critical question: "Could I give up my attachment to him who I love[?]" Could she incorporate an earthly love into her heavenly calling? And how could she be sure of herself when, as she admitted, "I doubt my sincerity"? She reached a tentative conclusion: "I did <u>not feel</u> that He required that sacrifice." God *would* allow Robert a place in her heart after all—probably. "On that subject I prayed most fervently & now I feel most easy. Oh my kind & merciful Father, if I am deceived by Satan open then my eyes but it is sin to doubt thee."

But what of his place in her soul? Robert's priorities were more earthly than heavenly. He did not share a conversion like hers, a deficiency that could impede their marriage and, she feared, even contradict God's will. God could resolve the matter simply, so Mary prayed, "Oh draw him also to Thee, that we may with one heart & one mind live to the glory of our Redeemer."[16] All would be well if he only converted.

Divided by a Common Faith

Robert showed no disposition to join in her enthusiasm. His mind was on marriage, not God. From Arlington on furlough, he wrote Carter of the engagements of friends and relations, then slyly added, "last though not least I am engaged to Miss Mary C. Think of that . . .—That is, She & her mother have given their consent. But the Father has not yet made up his mind, though it is supposed will not object." While the father did not object, he also did not consent, initiating a long limbo that proved as frustrating for Robert as Mary's spiritual tug-of-war. Eight days after sharing his news, he updated Carter, "The Wedding if there is one, will not be till next spring (so she says) and I am not going to resign, till God knows when, for I don't."[17]

Unlike Mary's, Lee's references to God remained conventional rather than spiritual. But they betray seeds of doubt: "The Wedding *if there is one*": What might preclude it?

Major Custis's reservations posed one obstacle. Lee knew of his reticence but not the reasons for it. There could have been many. Mary, as an only child, provided the only way to perpetuate the Custis line and retain the property within the family. Robert's family, though noble, had been besmirched by his father and half brother; Custis may have feared Robert's following in the family's less savory ways. Or he may simply have been loath to give up his daughter.

Mary had reason for concern. She was twenty-three years old at a time when women generally married between fifteen and eighteen. But marriage was not to be taken lightly, especially by one of her standing. Because laws did not yet allow married women to own property, the heiress of Arlington and Ravensworth could jeopardize her inheritance if she married irresponsibly. Robert brought into the marriage only those virtually valueless acres on the Virginia frontier. Matrimony marked a young woman's transition from the idylls of girlhood to the duties of adulthood: supervising the home, overseeing the servants, and—not least—bearing children, which remained a dangerous proposition. Worse yet, not only were the financial prospects of a young officer poor, but he was also subject to the orders of an army that would send him where it needed him regardless of family concerns. Mary would have to leave her mansion for officers' quarters in far-off posts like Cockspur Island.[18]

Underlying all else, Mary and Robert seemed to be walking different paths of faith. In late September 1830, when Lee spent a few weeks at Arlington, he wrote Carter of their plans for marriage. Mary meanwhile recorded in her diary her joy not that her beloved was near but that she had "been enabled to pray regularly & always with earnestness & to feel a hope that I was growing in grace"—and therefore she could pay closer attention in church.[19]

So it continued, Robert writing her of temporal pleasures, Mary meditating alone on heavenly duties. On Saturday, September 11, visiting family, he cheerily described the hubbub engendered by news of their engagement. The next day, she recorded a Sabbath meditation: "I have mourned through the week the want of lively feelings yet I think I feel more that thirst is all in all & that I am nothing, been much tempted with gloomy views of Religion & always fear lest when I engage in any religious duty I may find it a burden yet I have been much interested in my prayers at times."[20]

One way to resolve any competition between God and Robert would be to win Robert to God. "There is nothing I have so much at heart as your true interests & for these my petitions are daily offered to my Heavenly Father," she wrote him. "I cannot say all I would on this subject for I might weary you & I know how I <u>once</u> felt. I only beg you to consider it & not banish it from your heart." Before rushing off to sit for her portrait by Auguste Hervieu (not catching the irony of so worldly an endeavor), she added, "That God may protect & bless you & above all things may turn your heart to Him is my unceasing prayer for you. Then I should have nothing more to wish for on earth with regard to you."[21]

In wishing for Robert's spiritual awakening, Mary had an ally: her mother. Molly Custis kept herself well informed about the state of Robert's soul, for she read her daughter's incoming letters. In his lighthearted way Robert groused that he would write in a "less stiff & more natural way" if he knew her eyes would not see what he wrote. Mary apologized, but added, "Mother says if her eye is so appalling to you she will promise not to require a sight of your letters though I told her I could not imagine any thing you had to say that she might not see."[22] Young Lee was learning that to marry the daughter is to marry the entire family.

To Mary, Lee poured out his heart if not his soul. After enjoying a leave from Cockspur, he hated to return and told Mary so. He added a telling confession: "The truth is, that I have been for so many years in the habit of repressing my feelings that I can now scarcely reallize that

I may give vent to them, and act according to their dictates, but this is fast recurring to me, so you may be prepared for their expression."[23] This was a startling admission of a reality that reflected both the evangelicalism of his mother and the near deism of his father—the one with its emphasis on God, the other with its stress on virtue, both of which emanated in a high emphasis on duty. Neither left room for this sort of complaint, any more than West Point had. Yet the romantic movement then at its height stressed feeling, in reaction to the Enlightenment's rationality and Calvinism's rigidity.

Just sentences later, Lee's jauntiness had returned. Still, he had made a major confession. He had admitted his habit of repressing his feelings. Now he allowed himself to vent them, and vent he did. Returning to Cockspur after extended visits to Mary, family, and friends, Robert found that tides and weather had undone much of the previous spring's progress, some "beyond repair." His commanding officer was absent, probably drunk, and abandoned by his wife, and the threat of his return alarmed the men. Above all, he missed Mary. "Oh! cousin you don't know how much I have thought of you within the last four days," he wrote, "so much that at times I was entirely unconscious of the tossing of the little vessel, and though[t]less as to its consequences." He could not focus on "the very book you gave me to read, and which I promised so fairly to do"—likely a collection of sermons. Robert was, in a word, miserable.[24]

In Mary he was seeking an emotional mate. But he was not her *spiritual* mate. She shared her conflicts with her diary, not with him, as on Halloween 1830: "Not much change in my feelings for the last fortnight I have been enabled to observe my stated seasons of prayer & generally to find comfort[.] Indeed I am blessed far beyond my deserts & only mourn that I do not live as I ought, that my heart should ever wander should ever be insensible to such amazing love— . . . I have been quite desponding but a passage in the sermon today a farewell sermon from our Minister Mr. Maguire comforted me. He said the Christian does not expect a <u>rest</u> in this world."[25]

In reality, Robert and Mary were not as spiritually disparate as might appear. They were Episcopalians sitting on opposite sides of their church. Each reflected a strong tradition within Anglicanism. Mary exemplified the ascendant evangelicalism, a modified Calvinism shorn of the dark dichotomies of predestination. As moderated by John Wesley, made prominent by William Wilberforce, and championed in Virginia by Bishops Moore and Meade, it prized the individual soul's personal conversion to Christ in a moment that could be specifically identified. Mary most certainly could identify hers: July 4, 1830.

Robert, for his part, reflected an older version of Anglicanism that emphasized reasoned religion that reacted against the orthodox dogmatism that reached its height during the English Civil War and commonwealth. What mattered was not so much a moment as a lifelong pattern of devotion, what William Law had called "a devout and holy life."[26] Lieutenant Lee did what he had been taught to do: go to church, do his duty, listen to sermons, observe the church year, and, perhaps, say his prayers. He practiced his faith according to the old Virginia tradition, even if he was not as immediately transformed by it as the evangelical women around him believed he should have been.

As a couple, could they respect the tradition and experience of each other, within one household? Having gravitated toward different sections of the same church, could they unite at the altar as husband and wife?

Groping toward Marriage

Robert wrote Mary often. She responded far less than he wished. When she did, she apparently scolded him for complaining. "But cousin," he retorted, "are we to indulge no wish that is in vain? See then what piles and <u>heaps</u> of sin you cause me daily to comit. . . . I thought it was hard enough to be obliged to come away, but to come to <u>Cock-Spur</u> and yet not be allowed to wish to return, is too hard. . . . I don't think that even Cousin Molly will think it wrong."[27]

Both women took ill in November. Mary and Robert responded to the ailment, whatever it was, in ways typical of each. Wondering if "this might be my last sickness," Mary turned to God for solace. "I have often thought . . . that He designed me for an early tomb, for certainly it is a great mercy to his children when He makes the period of their probation short. That He may be glorified in my life & death is my earnest prayer." Robert came to share her view of earthly life as a "probation" for eternity, but not then. Instead, ever duteous, he wanted to take their illnesses on himself. "Could I have known that it would have relieved those whom I so much love, I am sure I should not only have borne it patiently but have rejoiced in its duration. But you are well now, & I hope becoming fat & rosy again"—plumpness being a sign of health. Yet, while avowing love for his future mother-in-law, he still felt the sting of her disapproval. In a postscript describing his role on the island, he added, "Tell cousin M[olly] I do teach those men something Good, for I learn them to do their work faithfully handsomely and scientifically."[28]

They each attended church on Sundays and holy days whenever they could, but reacted differently to sermons they heard. On December 12, Mary heard an "awful warning" from Luke 17:32, "Remember Lot's wife," about the woman whom God made a pillar of salt for looking back at the destruction of Sodom and Gomorrah. Mary took it as a plea to turn away from worldliness. "Lord may I never be found casting a single glance at those pleasures I have forsaken but may I press onward & so sure as to obtain the price of my high calling." Robert, who "followed your wishes exactly & went to Church" on Christmas, "listened to the sermon about which I will not tell you a word, as I am sure it would not make you in the least better." At least he enjoyed Savannah's holiday parties, which he described to Mary in detail.[29]

As 1831 dawned, their moods began to reverse: Mary more joyous, Robert more morose than ever. In mid-January she admitted, "My soul is often overwhelmed with a sense of this unmerited condescension & explaining why oh why [I] was not left to perish, & then again it is melted into tenderness & joy to think of my gracious Redeemer." He, though, confessed to remaining "the same sinful Robert Lee. Now don't be too much distressed, perhaps I may be better, but I see no prospect of it now." He was referring to his too-infrequent letter writing, but a deeper sensitivity slipped into a postscript to Mary's mother in "a small complaint against your Sweet daughter": "Well Ma'am you see she writes me little sermons every time, neither does she let a single opportunity pass of dilating upon the ambition of mankind. . . . [T]hats at me, & so she boxes all around the compas, giving me no respite at all. Again Ma'am I have to beg that you will take my spiritual affairs <u>entirely</u> in your own hands, as they are in dreadful keeping in hers, in as much as she is young yet & knows nothing of human nature, & with the best intentions in the world, for which I give her full & grateful credit, she will make bad, worse."[30] His half-joking message conveyed a serious point: Robert was practicing his faith exactly as he—and Mary—had been taught. Now, she implied, it was not enough, even as he wallowed in muck experiencing human nature far more than she in her mansion could possibly realize.

For Mary's father to go on postponing his decision whether to permit their marriage made his mood no better. After six months, Mary determined to approach the major. Lee recalled his own nervousness when he had broached with Custis the notion of marrying his daughter. "How did you find courage to speak to your Father? Whenever I think of that morning, the same feeling returns which I then had. I know it must be very hard for him to give away his dear daughter, but he can't expect to have her with him always. Is she not coming to Cockspur next Fall, merely for her health tell him. The climate is so warm, and the Island is so pleasant & the Quarters so comfortable." Then he added one of his first theological reflections. "I have one thing to be extremely grateful for. And in loving the gift I will try to remember the giver": in Mary, he perceived a blessing from God, and for that, he was thankful. Yet he remained defensive: "Now don't give me a lecture in your next for indeed I will not read it."[31] And still Custis delayed.

With Lent approaching, Lee attended a dance in Savannah, doing what he loved and Meade loathed. "You cannot expect me to give you an account of so wicked a place as a dance," he told Mary on Valentine's Day. "So I will only mention that the ladies looked very beautiful, that we were very happy (which I hope was not a very great sin)." After reporting other social news, he asked, "Now don't you think I deserve a good lecture for behaving so in the first place, and then telling you of it? Well give it to me then. I'll read it. I am sure I allow you the 'same priviledge' Miss Molly, so write what you choose, though I could not leave you in such great error, could I?"[32]

He was tiring of the religious hectoring from the two women. In a postscript to Mrs. Custis, he expanded on his earlier complaint: "You will at once think that I allude to those 'little sermons.' Now Cousin you know I wish to hear of other matters from her. And I sometimes think I would rather learn from any one else how wicked all men are in general, and I in particular, that there was no happiness for me in this world, and that I had nothing to do but die & go elsewhere. Is this natural? If it is not, it is still true." He said it, then retreated. "I will not enter into any arguments on this subject as I at first intended, but will think that in this care, as in every thing else, you are right & I am wrong. And that I have only to try to believe as you do." He avoided answering theological questions that Mrs. Custis evidently raised in a letter now lost. But something she wrote bothered him. "I should like to know whether that last sentence was intended for me. If it was I [am] glad to say that you were mistaken. And as bad as I know myself to be," he concluded defensively, "I believe I am not altogether as much so as that you would make me."[33]

While Robert danced, Mary pondered her spiritual progress. She observed Ash Wednesday in "fasting & prayer yet Oh Lord how feebly." By the first Sunday in Lent, she had resolved "to perform my devotions & charitable offices" early in the day when she was least likely to be interrupted. At church she had "the blessed privilege today of hearing Christ Jesus preached by one whose heart could witness that He is indeed our Saviour the divine Jehovah." The service may have included a hymn, for she wrote out a verse:

> We are travelling home to God
> In the path our Father's trod
> They are happy now, & we
> Soon their happiness shall see.[34]

But who would accompany her on her journey?

By early March, Custis still had not agreed to the nuptials. Robert wrote Mary, citing Matthew 6:34, "You know that your maxim is 'sufficient for the day is the evil thereof.'" He offered to write her father directly, but admitted, "I am the worst coward in this affair, & am almost afraid to think of it."

Meanwhile, the religious tension between him and the ladies of Arlington persisted. "Recollect how <u>good</u> I am," he pleaded to Mary, "and do not <u>presume</u> to lecture." Then he added another postscript to Mrs. Custis, taking umbrage at her evident allegation that "I do not believe":

> Did Miss M. tell you so? . . . Such <u>words</u> as I ascribed to her, are no where to be found in her letters. You may send me as many "written sermons" as you choose, for all of which I will be truly grateful. As for "Preached ones" I have less opportunity of hearing them than I could wish. . . . For it is too far to go & return the same day & I would be unable to do so unless the tide suited. . . . However Ma'am you may now give me a little "just commendation," for I walked in from the Garrison (one mile) through a hard rain last Sunday & returned. I [w]ish I could be sensible of <u>my merits</u> in all those relations of life or even pro[mise] to shew them in one.[35]

By now, even Lee's brothers worried over Mary's religious obsession. Carter advised their half brother Henry that Fitzhugh's death "afflicted the sweet girl with a little of that over-righteousness which the blue-lights brought into Virginia." Ironically, Carter could have described his own mother, given what she wrote to him at Harvard.[36]

But Mary was emerging from the darker shades of whatever the evangelical "blue-lights" brought. "Another bright Sabbath dawns for me in peace, the enjoyment of all the blessings of life, the presence of my reconciled father & the hope of a glorious immortality," she noted on Sunday, March 13. Her cheerfulness, though, could not let her avoid her abiding question: Would marrying Robert be an act of faith or a defection to worldliness? A week later she wrote: "Have been somewhat cast down the past week on account of unbelief & a sense of my own ingratitude & want of self denial in renouncing all for my precious Redeemer even him whom my soul loves, yet blessed be his glorious name his mercy still upholds me & the consolations of the Holy Spirit gladden my heart."[37] Who does she mean—Jesus, or Robert? It may be her Redeemer whom her soul loves; but if she wonders about "renouncing all[,] . . . even him whom my soul loves," then she ponders anew giving up Robert as an act of self-denial. Yet given what marrying him would entail—losing the mansion, the servants, the wealth, while taking on responsibilities of wife, mother, and junior officer's mate—would marriage actually be the greater denial of self?

Easter approached. Robert grew increasingly impatient. Mary had apparently let him know that her father had finally consented but, for reasons not revealed, now *she* wanted to delay. Robert was nearly beside himself. He teased her with a plot to dock at Arlington at sunrise in early July armed with a marriage license and, joined by a Presbyterian minister who would ask no questions (as Episcopal clergy might do) about the state of his soul, marry her when she took her morning walk. "I am sure there can be no objection to this Plan."[38]

The spiritual gap between the two persisted. In the same letter, Robert spoke of going to church the next day, Easter Sunday. He also described attending a "Fancy Ball" and the costumes people wore to it. He related the news of the death of his slave Nat, whom he had taken south in an unsuccessful attempt to improve his health. Meanwhile, Mary was again ill. Though "debarred by sickness" from attending Easter service and receiving Communion, she "renewed my covenant with my Redeemer." She wrote of heaven, not of Robert.[39]

True to his word, Robert celebrated Easter at church in Savannah ("come," he begged her parenthetically, "more 'just commendation'"). As usual, he dined with the Mackay ladies, receiving later a touching note from Mrs. Mackay "wishing me all manner of happiness both in this world & thereafter. I do not know why, But I have never yet received the Blessing of the <u>Good</u>, which we are taught 'availeth much' without being moved almost to tears & sometimes it is with difficulty I can restrain them. And so it was in this case"—perhaps because he yearned for encouraging words to help him persevere against the uncertainties of his marriage? In any event, he seemed to welcome positive words from someone who cared about him. At about the same moment he wrote his letter, Mary recorded "much comfort & peace of mind" from her "resignation to God's will whatever he may in his infinite wisdom see fit to appoint for me."[40] Did this "resignation" include marriage?

Mere "resignation" was not at all what Robert wanted. Since she rejected his earlier plan, he, increasing in boldness if not irritation, suggested getting married at Christ Church.

> I will meet you in Alexandria the first Sunday in June (since you prefer that month) and between the service & sermon we will walk up to the altar <u>two</u> & come away <u>one</u>. Now will <u>this</u> suit you. Do pray do not object to it, for I am at my wits end to accommodate you. Yours is a most horrid plan, you know if all those people get to Arlington they will stay there a month & instead of my indemnifying myself for this great loss of time. <u>I</u> should be the Lion of the house & would have to enact daily. But I will not object to this or any other thing so it is brought about in the quickest possible time, though if it waits my <u>leisure</u> I am afraid it will be a long time off. I cannot help admiring your ingenuity in placing that interval of a month to <u>my</u> account instead of where it is due.[41]

At least they were now discussing wedding plans. Again differences arose. She preferred a service at Arlington; he wanted one that was short, simple, soon, and in church. He was pining for her: "Do you ever think of me My own Sweet Mary?" he wrote in May. "And how much do you want to see me? Not half as much as I want to see you." He yielded utterly to her wishes. "Have every thing your own way since you will not have mine & tell me when I must come up." He would ask for a furlough, and if he did not get one, "I will take it" anyway. "For I declare

69

that I cannot wait <u>any</u> <u>longer</u>." The general "& his Uncle Sam may go to—France—For what I care."

Lee was as wretched, and as candid about his wretchedness, as at any point in their correspondence. "As I am now I am sometimes miserable & oftener of late than formerly, which I know would not be if I was with you. . . . Could you know my feelings, you would <u>Pity</u> me." Frustrated that military duty kept him apart from her, he questioned his vocation. "How I wish I had taken my Poor Mothers advice & never entered the Army. But then I thought & intended always to be <u>one</u> & alone in the World for I never expected You <u>would</u> be mine & you see how it has turned out." He was in a "bad humour" indeed.[42]

Pressure mounted on Mary as well. On May 17, about the time she would have received his self-pitying letter, she wrote in her diary, "Oh let my prayers & the desires of my heart which are in accordance with thy blessed will be granted at the time & manner which thou seest." Still, she sought to postpone the nuptials until fall, implying it was Robert's desire. Not at all, he retorted, "but <u>far</u> from it & I do beg that it may take place some day in <u>June</u> if <u>Possible</u>." Mary's mother apparently worried that June would be too cold; a cousin feared it would be too warm; Robert did not care. "I will not consent that every body should yeild to my wishes. But there is no reason why it should be deferred, Is there Sweetheart?" His humor returned: "I will be an old Man soon, Bald, toothless & every thing else."[43]

At last it was decided. A June wedding it would be, pending only his receiving leave. At once, marriage plans preoccupied them both. Her bridesmaids, she informed him, "will not let you off & you must wear your <u>uniform</u> that you may be more <u>captivating</u>." Mary proposed June 23 as the date, then closed with affection he must have relished: "I have so much to do this evening & I don't want to get thin before you come Farewell farewell my own love."[44]

At long last, her mind was firm, her myriad questions answered, and her soul satisfied. Marrying Robert, she concluded, would not contradict faith but rather be a means by which to live it. "O Lord suffer me not to be drawn aside from thee in the new situation I am about to enter on but with a single eye may I then live to thy service & by a blameless life & conversation endeavour to shew forth thy praises." True, getting married posed distractions all their own; her heart, she confessed, "is too much engrossed with this approaching bridal." Still, the Bible seemed to justify what she was doing: "Oh Thou who of old didst honour a marriage feast with thy glorious presence wilt thou deign to be present on this occasion & comfort the heart of thy servant with the sweet influences of thy spirit & the sense of the favour & forgiveness[,] Thou who art the light of joy of my soul."[45]

Details began falling into place. Robert received orders to Fort Monroe, blessedly located in Virginia. Mary would join him. So would her mother; if the newlyweds could not be in Arlington, then Arlington would come to them. Then Mrs. Custis became ill and reconsidered. "Do not be frightened," she assured Robert, adding that their "two little rooms" would better accommodate his sister; they seemed destined not to begin married life alone. Robert gracefully expressed his hope to "Miss Molly" (his fiancée) that "Cousin Molly" (his imminent mother-in-law) would "get rid of her chills" in time for the June 30 wedding, the day his furlough began.[46]

Almost overnight, the couple's correspondence turned to the myriad details of arranging a wedding. He retained his humor but admitted to a good case of the nerves, which perhaps Mary shared. "No Miss Molly it is too late to change your mind now, & all that I hope is you may not too soon repent of not doing it before. From your enquiring about my Courage, I am afraid yours is oozing out at your finger ends." He confessed to his own apprehension. "For my part I am getting so anxious as the time draws near, that I would not be surprised if I gave myself a fever which would be a fine accompaniment to your chill."[47]

Chills or not, a week later Mary felt "languid both in body & mind but blessed be his tender love who has supported this fainting spirit & not suffered it utterly to be cast down & drawn away by the snares of the world."[48] Robert fretted more over learning his vows. "So Miss Molly you must be ready & not only have your part by heart, but mine also & prepared to promise for I cannot find a book [Book of Common Prayer] even to read it over in." Though his garrison had plenty, he felt too "awkward" to ask for one. But, he assured her, he understood the "principle."

Then, after dealing with still more details, he asked, "I wonder if you are as anxious as I am." He referred to the wedding. But he also worried about their future. She had been sheltered, seeing "so little of mankind . . . that you will not be prepared to find them as they are, & the change from Arlington to a Garrison of wicked & Blasphemous soldiers will be greater & more shocking to you than you are aware of. Have you," he asked, "thought of these things or not."[49]

Mary may have "thought of these things" far more than either of them realized. Their engagement coincided with a year of intense struggle for her. Of the two, marriage had vastly more practical effects on her life than her spiritual rebirth. Mary Custis was about to descend from Arlington Heights to the depths of worldliness the likes of which she had never known. If this prospect gnawed at her heart, she never admitted it to her diary. Then again, she never mentioned Robert by name. Yet the tension between heaven and earth never left her, throughout the year, and ever afterward.

Finally the day arrived and, with it, torrential rains that thoroughly soaked the poor Mr. Keith. He had to borrow clothes from the very much smaller Major Custis, producing a less-than-reverent appearance that evoked titters from the bridesmaids. Still, the hilltop mansion beamed forth light. The vows were said, the couple married. The party begun. Festivities extended beyond Arlington for weeks to come, as the newlyweds, following good Virginia custom, made a circuit of homes and parties.[50]

Lee was devoted to Mary, and Mary had committed her life to him. Yet what of Mary's other love? That Sunday, the eve of the first anniversary of her conversion, writing amid the continuing "frolick," Mary never mentioned her nuptials. "What can I say for this week but that in the circumstances with which I am surrounded my poor vain foolish heart has been too much drawn aside from Thee O my Father in Heaven to whom I owe all both for time & eternity[.] Oh listen to the voice of thy child & when thou hearest pity & forgive."[51]

Within the tension of her two loves, she came to see that one did not exclude the other. They might even correlate. Whether marriage would enhance and sustain her faith remained to be seen. If she harbored doubts about what she saw as her new husband's less lively faith, then in marrying Lieutenant Lee she made the greatest leap of faith in her life. Whatever her doubts or her faith, as the parson had declared from the Prayer Book, the two, by God, had become one.

As for her husband, he had kept his eye on the prize, winning her without sacrificing his own convictions in the process. He would grow to share hers more fully. But he did so on his own terms, in his own time, and in his own way of believing. Little did Lee realize that he was following a classic pattern in Anglican spirituality: he was being transformed.

CHAPTER 8

"Christ's Faithful Soldier and Servant"

~

Lee, Family, and Church

After a week of wedding festivities at Arlington, Lieutenant and Mrs. Lee set off in their own carriage to visit friends in the Blue Ridge. In August, the couple—and just the couple—settled into married life at Fort Monroe, on Old Point Comfort in Hampton Roads, where the James River flows into Chesapeake Bay. Not even the threat of Nat Turner's slave revolt could dim their joy, though the rebels had planned to attack their very fortress. If Lee was alarmed, he masked it in the lightness of his account to Mrs. Custis.[1] But the incident terrorized whites in Virginia and, indeed, the entire South.

As Robert foresaw, Mary entered a strange new world: an army post, located in Virginia but still far from her home. She ruled over an empire of four small rooms, twice what Robert had predicted, with a man she had seen only rarely in the previous few years. Robert filled his natural niche in his army job; she found hers in a chapel chair. He joined her every Sunday he could. For him it was a duty from childhood, a habit from his youth, a chance to socialize, and now a means to support her. Going to church gave Mary an escape from her tiny home, a way to connect with others, a fulfillment of her spiritual obligations, and an outlet for the passion of her faith. Each held motives that allowed them to coexist within one household of faith.

In time, theirs grew into a stronger union. Over the next two decades, Lee avoided the spiritual flames that inspired his mother, his mother-in-law, and his new bride. He did, though, involve himself afresh in the church of his childhood. As a family man, Lee attended the Episcopal Church with his brood when he could. When he was away from home, he described his experiences of congregations, sermons,

73

and clergy, for his military postings and travels gave him the chance, rare in his day, to encounter a diversity of churches. He developed an increasingly active interest in parishes where he was stationed, in issues confronting his own denomination, and in the Christian faith at large. He developed into a good churchman.

Mary, meanwhile, struggled incessantly between the claims of earth and heaven. Her newfound obligations as army wife, as housekeeper, and eventually as mother reduced the number of her diary entries, but not her letters home expressing her abiding struggle between temporal and spiritual demands. In church she found a sanctuary that helped her and Robert to meet their responsibilities of family and of faith. It served to unite them even more fully.

A Mighty Fortress Is Our Church?

Robert rightfully feared that Mary faced a hard adjustment. For her, everything was new and different. By leaving Arlington House for army barracks, she also exchanged the vibrancy of Christ Church for a struggling little Episcopal congregation meeting in a chapel room with a parson of uncertain ability.

The Lees arrived in the fall of 1831 just as the Reverend Mark L. Chevers took on the unofficial role of chaplain as part of his responsibilities as rector of St. John's in nearby Hampton.[2] The priest faced hefty challenges. Enlisted men attended regularly and participated actively, using the Prayer Books they brought with them. Officers, though, "scarcely even attend except one or two of the married ones. They all make the preacher an excuse for their neglect of this duty." Not Robert, who, Mary reported, "goes with me always," but, hinting why other officers stayed away, he "seems to feel but little respect for the preacher": Chevers's "deportment does not command a great deal but as a minister of Christ & one who really feels zealous in the cause we might[?] so regard him." Mary wished for "a minister here more distinguished though I know not whether his preaching would be better attended." She was learning the realities of parish life.

Mrs. Lee held two other misgivings. One was the singing—so much "that the appearance of sanctity is in a great measure destroyed & it is only in the retirement of your chamber that you can feel it is a holy & solemn day." Counter to the evangelical trend, she preferred a quieter

service. Even worse, she perceived a troubling trend in the churchmanship that soldiers brought from outside Virginia. She commended their
avid participation in the service, but fretted, "They have probably been
brought under the religious influence prevailing at New York." While
Virginians stressed one side of Bishop White's old duality, that of individual spiritual renewal and relationship to God, New Yorkers valued
the other side, a tradition of order, sacraments, and rites, in what Virginia Theological Seminary professor William H. Wilmer scorned as the
"zeal . . . for externals." Mary feared the same force that drove McIlvaine
from West Point slinking into Virginia.[3]

Mary kept her mother apprised as spiritual devotions led her further into practice. In "a little serious conversation," she admitted, "I
know you feel most anxious to know how my soul prospers. What must I
say to you but that I still feel the consolations[,] the soothing influences
of Religion, still feel an anxious desire to do something to show forth
my gratitude to that all merciful saviour who has done all for me but it
is hard to find what I can do." In other words, she wanted to work for
the Lord. But she was lonely. "The only actively pious family here" had
not visited because of "sickness or some other cause." Other wives appeared to see no need to "influence the condition of the people here,"
she wrote, then quickly added, "I may be representing them uncharita-
bly, for I am so little acquainted here & their benevolence may be of that
unobtrusive kind" known only to those who receive it. That they might
have seen the lady of Arlington as too formidable to visit seems not to
have occurred to her.

"High church" or not, Chevers's little congregation adopted two
by-products of the Second Great Awakening, each a priority for Bishop
Meade. One was a Sunday school. In the absence of good public education, Sunday schools in that era taught the fundamentals of reading
and writing as well as of religion.[4] Mary heard that "the soldiers seem
to think it quite a condescension to send their children." In short, it
was small.

In a second innovation, Mary reported, a "black man" held "coloured meetings." The willingness of white congregations to reach out
to slaves grew from the evangelical imperative, expressed especially by
George Whitefield, to save all souls. Customarily, slaves would attend
the same services as whites, sometimes seated in a segregated area of
the church. No such seats were provided for them at Chevers's services;
"consequently they never go which seems . . . a great omission, as it

might keep them at least part of the day out of mischief"—she added, "if this was the only light in which they would view it here." Mary Custis Lee, the slaveholder, looked askance at a common white stereotype of slaves getting into trouble in any free time they could find. Fortunately, from her view, the church allowed blacks to worship separately with one of their own leading the service, evidently without Chevers or another white being present.[5]

Teaching, she could do. Following her mother's example, she began instructing enslaved children. She asked her mother to send materials from Arlington. Soon, the number of her students grew "quite large"; she led a "black class of 6[,] 3 of whom read quite well."[6]

When the General Assembly of Virginia finally responded to Nat Turner's revolt, one of its acts forbade religious assemblies of blacks, even freedmen, unless they were led by a licensed white clergyman. Another banned the teaching of slaves, making illegal Mrs. Custis's classes at Arlington and Mrs. Lee's at Fort Monroe. Mrs. Custis, at least, went right on teaching enslaved children to read God's Word, whatever politicians mandated. "Has she forgotten that the Laws of her State forbid the instruction of slaves in reading & writing," remarked one shocked young cousin, "or does she think that there are acts of justice that must be performed, the 'laws to the contrary notwithstanding'?"[7]

In time, Mary reported more good news. "Yesterday I got out to church," she wrote her mother. "The sacrament was administered to the small number of 6. The text was 'The Lord will not forsake those who trust in him' very comforting to those who feel they can have no other reliance. Most of the ladies were at church and some of the soldier's [*sic*] wives"; not all in attendance took Communion. On another Sunday, a visiting cleric pleased her greatly. "Dr. Ducachet preached 2 excellent sermons last Sunday the one in the morning was particularly addressed to young officers. It was an eloquent learned & earnest discourse from the text 'There is a lion in the way' answering all the arguments against religion & most affectionately urging all to embrace it. . . . I was glad to see the house crowded & some very attentive hearers, particularly so many of the soldiers. I hope some good may have been done."[8]

She welcomed the newcomers she deemed "decidedly pious," especially an officer and his wife who brought to church "all the soldiers" in his company. The chapel "was quite filled & lost its desolate appearance," and, she hoped, encouraged Chevers. Meanwhile, she knit socks for a ladies' society to sell to support itself and begged her mother to send more wool.[9]

Soon success showed. "Some spirit of usefulness is abroad" in the parish, Mary exulted to her mother in March 1833. "Some other of the young ladies have become teachers in the S School so that it is well supplied & they have formed themselves into a working Society who meet every Wednesday & devote the proceeds of their labour to procure Books for a library." They wanted Mrs. Custis's help in getting more. Even Mr. Chevers was improving; he "preached an excellent sermon on Sunday." As for their ministry to slaves, the chaplain "read to our servants some of the Bread of Deceit but they did not seem to be particularly interested in it."[10]

While Robert rebuilt the fort as the army assigned him to do, Mary worked on building up the church. "I have promised to visit the working Society though my family duties will not permit me to remain during all their meetings," she wrote her mother. At first, leaving Arlington had brought no change in her spiritual life. "I have been enabled to go on regularly with prayer & bible but ah my dearest Mother how often do I find myself listlessly perusing what ought to be my highest pleasure. . . . [P]ray for your child that she may be quickened & animated in her Christian course."[11] Now, more and more, she saw her labors bearing fruit, in her view, for God.

Mary showed more interest in the house of God than in her own little house of Lee. Church engaged her spirit, offered a social outlet, and provided a means to contribute to society. At home, she struggled alone with daily chores. Robert wrote a fellow soldier, "Tell the Ladies that they are aware that Mrs. L is somewhat addicted to laziness & forgetfulness in her Housekeeping. But they may be certain that she does her best. Or in her Mother's words, 'The Spirit is willing but the flesh is weak.'"[12]

Lee still lacked Mary's zest for spiritual nurture and community. If Robert was not concerned for his soul, Mary was. She mentioned to her mother in 1834 that he lacked "the one thing needful without which all the rest may prove valueless."[13]

Precisely as Mary fretted, Lee remained fond of this world. He especially welcomed the company of women. He was utterly devoted to Mary and did nothing to jeopardize their bond. Still, he prided himself on being a ladies' man. Just a year into their marriage, Lee boasted, "Let me tell you Mrs. Lee, no later than to-day, did I escort Miss L. to see Miss Kate! Think of that Mrs. Lee! . . . How did I strut along with one hand on my whiskers & the other elevating my coat tail! And my whole face thrown into the biggest grin I could muster. Surely it was a sight for the Old Pointers to see, and I only wish you could have been one of the number. How you would have triumphed in my happiness & then Molly I would have been happy." Two years later, he tantalized Jack Mackay with tales of the local belles. "As for the daughters of Eve, in this country they are framed in the very poetry of nature & would make your lips water & fingers tingle. They are beginning to assemble to put their beautiful limbs in this salt water."[14]

Other aspects of his army world bothered Lee. He remarked to Mackay that the boredom of peacetime life in garrisons caused "minds, formed for use & ornament, [to] degenerate into sluggishness & inactivity, requiring the stimulus of Brandy or cards to rouse them to action, apparently a burdon to the possessors & perhaps an injury to their companions."[15] His remark portrays a conscience formed by William Meade, who disparaged such turpitude; and Lee, though he enjoyed the company of women, was never much given to games or alcohol.

As for Meade, the bishop kept appearing in the young couple's life. In 1833, the bishop/godfather accompanied Lee's wife and year-old son from Fort Monroe back to Arlington, "where," Lee noted, "they are all as happy to have them as I am sad to lose them." To the end of Meade's life, they continued to meet up with the bishop in one place or another.[16]

For children had started arriving. George Washington Custis Lee, formally called "Custis" but, given the parental penchant for nicknames, dubbed "Boo," was born on September 16, 1832. "I have got me an heir to my Estates!" Lee wrote Carter. "Aye, a Boy! to cherish the memory of his Father & 'walk in that light of his renown.' His mother is quite well & would never forgive me did she not think I was describing all the Beauties & rare accomplishments, which she daily discovers."[17] The first of seven, Boo was followed by Mary Custis ("Daughter") in 1835, Fitzhugh ("Rooney") in 1837, Anne Carter ("Annie") in 1839, Eleanor Agnes ("Agnes" or "Wig") in 1841, Robert Edward Jr. ("Robertus Sickus" or, more reasonably, "Rob") in 1843, and Mildred Childe ("Precious Life") in 1846.

Marriage and family life, along with frequent and long separations from wife and children, intensified Robert's concerns. When Boo was six, Lee fretted to Mary, "I pray God to watch over and direct our efforts in guarding our dear Son, that we may bring him up 'in the way he should go.'" After Annie, their fourth child, arrived, Lee wrote his mother-in-law, "We have a nice little parcel of [children] now.... God grant that they may all be preserved to us, and grow to be our joy and comfort."[18] His references to the Divine had become more reverential than his offhand "God knows" a decade earlier.

Family religious life took practical shape at home. At Arlington, which became their primary residence, they joined in the household prayers led by Mrs. Custis. Having led a little school for black children at Fort Monroe, Mary Lee would have done no less for her own.[19] Their education would undoubtedly have included matters of faith, based on the same catechism that Robert had recited to Parson Meade a generation before.

The Faithful Churchman

Like a growing number of Americans of that day,[20] the Lees went to church, often. They attended the local Episcopal service if possible, but circumstances exposed them to other denominations as well. Being transferred from post to post and serving on temporary assignments allowed Lee to sample varieties of worship. On his trips, Lee often described to Mary his impressions of clergy, sermons, and congregations. When she accompanied him to a billet, they both found a place in the nearby parish. Together, they stumbled into politics at work at Christ Church, St. Louis, Missouri, in the late 1830s. Early in the next decade, when Robert was stationed at Fort Hamilton, to oversee repairs at military installations in New York Harbor, they discovered divisions within the Anglican Communion causing tension within St. John's in Brooklyn. During the Mexican War, Lee encountered Roman Catholicism. After the war, they attended Mount Calvary, Baltimore. By then, the Lees had become conscientious churchfolk, frequent in attendance, in Robert's case serving on the vestry, and becoming increasingly aware of issues facing congregations, their denomination, and beyond.

When living at Arlington, the family ventured to Christ Church, Alexandria. Usually they sat in the gallery, where they endured what one cousin called "the hardness of the pew and the tedium of the sermon," which could last an hour. If family members could not join Lee, or if he was away from them, Lee attended services alone. One Sunday in 1847 with Mary away at Arlington, Lee was tending to two sick children but still got to the service at Mount Calvary.[21]

Baptisms were important to the family. All but Custis/Boo were born at Arlington House, even if army assignment precluded Robert's presence. When Agnes was born, he wrote Mary from Fort Hamilton in New York, "I long very much to see the dear children, & <u>especially</u> Miss Agnes. I told you she was the finest child that was ever seen, but you would not believe me." Then he asked, "Are you going to have her christened before you come on?"[22]

Robert and Mary kept abreast of news and views of the Episcopal Church through Virginia's diocesan newspaper, the *Southern Churchman*. It was designed to reach a more general audience than the *Washington Theological Repertory*. Beginning in 1831 it published sermons each week from around the country by evangelical notables such as McIlvaine, devotional articles of piety, poetry, seasonal reflections, news of churches and missions, historical notes, articles about the denomination such as one titled "Excellence of the Episcopal Church," and even personal announcements of marriages and deaths. It bore Meade's unmistakable stamp. In February 1839, he reported on the consecration as bishop of Leonidas Polk, McIlvaine's first convert at West Point. "A Short Sermon on Horse Racing" sounded for all the world like Bishop Meade, as did an editorial blasting the "dangerous doctrines and pernicious tendencies" of the "Tractarians," who, in Meade's view, were reviving Romanish practices in the Church of England. From England came a statement of the bishop of Norwich opposing private baptisms precisely as the young deacon Meade had done when he arrived at Christ Church, Alexandria. The newspaper featured an appeal for the Virginia Colonization Society and a report of its annual meeting.[23]

Lees and Custises avidly read and supported the periodical. Mary, in Fort Hamilton, commented to her mother on remarks she saw in the *Churchman* from Meade and the head of the Colonization Society.[24] Cousin Cassius served as its "agent" in Alexandria. A May 1839 issue recorded that "Mrs. Custis" of Alexandria and "Lt. R. E. Lee of St. Louis, Mo." had renewed their subscriptions—as usual.[25] Robert, stationed in Texas in 1856, reported comparing copies of the *Southern Churchman* with the "high church"–oriented *New York Churchman*. During the Civil War, he made sure Mary paid the subscription, and after the war sent five dollars to revive it.[26]

The Divisive Spirit of St. Louis, and Beyond

Stationed in St. Louis in 1839, Robert would have particularly noted a *Churchman* article reprinted from a Missouri paper describing the consecration of Christ Church, the very church he was attending.[27] It was the parish that exposed him to church politics as never before.

Just after Rooney's birth in 1837, Lee left for St. Louis, assigned to remove snags and silt from the Mississippi River that threatened to close the port. Missouri did not impress him at first; he described the countryside to Carter as "<u>bloody humbug</u>" and complained to Mary of "<u>astonishingly</u> hot" weather and dust that reached his ankles. Later he noticed that the "<u>magnificent</u>" soil yielded marvelous produce.[28] When ice floes put an end to work for the winter, he returned to Arlington in time for Christmas. In the spring he returned to St. Louis with Mary and the two boys while daughter Mary Custis stayed with her grandparents.

Leaving Episcopally dominated Virginia, the Lees encountered a diversity of religious persuasions, among them what Lee's mother twenty years before had condemned as "Socinian." Mary wrote her mother, "The Unitarian Clergyman Mr. Elliott . . . is quite the fashion & is said to preach very handsomely." An army captain "lives here & is a Unitarian so I hear more of it than ever I did before & am more astonished that any one who professes to believe the Bible can hold doctrines so contrary to it." Fortunately for them, Episcopalians had arrived too. In Christ Church, now the cathedral of the Diocese of Missouri, the family found a new building, a growing congregation, and a proper welcome from the rector's assistant. The Reverend Peter Richmond Minard and his wife called on Mary, who candidly told her mother, "He seems to be an excellent man & gives us very good sermons but he is not a man of much talent" (she did not say why).[29] They also found a congregation in turmoil.

In 1829 Christ Church completed its structure, ambitiously designed to seat 250 worshipers. Its second rector, William Chaderton, left in 1835 after only three years. About this same time, Jackson Kemper was chosen the first "missionary bishop" in the United States to serve the vast American Midwest. Since St. Louis was centrally located to his jurisdiction, he made the city his home, whereupon the church's vestry asked if he would serve as rector. Like the first American bishops, Kemper found his chief financial support in serving as a parish priest.

His frequent absences as bishop, however, required him to hire assistants, first Minard, then the Reverend William Grant Heyer.[30]

In 1839, after Mary returned to Arlington to give birth to Annie, Christ Church again needed a priest. The reason is unclear. Kemper is listed as rector until 1840. But his diocese was huge, he was often away tending it, and he may have voluntarily stepped aside. Whatever the cause for the vacancy, Lee told Mary of the growing debate over who would fill it. One faction favored Minard, the other Heyer, pitting one assistant against the other. The vestry asked the bishop to resume his rectorship. Kemper agreed, but only if Minard and Heyer were not candidates. The vestry informed him that they were not; that may have been officially true, but partisans of each candidate did not get the word. So Bishop Kemper returned to a deeply divided congregation. Some laity refused to attend services if the bishop remained there. Others created new churches so that Minard and Heyer each could have his own pulpit. Lee reported, "I do not think more than 1/4 has attended since my return from up the river that did during the summer." He added dryly, "Perhaps the novelty of the new church has worn off."[31]

A year later, a new rector arrived, and Lee was present for his first sermon. Ironically, Frederick Foote Peak had been yet another assistant at Christ Church. All the more reason, as Lee described to Mary, that he "laid down very plainly his own line of conduct, duties, trial etc." and "was equally plain in what he expected from them." Lee seemed to approve. He added, "The Bishop is now absent & Mr. Minard has a new church in the upper part of town."[32] The congregation could begin to heal.

Lee was discovering the politics of personality and authority that can beset churches. He was learning what it meant to be a churchman. He saw firsthand forces that could divide a congregation. He would soon encounter forces that could divide a denomination.

Discovering the Larger Church

Far from being discouraged by the maneuverings that plagued Christ Church, Lee took an even more active interest in his next church, St. John's in Brooklyn. For five years, Lee oversaw repairs to military facilities in New York Harbor. Fort Hamilton became the family home, and St. John's the church the family attended, including a unique addition.

As Lee was arriving in 1840, he rescued a spaniel that had fallen into the Narrows. When she produced puppies, Lee let the children keep one, whom they named Spec. Wherever the youngsters went, Spec was sure to go—including to St. John's. Unlearned in Episcopal ways, Spec responded to the liturgy at all the wrong times. Confined at home the next Sunday, Spec jumped out an upstairs window and caught up with the family at the church door. He went with them ever after.[33]

This tour of duty gave Lee the time to become more involved in the life of the parish. Elected to its vestry, he encountered a clash within the congregation, not over personality as at St. Louis, but over theology and liturgy in a controversy then raging on both sides of the Atlantic. A "catholic" revival had begun to grow out of intellectual ferment in England. First, a small group of Oxford dons, most notably John Keble, John Henry Newman, and Edward Bouverie Pusey, published widely circulated tracts that led them to be called Tractarians. Also known as the Oxford Movement, the group derived a third moniker based on the name of one of their leaders: Puseyites. Though sharing with resurgent evangelicals a reaction against the dry, reasoned faith of the Enlightenment, they differed sharply over the nature of the church, the efficacy of sacrament, and the importance of the episcopate. Then in Cambridge a parallel group emerged with the goal of improving the church's worship by adapting to religion the principles of romanticism, notably an appreciation of England's medieval past, then pervading literature and the arts. One of them, A. W. N. Pugin, was designing churches in a Gothic style that won popularity with many Episcopalians and others. Music, art, and architecture—the veritable fabric of worship—became the concern of the Cambridge Movement, which also became known as the ritualist movement. Oxford's was more theological and ascetical, Cambridge's more liturgical and aesthetical. Both proved controversial.

New York had long been a center of "high church" doctrine, emphasizing episcopacy (the place and role of the bishop), worship, and sacrament; Mary alluded to this threat when she worried over the "New York influence" on soldiers at Fort Monroe. That diocese provided a fertile ground for the seeds of these newer forms of "high church" doctrine and liturgy. One place they rooted was St. John's, Brooklyn.

Some elements of the movement pleased the Lees, like Christmas greens in the sanctuary. On the night of December 25, 1845, Mary reported to her mother from New York, "I took Annie & Wig to church which was beautifully decorated with Evergreens & Mr. Calder gave us a very good sermon & then administered the communion." Decorations were definitely not the Virginia evangelical way: a successor to Meade eventually forbade greens and flowers in churches of his diocese.[34] Whether Tractarian ideas or ritualist decorations, such imports from Oxford and Cambridge bordered on popishness, and Meade abhorred them all. "The Oxford writers," he sputtered to a newly consecrated bishop, "are I think blinded by prejudice sometimes nearly mad thro much learning—and have fallen into many mischievous errors." Fortunately, he claimed, "Hitherto in Virginia we have been happily very free from any such things, and therefore been united and harmonious." Still, to protect against even the slightest of such errors, he insisted that even church furniture retain Protestant integrity. When a Suffolk parish built a new church in 1843, Meade warned against incorporating a "Romish altar, with a view of magnifying the Lords Supper at the expense of preaching and reading the word of God." A simple, four-legged table would do, just as the 1552 Prayer Book prescribed.[35]

Even so, Mary liked the greens. Yet already she had endured a related controversy spawned by a guest preacher in the St. John's pulpit. In 1843, after updating her mother on Boo's fall wardrobe, Mary added, "I forgot to tell you that Mr. Carey the Puseyite preached for us today a very indifferent sermon tho' the subject was interesting from the text 'search the Scriptures.' He touched on no doctrinal points & we were quite surprised after church to hear who we had been listening to."[36] Arthur Carey was a young Englishman who had attended General Theological Seminary, where he expounded Puseyite teachings so fiercely that he was accused of espousing "Romanism." At his ordination as deacon in 1843, several people rose in protest. The officiant, Bishop Benjamin Onderdonk, was subsequently tried and suspended on various charges—ordaining Carey being one—levied by, among others, William Meade.

"Low church" parishioners reproved their rector for inviting Carey to the pulpit. They called him a closet Puseyite, the more so because of "suspicious prayers that he used to which they had not been accustomed." Lee never spoke publicly about the matter. Then, according to Henry J. Hunt, a junior officer at the fort, one evening Lee joined a gathering of some younger officers and civilians in the bachelors' quarters.

> Soon the inevitable subject came up and was discussed with considerable warmth, and, on the parts of two or three, with some feeling.

Captain Lee was quiet, but, to those who understood him, evidently amused at the efforts to draw him out. On some direct attempt to do so he turned to me and in his impressive, grave manner said, "I am glad to see that you keep aloof from the dispute that is disturbing our little parish. That is right, and we must not get mixed up in it; we must support each other in that. But I must give you some advice about it, in order that we may understand each other: *Beware of Pussyism! Pussyism* is always bad, and may lead to unchristian feeling; therefore beware of *Pussyism!*"

Laughter over his deliberate mispronunciation broke up the discussion. Lee had used a vulgarism that, then as now, held a scatological double meaning. Lee perpetuated the joke, for sometimes when encountering Hunt he would shake his head and say, "Keep clear of this *Pussyism!*"

Hunt had his revenge. During the Mexican War, after the surrender of Veracruz in 1847, Hunt decided to attend a local Roman Catholic service. He found the church filled with Mexican women and many American soldiers getting their first exposure to a Catholic service. General Winfield Scott, the commander of the American forces, was there with Lee and other officers, sitting on the only bench in the church. Hunt divined that this was a festal day. An acolyte brought a thick wax candle that he handed to Scott, left, then returned with a smaller one; but Scott had passed the large candle to one of his officers. The acolyte blew out the small candle, then left to get another fat one for Scott, and other small ones for the officers. Finally, with tapers in hand, two by two, led by priests "in gorgeous vestments" and followed by Scott and his staff, the procession filed around the church as "very good" music was performed. As Hunt described the scene, "We had passed the altar, when . . . I touched Captain Lee's elbow. He very properly gave me a rebuking look, but upon my repeating the touch he bent his head toward me and whispered, 'What is it?' —'Captain Lee?' —'Well?'—'I really hope there is no *Pussyism* in all this?' I glanced at him; his face retained its quiet appearance, but the corners of his eyes and mouth were twitching in the struggle to preserve his gravity."[37]

Discovering the customs and convictions of other churches caused Lee to value his Episcopal tradition all the more. Encountering varieties of Episcopal customs and trends fostered his appreciation of the ways he had known in Virginia. One of these was a respect for the Bible, the book that Bishop Meade believed communicated "divine truth," to be read prominently, propounded effectively, and heeded carefully.[38] In that spirit, Lee often commented to Mary on sermons he heard. He was often impressed—just not always favorably. Visiting Trinity Church in Newport, Rhode Island, in 1849, he encountered, in the small worlds of the Episcopal Church and the military, a West Point classmate named Frank Vinton, now a clergyman whose name Mary would have recognized from Brooklyn. "The subject of his sermon was the sale by Esaw of his Birthrights. His application was pretty unusual. To all those who had been babtized & who had not been babtized, & despised the birthright to which they had been born. As far as I could understand we were all modern Esaus. I never heard him but once before, in this same church, I did not admire his sermon then more than the one today. I suppose the fault is in me & not in him." It was a small world indeed: he went to Trinity Church with two friends, ran into other acquaintances, and missed chatting with still more. "I was told that Mrs. Eustis & Mrs. Pinckney were in church but did not see them. In a pew just before one sat Mrs. Rives," he told Mary. "Miss Grace Sears whom I told you I saw in Boston last winter."[39] The Lees had connections seemingly everywhere they went.

Lee had developed into an educated layperson. He knew enough to distinguish wheat from chaff and was sensitive enough to doctrinal and pastoral issues to assess the preacher's remarks. After daily prayers Mary and her mother regularly read books relating to their faith. Though Lee probably heard them when he was at Arlington, no evidence indicates that he read devotionally on his own. But he did peruse the *Southern Churchman*; he listened to sermons; he was aware of developments in his denomination.

Lee was becoming a mid-nineteenth-century Protestant evangelical Episcopalian imbued with the principles of the Diocese of Virginia. In the years to come, he would grow ever more fully into this definition.

CHAPTER 9

"This Our Bounden Duty and Service"

From Peace to War

If Lee learned any lessons growing up, doing one's duty ranked high on the list. In the second half of the 1840s, he put the lesson all the more to use.

The concept of "duty" permeated the teaching of the eighteenth century. His father's generation considered it a fundamental component of "virtue," emphasized by both the classical and the Enlightenment philosophers. Henry Lee commended for his sons' education a book by Cicero, the ancient Roman author, extolling duty. Meanwhile, the German philosopher Immanuel Kant, one of the brightest stars in the constellation of Enlightenment writers, made doing the "right" thing the very foundation of his ethical theory.

Not only did secular philosophy stress duty, so did the religious authorities respected by both of Lee's parents. Tillotson and Butler stressed the importance of duty. Virginia preachers endorsed it from the pulpits of colonial churches. William Meade included in his compendium for families a prayer of Bishop Thomas Wilson "for grace to know our duty, for willing minds to desire to do it, for strength to perform what thou requirest of us."[1]

Reciting his catechism to Pastor Meade, the young Lee would have identified his duty to God and to neighbor, one element of which was "To honour and obey my Civil Rulers." Each time he attended Holy Communion, Lee was reminded of his "bounden duty and service" to offer and present "ourselves, our souls and bodies, to be a reasonable, holy, and lively sacrifice" to God. Doing one's duty was the Christian obligation of Virginia Episcopalians, especially if one's name was Lee.

In becoming an active churchman, through his attendance at ser-

87

vices, through keeping up with developments, through serving on his parish's vestry, Lee was doing his duty to his church. With the coming of war with Mexico, his horizons expanded in very different ways, particularly as he faced battle and death—potentially his own—in another nation. He discovered much of himself, much of other cultures, and much of the duty required in the venues to which he was called, all while fulfilling his duty to his country.

The Onset of War

On a fine Sunday, June 7, 1846, Lee attended church on Governors Island, in the New York harbor. There sat Fort Columbus, among other things a major recruiting depot for the army. The Reverend John McVickar, its chaplain, also taught religion at Columbia University, yet he cherished the pastoral connection with the soldiers. He had not yet succeeded in building a church, so the service was held beneath willow trees near a graveyard. Lee was impressed with the sermon and the scene, as he shared with Mary, who had returned with the children to Arlington. "The close ranks of the Soldiers, the Squads of Recruits, the groups of women children & citizens scattered on the grass made a pleasing as well as picturesque scene. The music from the Band was appropriate & solemn & I have never witnessed a more imposing service." But a sense of foreboding loomed over the lovely island. "Its smiling face of peace has been changed for the grim visage of war."[2] The conflict with Mexico had already begun.

Though an army veteran of fifteen years, Lee had never seen battle. Ever since the War of 1812, the country had avoided major conflict. But the spirit of "manifest destiny" took hold. Americans looked longingly toward Texas, which had seceded from Mexico, and pondered how to seize the great southwest. Soon, border skirmishes fed a frenzy that gladly remembered the Alamo and provided a pretext for Yankee intervention.

At Fort Hamilton, Lee was not impressed. "I fear the Country is already disgraced for its puerile conduct," he confided to Mary after President James K. Polk ordered General Zachary Taylor into Mexico, an act that Lee feared would unite Mexicans behind a war. "The result is not in our own hands & we must take the chance of war, in which victory is not always to the strong." Strategic decisions bothered him. So did moral considerations. "I wish I was better satisfied as to the justice of our cause," he observed; but, as an officer, he added, "that is not my province to consider, & should any services be wanting I shall promptly furnish them."[3]

Lee was by no means alone. A first-term congressman from Illinois, Abraham Lincoln, raised similar questions. Henry David Thoreau wrote *Civil Disobedience* to protest the war. Ulysses S. Grant, who distinguished himself during the conflict, later called it "the most unjust war ever waged by a stronger against a weaker nation."[4] Indeed, historians have found Lee's reservations credible. Polk, a Democrat, was elected to annex Texas. A passion to rule North America from sea to shining sea was in the air. The family in Arlington, like many Episcopal evangelicals, preferred Whigs to Democrats, but Robert studiously avoided partisan politics. As an officer and a Christian, he had pledged to do his duty to his civil rulers, regardless of party.[5]

Civil rulers wanted his services. It was his duty to obey. Reservations or no, he was not loath to go. In mid-June he wrote his commanding officer, "In the event of war with any foreign government I should desire to be brought into active service in the field with as high a rank in the regular army as I could obtain," if not with the engineers, then with the artillery.

On receiving orders to Mexico, he began readying himself for war, which realistically meant preparing for the worst. He asked his brother Carter to get what they could for their "Floyd land," those twenty thousand acres that the three brothers owned jointly. He could use the proceeds to support his children's education, a duty that weighed on him. "My pay seems to decrease as my children increase," he bemoaned. "The first has been reduced to $1350. & the second raised to 7. See how little way the former will go with the latter & of the necessity of augmenting it even in this small way." Six weeks later he complained again about his relative poverty as he faced the costs of clothing Custis and Fitzhugh for school, transporting his servant and himself to Mexico, and buying horses, none of which the army paid for. Since he had only a day to sell his household goods at Fort Hamilton, "everything went very low. Such is the fortune of War."[6]

The Lees were not impoverished. The family spent most of their days at one of the grandest estates in the country. Lee himself drew investment income of about $2,000 per year at a time when average per capita wealth in the United States stood, by one estimate, at $363.[7]

But he had to maintain an army residence, pay his own professional expenses, and clothe and educate seven children. He felt the stress.

He was also facing battle and the possibility of death. In March 1846, while sabers rattled in Texas, he related to Rooney the lugubrious tale of a New Hampshire boy who had accompanied his father into the forest to cut lumber. The boy left the father briefly. When he returned, he found him dead beneath a trunk. He extracted the body, brought it home, and was greeted by a mother "greatly distressed at the loss of her Husband, but she thanked God, who had given her so good & brave a Son." Lee provided a moral for Fitzhugh. "You & Custis must take good care of your kind mother & dear sisters, when your father is dead. To do that you must learn to be good. Be true, kind, & generous, & pray earnestly to God to enable you to keep his Commandments & walk in the same all the days of your life."[8]

When war was declared, Lee gathered his papers and entrusted them to a bank for safekeeping. He told Mary that his will left all his property to her to educate the children, leaving it to them at her death "in such proportions as their situations & necessities might require, making special provision if need be for dear little Annie." She had been born with a birthmark and, worse, as a child had scarred her face so badly that they feared she would never marry, nor acquire thereby the financial security that matrimony was expected to provide.[9]

This letter, written from a ship taking him to war, raises the unanswerable question of why he and Mary had not arranged his affairs earlier, and in person. In an era when infant mortality claimed one of every five infants,[10] when Mary was her parents' only surviving child, the Lees had been exceptionally fortunate. All seven children attained adulthood. Lee's parents had died, but the Custises enjoyed good health. Army service, moreover, had never placed Lee himself in particular danger. Death was not the Lees' companion, as it was to so many of their day.

Going to war made the threat more real. Just before he left Arlington, he closed a letter to Carter with, for him, an unusual benediction: "God bless you my dear brother & may you prosper in all things. Adieu." To Mary, from the ship, he sent a different valedictory: "I cannot express to you my dear Mary my distress at leaving you, & I always think at those times that it would be better to be fixed permanently in some humble home than to be living this roaming life in the world we do." But soldiering was his profession. It paid their household bills, letting him devote his "private income" to the children's education. He knew he was leaving her with a "heavy responsibility" for their offspring that "will require anxious consideration, watchfulness & firmness on your part. As you may however be called upon to exercise the sole care of them, it may be as well for you to prepare yourself by taking it at once; I believe I said all that was necessary in reference to Custis & Wm. You must endeavour to make that dear little Rob better & must begin by making him more obedient. A little firmness & an <u>undeviating course</u> will easily accomplish this, which you ought also to extend to the girls."[11] Lee often advised Mary on child rearing, but never before when he was heading into battle, and never had he admitted that she might need to rear them alone. He was passing that duty on to her.

Death quickly became a reality. George W. Williams, father of Mary's intimate cousin Martha Custis Williams, the "Markie" with whom Lee often corresponded, died in the Battle of Monterrey in September. "His end was a glorious one for a soldier, on the field of battle with the cry of victory in his ear," Lee wrote Mary. "Tell Markie she has my deepest warmest sympathy which no words can express."[12] Death was the inevitable companion of soldiers, but losses were to be mourned nonetheless.

Along with death, Lee encountered an entirely new culture during his first excursion onto foreign soil. Like that of many newcomers to a country, his first impression was of the cuisine. Soon after crossing into Mexico, he tasted "a small red pepper . . . of which they are very fond which to me is as hot as a coal of fire." He was less impressed with the people, whom he found "amiable but weak . . . Primitive in their habits & tastes. Their towns are all alike."

He also experienced their religion.

As I passed through Monclova Sunday mor^g I went in to the Church or Cathedral to witness Mass. There were several officers & soldiers present, the main part of the Congregation was composed of Mexican women. They were on their knees, their heads enveloped in plain coloured scarfs or shawls, concealing the lower parts of their faces & shoulders, but giving them free use of their eyes which they used unconcernedly & freely. The Church was large, in the form of a cross without seats or pews, arched & ornimented with some small images of our Saviour & the Virgin. There was rather a meager allowance of candles, pretty good instrumental music & the priest in a very rich dress was closing the usual ceremonies.[13]

He would deepen his opinions of Roman Catholicism in years to come.

An intense longing for home soon came over him, especially when the army was not moving and Lee had time on his hands. "When shall I see you all! You are always present to me," he wrote Mary four months after leaving Arlington. "May God keep you & preserve you & all with you that I so much love." On Christmas Day he rushed from breakfast to prepare for a battle that did not occur, returning to an unexpected holiday feast "under the indulgent colouring of candlelight" that featured "an ample supply of the Parras wine." They "drank many patriotic toasts nor were our wives & sweethearts forgotten." Pleasant as it was, the Lees had never before been "entirely separated" such that Robert could not join the family at all during Christmastide. He roused himself from gloom: "We have therefore nothing to complain of & I hope [my absence] has not interfered with your happiness, surrounded as you are by father mother children & dear friends. I therefore trust you are well happy & that this is the last time I shall be absent from you during my life." He concluded with words that were becoming a common part of his letters: "May God preserve & bless you tell them & forever after is my constant prayer."[14]

Indeed, language about God entered increasingly into Lee's correspondence, especially as he thought of his "dear children." To Molly Custis, whom he addressed as "my dearest mother," he confided "my earnest prayer . . . that they may continue through life to grow in wisdom & goodness & my greatest wish is that I might be able by example & precept to aid them in that course." However, to the same person who had doubted the state of his soul, he confessed that, reviewing his life, he had more precepts than examples to offer "my dear boys."

> I have done no good. I hope I have escaped any great crime. In that respect then they would derive little benefit from my presence, & they are with those better able to advise & direct. I trust they will be able to present to them in so strong a light the advantages of virtue & religion that they can. I refrain from following their dictates. But oh what pleasure I lose in being separated from them. Nothing can compensate me for that. Still here I must remain, ready to perform what little service I can & hope for the best. But I did not sit down to impose upon you my troubles. Those I must keep to myself & will therefore speak of something else.[15]

Since Lee could not set an example in person, at least he could advise and admonish by mail. He assured Custis and Fitzhugh "that I am thinking of you & that you have constantly the prayers of your affectionate father."[16] To his oldest son he was more direct. He complimented Custis on his progress in school. "This is delightful to me & I pray that you may always preserve your innocence & rectitude. Such horrid forms of vice meet one at nearly every step that I am sickened by its contemplation, & would prefer a thousand deaths than to see the least, practiced by any of my children. It is distressing to see the depravity to which human nature falls by indulging their selfish passions & which can only be avoided by guarding well our conduct & governing our thoughts & wishes." After all, a priest prayed over them at their baptism "that all carnal affections may die in [them], and that all things belonging to the Spirit may live and grow in [them]," that they might "triumph against the devil, the world, and the flesh." Lee took such things seriously.[17]

To Agnes, as with his children generally, he was more lighthearted, though still pointed. "You must be quite learned, studying so many branches & I suppose are becoming quite a <u>Philosopher</u>." He also fostered their religious sensibility by describing his own experience of worship. After capturing Mexico City, the Americans took over Santa Anna's palace, and converted a "richly furnished" reception room into a Sunday chapel. "Santa Annas large arm chair is brought forward to the front of the dais," he told Agnes, "before which is placed a small desk, where Mr. McCarty our chaplain reads the Episcopal Service & preaches a sermon. Genl Scott & the officers & those soldiers that wish to attend sitting below him."[18]

Captain Lee's War

To his mother-in-law, Lee admitted his chronic spiritual insufficiencies, but in war he attained stunning success. He served on the staff of Winfield Scott as a member of what Scott called his "little cabinet," giving him an influence beyond his rank. He had started inauspiciously: he and First Lieutenant P. G. T. Beauregard had been scouting enemy lines when, suddenly, twelve feet away, a man challenged them and almost immediately fired his pistol. The round passed between Lee's arm and body. After subduing their attacker, they discovered that the first time Lee had ever been shot at, he was almost killed by friendly fire.[19]

93

At the Battle of Veracruz, Lee directed first the placement of artillery that sailors had dragged ashore, and then the fire that forced the city to surrender on March 26, 1847. His brother Smith, a naval officer, was in the thick of the cannonade.

Two weeks later, when American troops approached a much larger force at Cerro Gordo, Lee and another soldier were assigned to reconnoiter a route around the Mexican positions. As they scouted the territory, they came to a spring of water. Suddenly they heard voices speaking Spanish. Mexican soldiers were approaching. Lee's companion hid himself nearby, but Lee had time only to hide beneath a log. There he stayed, motionless, while the troopers drank from the spring. All day long, Mexicans kept coming, even stepping over the log—and Lee. Only at dusk did they leave, and Lee could escape. He brought back a plan to skirt the enemy's positions by carving a trail around their rear. It led to an easy victory over a much larger Mexican force.[20]

Then, his reconnaissance found a route through a huge and desolate lava field that allowed American troops to flank Mexican forces, leading to a series of American victories that opened the way to capturing Mexico City. Afterward, Scott commended "the gallant, indefatigable Captain Lee" for "the greatest feat of physical and moral courage performed by any individual in my knowledge." By war's end, Captain Lee had become Lieutenant Colonel Lee by "brevet," or temporary battlefield promotion.[21]

Of these exploits, Lee wrote nothing in his letters home to Mary, his children, or his brother. On the contrary, he instructed Carter not to "think that I consider [that] I have suffered any neglect for my slight services in the line of my duty. The consciousness of having endeavoured to perform that duty is the only satisfaction I expected, or coveted." As duty was a virtue commended by his father, so was modesty. Lee had seen all too many soldiers, from generals down, who sought acclaim and adulation. As a junior officer, he knew his place. He did share with Carter his opinions of the war and the political infighting within the army. He harshly criticized some of the commanders. But, he quickly added, "Military discipline requires subordination of ones feelings as well as conduct & those whose duty it is to preserve it, cannot be too cautious how they encourage the exhibition of it in subordinates against their superiors. It is sapping the foundation of all military organization. I sat down to be very moderate, but you see I have been unusually led into discussion."[22]

94

He was writing of some tiff among generals causing dissension in the ranks. It was not his place to speak, except to immediate family; but to Carter he described his fruitless efforts to promote harmony for the sake of cause and nation. "I have done all in my power to allay the feelings of the parties from the first, but without success. I knew it was a contest in which neither of them had anything to gain, & the service & perhaps the country much to lose. The latter is always first in my thoughts & efforts, & the feelings & interests of individuals should be sacrificed to its good. But it is difficult to get men to act on this principle."[23]

The war had given Lee plenty to ponder. He had seen battle and distinguished himself. He had faced fire, both friendly and hostile, and survived. He knew many who did not, and mourned their loss. Encountering John Macomb, a friend from West Point who had recently lost a cherished relative in battle, Lee lost his composure. "Meeting me, he suddenly saw in my face the effect of that loss, burst into tears," Macomb related, "and expressed his deep sympathy as tenderly in words as his lovely wife could have done."[24]

Lee worried that political spats might endanger the fruits of victory and jeopardize the dearly won peace. He perceived the fallibility of the nation he served. "It is true we bullied her," he wrote Mary of Mexico. "Of that I am ashamed, as she was the weaker party"; virtue was not, for him, a matter for individuals alone, but also for nations to practice. Yet their adversary shared blame for a conflict that had been "continued if not provoked by the wilful ignorance & vanity on the part of Mexico." As victors, the United States, having "fought well & fought fairly," deserved compensation for the costs it bore. "It would be curious now if we should refuse to accept the territory we have forced her to relinquish."[25] Virtue also justified the victor receiving the spoils.

Mary, too, had taken a dim view of the war, but felt no constraints in expressing it. She wrote to a friend in Savannah, "You can scarcely realize so far off the misery the war has occasioned, how many hearths have been made desolate and we can as yet see no termination." She, too, looked askance at the politics surrounding it. "I should think your friend Mr. Polk was now sufficiently glorified but I believe he is quite at a loss how to get out of the scrape."[26]

Lee also pondered his obligations to his own family, even whether he should leave the army to be closer to his wife and children. That would be no small sacrifice. He derived great satisfaction from military duty. He had been promoted, if only temporarily. He found the "friend-ship & kind considerations of my brother officers" to be "a constant source of warmest pleasure." But, he continued, "My children require more attention than I have ever yet been able to devote to them. I shall have been in the Pub. Service nearly 20 years. It has had my best days & energies. A young family has some claims." As well, he saw a need to help his sister Lucy, who was expecting a child.[27]

After he returned from the war, Lee found it possible to balance military tasks with family life. He received orders to Baltimore and then to West Point, positions that kept him busy yet still allowed him to pay greater attention to the children. He would not have to impose sole re-sponsibility for their care on Mary after all. At least for a while.

CHAPTER 10

"That, as We Grow in Age, We May Grow in Grace"

~

Father and Superintendent

In June 1848, the residents of Arlington House eagerly awaited the return of Robert E. Lee from Mexico. Listening intently for the carriage they had sent to carry him up the hill, they failed to notice the entrance of a bearded gentleman who had climbed off a horse and walked in. Suddenly Spec bounded over to the stranger with what his youngest son Rob called "demonstrations of delight": a terrier was the first to recognize that Lee had come home.

The joyous family crowded around him. Suddenly Lee exclaimed, "Where is my little boy?" He went looking for Rob. The five-year-old was as anxious to see his father as his father was to see him. Rob had carefully chosen a blue outfit adorned with white diamond figures. Face scrubbed, golden ringlets combed, he watched for his father with the throng that included a friend of his mother's and her son, who was the same age as Rob. When Colonel Lee stooped down to pick up his "little boy," he scooped up Armistead Lippitt instead.

Nearly sixty years later, Robert E. Lee Jr. began his otherwise glowing reminiscences with this, his first clear memory of his father. "I was shocked and humiliated." Then, he added, Lee "made ample amends to me."[1]

For the next seven years, Lee had the time to make amends. He savored a summer's respite in Arlington. Then, after temporary duties took him from Rhode Island to Georgia, he drew a three-year stint in Baltimore, then another three years as West Point's superintendent, both assignments on which the family, save those at boarding school, could join him. For six years, Lee could nurture his relationship with his family—and with his church.

In Baltimore, Lee's task was to lay the foundations of a structure that would replace the legendary but obsolete Fort McHenry to defend the city's harbor. He rented a townhouse at 908 Madison Avenue, a not-quite-finished house owned by an uncle and near the home of his sister, Ann Marshall, and her husband Louis, the US district attorney. These familial connections opened the city's social life to the Lees—once they settled in. Prying Mary from Arlington took some effort. First, the house remained uncompleted. Then, when it was ready, Mary delayed leaving her parents' home for as long as she could. So Robert lived in Baltimore alone for nearly a year, returning for weekends at Arlington until the family finally joined him in August 1849.[2]

His work seems not to have thrilled him. "My days are spent pretty much at Fort Carroll," he wrote Markie. "My thoughts are engrossed with driving piles laying stone; & my imagination is exercised in the construction of cranes, Diving bells, Steam Pile drivers, etc. . . . If it was not for my heart, Markie, I might as well be a pile or stone myself, laid quietly at the bottom of the river."[3] The glory days of Mexico seemed long past.

On moving to Baltimore, Lee began attending the nearby Episcopal parish. Mount Calvary, founded in 1843, anchored the same new residential neighborhood that attracted not only the Lees and Marshalls but also the bishop of Maryland, William Whittingham. All of them went to Mount Calvary. The church held an irony for Lee, given his comments on "Pussyism," for it was at heart a Puseyite establishment, designed to embody Tractarian principles. Its architect had intended to create a "God-centered church," inspired by the Cambridge movement, and in the English Gothic Revival style. A solid altar stood prominently in the center, precisely the kind that Meade forbade in Virginia. Although not for twenty years would Mount Calvary celebrate the Eucharist every Sunday, at that time it did so more often than most parishes. Morning Prayer was said there each day, drawing Whittingham (who at times also served as its rector) so often that Mount Calvary became known as "the Bishop's Church." That led to an irony for the bishop too, twice over. He was a "high" churchman of the old New York school, which was opposed to the Catholic style that Mount Calvary represented even before vestments, candles, crosses, and other elements of the ritualist movement made their appearance. As well, Whittingham had been the new bishop who received Meade's warning of insidious English influences.[4]

Lee worshiped regularly at Mount Calvary. This was the church he left his children's sickbeds to attend, and where he observed Good Friday in 1850.[5] It was his soul's duty, and it became his ecclesiastical responsibility as well: he was elected to the vestry. Old Maryland law allowed anyone to serve even if he, like Lee, had not been confirmed as an Episcopalian (or, for that matter, baptized as a Christian).[6] Mount Calvary may have lingered in the family's memory, for the steeple of the church that Lexington Episcopalians built to memorialize Lee a quarter-century later with the children's advice and help bears a striking resemblance to that of their parish church in Baltimore. If so, the Lees would have slipped a bit of Puseyism into Virginia.

Lee's work in Baltimore allowed him to pay closer attention to his children. Sometimes he would take Rob with him. The two would ride a horse-drawn bus to the Sollers Point wharf, near where Fort Carroll was being built just offshore. Rob spent the day in the safekeeping of nearby residents who then invited the two Robert Lees to enjoy a "country dinner" with them. On evenings when Robert and Mary dined out, as they often did, the children bade them farewell, he in uniform, she in her elegant gown. Rob remembered drifting off to sleep "with this beautiful picture in my mind" of his father, "the golden epaulets and all—chiefly the epaulets." Such events left Rob with better memories than his first, of "my father, his gentle, loving care of me, his bright talk, his stories, his maxims and teachings. I was very proud of him and of the evident respect for and trust in him every one showed."[7]

Bringing Up Children the Way They Should Go

By this time the family followed an established pattern: attending church often, teaching the younger children at home, advising them when they were away. Family letters rarely cite daily prayers or Christian education, but both were as much a part of life as eating breakfast, so ordinary as not to warrant mention. Mary seems not to have involved her children in a formal program like the one she established as a newlywed in Fort Monroe, but she undoubtedly continued the practice of family devotions as at Arlington. The boys attended local schools, and Mary taught the girls, who, when they were older, went to boarding school.[8]

In rearing their seven children, Robert seemed to echo his father. Nearly every letter to or about Custis, the firstborn, contained discourses on the importance of duty, responsibility, and accomplishment. "I am sorry indeed Custis has recd so many marks of demerit," he complained to Mary from Fort Hamilton. "Although they may be for <u>trifles</u>, yet still if they are required to be observed, they become of <u>importance</u>, & cannot be considered beneath his attention." He took personally what Custis did—or did not—do: "I shall be very much mortified, if after behaving well so long, & acquiring a character, for attention & good behaviour, he should now, when a stricter observance of the regulations could be more easily expected of him, forfeit the good standing he has hitherto held."[9]

He expected much of both of his older boys. From Mexico, he wrote them both that "it is the highth of my wishes that you should be <u>good</u>, <u>wise</u> & <u>true</u>. You must therefor try hard to be all these, & when I come back give me the joy & satisfaction of finding you so." All his sufferings and separations "will be more than compensated to me, by such a result."[10]

Custis always bore the greatest burden. Finishing second was never good enough. "I am glad you have attained the Corporalcy," Lee wrote his son at West Point. "I should have preferred it to have been the first, but it will lead to that yet, if you will prove yourself, as I hope you are, the <u>best soldier</u> in your class." His father exhorted him to achieve even greater success: "Do your duty, <u>honestly</u>, & <u>faithfully</u>: Without <u>favour</u> & without <u>partiality</u>. Do not seek to report, but let it be seen that though it gives you <u>pain</u>, still you <u>must</u> do your duty. That this duty is <u>equal</u>. Never more or less rigid, but always the <u>same</u> & your <u>duty</u>. The same as regards your dearest friend or worst enemy. You will thus gain esteem & affection & not dislike or hatred. The <u>Just</u> are always loved & never hated."[11]

Rooney, the proverbial handful, was a different story. In 1845, alone and bored in the Fort Hamilton home, the eight-year-old transgressed parental boundaries and wandered into a barn, climbed into the loft, played with a pair of straw cutters, and cut off the ends of two fingers. Attempts to reattach them failed.

Did Custis, then at school in Virginia, ever hear about *that!* After chiding him on low marks in algebra despite his having "some talent for mathematics," his father described the "calamity" that his brother might "lose his fingers & be ruined for life." Soon after, Custis received a letter supposedly dictated by the injured Rooney to his father in which the victim confessed his sins to his brother. "I hope neither of us will disobey our parents for the future & that a similar accident may never happen to you." Then Lee added in his own voice, "My only consolation is that this severe lesson will never be forgotten by himself or his brothers & sisters." He referred to Annie's having lost an eye when playing with scissors. "See how two have been punished for their inattention & disobedience. One with the loss of an eye, another with the amputation of two fingers." Suddenly two of Custis's siblings had become moral examples. "If you ever acquire [*sic*: aspire?] to be strengthened or confirmed in the path of rectitude, let the fate of these two be then before you." Lee added, "If children could know the misery, the desolating sorrow, <u>with which</u> their acts sometimes overwhelm their parents they could not have the heart thus cruelly to afflict them. May you never know the misery I now suffer & may you always be preserved to me pure & happy." At least he praised Custis's latest report card.[12]

One biographer wonders if Lee's moralizing reflected contemporary theories of child rearing. Perhaps it did, but Lee may also have been remembering his youth. His father strove mightily to instill duty and virtue in his sons, Carter in particular, which resembled how Lee commended and, more often, chided Custis. Lee strove to guide his children, notably his oldest, encouraging and admonishing with high standards, doses of guilt, and the promise of prayers.

Yet the same biographer points out Lee's tender devotion to his children. "I am now watching by [Rooney's] bedside lest he should disturb his hand in his sleep." The stern father was also loving and attentive. Without question he was proud of his children. When Rob was a toddler, Mary complimented a youngster she saw. Lee retorted, "I see she does not in your opinion bear a comparison with my Rob. Indeed I don't see how anything could. I long to kiss that fragrant mouth & feel that little heart fluttering against mine." On his way to war, he even dreamed of being in bed with his children crawling around him, a common practice in the Lee household. He fascinated them with stories, but only if they tickled his hands and feet.[13] How his relationship with his children contrasted with anything he could have had with his father.

Lee's letters preached to them on discipline, duty, and morality. Mary sent books. She who had forwarded sermons to her affianced in Georgia in a vain attempt to convert him before their wedding now mailed religious works of various sorts to her children old enough to be away at school. Custis thanked her for sending him *The Young Man's Friend and Guide through Life to Immortality* to read during leisure moments at West Point. He was prudent enough to peruse at least one sermon, which contrasted filial "undutifulness" with "dutiful conduct."

Custis thanked her with the "hope that its pleasant truths have not been entirely lost upon me. . . . The profit to me may I hope equal its cost in money." He diplomatically added that "it can in nowise compensate for the affection which prompted the gift." He, like his father, was learning to be tactful.[14]

Meanwhile, Mary Custis, "Daughter," at age fifteen at school in New York, exchanged notes with her mother on sermons. Mary, Daughter, and Annie continued a tradition of Custis women by organizing epistolary discussions of religion; one discussion concerned letters written by the English evangelical Henry Venn.[15]

Mary and Robert took great pride in their children's achievements. She bragged to a friend about Custis, then a new West Point cadet. "He is doing very well so far not a single demerit—but he has only been in camp has not commenced his studies." She could have spoken for them both. "We begin to feel quite patriarchal with our sons & daughters growing up around us." Like Robert, she sent exhortations, though they, like the books she sent, had a particularly religious point. She wrote Custis midway through his plebe year, "I am . . . very anxious you should preserve your post as the head of your class." She added, "Above all my son do you read your bible. Do not neglect that most important of all books for your mother's sake if not for your [own]."[16]

To varying degrees, at least outwardly, the lessons were shaping the next generation of Lees. Like his father when fresh out of West Point, Custis, newly posted to Amelia Island off the Florida coast, attended church at least occasionally. He had the wisdom to tell his mother of it. "Last Sunday I hired a little boat and two men and went to church 'on the main' [mainland] to a little log country meeting house, where I heard a tolerably good sermon upon the resurrection of Christ from a methodist minister by the name of Tidings." Again like his father, he enjoyed being invited to dinner afterward.[17]

Rooney followed a different path from his brother and father: he went to Harvard. There he accomplished nothing of which his parents could brag. "He thinks entirely of his pleasures, & not of what is proper to be done," Lee groused to Mary after Rooney, whom he called "dearest Horse," abandoned—in Lee's view—his ailing mother to return to Cambridge in the fall of 1856. "I fear he pursues the same course at college, & has never seen the necessity of his being there." A Harvard classmate, Henry Adams, tended to agree. The descendant of the nation's second and sixth presidents, whose family was a Massachusetts equivalent to the Lees of Virginia, Adams knew "Roony" well (if not well enough to spell his name as the Lees did). He liked him, too, though in his autobiography he depicted Fitzhugh as a "Virginian of the eighteenth century" who "had changed little from the type of his grandfather, Light Horse Harry." With a "habit of command," the Lees' second son soon became "the most popular and prominent young man in his class." But he was "simple beyond analysis," Adams stated. "No one knew enough to know how simple he was. As an animal, the Southerner seemed to have every advantage, but even as an animal, he steadily lost ground," including academically. Every student needed to learn to "read mathematics," but young Lee "never reached the alphabet."[18] His parents never said any such thing. They never mentioned his faith, either.

Lee's religion, meanwhile, was growing more intense as well, even as his military career received its first, if unwanted, reward.

Duty, Honor, Country

Lee had made the ideals of the United States Military Academy—duty, honor, country—part of his life long before they became West Point's motto at the end of the century. In May 1852, the army made him its superintendent.

Lee took the post reluctantly. He had graduated from the academy second in his class with an honorable record in every way. He had shared in examining cadets while he was stationed downriver at Fort Hamilton. He had distinguished himself in war, winning the utmost confidence of his wartime superior, Winfield Scott, who in 1852 still commanded the entire US Army. In short, Lee was an ideal candidate for the job. But Lee resisted. In 1839 the chief of engineers, Joseph Totten, had suggested that Lee teach at the academy. Claiming "[t]he duties of an Instructer being very foreign to my taste and disposition," Lee turned him down. To a friend, Lee explained his preference for construction over instruction, especially "having experienced the disagreement attending the duties" of teaching just after his graduation, so "it would have been uncandid to have induced" Totten "to believe that I possessed the taste and peculiar zeal which the situation requires." Nor, he added, was he qualified.[19]

Thirteen years later, eleven days after receiving his orders, Lee protested to the same superior that the job demanded "more skill, & more experience than I command." This time Totten had none of it. Silence conveyed his answer. Lee got the message. In July he confessed that he had never taken any post "with such reluctance." On September 1, "in obedience to the instructions of the Secy of War," Lee assumed the superintendency.[20] Duty had called.

Brevet Colonel Lee journeyed to his new post, once again, alone. Eventually, some of the family joined him. By that time, Custis had attained respect in the corps for his achievements. Suddenly he found his own renowned father as his superintendent.[21] "Daughter" and Rooney came too, then headed to schools in the New York area. Annie and Agnes remained at Arlington with their grandparents and their governess for a time. Only the youngest, Rob and Mildred, lived in the superintendent's quarters with their mother and father, though Custis savored his chances to visit.

Lee's tenure fell within what some have called West Point's "greatest age," 1840–1860. Its officers had performed brilliantly in the Mexican conflict. In the corps and on the faculty were hosts of future officers who distinguished themselves in the next big war. Lee brought a stature beyond his ability to comprehend. Some considered him the army's most promising officer. Scott saw Lee as his successor as general in chief. Cadets admired him. One observed that "by his generous, manly and consistent conduct he has won the respect and esteem of every Cadet in the Corps."[22]

Golden age or not, Lee as superintendent confronted serious problems. Despite relatively low standards for admission, half of the candidates, mostly from the South and the West, failed the entrance examinations. The war with Mexico revealed deficiencies in a curriculum that had not changed since the 1820s. Lee urged Congress to extend the course of study to five years, allowing an extra year for English, military law, and field instruction. Since few of the officers spoke Spanish, Lee introduced the language into the curriculum. He also altered the uniform, redesigning the traditional cap because its heaviness caused "headaches and dizziness."[23]

Concern for the cadets extended beyond relieving their aching heads. The Lees invited groups to small dinners and larger parties, getting to know the young men personally, and giving the cadets relief from the woeful fare served in the mess hall.[24] For their part, cadets marveled not only at George Washington's personal silverware but also at the character of their host.

Cadets learned to respect his administrative wisdom. On one occasion, two of them, Archibald Gracie and Wharton Green, got into a fight. Gracie was caught. Green was not, but turned himself in anyway, asking Lee to administer to him the same stiff penalty Gracie faced. Lee punished neither. "Don't you think," Lee asked Green, alluding to Psalm 133:1, "that it is better for brothers to dwell together in peace and harmony?" "Yes, Colonel," Green replied, "and if we were all like you, it would be an easy thing to do." Just moments later, Gracie entered the room with an orderly, seized Green's hand, "and the breach was closed."[25]

Lee related to the cadets but retained his reserve. One, the future Union general O. O. Howard, concluded that "probably no man better combined the dignity of a proud man with the geniality of a friendly spirit" than Lee. Lying in the post hospital after a riding accident, he opened his eyes to see the superintendent at his bedside. "I said to myself: 'Colonel Lee is my friend, but I must never approach too near him; he is gracious, but evidently condescending.'"[26]

As superintendent, Lee had authority on rare occasion to bend rules. He allowed a Cadet Gracie—the same one involved in the scuffle?—to attend a family wedding because of his mother's poor health, hoping that Gracie's "visit will afford relief as well as gratification to his mother, & make him the more diligent in his studies & attentive to his duties."[27]

More often, he had to reject requests, yet in so doing he always kept the cadet and his family aware of larger goals. Out of fairness, what he offered to one, he had to offer to all. The exception Gracie received was genuinely exceptional. To a father requesting a similar pass for his son, Lee cited the broader responsibilities that a cadet carried: "The Cadets are placed here for a particular object & if the indulgence in question is granted to one, it must be extended to all. You therefore see it would materially interfere with their course of studies & instruction. Their presence at this time, to prepare for the approaching Jany. [January] examination, is particularly important to them, & it may be of more advantage to your son, to maintain his present high standing in his class, than to enjoy the gaities of the wedding. He will have other opportunities I hope to participate in these hereafter."[28]

Eternal vigilance was the cost of superintendency for Lee, as it had been for Thayer. Lee notified an officer that on Wednesday, February 23, 1853, "one of your pupils whose name is Cooper was seen to bring from

Mr. Clark's store a quantity of tobacco, about a dozen papers, & give them to some cadets who were standing near the shoemaker's shop." He gently suggested that "perhaps this was done by the young gentleman in question, without knowing he was violating the regulations of the Academy, or considering the injury he was doing to the cadets." Lee made clear that the act was not to be repeated.[29]

Lee had his duty to perform. So did the cadets. He would not allow Christmas celebrations to last for more than one day lest they distract cadets from preparing for exams. He would not release Episcopal cadets assigned to guard duty to attend evening prayer at their church (and his). When a cadet failed in either responsibility, military or academic, Lee reported his deficiencies to his family. He wrote many such letters, as tactfully as he could. "Although he has not committed any serious offences," he informed one father, "his conduct has not been marked by that attention to his duties necessary to the character of a Soldier." Invariably, Lee looked to what good might result from the boy's failure, hoping that it "may serve to stimulate him to greater exertion, & by showing him the necessity of diligent application & steady attention to whatever he undertakes, may tend to his ultimate welfare." He consoled a guardian of another cadet accused of a serious fault: "Whatever may be the result of his trial, I hope his connection with the Military Academy will be of no ultimate disadvantage to him, but will teach him the importance of earnest attention & application & thus pave the way for future success."[30]

He applied these same principles in dealing with cadets' religious duties. Cadets and officers were required to attend Sunday morning chapel services unless, as he explained to a concerned father, "they entertain conscientious scruples at attending the worship of a different denomination." As in Lee's cadet days, the chaplain was also professor of ethics and moral philosophy. After McIlvaine, the Episcopalian, left under duress, the chaplaincy reverted to the Presbyterians. In 1853, the Reverend William D. Sprole conducted services "according to the forms of that church." But, Lee assured one father, "I think there is little danger of the feelings or principles of other sects being violated, or that the moral & religious culture of the cadets will suffer more by their attendance there" than in the Presbyterian chaplain's classroom. He told a worrying mother in Baton Rouge, "His discourses are addressed particularly to the Cadets [and] are free from doctrinal questions, & calculated to inculcate principles of piety & morality." Lee's father, though not his mother, would have been relieved to know that the chaplain's talks to the cadets were "free from all doctrinal or sectarian questions."[31]

For cadets with strong denominational ties, Lee granted some latitude. Roman Catholics could attend Mass at their church on the other side of the Hudson, and a priest officiated at the academy itself on Sundays. With "pleasure" he granted cadets the right to attend churches of their denomination on Sunday afternoons, if the church was not far off, if assigned duties did not preclude their attendance, and if they attended the mandatory chapel service on post. The Episcopal church was one that cadets could attend when Communion was offered. Unfortunately, the Methodist church was too far afield, in Buttermilk Falls, where, except for the "particular occasion," "it is not considered adviseable for the Cadets to visit; being beyond the influence of their Officers, & where there are temptations to violate the Regulations."[32]

Lee had no patience with those who abused the privileges he extended. Three months into his tenure, he learned of Cadet Dwight's absence from chapel. Two years earlier, with his father's approval, Dwight had declared that he "he could not conscientiously attend the Presbyterian form of worship." The secretary of war, no less, gave his approval. Instead of meditating in chapel, however, the cadet felt inspired to contemplate in person the allures of New York City. Lee reported Dwight to the authorities in Washington, no doubt to his future detriment in the Corps of Engineers.[33]

Because officers as well as cadets were expected to attend chapel, Lee and his family set an example. Rob recalled his father's being dressed in uniform ready for church before anyone else, "jokingly rallying my mother for being late, and for forgetting something at the last moment." If she tarried too long, he left her behind, taking any of the children who were ready to go. Arriving at the chapel, he strode to a seat "well up the middle aisle." Occasionally, he "took a little nap during the sermon." His drowsiness was "something awful" to Rob, who suffered the same weakness but could not understand "why he, who to my mind could do everything that was right, without any effort," could have such a fault. But the superintendent was not alone. Agnes, who generally liked Chaplain Sprole's sermons, sometimes dozed off at the start, though she awoke in time for his strong finish. One Sunday she watched "one poor cadet whom all the parson's eloquence could not rouze." He yawned, shook himself, tried everything he could to stay awake, but inevitably "would sink back upon the bench & go fast asleep."[34]

Family prayers remained a standard practice when Lee was superintendent. As well, on some Sundays and on various feast days, they, like some of the cadets, worshiped at the Church of the Holy Innocents, the local Episcopal parish about a mile and a half away. Agnes, aged twelve, deemed it "very pretty but a little too much like a catholic one."[35] It was, after all, in the Diocese of New York, where, to a young Virginian, ritualism was rampant.

On Easter Day 1855, the three older Lee daughters went to the academy chapel while Superintendent and Mrs. Lee "attended the H.I." It was their last Sunday at the Point. Lee had been appointed second-in-command of the Second Cavalry, an elite new regiment raised to guard the Texas frontier. On the eve of their departure, the cadets serenaded the Lees. Earlier that day, Robert and Mary partook of Holy Communion.[36] Robert could now receive the sacrament. While overseeing the moral and religious welfare of his own children and the sons of many others, he had considered his own faith and, as a result, was confirmed in the Episcopal Church. He at last became a "communicant."

CHAPTER 11

"That He May Continue Thine Forever"

Lee's Confirmation

For all Lee's involvement in the church, his oversight of his children's upbringing and of cadets in their religious activities along with everything else, he himself had never made an adult commitment to his church. He had never been confirmed into the Episcopal Church. Thus, he most probably had never received Communion, the central act of worship for Episcopalians. In 1853, that changed dramatically.

In the Anglican heritage, the rite of confirmation held an honored place. Though departing from Roman Catholic tradition in not counting confirmation as a sacrament, English reformers valued it as a rite, included it in the Book of Common Prayer, and deemed it important enough to be administered by only bishops. Usually, children who had been baptized as infants were confirmed when they had come to what the Prayer Book called "the age of discretion" and could take upon themselves the fundamental commitments of a Christian. They were then "admitted to the Holy Communion."[1]

In Virginia, however, as generally in colonial and newly independent America, its practice was necessarily irregular. America had no bishops until 1784. Rigorously enforcing the rubric that only bishops could administer the sacrament would have effectively barred from the communion rail all but a handful of faithful members. That did not happen, thanks to another rubric, in the 1662 rite, that allowed some exceptions. So Martha Washington regularly received the sacred elements even though she could not possibly have been confirmed. An early American bishop, John Henry Hobart, writing in 1819, justified that practice for pastoral reasons. Because Jesus said at the last supper with his disciples, "*Do* this in remembrance of me," Hobart argued, "the reception of one ordinance of the Gospel [confirmation] cannot exempt us from the obligation of observing the other institutions which it prescribes"—namely, Communion.[2]

Even when bishops, and confirmation, became available on American shores, the theological question remained of what the rite *was* and *meant*, especially in relation to baptism, which confirmation in some way reaffirmed. Hobart held a "high church" perspective that stressed the importance and efficaciousness of sacraments, and differentiated baptism from confirmation as "between *Regeneration*, or the change of our spiritual state; and *Renovation*, or the change of heart and life." Confirmation for him was a "renewing of the mind" that "can alone secure . . . the privileges of baptism." In short, confirmation fulfilled baptism.[3]

Others saw it as a sign, virtually as an adult reiteration of baptism. A Philadelphia rector in 1829 called it "a transaction, not for time, but for eternity," in which a believer enters "into a covenant of love and service with the great and holy God."[4]

Evangelicals accepted this sense of discipleship even while stressing confirmation as an outward sign of inward conversion. For Charles McIlvaine, confirmation was not merely a nourishing of faith, but also a forthright expression of it. Confirmation demanded a visibly Christian way of life. McIlvaine's equally fervent brother bishop in Tennessee, James Otey, complained of "the lukewarmness, not to say careless lives, of many who have renewed their Baptismal vows." He blamed a lack of preparation for confirmation—on account of "Parental neglect and Ministerial unfaithfulness"—resulting in young people avoiding the Lord's Supper and older people living "in such habits of worldliness" as to make one wonder if they took seriously their "professed obligations."[5]

To varying degrees, midcentury Episcopalians generally held that confirmation signified more than an adult's reaffirmation of baptism. At the least, it renewed the fundamental commitments to Jesus Christ as Lord and Savior, and, as a result, the Holy Spirit provided a refreshment of grace.

Evangelical Episcopalians went further. They considered confirmation nothing less than an outward and visible sign of one's conversion to Christ, through a public confession. If baptism opened the gates at least to the possibility of eternal life, confirmation provided the means by which one might walk through them, and proceed along the heavenly way. Eucharist regularly refreshed one's baptismal vows once one was confirmed. Because the rite marks the act of a converted Christian, receiving Communion must be limited to the confirmed.

This was William Meade's perspective. As early as 1831 he prepared a guidebook that paralleled his book on the catechism to help the candidate for confirmation. He saw in preparing for the rite a moment for genuine soul-searching, for "ascertaining what is my real state and condition before God, that I may either bless him publicly for having granted me his renewing grace, or else, finding that I am still in a state of sin and death, may seek deliverance without a moment's delay." Death always stood near to nineteenth-century Americans, so urgency was always great. For those looking for God's saving grace to "overcome their rebellious hearts," whatever their age, "this Rite is for them."[6]

Anyone confirmed became a "communicant," in communion with Christ through receiving the sacrament of his body and blood. In Meade's view, any person in so intimate a relationship with God would behave in a particularly uplifted way. The conduct of communicants that appalled him at Christ Church in 1811 inspired his lifelong quest to elevate the moral behavior of all his people but principally of those who partook of the Lord's Supper. Meade at last succeeded in having his diocese set a particularly high bar for confirmation and even Communion. Confirmation presupposed a conversion to Christ. Communion demanded not only faith (established in confirmation) but also a rigorous if not austere religious life. The Diocese of Virginia officially expected much from its communicants.[7]

The young Robert Edward Lee was baptized and catechized with the clear understanding that, as soon as he could say the creed, the Lord's Prayer, the Ten Commandments, and other requisite parts of the catechism, he be brought to the bishop for confirmation.[8] Why was he not? There is no obvious answer. Lee himself never seems to have addressed the matter, and several possible explanations fall short. Some families might procrastinate. The Lee household in Robert's teenage years was tumultuous, with his mother ill and his father absent, so perhaps they simply did not get around to it. Yet Ann Carter Lee's religious passion makes it unlikely that she would neglect what was becoming, in her era, an especially important step for her son. It is improbable that she would forget or delay.

Confirmation required episcopal hands. The lack of a bishop at an opportune time might be a second explanation. But the Custises and the Lees kept in close touch with the bishops of Virginia, especially

Meade and Johns. Even if Robert had consistently been away when bishops visited congregations for confirmation, they of all people could have arranged an alternative.

Robert, as a teenager, may simply not have been ready for what was becoming so momentous a rite. He may have been unwilling to assume the high responsibilities the Diocese of Virginia expected of a confirmed communicant. As a fiancé, Lee withstood the religious hopes and hints that his bride and her mother tried to impose on him, a sign that he would not sacrifice his own convictions, or the absence of them, to meet the expectations of others. He also truly enjoyed some of the worldly pleasures that Meade and the diocese condemned, such as dancing. "I never have been able to see any sin in the exercise," he once wrote Mary.[9]

The notion of enjoying life, of "sowing wild oats" in youth before getting serious about faith, extends far back in Christian history. Saint Augustine of Hippo, another son of a devoutly faithful mother, delayed baptism for just this reason. Perhaps this was why Lee delayed confirmation.

Lee never explained why he did not seek confirmation earlier. But, when he was forty-five, a family sorrow shook him to the core of his being. His mother-in-law died.

"Irreparable Loss"

On April 25, 1853, Lee had terrible news to convey to his children. "I have to communicate intelligence of the most afflicting calamity that has ever befallen us," he wrote to Daughter, Mary Custis. Her grandmother had died. She "has been called by her God whom she so fervently adored & earnestly served, to worship in his presence forever & ever!"

For the Lees, it was the worst crisis they had faced. In Robert's era, death visited homes with regularity. But not for a remarkable span of twenty-three years, since Ann Carter Lee died, had the Lees suffered a loss in their immediate family. For Mary Lee Fitzhugh Custis, the end came unexpectedly. Though her health had declined, when she complained of a headache her doctor saw little reason for concern. By the next day she was dying. As her husband knelt by her bedside "& implored God to spare her or to make him submissive to His will," she clasped her grandchildren, said the Lord's Prayer, and, on the day after her sixty-fifth birthday, breathed her last.[10]

Mary rushed from West Point to Arlington, but arrived only in time for the funeral on April 27. Lee could not attend. By law, an officer of the Corps of Engineers had to be present to command the academy. At that moment, the superintendent was the only such officer at West Point. Only his own death, he told Daughter, would allow him to relinquish his post. So he mourned from afar. "I have no words to soften the anguish it will occasion you, or power to mitigate our suffering & sorrow."[11]

Unable to console his wife in person, he strove to comfort her by letter. Lee knew the changes arising from Mrs. Custis's death, the magnitude of the loss, the burden Mary would shoulder. "How sad to realize the change from other times, when that farm and that house overflowed at your approach with love devotion & tenderness!" he wrote on the day of the funeral. "May God give you strength to bear it & enable us to say, 'his will be done.' The more I think of our irreparable loss the greater is my grief." But, he insisted, he grieved more for the living. "Not for her. She has gone from all trouble, care & sorrow to a happy immortality! There to rejoice & praise forever the Lord & Saviour she so long & faithfully served." Her death conveyed a lesson for them all. "Let that be our comfort & that our consolation. We must discard all selfishness & all egotism & so act & live as she would have wished. May our death be like hers & may we all meet in happiness in Heaven."[12]

Both parents drew the attention of their children to the moral lessons of death. Lee exhorted Daughter, at boarding school in New York, to remember her grandmother's example in order that it "teach you what a woman should be."

> Know what will procure you real happiness. Follow that steadily & directly. Be above the fashions of the thoughtless & the enticements of the silly. Above all, weigh & consider the perishable & fleeting nature of all things here, & the everlasting fixedness [?] of that eternal world to which we are daily progressing. Let the feeling of the woman in the wilderness be always over you, "Should God seest me," & let that knowledge chasten & pacify [?] your thoughts, word, & actions. The first step to improvement is the knowledge of its importance. If you begin to perceive what you lack you will the more readily strive to prepare yourself. I am not therefore discouraged at your confession

of a want of preparation to take your place in the world. You must be the more earnest in your efforts guarded in your acts.[13]

Lee's children also expressed moral lessons. Two days after the burial, a grief-stricken Rooney advised his mother, "You must not make yourself sick, but as you would if she was living and happy, she is now looking down upon us all and sees all our actions, may none of us do wrong."[14] He had learned from his parents to accept the deaths of others and to grow from them.

Molly Custis's death inspired Lee to ponder his relationships and his mortality. "As a son I have always loved her, as a son I deeply mourn her," he wrote his wife the following week. He had known Mrs. Custis since early childhood. She filled the place of his own late mother. "My heart will cherish her affection . . . till it too ceases to beat, when"—he added—"I pray & trust I may be priviledged to join her." The advice he had given Daughter, to look beyond this life, he now took himself: his mother-in-law's death put him in mind of his own.

Lee also pondered the works of providence, even in his not attending the burial. Of course, he wanted to be present, but "it was otherwise ordered by him too wise to err & too good to be unkind."[15] He saw not the hand of the army, but the hand of God preventing his presence.

He may have wondered how else the hand of God might be guiding him. What other orders did the Almighty have in mind for him? How much time might he have on earth? Or, as Meade asked confirmands to consider, "How is it with thee, O my soul!"[16]

How it was with Lee's soul he does not say, even to Mary. But many searched their souls at times of death, as Mary did after her uncle Fitzhugh died in 1830, with her conversion as a result. Lee's confirmation might well have been his response to his mother-in-law's death.

Furthermore, Lee's religion had been becoming more serious even before Mrs. Custis's demise. He had seen the horrors of war. He had consoled relatives and cadets. He had supervised young men's lives. Human nature was ever before him. He paid close attention to what was required of him, and tried to instill a sense of duty to others.

It so happened that Bishop Johns was coming to Christ Church, Alexandria, where he would administer confirmation to Lee's two older daughters. If God could keep Lee from attending a funeral, might God be providing the chance for a religious commitment?

Confirming Faith

On Sunday evening, July 17, 1853, Mary "had the inexpressible happiness" of watching Mary Custis and Annie, "with their dear Father," kneeling before Bishop Johns as he confirmed them all. Whether he was motivated by his own religious impulse or by a desire to set an example for his daughters, or simply to preclude any question of why they should be confirmed when he was not, Lee never explained in writing. But there he knelt.

Agnes found the service of confirmation deeply moving. "I don't think I ever heard such a sermon before," she recorded in her diary. Johns so inspired the "almost breathless" Agnes with his "invitation to come to Christ" that she "solemnly determined to dedicate myself to God & I have tried, but Oh! I don't think I have improved in the least. . . . I wish I was a christian! but it is so hard to be one." What effect Johns had on Robert, Mary Custis, and Annie is not recorded; but, after the sermon, the three of them were confirmed. "They have promised to be Christians," Agnes wrote. "May they have strength given them to keep their vows."[17]

Mary Lee saw the rite for her children as a coming-of-age. She looked forward to having Daughter's help in managing affairs at Arlington in her mother's absence. But, before the service, Mary also encouraged Mary Custis to understand the spiritual significance of the vows she was about to make.

> The Holy Spirit can guide you into all truth & righteousness. Pray earnestly that He may take possession of your soul. . . . Perhaps you have already offered that soul to God. Do not hesitate[,] this is a golden period with you, the turning point in your life. Let it be established that you are truly a member of Christ, a child of God & an Inheritor of the Kingdom of Heaven. Confess Him before men who at the last day will acknowledge you before the assembled universe[.] That will be a proud recognition for you. Be assured my child from the experience of one who in early life culled all the choicest pleasures of the world & before they had begun to lose their freshness & zest, found in Religion a happiness & comfort far above all & which as the world cannot give it can never take away.

Annie, apparently, understood the vows' importance on her own. "My dear little Annie seems to be deeply impressed tho' I have not conversed with her particularly on the subject, to her gentle meek spirit the change will be hardly perceptible at first even to herself."[18]

For his part, Robert had taken another step in the process of transformation. Soon thereafter, he took another: he received Communion. "Today I knelt with my husband at the supper of our blessed Lord," Mary jubilantly wrote in her diary. "Happiness long waited for yet it could only be expressed in silent tears of joy." Only her mother was missing. She would "have cried to see this day!," for Mrs. Custis had longed for it as much as Mrs. Lee had. "Yet the knowledge of it may have swelled the full tide of joy in which her spirit now floats."

Mary knew that, according to the doctrine of confirmation as taught to Virginia Episcopalians, this marked just the beginning of a life of dedication and service. She sensed that she and her husband might offer significant contributions in the future. Perhaps this was one more event in the process of God's fulfilling the destiny appointed for them. It might inaugurate what she wrote to Daughter, "a golden period, a turning point" in their married life. She was ready, and seemed to believe that her husband was ready too. "Shall we not be able now to do something more for the glory of God," she asked. The answer was in the hands of the divine. "How much is to be accomplished our Lord direct & guide us."[19]

Little did she know what lay ahead.

CHAPTER 12

"Of the Traditions of the Church"

Lee the Episcopalian

Lee's confirmation may not have been *the* turning point in his religious life. Had it been a conversion similar to Mary's, she would have filled her diary with thanksgivings for it. Robert did, though, increasingly articulate his religious principles more consistently, candidly, and cogently. His letters reveal more of the content of his faith. They also show, within the panoply of American Protestantism, how deeply Anglican he had become. He had matured into the tradition that had been his since birth. It would continue to influence him for the remainder of his life. For that reason, it bears exploring.

No one ever accused Lee of being a theologian. He lived the life of a soldier, and within that orbit, of an engineer. In this he resembled his wife's forebear whose example stood ever before him, George Washington, who "was a military man, not a theologian or philosopher. There was an assurance and a practical bent to his faith, rather than continued questioning or a need to search deeper for answers."[1] They both grew up among Virginians who thought seriously about matters of religion, albeit in ways more pragmatic than dogmatic. Lee's faith, too, fell short in doctrine but loomed large in practical application. His was not so much a "theology" as a "spirituality." His faith depended on a few central tenets, notably that of "providence," while relying more generally upon a strong spiritual tradition to guide him through life. As he encountered other Christian expressions, his appreciation grew not just of them but also of his own Episcopal Church. It fit him well.

The Two Books

On the plains of Texas in 1857, Lee, by then a colonel commanding a cavalry unit, had the terrible duty of officiating at the burial of the young son of one of his soldiers. "For the first time in my life, I read the beautiful funeral service of our Church over the grave," he wrote Mary, referring to the Order for the Burial of the Dead in the Book of Common Prayer.[2] Lee maintained a lifelong appreciation for his church's Prayer Book. He grew up with it; he carried it with him on his travels and through the war; its words were among the last he heard; and the same service he read over the grave of the child in Texas was used at his funeral in Lexington.

The Book of Common Prayer was one of the two volumes his forebears brought from England. The other was the Bible. These "were the twin pillars" of Anglican spirituality from the sixteenth century onward. In Lexington, he kept a copy of each near at hand in his office until the day he died.[3]

The Lees, along with most Protestants, cherished their Bible. Mary read the Scriptures regularly, if not always with the attention she believed they deserved.[4] She exhorted her children, as she did Custis at West Point, not to "neglect that most important of all books for your mother's sake if not for your [own]." After commending several books to Mildred, then away at school, she remarked that "in your Bible you will find all you need. Study it daily & you will find it a light to your feet & a lamp to your paths."[5]

Lee esteemed it too. Nine months after his confirmation, Markie Williams found him perusing it in the Arlington House parlor. During the war, he asked his daughter Mary to send him a copy to carry with him on campaigns. She sent a different edition from the one he had in mind, which proved "the more agreeable for my eyes."[6] That he quoted the Bible in his younger days suggests his early familiarity with it. His citations increased after his confirmation.

The Bible served several functions for him. It was the standard by which he measured sermons. On Christmas Day 1856, Lee listened to the Episcopal rector in Brownsville, Texas, preach, naturally, on Christ's birth. "It was not as simply or touchingly told as in the bible," Lee noted dryly.[7] He considered the Bible the basis for spreading the faith. When some Georgians in 1863 made him a life director of the Bible Society of the Confederate States, he lamented to Mary, "I wish I could feel worthy

118

of these attentions or do anything for the glory of God, or the diffusion of his holy word."[8] Three years later, accepting a Bible for Washington College, Lee assured the donor that he would place it in the chapel "where I trust its simple truths will be daily learned, & thoroughly appreciated, by all the students." When the Rockbridge Bible Society reorganized itself in 1868, Lee became its very active president.[9]

Lee's appreciation derived from both elements in his background. He took his mother's and his wife's evangelical perspective on the Bible as his own. The "enlightened" tradition of his father also recognized the inherent value in the Bible. Henry had encouraged Carter to study it to grasp the life (if not the divinity) of Jesus, and figures such as Thomas Jefferson often stressed its moral teachings—what they too would have considered "its simple truths."[10] The combination also aided Lee in resolving in his own mind a controversial, and not so simple, contradiction.

Lee, Science, and the Bible

For many Americans, and Europeans too, the Bible's "simple truths" included the creation of the earth in six days, as related in Genesis 1. From the late eighteenth century, empirical studies of the earth's structure led to the very different conjectures that its formation occurred vastly earlier than nearly anyone had dreamed possible. Geologists also discovered fossils that inspired early speculations on an evolution of species. A leading English scientist, Sir Charles Lyell, visited the United States with his wife in 1846–1847, bringing his theory of a "successive creation of new species" that appeared, adapted, or vanished as environmental conditions changed. His sharing it in Boston aroused, as one newspaper put it, charges of "rank heterodoxy by those of the old Noah's Ark belief, though it may be none the less true for all that." In Pennsylvania the Lyells viewed newly discovered fossils and human-like footprints and pronounced them of great antiquity, earning fiery denunciations from Catholic and Protestant clergy. By contrast, the Lyells' days in Richmond on December 19–21, 1846, featured social events rather than geological expeditions, including one at which Carter Lee amused the English couple by imitating accents from New England and Mississippi.[11]

Carter's younger brother Robert quietly followed the scientific advances—and controversies—in geology and biology. To the privacy of his diary, most likely after the war, he confined thoughts that placed him, if not in the vanguard of contemporary thinking, at least toward its front, putting him greatly out of step with most of his fellow evangelicals. His training as an engineer had opened his mind to science. So too had the Enlightenment tradition of his father, which looked to nature as the sourcebook for creation.[12]

Lee marveled at the revelations of the geological discoveries. The science "has given us a view of the earths history, while as yet no human beings lived upon it. It appears that this space of time was vast beyond all that [we] could have supposed." Along with the changes to the earth's structure—"beds of rock being formed at the bottoms of seas, other rocks thrown up by subterranean forces"—life itself emerged as

> a succession of animals, beginning with those of simplest form, & advancing to others of higher character, until those nearest the human figure appeared, these animals being of different species from any which now exist. All these facts have been ascertained by investigating the rocks which compose the earths crust, in which are found the remains, more or less preserved of the animals in question, as well as of a similar succession of plants, the order of existence of both animals & plants being established by an order which is ascertained with regard to the age of the rocks.[13]

In good Enlightenment fashion, Lee identified the source of this knowledge as nature itself. "It is interesting to reflect, that this history has been compiled, not from family or state documents, but from facts placed before us by nature," he wrote, "& such is the character of this evidence, that events which took place thousands of years before the existence of the human race, are clearly ascertained." Though his chronology erred by eons, he clearly relied on scientific observation and not tradition (those "family or state documents") as the basis for this learning. As well, religion influenced by the Enlightenment prized scientific discovery as a means of discerning theological truths. God's world revealed God. Matthew Tindal had titled his major work *Christianity as Old as the Creation* with that in mind. Clergy of many denominations, Anglicans included, experimented with flora and fauna when not tending to their human flock. The most famous student of John Stevens Henslow, who combined parish priesthood with Cambridge professorships in geology and botany, was Charles Darwin.[14]

Lee's father, too, had stridently commended scientific learning as a means of discerning divine truths. To his son Carter in 1817, he conveyed lessons he had learned at Princeton from John Witherspoon on the moral as well as scientific importance of Isaac Newton. "Sir Isaac has not only been an eminent benefactor to the human mind in opening to its view the frame of the universe and the action of all the primary parts, but by so doing has contributed more than any other man, to knock down fate and confirm Providence, destroying atheism and upholding theism." He exclaimed, "The man must be blind, who, after understanding Sir Isaac's works, cannot discover the infinite goodness and wisdom of Almighty God," to whom "we men can only be acceptable by the practice of virtue and abhorrence of vice." Scientific learning leads to theological insight, which inspires ethical behavior.[15]

Carter had forwarded this letter to Robert for inclusion in his introduction to a reissued edition of their father's war memoirs, probably at about the same time Robert jotted his back-of-the-diary thoughts. Robert likewise saw no conflict between science and religion. He presumed that general opinion had come to agree. "It was at first thought that these revelations of science militated against the account of the creation given by Moses in the Book of Genesis, but this supposition is now dismissed & a conviction exists that there is nothing in the one history to interfere with the truth of the other." For him, the Bible provided one source of knowledge, science another, and the two could be reconciled. In America and England, some scholars had already suggested as much. The Yale science professor Benjamin Silliman argued in 1836 that the Bible was not a scientific textbook, and the Hebrew word for "day" as used in Genesis should be construed as "eon."[16]

But on both sides of the Atlantic, far more people rejected than accepted such attempts at reconciliation. The furor that surrounded the Lyells' visit only intensified, especially when the fruits of Continental biblical research appeared in what many perceived to be a double-barreled attack on the authority of Scripture, and thus the Christian faith. At the same time that geologists were probing the earth, biblical scholars especially in Germany had proposed theories that, among other things, challenged the traditional notion that Moses had written the Pentateuch, the first five books of the Hebrew Scriptures. When a small group of Oxford scholars shared those radical notions in *Essays and Reviews* in 1860, just one year after Darwin's *Origin of Species*, English evangelicals joined with their ecclesial archenemies, the Anglo-Catholics, to combat what they saw as outright heresy. Their ire intensified after an Anglican bishop in South Africa, John Colenso, published books in 1861 and 1862 that challenged the historical accuracy of the Old Testament. Americans at that moment held other preoccupations; but by the end of the 1860s, the controversies took hold, all the more ferociously because the revival of the previous decades had bred no small degree of anti-intellectualism.[17]

Lee gracefully accepted the scientific advances of the "new geology," though he naively expected a far wider acceptance of them than in fact developed. Whether he even knew of similar advances of the "new theology" is less likely, given his traditional view that Moses was author of the Pentateuch. Ironically, this placed him in a category similar to the Oxford Tractarians whom he otherwise despised, for they, like the authors of *Essays and Reviews*, compartmentalized science and religion in separate, noncompeting categories. In any event, President Lee saw to it that geology was taught at Washington College at a school of "Civil and Mining Engineering" that he created.[18] At the same time, he remained confident of the Bible's "simple truths," taking seriously the Prayer Book's injunction to "read, mark, learn, and inwardly digest the Holy Scriptures."[19]

Of God and Mortals

Lee took a similarly uncomplicated view of the Divinity. Nowhere in his extant writings did he plumb the mysteries of the Trinity. While he cherished the "touching" story of Jesus's birth, he never seemed to consider relationships of Father and Son. Rarely if ever did he refer to "Christ" or "our Lord," nor by any term to the Holy Spirit. This silence does not imply that Lee was a closet Unitarian. Presumably he accepted the standard Episcopal doctrine of the Trinitarian Godhead as articulated in the creeds, but perhaps without feeling much need to plumb their depths on his own. The modern theologian John Macquarrie has asserted that "a majority of Anglicans have been happy to refrain from close dogmatic definition." Such latitude does not preclude a recognizable theology (witness Meade). Rather, Macquarrie suggests, the lack of "detailed doctrinal statements" results from "the somewhat empirical and pragmatic temper of the English people"—the very sort who colonized Virginia.[20]

Lee may not have recited the creed as often as the Prayer Book anticipated, twice daily and at least once each Sunday. However, he certainly appreciated its first article: "I believe in God, the Father Almighty, Maker of heaven and earth." Even in the midst of war, he paused to admire nature. "The country here looks very green & pretty notwithstanding the ravages of war," he wrote Mary in the hard days of June 1863. "What a beautiful world God in his loving kindness to his creatures has given us." He expressed a centuries-old Anglican perception of the link between God's grace and nature itself. Tindal based his deism on concepts of God as Creator. Paley saw in nature itself "evidences" of God. So did Lee.[21]

That God rules nature was for Lee a given. From the Divine come the warmth of summer and the rains that relieve it. Amid a brutal heat wave in Texas, Lee wrote Mary that he had not heard that Virginia was suffering "the common calamity" that would jeopardize their crops—a major concern since Lee had assumed responsibility for the family estates after his father-in-law had died. "Man proposes, but God disposes," he wrote—Mary often quoted the phrase, which came from the medieval German monk Thomas à Kempis—"& we must be content." To Annie, he described a period of "excessive hot weather" giving way to "some refreshing rains, that have ameliorated the atmosphere, refreshed the parched earth & revived the grass. How good is God! Nature is smiling again, & man encouraged. Forgetful I fear of the Giver of all good, & thankless for his benefits."[22]

Yet Lee well knew that the vision of harmony does not always accord with earthly reality. The problem abides with mortals. For one thing, as he had written Annie from Texas, people forget God's blessings and fail in their thankfulness for them. For another, he added in the same letter, "Man cannot bear unmitigated good." He made his point playfully, saying that as cooler weather returned, so did insects. "Our flies & musquitoes are reanimated too. They could not endure the heat meted out to the Shadrachs, Mesheks & Abednigos of the county & had entirely disappeared."[23] Beneath the joking, he alluded to humankind's always falling short. People err and go astray. They sin. They harm what God has created, and detract from what God intends. Soon after arriving in Lexington, he and Custis rode south a dozen miles to view the Natural Bridge, one of the wonders of Virginia. "The scenery along our whole ride was beautiful," he reported, "& there is a grandeur as well as beauty in the scenery at the bridge. One of its great beauties is the entire absence of all work of man. All is the work of God. Differing in this respect from Niagara," where human hands had defaced the Creator's masterwork—ironic words from an engineer.[24] The war itself gave Lee plenty of opportunity to meditate upon sin.

Each soul faces the tension, he believed, between "the infirmity of human nature, & the aspiration for a high & holy spirit to accomplish all that is right." It is not possible, he wrote Markie in 1854, quoting Paul, "for us always to do 'the good we would,' & omit 'the evil we would not.'" But failure should neither discourage our efforts nor dim our hopes. "Toil & trust, must be our aim, as it is our lot."[25]

Lee took both abstracts—the theology of the creator God's goodness, and the anthropology of human depravity—intensely seriously, and applied them comprehensively, even to the minutiae of life. His was, in the word of medieval English spirituality, a "homely" faith: down to earth, practical, habitual. Lee perceived God's blessings in being provided a piano in their postwar home in Lexington. He hoped Mildred would learn to play it to entertain "her self & others, & promptly & gracefully whenever invited. I think we should enjoy all the amenities of life, that are within our reach, & which have been provided for us by our Heavenly Father." Likewise, realities of mortal frailty hit close to home. Though in 1831 he may have referred to himself in jest as "sinful Robert Lee," by middle age he meant it seriously. In 1847, having survived battles in Mexico, he assured Mary, "I endeavored to give thanks to our heavenly Father for all his mercies to me, for his preservation of me through all the dangers I have passed, for I know I fall short of my obligations." In 1854 he tried cheering Markie Williams by reminding his younger cousin of what joy she brought to others. He added, "The world is full of pleasure for you, & a blessed immortality I trust laid up for you in heaven. We are all prone I think to undervalue the gifts of a merciful God, & to make our own unhappiness. I am conscious of my faults in this respect & make many resolutions & attempts to do better, but fail. I will continue my efforts & am resolved to improve. You who know my weakness will I fear have little confidence in my success." When in 1860 his son Rooney and his wife Charlotte named their first child for him, the new grandfather confided to Mary, "I wish I could offer him a more worthy name and a better example. He must elevate the first, and make use of the latter."[26]

Lee was not telling his highly religious wife what she wanted to hear. His pattern of such statements is too consistent throughout his life. But then, both the temper of religion in his day and the tone of his own denomination encouraged the dynamic of humble penitence and humble thanksgiving. Though disputing details, Christians across the spectrum, and especially evangelicals, agreed on the ever-present reality of human sin that affected every individual.[27]

For the devout Episcopalian, each day began and ended with repentance. The "daily offices" of Morning and Evening prayer in the Book of Common Prayer start with a "general confession": "we have erred and strayed from thy ways like lost sheep." So too, before receiving Communion, the congregation acknowledges "our manifold sins and wickedness, which we from time to time most grievously have committed." Later, they might pray, "We are not worthy so much as to gather up the crumbs under thy Table." The Prayer Book, in general, stressed penitence. So, certainly, did Meade.[28]

Yet it also highlighted thanksgiving. Morning and Evening prayer each conclude with a "general thanksgiving" that also begins on a note of humility: "we, thine unworthy servants, do give thee most humble and hearty thanks for all thy goodness and loving-kindness to us, and to all men." As the daily offices concluded with thanksgiving, so did the eucharistic rite, especially regarding the blessing of God in Communion, of God's "favour and goodness toward us," of sharing in "the blessed company of all faithful people," and for being "heirs through hope of thy everlasting kingdom." Dozens of other prayers expressed thanks for specific blessings. Lee shared in them. When Markie informed him that all were well at Arlington, he responded from West Point: "Whenever & as often as such joyful tidings reach us, I breathe a long & fervent thanksgiving to the merciful & Almighty father in Heaven for its continuance & pray for the preservation & happiness of you all."[29]

The Anglican Way of Life—and Death: Jeremy Taylor

By 1853 Lee had assimilated long-standing Anglican understandings of life and death itself. Shaped by the Prayer Book, articulated by preachers, Lee's views echoed those of the seventeenth-century bishop Jeremy Taylor. Lee may never have read any of Taylor's voluminous works, though he might well have found them on the shelves of Ann Lee or

Mary Custis. But Taylor influenced Thomas Wilson, and Meade borrowed from both of them in his *Family Prayers*—even attaching a portion of Taylor's very long litany of confession.[30] If Lee did not know of Taylor directly, he bore an indirect spiritual kinship. His letters show it.

Taylor (1613–1667) led a hard life in a grueling era. Caught up in the English Civil War as a chaplain to King Charles I, and briefly imprisoned, Taylor found refuge in the Welsh home of the Earl and Countess of Carbery. There he composed his two most famous devotional works, *The Rule and Exercise of Holy Living* (1650) and *The Rule and Exercise of Holy Dying* (1651), along with treatises on toleration, sin and repentance, and moral theology. With monarchy restored, he received bishoprics in Ireland but, given his incessant conflicts with Presbyterians and Roman Catholics, these were no great prize.[31]

Personal sorrows matched wider turmoils. Just one of his five sons reached adulthood. He wrote *Holy Dying* after the deaths of Lady Carbery and his own wife in the same year. He intended it, like *Holy Living*, to be a practical, pastoral guide to support the Christian believer in times of sorrow. He depicted a road he had traveled himself.[32]

Yet Taylor retained a sense of hope and joy that first arise from a creation infused with divine grace. On that basis, Taylor discerned a relationship that mortals first experience as "God's goodness and bounty," which then inspire "the first motive of our love," rather like a child learning of love from the abiding love of a parent. Like a parent, too, God remains active, through "profitable and excellent emanations from Him." In so doing, this grace and love provide "the image and little representation of heaven."[33]

Divinely ordered unity, for Taylor, characterizes human life itself, from birth to death, in which, ideally, an ongoing process transforms the person to become ever more Christlike. What matters is not so much the specific moments in life, even ones directly inspired by God or blessed in a Prayer Book rite, but rather how one grows in deed as well as belief. Growth, though, relies on freedom: the freedom to act in response to God's grace (which he deems essential), but also to err and thus find the rewards of being forgiven. Taylor defines faith as "an act of the understanding" that represents "the gate of duty, and the entrance to felicity."[34]

Lee's unfolding religious experience resembles what Taylor described. His confirmation denoted not so much a moment of change as a decades-long process of spiritual evolution. To be sure, Lee seems to contradict this point when, in Texas, he received a letter from Annie indicating her intention to "declare [her]self, before the world on the Lord's side" in the presence of Bishop Johns, and jotted to her, "My dear daughter <u>Annie</u> declaring her determination to become a <u>Christian</u>." Of course, Johns had confirmed her alongside him and Mary Custis when, as Agnes recorded in her diary, all three "promised to be Christians."[35] Yet, while Lee may be reflecting an evangelical understanding of conversion, he also notes his daughter's process of growth and increasing discernment, along the very lines that Taylor described.

The Lees also saw the importance of living out a holy faith, in Taylor's words, conjoining "the gate of duty" with "the entrance to felicity." Mary had wondered what God would ask as a result of Robert's confirmation. Lee challenged cadets to rise, actively, to adversities they faced: they had that moral obligation for, as Taylor put it, "Commanding us to do all that we can . . . does invite our greatest endeavors."[36]

They also followed Taylor's teaching regarding what the Prayer Book called "trouble, sorrow, sickness, or any other adversity." Having faced them himself, Taylor counseled others to recognize their inevitability, but to perceive their limits and the opportunity they provided. After two of his sons died, Taylor wrote to the diarist John Evelyn, "I bless God [that] I have observed and felt so much mercy in this angry dispensation of God, that I am almost transported, I am sure highly pleased with thinking how infinitely sweet His mercies are when His judgments are so gracious."[37] From this, several points emerge: that God sends adversity (though none that one cannot bear); that amid adversity, God's mercy abides; that in the process, the person may draw closer to God. Sickness, for example, "may serve the ends of the spirit, and be a messenger of spiritual life, an instrument of reducing [one] to more religious and sober courses." It is a godly tool for human transformation.[38] War gave Lee ample occasion to make similar observations to Mary as he meditated on why sin and evil remain ongoing verities of life in this world.

Taylor writes, too, that "no evil is immortal." Death, when it comes, takes a person into "that harbour, whither God hath designed everyone, there he may find rest from the troubles of this world." Nothing in Taylor speaks so clearly about how a person lives as how he or she dies. Both of Taylor's major works stress the importance of living with death in mind; the best way to have a "holy death" is to lead a holy life, a life that draws a person ever closer not only *to* God but also *into* God.

An awareness of death's inevitability promotes a recognition of one's sin, and thereby inspires repentance.[39]

As if to prove Taylor's point, both Lees responded to the suffering of grief with acts of religious faith. Her uncle's death led directly to Mary's conversion. Though Robert showed profound grief at his mother's death in 1829, it was his mother-in-law's sudden demise that was followed by his confirmation. Taylor would have said that the timing was not coincidental.

Indeed, an awareness of death should promote living into the fullness of life. One should not seek death, Taylor cautioned; it will come soon enough. Rather, a person should take care of oneself, "that we may better exercise the labours of virtue."[40] Ultimately, all things focus upon one goal, a goal that Thomas Wilson articulated a century after Taylor: "The end of Christianity is to perfect the human nature by participation in the divine."[41]

William Law, whose concept of "holy worldliness" had spoken to Lee's parents' generation, summarized classic Anglicanism in the words of a father to a son. "Fear and worship and love God. . . . All things that you see are so many marks of his power and presence, and he is nearer to you than anything you can see. Take him for your Lord and Father and Friend." He added, "You cannot please God except as you strive to walk in love, wisdom, and goodness. . . . When you love that which God loves, you act with him, you join yourself to him. When you love what he dislikes, then you oppose him and separate yourself from him." Then, later: "Banish, therefore, every thought of self-pride and self-distinction, and accustom yourself to rejoice in all the excellencies and perfections of your fellow creatures. Be as glad to see any of their good actions as your own."[42]

It was simple, straightforward, practical advice. Whether or not Lee ever read Law's book, or Taylor's, he adapted their lessons into his own life in his own day, in his own way, as he sought to worship and serve a providential God.

CHAPTER 13

"Whose Never-Failing Providence Ordereth All Things"

~

Lee's Central Tenet

Spring 1857 found Lee commanding a cavalry unit in a remote camp on the frontier of Texas. One languid Sunday, he virtually summarized his theology in a meditation for Mary. "I feel always as safe in the wilderness as in a crowded city. I know in whose powerful hands I am, & in them rely, & I feel that in all our life we are upheld & sustained by Divine Providence. But that Providence requires us to use the means he has put under our control. He deigns no blessing to idle & inactive wishes, & the only miracle he now exhibits to us, is the power he gives to truth & justice, to work their way in this wicked world."[1] Lee perceived God as all-great, all-good, and all-knowing. Whatever happens—other than as the result of human sin—happens because God wants it that way: God rules his creation, and, because God also knows what is good, what happens is, in the end, best.

But God does not control human beings. They can accept God's designs as expressed in nature or events. If by rejection, passivity, or outright sin they do not accept God's designs, they make the world more wicked. When mortals use the powers God "has put under our control," Lee believed, they further God's will.

Lee shared this concept of providence to a greater or lesser extent with Abraham Lincoln, Stonewall Jackson, and countless Americans of his day, Episcopalians included.[2] It furnished Lee with a pragmatic way of understanding what happens in the world and knowing how to respond personally and appropriately. This conviction, more than any other, guided him in his thinking and in his life. It sustained him in war, and directed him in peace.

The Doctrine of Providence

The concept of providence emerges in the first book of the Bible. Genesis 22 describes Abraham walking up a mountain, intending to offer his only son Isaac as a sacrifice to God. The unsuspecting boy asks his father, "Where is the lamb for the burnt offering?" Abraham responds, with poignant irony, "God will provide himself the Lamb for a burnt offering, my son." After laying Isaac on the altar and unsheathing his knife, Abraham hears a heavenly voice commanding him to stop; Abraham then sees a ram caught in a thicket, which he sacrifices in Isaac's stead. Abraham named that place "the Lord will provide."[3]

From stories such as this grew the concept of God providing for his people, whatever their need. The Hebrew and Greek words for "providence" relate to "foresight" (*pro-videre* in Latin), an attribute of an omniscient God. Going one step higher, the Apocrypha uses the word *pronoia* as a name for God. The term came to denote not just a quality of God but also a description of God's very being, precisely the double sense of the English word "providence" as employed by George Washington and hosts of others, including Lee.[4]

The concept of God exerting his divine will in the world—*providentia*, the Latin counterpart to the Greek *pronoia*—has long occupied theologians. In the fifth century, Augustine argued that God "is the Cause of all causes" but "not of all choices." During the Reformation a millennium later, Ulrich Zwingli stated, "Providence is the enduring and unchangeable rule over and direction of all things in the universe," so that nothing could happen by chance, not in a world in which a supremely good God rules over all. John Calvin agreed: "There is no random power, or agency, or motion in the creatures, who are so governed by the secret counsel of God that nothing happens but what he has knowingly and willingly decreed." The world could not be otherwise, being ruled by an ever-vigilant, omniscient, omnipotent God who brings all things to ultimately good ends.[5]

How much freedom did that leave the individual? Calvin answered, not much. His rigorous idea of predestination propounded that God had eternally foreordained some to salvation and others to damnation, sealing one's everlasting fate even before creation. That doctrine found its way into the Church of England's Thirty-Nine Articles.[6] But it did not quell disputes over whether the beliefs and actions of a lifetime might have some effect on one's eternal fate or over God's role in determining personal action, from what one eats for breakfast to how one helps a friend. Augustine, after all, had referred to a "Cause of causes" but "not of all choices." In other words, how deterministic was God? That is, to what degree did God control one's ultimate destiny or even one's daily life? Do one's choices matter?

In the seventeenth century, the Dutch theologian Jacob Arminius argued that human free will might well have some influence on one's eternal future. Anglican leaders came to favor this less-harsh interpretation, to the disgust of hard-core English Calvinists who found in rampant Arminianism yet another reason to flee to Massachusetts. Virginia's colonials, however, cared much less about who was predestined to heaven or hell and more about why God might be afflicting them with hurricanes. What they did or did not do mattered greatly.

Scientific advances of the Enlightenment seemed to provide objective proof of providence. Newton's *Principia* (1687) discerned principles of force and motion that guided the planets themselves, inspiring a sense of orderliness to a universe overseen by God. British theologians used this perspective in describing the Spirit of God at work in the cosmos and in the individual. In both ways, they claimed, God strove to reclaim them from evil and guide them toward good.[7]

A synthesis regarding God's involvement in history emerged just before the American Revolution. An Anglican, Thomas Hunter, in his *Moral Discourses on Providence* (1774), and a nonconformist, Richard Price, in *Four Dissertations* (1768), made three points: that God controlled everything that happened on earth; that nations rise or fall as a result of God's will; and that their destiny, and the process by which they advance or decay, results from their political or moral conduct in the eyes of God. Their thesis, read widely throughout the British Empire, influenced thinking regarding both church and state. The God of nations paid attention to how both mortals and societies behaved, an idea that influenced the Declaration of Independence and the new republic.[8]

Newly independent Americans across denominational and geographic lines largely accepted this concept of God's beneficent care. They used it to explain the evolution of the new nation and the setbacks it suffered, even if they did so to suit their own conclusions. Federalists who opposed the War of 1812 pointed to the British capture of Detroit as an example of divine judgment on the conflict. Republicans who favored the war countered that God would use the event to bring good out of defeat. In that context Hezekiah Niles of South Carolina, probably the most influential journalist of the early republic, opined that "the ways of Providence" were "inscrutable" and that "apparent ills" often brought "real blessings."[9]

Episcopalians likewise grasped the concept of providence. Their Book of Common Prayer enshrined it, but in ways that the enlightened and the evangelical could each support. On the one hand, providence could refer to God's overarching governance of the universe. This concept of "general providence" fit well with the deistic notion of the one whom the Declaration of Independence termed "nature's God" and "supreme governor," standing above and beyond this world while directing its overall forces of nature and history. The Prayer Book referred to God's providence in great matters, such as providing rain and ordering the ministry of his church. On the other hand, it also upheld notions of "specific providence" such as God's delivering individuals from the dangers of sickness, childbirth, and the sea. Many if not most evangelicals accepted the role of providence in such personal matters. If something happened, then, barring interference from sin or Satan, God was most likely the cause.[10] The evangelical soul could thereby sense the ongoing presence of God, taking comfort in the good things that happen in life, while also recognizing the impact of sin that evokes a reaction from God. This, in turn, led to the explanation of why bad things happen to good people: God, the ultimate disciplinarian, is teaching a person or a nation some needed lesson. The God of persons could also be the God of nations.

Lee and Providence

Lee took a while to reach his wife's evangelical understanding of providence. "You say everything is for the best," a lonely young Lee wrote to Mary, who had left Fort Monroe for Arlington early in their marriage. "I must acknowledge it sometimes passes my poor comprehension to understand it." Mary had understood it at least as early as her conversion, and applied it during the Civil War. She concurred with a friend that she was "sick of hearing of marches & countermarches, & of having my mind continually kept on the stretch." But, she added, "While we can trace the hand of God stretched out for our protection let us not provoke him to withdraw it by undue exultation but go on in an humble trust upon Divine Providence to defend ourselves." By then Robert had long caught up with her, seeing God at work through "general providence" over nations and "specific providence" in something so intimate as his brother and family appearing just in time to help Mary find relief for her arthritis at the spas of Bath County. "See how kind our Heavenly father is to us. Always arranging for us better than we could for ourselves, & preparing blessings that we could not anticipate."[11]

In bestowing blessings, Lee believed, God had some purpose, such as to remind recipients of his nature and to nurture them in his ways. "May he always preserve in us such a clear sense of our obligations," Lee reminded Mary in 1857, "that upon the receipt of every favour we may immediately turn our eyes to him from whom all cometh, & praise him & adore him as we ought."[12] God's blessings always demand a human response.

If good things come to mortals for some godly purpose, bad things do too. But because God is good, whatever seems bad must lead to ultimate good. When Lee's sister Mildred died, Mary pondered the unanswerable question of why the youngest sibling went first and an older, debilitated sister, Anne, lingered. "Truly the ways of Providence are past our finding out. God grant that we may all be found watching & waiting for the coming of our Lord." One's own illnesses, troubles, and griefs helped to prepare a person for the ultimate. Lee advised his daughter Mary Custis that "occasional ailments are necessary to remind us that we are not immortal, & to hasten our preparations for our transit from this transitory world." A person should strive for good health, because it "is allotted us by our allwise Creator, that we may do our duty in life, & accomplish all the good we are capable of."[13] Lee echoes the Wisdom of Solomon (17:2) on the dangers facing those who make themselves through ignorance or lawlessness "exiles from eternal providence"—as during the war he came to fear that the South would do just that. His advice also resembles Jeremy Taylor's sense of adversity as a potential tool for human benefit and of the obligations to respond appropriately.

For Lee, mortals bore responsibility for the sins of the world. Though the Litany asks God's providence in addressing "those evils which the craft and subtilty of the devil or man worketh against us," Lee saw plenty for which to blame people but nothing, apparently, to pin on Satan: the devil was a topic he did not seem to address.[14] Intentional or not, his silence has the effect of focusing on human moral responsibility: no one, for Lee, can escape duty by claiming, "The devil made me do it."

Finally, providence could work its ways, even through the same event, differently for different people but always for ultimate good. Lee told Mary of a New Englander named Marsh who suffered severely from illness. For the sake of health, Marsh and his wife moved to the warmer climes of Texas. Though he improved, his condition kept him from earning a living, so his wife had to work as a milliner and dress-maker. She prospered. But the heat that benefited him forced her to work principally at night. "What astonishes her more than anything else," Lee added, "he does not suffer at all from the heat, that to her is intolerable." Lee appended the inevitable moral to the story: "They illustrate the mercy of divine providence, that in sending us affliction, always mixes with them some solace, & in afflicting him has given him a wife to take care of & nurse him."[15]

Since God's providence intends the best for his people regardless of earthly appearances, how can the individual respond? For Lee, one can only accept whatever God wills. Thomas Wilson and William Meade had often made the point. Wilson saw "whatever shall befal me" as "the Lord's doing, and to come from [God's] Providence, and not by chance." God "alone knowest what is best for us"; therefore, "let me never dispute thy wisdom or thy goodness" but "be ever prepared for what thy Providence shall bring forth." Meade suggested praying for "a will always readily and cheerfully acquiescing in all the dispensations of Providence."[16]

Lee, like Wilson, often described this kind of acquiescence as "res-ignation." While "submission" constitutes part of the definition, the word "resignation" meant far more than merely giving up. In one of his prayers, Wilson commended "an humble and *resigned* heart, that, with perfect control I may ever acquiesce in all the methods of Thy grace; that I may never frustrate the designs of Thy mercy by unreasonable fears, by sloth, or self-love."[17]

Far from implying abject surrender, resignation involves actively participating in God's will. Mary understood that key distinction. Soon after her conversion, she wrote, "I feel a perfect resignation of will to his disposal & a disposition to be as whatever he may appoint me." For his part, Lee increasingly applied this definition of resignation to what he faced in the 1850s. When as superintendent he learned that a cadet's brother had died, he consoled the bereaved father with hopes that the cadet "will bear this painful bereavement with fortitude & resignation" and—always looking ahead—"endeavour to supply to you the place of one, whose loss you must so deeply feel." As husband, Lee sought to comfort his increasingly disabled, arthritic wife with the thought that "should it not please God to grant our prayers, or favour our efforts, we must not repine, but be resigned. Knowing that he will never afflict us but for our good, which though it may be hid to us is clear to him." But she could, and must, do her part: "Relax no efforts though dear Mary that affords a reasonable prospect of relief, & do not be deterred by the trouble or expense of doing that which promises probable restoration."[18] One should not "repine," that is, grumble, complain, or resign, in the sense of giving up. Instead, in "resigning" one yields to another's care or guidance, and subordinates one's own will to that of another[19]—in this case to God—and exerts oneself actively as a result. The Bible did not say that the Lord helps those who help themselves, but the Lees believed that was exactly what God did.

Lee's Resignation: Christian, Fatalist, Stoic?

Ideas of specific providence and of "resignation" to it were nothing new to Lee. As his wedding day drew near, Robert expressed to Carter a form of fatalism more Shakespearean than biblical. "I can tell you I begin to feel right <u>funny</u> when I count my days, especially when I consider the novel situation in which I shall be placed. However Nym says 'Things must be as they may & that's the certain of it' which is a good doctrine too."[20] More lighthearted than philosophical, he hinted at a pattern of accepting whatever happens simply because "things must be as they may."

Early in their marriage, Mary expressed a different viewpoint, more theological than her husband's. She depicted her illness following Daughter's birth as an "alarming visitation of Providence." She understood sickness as Jeremy Taylor did, as a means that God may use (if not also cause) to promote spiritual reflection.[21]

Ten years later, Lee's own language had become more theological. He wrote from his post at Fort Hamilton, New York, to Mary, again in Arlington with the family, regarding an injury to Rooney's hand. He directed how to care for it, then closed, "God grant that all may have a happy issue & that all may work together for the good of us all." Here he combined paraphrases of an Episcopal prayer for "a happy issue out of all their afflictions" and Romans ("And we know that all things work together for good to them that love God").[22]

By the 1850s, Lee had grown more theologically sophisticated. He had also dealt directly with war, the death of his mother-in-law, the vigor-sapping illness of his wife, and major troubles of others. Lee advised being "resigned" to whatever they faced in life, notably its woes.

Such language has led to depictions of the Lees, Robert in particular, as "fatalist" or "stoic," or even as a "Stoic" in the tradition of classical philosophy. Given his religion, notably his concept of providence, none of these apply.

Many have described Lee's attitude as "fatalist."[23] His quotation from Nym encapsulates the thought: what will be will be. Events and natural law, if not God, create inevitable scenarios that determine human actions. Free will does not really exist.[24] But Lee wrote this as a young bachelor eagerly anticipating his wedding. His more mature providential theology presumed human choice. God is not a divine manipulator but rather the source of inspiration, guidance, care, and, in the end, accountability. Whereas thoroughgoing fatalism ultimately precludes human responsibility, Lee's sense of providence underscores it.[25]

Some, like his wartime aide Walter Taylor, applied the term "stoic" to Lee's character.[26] As an adjective describing stiff-upper-lip fortitude, it might well apply. Lee suffered much and advised others to bear their sufferings with good grace.

Other historians have gone further, classifying Lee as a Stoic—a follower of that ancient philosophy itself. Michael Fellman links the words "Stoic" and "Christian resignation" with great, and undue, frequency. He repeatedly describes Lee "as a Stoic and Christian of the highest social order." Lee's youth provides some reason for such a conclusion. Henry Lee was a deistic Christian who was schooled to appreciate classical writers and who commended to his family the Roman writer Seneca. Seneca and other Stoics presumed an orderly, interconnected universe imbued with divine reason and ordered by divine fate. They upheld virtue as the source of happiness, much as Tindal and other Enlightenment authors on the left wing of Anglicanism did. Moreover, Robert E. Lee on occasion quoted Marcus Aurelius, the Stoic Roman emperor. Douglas Freeman asserts that during the war, Lee jotted "reflections that somewhat echo Marcus Aurelius, who seems to have been one of Lee's favorite authors." This Stoicism, it is argued, led Lee toward *apatheia* and *euthymia*, the spiritual peace and well-being that results from virtue and leads a person to resemble the deity and is the ultimate goal of human life.[27]

Freeman is right to be tentative in his "seems to have been": linking Lee with Stoicism rests on shaky evidence. Though Lee, as a schoolboy, may have known Marcus Aurelius well enough to quote him, as he reportedly did to the sculptor Edward Valentine, historians cite few corroborating examples. Fellman rests his case on the presence of a "well-worn *Meditations*" of Marcus Aurelius on Lee's desk when he died, but that assertion rests on slim and questionable evidence.[28]

Of course, likenesses exist between Christianity and other philosophies and religions. For example, the "golden rule," often attributed to Jesus, has parallels in many religious, and secular, traditions. Moral teachings are rarely unique. Lee need not have been a Stoic to quote aphorisms of Marcus Aurelius, though he may have appreciated them the more out of the classical influence of his father and of his own studies, and also the values he held as a Christian.

More significantly, the philosophy of Stoicism and the theology of Christianity ultimately clash. Though generalizations are dangerous, Stoics often identified events with fate, which they equated with the divine will. Many equated virtue with adapting oneself to the inevitable. A person could not positively influence the outcome and therefore had to deal with it accordingly. Seneca, whom Henry Lee commended to his sons, admired Cato the Younger, who, facing certain capture by his foe Julius Caesar, committed suicide.[29] By that standard, Lee should have fallen on his sword at Appomattox.

Blending Stoicism with Christianity resembles shaking vinegar and oil in a cruet: eventually they separate. While each uses the terminology of religion, and each concerns both the individual and God, Stoic philosophy focuses more on the self, and Christian theology ultimately on God. Stoics consider virtue to be the highest good, the *summum bonum*. Christians reserve that status for God. A scholar of Stoicism, John Sellars, concludes that there is "a basic incompatibility between Stoic philosophy and Christian doctrine." Randolph McKim, a Confederate veteran who became a wartime chaplain and, during Lee's final years, was rector of Christ Church, Alexandria, rejected this description of Lee altogether. "He was not a second Marcus Aurelius—the noble stoic, the sad-hearted royal philosopher. No, he was a Christian—a Christian optimist" who, while perhaps pessimistic at the end of the war, "was always hopeful." McKim went further: Lee exemplified the difference between a Stoic and a Christian.[30]

Lee insisted that Christians had the responsibility to pursue good, no matter what may befall them. As a general, he looked to God's providential power to win battles, of which God already knew the outcome, while urging his men to fight their hardest with the promise that their efforts would make a difference; he did so presumably unaware that Augustine had made the same point: "that God knows all things before they happen, and that by our own will we do whatever we know and feel could not be done by us unless we willed it."[31]

Probably without realizing it, Lee had assimilated a perspective consistent with these viable strains of Christian theology. He was neither fatalist nor Stoic. Even as he faced reverses and defeats with resolve, he considered them neither inevitable nor hopeless; human beings could influence the course of events, and, even if those events ended badly from a human point of view, hope abided. Good could come from sorrow, even from abject defeat, under an all-knowing, all-merciful, all-powerful God.[32]

This concept of providence gave Lee an eminently pragmatic way of understanding both God and humanity. He could explain why things happen while upholding personal responsibility and personal acceptance of God's apparent will. It developed just in time for him to put it to practical use, for personal and national events required all the faith he could muster.

CHAPTER 14

"Under the Protection of Thy Good Providence"

⌒

The Lee Family

During the 1850s, Lee found ample reason to employ his religious and ethical convictions. Leading a cavalry regiment in Texas caused him to see the world from new angles, and to act in new capacities. His perspectives widened as he discovered unfamiliar cultures and encountered old ones anew. While recovering from sorrows in his own family, he confronted the troubles of others. To these experiences he applied his sense of providence, which confirmed his convictions all the more in the process.

As Lee's tenure at West Point drew to a close, Congress was expanding the army to protect settlers on the frontier. It created four new regiments, two each of infantry and of cavalry. Lee received orders to become second-in-command of one of the cavalry troops. Leaving the academy in April 1855, he met up with his new unit in Missouri. Since his superior, Albert Sidney Johnston, had been ordered to Washington, Lee took charge of organizing the unit. Still, over the next nine months he returned several times to Arlington, where Mary remained with all the children except for Custis, by then a soldier stationed in Florida, and Rooney, a student at Harvard. During his stays there, Lee shouldered the tasks of renovating the house and reorganizing the Custis estates that dotted Virginia, all of which suffered from his grieving father-in-law's always lackadaisical oversight.[1]

Lee's new army position finally earned him a permanent promotion. Captain Lee officially became a lieutenant colonel, while still bearing the honorific of brevet colonel. His duties took him through the Texas frontier from Fort Brown outside Brownsville on the Gulf Coast across the Rio Grande from Mexico, to the isolated Camp Cooper near the Brazos, some three hundred miles to the north. In letters home and in a diary, he documented his perceptions of Native Americans and Mexicans; Catholics and other Christians; grief and trouble; Episcopal churches and clergy; the way he spent his Sundays and, as always, how to guide his family.

Encountering New Cultures

Lee's new duties, far removed from where he had spent most of his life, exposed him more directly than ever before to different races, cultures, and their religious practices. In Missouri he toured a reservation of some three thousand Native Americans. A Jesuit mission led by three priests and five nuns operated two schools and at least one church. "There was a respectable congregation of men, women & children, who were orderly & attentive. The discourse was in the Potawatomie language. The dresses & appearance of the party were very[?] various & as multifarious in Indian as in mixture of blood. The tribe were out on their Fall hunt. The children that had been at the school one & two years, were well clad & clean. The new scholars were in their Indian costume & were listless & dirty."[2]

Lee found that his impression of these "new scholars," who had not yet assimilated the civilizing benefit of the mission, also characterized the Indians he next encountered in Texas. His job there ensured a conflicted relationship with the American Indians: he was to guard against any attacks on white settlers, while preserving Indian rights granted by treaties more often breached than observed by whites, and also protecting the Comanches who lived on reservations from those who did not. Government policy, moreover, strove to "humanize" or civilize the Indians according to Anglo standards, converting them from hunters to farmers. Unfortunately the Texas droughts that killed Lee's poor efforts at gardening also parched the farms of Indians, who then blamed the whites for angering the Great Spirit.[3] Glamorous duty it was not.

Lee shared the racial attitudes implicit in the federal policy. Visits to reservations only bolstered his bias that Indians were inferior to whites. Soon after taking command at Camp Cooper, he and the Comanche chief, Catumseh, called on each other. At one point Catumseh bragged that he had six wives. To his one wife, Mary, Lee recounted, "Their paint and ornaments make them more hideous than nature made them &

the whole race is extremely uninteresting"; although God-given nature made Indians inferior, nurture did them no favors.[4]

Native American nurture, he concluded, was perverting another group. Catumseh's tribe had captured twenty-five men and boys, and fifteen women and girls—all Mexicans. These prisoners had picked up their captors' ways, becoming, Lee claimed, "worse than the Indians in rascalities."[5] It was not clear which ethnicity Lee disdained more, Mexican or Indian.

In late 1856, Lee crossed into Mexico for the first time since the war. Visiting Matamoros and its unfinished cathedral evoked evangelical along with racial prejudices. He wrote Mary, "However little attractive in its exterior is still less so in its interior. I shuddered at the exhibition of ignorance & superstition in the worship of the true & living God, as indicated by the senseless images, & offerings, around the walls, & the uninterested, careless & wandering looks of the single worshipper on the floor of the building—& felt humbled that his creatures, upon whom so many blessings have been showered, should have so poor an appreciation of his majesty & goodness."[6]

He found the Mass, said in Latin, inscrutable. The chaplain at a nearby fort, Father Shane, visited Camp Cooper in 1857. "He performed the Catholic service this morn[g] for the benefit of the Catholics of the Command. I attended. The service was incomprehensible to me, but I hope it availed much those who did understand it." Lee did see some value in the sermon, on "What will it profit a man, if he gain the whole world & lose his own soul" (Matt. 16:26). The priest preached "in a very feeling & practical manner, which all could understand & profit by, & I hope his words sank into the hearts of some."[7] As always for Lee, a sermon's value depended on how much it helped its listeners become better Christians.

By 1860, Lee's eyes had become thoroughly jaundiced concerning Roman Catholic ways. He wrote of a baptism he attended: "I saw the poor little child pawed over, sprinkled, [illeg.] & salted, very much to his discomfort, surrounded by candles, in a hot close church & a service mumbled over him, not one word of which I could understand, or anybody else. I hope it will be of benefit to him, & that all the saints invoked may be present to him, & all the devils anathematised, may avoid him."[8]

A celebration in San Antonio encapsulated all that Lee disliked of Catholic Mexicans:

Yesterday was St. Johns day, & the principal or at least visible means of adoration & worship, seemed to consist in riding horses, so every Mexican & indeed others that could procure a qua[d]raped, were cavorting through the streets. With the thermometer over 100° in the shade, a scorching sun & the dust several inches thick, you can imagine the state of the atmosphere, the sufferings of the horses, if not the pleasure of the riders, as everything of the horse tribe had to be brought in requisition to accomodate the bipeds, unbroken colts & worn out hacks were saddled for the occasion. The plunging & kicking of the former procured excitement, & the distress of the latter, merriment, to the crowd. I did not know before that St. John placed so high a value upon equitation.[9]

More Familiar Ecclesial Territory

Lee found Presbyterian ways far more comfortable. He occasionally attended a struggling church in Brownsville on Sunday nights. When it held a "fair" to pay its bills, Lee supported it, choosing "to bestow my mite outright rather than exchange it in the way of trade" at the church bazaar, where he would know no one.[10]

In Episcopal churches he found himself most at home. Passing through Indianapolis late in 1855, he heard "a good sermon from the Revd Mr. Talbot" on the text "Who is my neighbour," which the preacher related to "the benefit & importance of domestic missions to which I added my mite to the contributions of the congr^n." Two years later he returned for services in morning and evening and "heard two good sermons from Mr. Spencer."[11]

Missouri was the exception. No services were offered at the Jefferson Barracks, where Lee prepared for his Texas assignment, because the chaplain, though "highly spoken of," was absent. He avoided the local church, "grotesque in its form, & ancient in its appearance." Instead, he assured Mary, he was "content to read my bible & prayers alone, & draw much comfort from their holy precepts & merciful promises; though feel unable to follow the one, & utterly unworthy of the other. I must still pray to that glorious God, without whom there is no help, & with whom there is no danger. That he may guard & protect you all, & more than supply to you my absence, is my daily & constant prayer."[12]

Reaching Galveston, Texas, in March 1856, Lee once again attended an Episcopal service, held in an old wooden structure. He praised the sermon by an "English" cleric on the text "All nations shall be shaken; & the desire of all nations shall come." The congregation was "not very large"; he received Holy Communion as one of just a "number of communicants." Catholics in town had built a large brick structure and Episcopalians were striving to do the same.[13]

Not until November could he again grace Episcopal doors. He left with mixed feelings. "Mr. Passmore has a small but good brick church in Brownsville & if all his congregation were present last Sunday it was certainly small too," he wrote Mary. "It was however very attentive, & among them were several soldiers & their wives. It was pleasant to join in the prayers again, & Mr. P— gave us a plain but good sermon." One week later he reported, "Mr. Passmore is not a captivating preacher, but I hope an efficient one." Lee returned that afternoon for Evening Prayer. "Whether the smallness of the congregation caused him to forget the sermon, or whether he usually preaches but once a day, I do not know. He is not a felicitous reader. But who can feel otherwise than diminutive in uttering the sublime exordium, 'The Lord is in his holy temple; let all the earth keep silence before him'!"[14]

By the third Sunday, the pastor had grown on Lee. "Mr. Passmore gave us a very fine sermon last Sunday from the book of Isaiah, 'The bruised reed shall he not break, & the smoking flax shall he not quench, etc.'" The sanctuary was appointed with "a small table" for an Advent Communion two weeks later. "I was sorry to see, among them only three officers" on a cold and rainy day. The parson "seems to be a very amiable and good man, kind & sociable. . . . I hope [he and his wife] are happy."[15]

Passmore's churchmanship troubled Lee, however. The cleric "has brought to this wilderness the colouring of the high church which had much better be left behind. There is already enough of Romanism in the country, inherited from Mexico, & there is more want of 'the worship of Spirit & of truth' in all the beauty of its sincerity & holiness." The "Puseyism" he had previously derided still rankled him. "When I see its perversion by man from the purity practiced by our Saviour," he said, referring to liturgical style, "there is an inward rebellion over which I have no control, & I think it better for me to remain in the wilderness from whence I came & adore the Great God with all the power and all the strength he has given me free from the detracting & distracting forms around me." It was a problem Lee the Virginia evangelical could not escape. He wrote again to Mary that Passmore "has a strong proclivity to High variance, of which I am not fond. Raising more serious objection, I think it unsuited to our people & institutions, & not calculated to extend episcopacy among the masses & therefore impolitic."[16]

Nevertheless, from afar, Lee kept up with news of his church. Passmore shared copies of the *New York Churchman*, which leaned toward "high churchism," and Mary regularly sent him issues of his beloved "low church" *Southern Churchman*. Far from home on Christmas 1856, after bestowing presents on some children near Fort Brown, he went to church where, for once, the congregation's numbers were "very respectable." Passmore delivered the sermon on the nativity that was "not as simply or touchingly told as in the Bible."[17]

Easter Day 1857 found Lee on the remote western frontier, thinking of his family at Christ Church. His services were "performed alone in my tent. I hope they have been performed with an humble grateful & penitent heart, & will be acceptable to our heavenly father. May he continue his mercies to us both, all our children, relations & friends; & in his own good time again unite us in his worship, if not on earth, forever in heaven!"[18] Often in Texas, Lee's worship had to occur in his tent or on his saddle. He may have been "grateful & thankful to the Great God, for his mercies & blessings," as he wrote in his diary, but the absence of water and grass to refresh his men and horses precluded the rest that he tried to provide for them on Sundays.[19]

Returning at the end of one foray, he found Camp Cooper as parched as the frontier. Its dire conditions bred enemies that Lee had not been sent to fight: disease and death. With no clergy anywhere nearby, he had to combine his role as commanding officer with an unfamiliar role as pastor.

Lee the Parson

The frontier proved deadly. "I cannot describe the pain I feel in now addressing you," Lee had to write a Pennsylvania congressman one hot day in August 1856. "Your son . . . is no more." The young man, a lieutenant in his regiment recently graduated from West Point, had died some days earlier from an intestinal inflammation. "He breathed his last & so calmly did he die, that we could scarce mark the moment. Not a sigh or movement denoted his departure from earth. He was conscious of his approaching end." His comrades buried the officer with military honors and Masonic rites. Lee sought to assure the grieving father of providential good prevailing over sorrow. "Let this then be your comfort, that your loss is his gain."[20]

Nine months later, Lee recalled the deathbed scene in writing the father again. "In addition to his remark that he was 'going to a better world,' a convincing proof that the eye of faith though dimmed to mortal things by the veil of approaching dissolution is clear sighted to the heavenly bliss opening to its pious vision, I have heard that he said, 'tell my mother I will meet her in heaven.' What more blissful message could he send! It is enough to change all grief to joy, all pain to happiness."[21]

For a young officer to die was difficult to take. For young children to die was even worse. Lee had to bury them, too. Some soldiers had brought their wives and children with them to Camp Cooper, exposing them to the extremes of Texas weather. In early June, temperatures climbed to 105 degrees. Disease soon claimed the life of a young son of a trooper. "He was the only child, & his parents were much affected by his loss," Lee told Mary. "They expressed a great desire to have him buried with Christian rites, & asked me to perform the ceremony." This was the moment when he appreciated so much "the beautiful funeral service of our Church." He added, "The parents were much affected."[22] So was Lee.

Not two weeks later, death struck again, this time taking the year-old son of a sergeant, a boy Lee had admired just before the child became ill. "His father came to me with the tears flowing down his cheeks & asked me to read the funeral service over his body, which I did at the grave for the second time in my life." After two funerals in ten days, Lee admitted, "I hope I shall not be called on again."

He found in his providential theology a context in which to deal with the double sorrows. "Though I must believe, that it is far better for the child to be called by its Heavenly Creator into his presence, in its purity & innocence, unpolluted by sin & uncontaminated by the vices of the world, still it so wrings a parents heart with anguish, that it is painful to see." He was striving to reason his way into reconciling his conviction in a providential God with the realities of earthly suffering. "I know [the boy's death] was done in mercy to both. In mercy to the child & mercy to the parents. The former has been saved from all sin & misery here, & the latter have been given a touching appeal, & powerful inducement to prepare for hereafter. May it prove effective, & may they require no more severe admonition."

It was a harsh implication he drew, showing the difficulty of conjoining the rational principles of the Enlightenment with the idea of providence to find reason in what seemed so unreasonable. If God is omnipotent and all-gracious, then God must have some purpose in mind to warrant the boy's death. From Lee's perspective as a father and a Christian, he concluded, much as Jeremy Taylor had, that the intention must be to educate those who remain alive. As he had seen Rooney's accident as a warning to children of the sorrow they bring on parents, he perceived God was now admonishing the parents to prepare themselves for their own destinies.

Death, providence, and eternity were ever on Lee's mind. In the same letter to Mary, he cited the death of Lieutenant Colonel Harry Bainbridge on the steamer *Louisiana* off Galveston. Bainbridge had left his unit to meet his wife and escort her back with him to Texas. "He was much elated at the prospect, & went off in fine spirits," Lee recalled. "How little we know when our wishes are gratified whether it is really for our good. In this instance I hope it was for his, & that an ever merciful Providence chose the time to perish his earthly cares, when his heart was most powerfully drawn to him & his pardon most truly sealed":[23] holy living, holy dying.

Building Up the Church

In Texas, on the fringes of civilization if not of Christ's kingdom, Lee prayed. He worked in ways he had never imagined. He also gave consistently and sometimes quite generously. By then he had become prosperous even apart from his wife's inheritance; his annual military salary barely exceeded $2,600, but by the time Lee deployed to Texas, he had accumulated investments totaling $64,500, no small sum in those days.[24]

He shared his wealth freely for religious purposes. Having contributed his "mite" to the Presbyterians in Brownsville, he gave toward repairs at the local Episcopal church too.[25] When Christ Church, Alexandria, required attention, Lee had Annie send a check for $25, adding, "I wish I could send more." They had long supported their home parish. Their rector, Charles B. Dana, thanked Lee in 1859 for an Eastertide contribution of $50, which he allotted to diocesan missions, the Sunday school, and the Education Society. The year before, the Lees purchased a pew—still a means of meeting Christ Church's budget.[26]

In 1860, during his short time in San Antonio, Lee developed a particular affection for St. Mark's Church. "The congregation is small at best, & poor at that, nor is this a country where religion ranks pre-eminent in the hearts of men." It met in a rented room "which is hot, small & noisy," and was recovering from a discouraging attempt to form a parish. Still, under its new rector, Lucius D. Jones, spirit was high. Jones boasted that his people "sang in hearty fashion the chants and tunes" of the Episcopal Church. They held aspirations to match, having hired Richard Upjohn, the nation's leading church architect, to design a new edifice. Lee especially admired the church's success in attracting his fellow soldiers. "I have been glad to see that the officers stationed here have been the most liberal subscribers to the church, though they of course have not a permanent interest in its erection, & those now here may never see its completion." Often, when Jones was away raising money for the building, the bishop's assistant, J. Hamilton Quinby, officiated "to the great edification of the young ladies of the congregation, and indeed to the admiration of some of the serious. He seems to be a promising young man, & with more study, practice & learning, will become a good preacher." But Lee preferred "Mr. Jones, who appears to have an earnest piety, which many disadvantages cannot repress." Of all churches he attended outside Virginia, Lee seemed most enthusiastic about St. Mark's. He wrote Annie, "The church here is in great need & I have had to help it all I could," which amounted that day to $150. He asked Mary, "If any of your rich friends could spare him $1000 or $2000 to aid in the completion of the church, it would be a good deed." St. Mark's Church, San Antonio, honors Robert E. Lee as one of its early members and benefactors.[27]

The Absent *Paterfamilias*

Meanwhile, in Arlington, Lee's family maintained their pattern of daily prayers and Sunday churchgoing. Along with Christ Church, they had their own house of God in which to worship. As early as 1805, the Custises had built a schoolhouse, about a mile west of the mansion, for educating the enslaved children. Rarely had it been used for that purpose. Instead, what they called "the station" morphed into a chapel. After his wife died, Major Custis often went to the Sunday evening services, frequently joined by his niece Markie Williams, others in the family, members of the public, and "chiefly" the "servants." Seminarians from Virginia Theological Seminary led Evening Prayer and preached, though often with mixed results. Henry Potter, later bishop of New York, recalled putting Mr. Custis to sleep. Markie once informed Potter that he "put the hay too high for the sheep of his flock"—that is, he spoke over the heads of the slaves (many of whom ultimately fled the church of their master for the more comforting arms of the Baptists). Robert went too. Potter remembered him as "singularly alert and reverent in his bearing" at the estate's "tabernacle in the woods."[28]

But Lee's time at home had become so rare that, by the mid-1850s, he had soured on the military profession. When Rooney pondered leaving Harvard to follow father and brother into the army, Lee advised, "I think you can be as useful & consequently as happy in other walks of life. . . . My experience has taught me to recommend no young man to enter the service." He recalled young officers whom he had seen graduate from West Point longing to "earn their bread in some other way." He cautioned Charlotte Wickham, Rooney's new fiancée, "A soldiers life is one of toil & self denial. A soldiers wife must practice hope & patience." His own wife patiently received his frequent complaints. "We must try to be resigned to God's will," Lee added to one letter. "Let us never murmur or be impatient under the troubles & trials of life, but yield a cheerful obedience to all his appointments."[29]

Lee also realized that serving in Texas kept him from meeting increasing responsibilities at home. Arlington House needed repairs. Mr. Custis's estates demanded more attention than the old man could ever provide, or ever had. Lee felt the obligation, "for the sake of her who is gone, & of those who remain, that I wish the place dear to their affections, to be properly preserved, & not either to suffer from, or exhibit neglect." Mary and he had to "fulfill our duties, & the work set before us, before we go hence," regardless of "who is benefitted by our labors" as stewards of what God had granted them. So, he concluded, "May God grant it be well done, & that we may earn the title of faithful servants."[30]

Even more, Lee was missing out on his children's growth. From faraway Texas, he tried to stay in touch by unreliable mails, frustrated that he could not more directly guide their spiritual progress. On that score, the Lees could not have chosen a more evangelical boarding school for Annie and Agnes to attend than the Virginia Female Academy in Staunton. Religious life was a central aspect of students' experience. They worshiped regularly at Trinity Church, three blocks away, and studied such works as *Evidences of Christianity* by the West Point chaplain-turned-bishop Charles McIlvaine, which relied on the same book by William Paley that Meade had studied years before. The school's revivalist spirit drew the enthusiastic attention of Bishop Johns as early as 1850.[31]

The Lee girls embraced that spirit. When Annie decided to kneel once again before Bishop Johns in 1857, Agnes yearned to do the same. Her spiritual longing led to a spiritual crisis one Sunday evening in 1857. She had not gone to Trinity for the evening service but remained in her room. She heard weeping from down the hall, which affected her deeply. "My sins seemed arrayed before me in all their hideousness. . . . I remember a sweet friend holding fast my arm saying 'Agnes what is the matter, you are *so* strange, tell me?' O I *longed* to tell her all, but she was not a christian. . . . At last the Saviour's, *my* Saviour's words seemed sent to suit my feelings, 'He that cometh to me I will in *nowise* cast out.' I clung to that." Agnes resolved, like her sister, to make a public profession before Johns. She informed her mother, "dearest Mamma, I will not hesitate to be confirmed. My desire grows stronger and stronger. I am sure I will feel strengthened and blessed. Much would I love to receive the holy communion. . . . May I come to Him with my whole heart!"[32]

Young Rob followed a similar path in his own way. Shortly before entering the University of Virginia in 1860, he underwent a full-blown evangelical conversion marked by "a change in his feelings, & the devotion of his heart to God." His father, then in San Antonio commanding federal forces in Texas, explained to Mary that Rob had informed him that he shared in the prayer meetings the boys in his boarding school had organized for themselves, "& I saw that he had become interested in the subject of religion, & felt the influence upon himself & schoolmates. I hope its noble truths & blessed prospect, may diffuse themselves through his life & actions, purify his heart, & fill his soul with love & gratitude, that he may worship & serve his Heavenly father in sincerity & spirit." Rob shared his experience with his youngest sister. "And how are you getting along with your God?" he wrote Mildred from Mr. Jefferson's university. "O my sister neglect not him. I have suffered much from neglecting him but I am glad to tell you that now my breast is comforted much by him & I am trying to live closer to him."[33]

Mary joined Rob in concern for "Precious Life's" spiritual condition. She assured Mildred, "Do not be discouraged because you see so much in yourself that is vile & sinful[;] that is the sure work of the Holy Spirit. Before His influence was shed into your breast, you could see none of your faults." Mary likened what Mildred faced to coming into a parlor where dust and litter had accumulated, unnoticed, until a ray of light shined on "every particle of dust." She counseled, "Commit all your hopes & fears, yourself to Him without reserve in the words of the Hymn, 'Hear [*sic*] Lord I give myself away / Tis all that I can do.' He will keep you safe." Two weeks later, she advised, "Study your Bible with constant daily prayer & you [will] grow in grace & be able to overcome all your evil & sinful tempers or at any rate to keep them in subjection." Evidently Mildred followed her mother's wishes, for in 1861, with war looming, Mary exhorted, "Strive to attain all the comforts belonging to your Christian profession."[34]

Lee's concerns for Mildred were more practical. Anticipating her schooling in the fall, he instructed Mary, "I wish her to be taught to danse, if she desires it, to learn how to control her movements, & give her a good carriage, of which she is in need." He hastily added, as if under Meade's disapproving spirit, "Not that I ever wish her to danse in after life, though I never have been able to see any sin in the exercise." Still, he held a greater purpose in mind. "Above all things impress upon her the necessity of learning to be useful, that she may have the enjoyment of doing good & of being appreciated by the wise & virtuous in the world, & of making some amends to her Creator."[35] He might have been speaking for himself.

Meanwhile, the forces he increasingly feared grew more ominous as he watched from Texas, threatening to draw him into a conflict of which he did not approve.

Ann Hill Carter Lee. *Courtesy of Washington and Lee University.*

Mary Anna Randolph Custis, portrait by Auguste Hervieu painted in September 1830, shortly after her engagement to Lieutenant R. E. Lee. *Courtesy of Arlington House, The Robert E. Lee Memorial.*

Robert E. Lee as a lieutenant in the Corps of Engineers, 1838, by William Edward West.
Courtesy of Washington and Lee University.

Henry Lee III, "Light Horse Harry." William Edward West, c. 1838, after Gilbert Stuart. *Courtesy of Washington and Lee University.*

William Meade soon after his consecration as bishop. *Courtesy of the Virginia Theological Seminary Archives, Bishop Payne Library.*

George Washington Parke Custis, by Junius Brutus Stearns, 1848. *Courtesy of Washington and Lee University.*

Christ Church, Alexandria, in the 1850s. *Courtesy of the Virginia Theological Seminary Archives, Bishop Payne Library.*

Lee as Superintendent of West Point, c. 1853. Photograph of the original at West Point.
Courtesy of Washington and Lee University.

Portrait of Lee taken by Julian Vannerson in Richmond in early 1864, one of several made for the sculptor Edward V. Valentine and sent through the Union blockade to him in Berlin. He used these to model a statuette of Lee. *Courtesy of Washington and Lee University.*

Lee while president of Washington College. Photograph by Michael Miley in late 1869.
Courtesy of Washington and Lee University.

Washington College, c. 1867, midway through Lee's tenure and prior to the construction of Lee Chapel. Photograph by John C. Boude and Michael Miley. *Courtesy of Washington and Lee University.*

The President's House, Washington College, during the last year of Lee's life. Photograph by John C. Boude and Michael Miley. *Courtesy of Washington and Lee University.*

Sketch of Lee's Funeral, William Nelson Pendleton presiding. Leslie's Magazine, November 18, 1870. *Courtesy of Washington and Lee University.*

Lee Chapel, c. 1880s. Photograph by Michael Miley. *Courtesy of Washington and Lee University.*

CHAPTER 15

"Help Thy Servants, Whom Thou Hast Redeemed"

~

Lee and Slavery

Deep in the heart of Texas, Colonel Lee grew increasingly concerned for the country, and for his wife's health. Conditions of each deteriorated as the 1850s wore on. As a soldier and a citizen, he had always stayed abreast of national issues. Now he, like so many Americans, was inexorably drawn into an ever-intensifying and increasingly inescapable storm over whether one set of human beings could own another set of human beings as property.

No Southerner could escape the issue of slavery, least of all the elite, who were the primary slaveholders. Even when most financially strapped, Lee's parents owned at least a few enslaved persons. Robert inherited several, one of whom he had taken with him to Georgia for the old man's health. He owned several more as late as 1846.[1] The Custises, of course, held hundreds on their estates. Their way of life relied on the institution.

Yet the ideals, political and religious alike, of the Lee and Custis families posed a fundamental disparity with that way of life. Nothing violated the Anglican vision of harmony nor the colonial Southern aristocratic image of benevolent patriarchy as much as slavery. Nor was the utter incongruity lost on Robert's father between the spirit of American independence and the denial of the rights of "life, liberty, and the pursuit of happiness" to ever-increasing numbers of black people. Henry Lee called slavery a "dreadful evil" that the Constitution should have resolved through gradual abolition. Likewise, evangelicals such as Mrs. Custis's kinswoman, Ann Meade Page, bore a profound sense of guilt over holding some of God's children in human bondage.[2]

Lee lived his life, then, immersed in the culture of institutional slavery, but his microculture was that of Southern moderates. Ann Page's brother, Bishop Meade, exemplified that microculture. A slave owner himself, he nevertheless advocated the humanity of the enslaved as children of God, and consistently commended their spiritual needs to his diocese. His pastoral letter of 1834 "on the duty of affording religious instruction to those in bondage" was reissued in the 1850s to accompany a book of sermons for "servants." In that spirit, for decades Mrs. Custis gave religious training to at least a few enslaved children. Mary continued the practice, as did cousin Markie when residing at Arlington in the 1850s. They taught other subjects along with religion, despite Virginia law that, after Nat Turner's rebellion, specifically forbade instructing slaves. No lawman dared arrest the women of Arlington.[3] When Mary was on her own, a newlywed at Fort Monroe, she took her godfather's words to heart by helping the chaplain at Fortress Monroe provide services for blacks. "I hope that we may be able to do something in time for the spiritual benefit of those poor neglected slaves," she wrote her mother.[4]

Teaching slaves, though, did nothing to end slavery. On that score, the women of Arlington House joined Meade's effort to resolve the problem by emancipating bondsmen and sending them as colonists to Liberia. Meade had already recruited uncles of Robert and Mary, along with Mary's father, to the Colonization Society. Mother and daughter ardently joined the project. Meade kept them apprised of the society's progress. When Congress failed to provide it with funding, he reassured them, "I suppose we are going on as rapidly as is good for us or Providence would speed our way faster." One "must not be disheartened at the backwardness of Congress, tho I think . . . that we should urge that coldhearted, sluggish body to do more than it has yet done." He placed colonization "as the first in importance to our unhappy and I must say grisly[?] land." It would be morally wrong, a guarantee of "misery & vice upon our children," were they not to adopt "the most effectual" means "of removing an evil"—slavery—"which grows with our growth & strengthens with our strength, and will soon outgrow us & heave us to the ground."[5]

Despite support for the idea even from such luminaries as Abraham Lincoln, Meade soon grew disillusioned when faced with its realities. Few of his own slaves whom he liberated fulfilled his visions for their future. Moreover, the inherent difficulties of colonization—the enormous cost of emancipation, the effort involved in migration, and above all, the reluctance of freed slaves to go to Africa—caused Meade to accept the futility of an inherently impracticable scheme.[6]

The Custises, especially the women, persisted nonetheless. Mary Lee yearned for her maid, Eliza, who served her at West Point and Arlington, to start a new life in Africa. "I have promised," she inscribed in her diary in 1853, that she "shall have her freedom to emigrate to Liberia in the course of a few years, no specified time. In case of my death, I hope my husband will send her as soon as convenient & practicable." A month later, Mary realized that Eliza might not wish to go. "If she should marry here & be unwilling to go, especially if she should marry a free man when she has either served in the family long enough to earn the sum of $200.00, or can pay that sum by earning it elsewhere, let her be free. If she will go to Africa she can have her freedom" (Mary here crossed out the word "unconditionally"). Eliza made up her own mind; Mary penciled a note in 1869 that "Eliza has her freedom & lives at Newport."[7] By then, of course, all slaves were free.

Christian Paternalism

The naive paternalism—or, at Arlington, maternalism—inherent in the colonizing scheme manifested a basic conviction shared by most whites throughout the nation: people of color were inferior to whites. Even Bishop Meade, whose family found slavery distasteful, whose sister considered it immoral, and who differed from most Southern religious figures in thinking of slaves as human beings that as children of God deserved to hear the Christian gospel, maintained nonetheless that whites were superior to blacks.[8] Custises and Lees took the same approach. Robert Lee believed in a racial hierarchy that placed whites at the top and Mexicans, Indians, and blacks somewhere near the bottom. Nevertheless, following Meade's pastoral advice, the masters of Arlington House felt the obligation to teach their "servants" reading and religion, encourage services for them and even build a place where they could worship (under white supervision, of course), and care for them in sickness and death. When two "servants" died in 1854, Mary confided to her diary: "I feel a heavy responsibility both for the bodies & souls of these poor creatures"—neither of whom she called by name. "Lord enable me to do my duty & give them for faithfulness & truth."[9]

Yet, of the hundreds of slaves the family owned, only a few could possibly benefit from their direct care.

Markie recorded the prevailing antebellum attitude at Arlington House. When *Uncle Tom's Cabin* scandalized Southerners and Northerners for diametrically different reasons, Markie defended slavery. "Certainly, Mrs. Stow has no counterpart of Arlington in her Book or of things as they are conducted here." Her uncle, she wrote, favorably compared "the life of his negroes and the best class of the poor in Europe so far as manual labor & comfort is concerned." Indeed, she continued, "To eat & drink & sleep are the only duties with wh[ich] he has anything to do. . . . They have their comfortable homes, their families around them and nothing to do but to consult their own pleasure. Their eating & drinking & clothing is all provided for them." If anything, "the master is the only slave. Uncle considers slavery a great curse to the country," as Meade had done, "& says it is his hearty wish that the first ship which sailed from Bristol England with slaves had been engulphed in the Sea." For her part, Markie justified it on religious grounds, as was her wont.

> I believe Providence has permitted things to be as they are and it is our duty to seek for light that we may do our duty as christians by them. Having for so many years been reared in ignorance and servility, they have not that keen perception of their degraded situation, that we, differently reared, might suppose them to possess. Hence, the mere fact of their position, is, I believe, not a source of pain to them, unless inoculated with those ideas by the whites. Whether they ought or ought not to have been thus degraded from the first, is another question and one exceedingly difficult to solve. It has involved discussions among the wisest of the earth and there is scarcely a hope of its being amicably settled. For myself, I am very doubtful of its propriety. There is certainly no institution wh[ich] admits of more abuses than Slavery.[10]

In truth, no amount of Christian paternalism could erase the realities of slavery. Though termed "servants" in the Lee vernacular, they were, in the end, property owned by the family. They could be bought and sold, rented out, retrieved if they ran away, whipped, and freed with or without conditions. Mr. Custis allowed his daughter's "girl" Judy to be bound over to Senator Albert Smith White of Indiana for three hundred dollars, after which she would be "considered as fully liberated."[11]

Lee knew all that. He had grown up with slaves. He absorbed lessons from dealing with them and choosing their overseers. "In his treatment of the negroes," he wrote his cousin Hill Carter in 1840, the manager needs "to be as attentive to their comfort & welfare, as to the discharge of their duties; and to be neither <u>harsh</u> nor <u>severe</u> in his discipline."[12]

An Unpleasant Legacy

Theoretical advice took on pragmatic reality for Lee when his father-in-law died on October 10, 1857. Having rushed home from Texas to tend to affairs, he confronted a huge problem. Mr. Custis's will was a legal and financial mess. Bequeathing his various farms to his grandsons—Arlington to Custis with Mary retaining a life interest; White House on the Pamunkey River to Rooney; Romancoke in King William County to Rob—he also promised $10,000 to each of his granddaughters. Robert himself received a city lot in Washington.

One last condition of Custis's will complicated matters all the more. "Mr. Custis directed that his slaves should be emancipated as soon as his debts & certain legacies could be paid," Lee explained in 1859, and within five years at most. He added, "Justice to the negroes requires that this should be accomplished as soon as possible."[13]

But his estates could not possibly fulfill all those terms. Proceeds from the sale of other properties such as Smith Island in the Chesapeake, which Custis expected to cover his debts and legacies, fell far short of filling the need. To meet it, the remaining estates had to become productive enough to provide the funds for the girls, farms for the boys, and freedom for the 196 slaves.[14] But those lands were far from productive. His father-in-law had not been effective as either farmer or businessman. He failed to provide the systematic organization or management that agricultural specialists of the era advised for plantations—or for himself. Markie walked into his parlor one afternoon to find papers strewn about which her uncle claimed were "<u>exceedingly valuable</u>." She wrote, "This utter carelessness of business matters, was so perfectly characteristic." Markie thought his neglectfulness charming. What Lee thought of it, he never seemed to say.[15]

As a result, Lee as executor faced a startling paradox. He believed he had to energize the slaves to make the farms more productive in order to meet the will's obligations, including their own freedom, and he had five years at most to do it. But, as the Lees assessed the situation, hard work was something the slaves neither were used to nor desired. Most of them, in Markie's opinion, lived in "idleness." Some expressed their discontent in their behavior. "Constant trouble in our domestic affairs," Mary complained in the spring after her father died. "I see nothing else before us & alas I fear no benefit to those who have caused it." She prayed God to "change their consciences so clouded by ignorance & sin & give them the true light to shine into their hearts." Her prayers were not answered as she wished. In August she wrote, "Have been made very unhappy by the sad[?] conduct of our servants. May God forgive them & lead them to true repentance." She assumed, of course, that God saw matters as she did.[16]

Other slaves became even less inclined to work once they realized they would be freed. Lee wrote to Rooney about "some of the people" who rebelled against his authority, telling him that "they were as free as I was &c &c." They were captured, tied, and jailed. Others ran away. It was an impossible undertaking. Mary complained to a friend that her husband

> has been kept very busy in trying to reduce these very complicated affairs into some order. It is very unsatisfactory work for the servants here have been so long accustomed to do little or nothing that they cannot be convinced of the necessity now of exerting themselves to accomplish the conditions of the will which the sooner they do the sooner will they be entitled to their freedom. What they will do then unless there is a mighty change wrought in them I do not know but at any rate we shall be relieved from the care of them which will be an immense burden taken from our shoulders.[17]

Further complications resulted. Reports in the Northern press accused Lee of mistreating his slaves. Anonymous letters from Washington appeared in newspapers in Boston and New York charging Lee with twisting Custis's will to extend his ownership of slaves, mistreating them brutally, even personally whipping a captured fugitive slave woman. He did have to deal with several slaves who escaped, and with others who resisted his authority. Lee sent them first to jail in Alexandria, then to a slave trader in Richmond, not to sell them but instead to put them to work for five years, after which they were to be freed. As for the news reports, Lee purposefully said nothing, except to lament to his son Custis that it was altogether "an unpleasant legacy."[18]

Lee's Ambivalent Views

Adding to the paradox, Lee held mixed opinions about slavery as an institution. He considered slavery to be an evil institution that brought some good to the enslaved. In an especially revelatory letter to Mary from Fort Brown in 1857, Lee declared, "In this enlightened age, there are few I believe, but what will acknowledge, that slavery as an institution, is a moral, political evil in any country. It is useless to expatiate on its disadvantages." But who was more disadvantaged? "I think it . . . a greater evil to the white than to the black race, & while my feelings are strongly enlisted in behalf of the latter, my sympathies are more strong for the former." Unlike Meade, who compared the condition of blacks in Pennsylvania to that of blacks in Virginia, Lee compared the condition of blacks in Africa to that of blacks in the American South. "The blacks are immeasurably better off here than in Africa, morally, socially, physically."

Lee shared Markie's belief—common to many white Americans[19]—that God would eventually resolve the problem. "The painful discipline" that slaves "are undergoing, is necessary for their instruction as a race, & I hope will prepare & lead them to better things." But when? "How long their subjugation may be necessary, is known & ordered by a wise & merciful Providence."

But *how?* "Their emancipation will sooner result from the mild & melting influence of Christianity, than the stormy tempests of fiery controversy," Lee continued. "This influence[,] though slow, is sure." The Savior himself, after two thousand years, had converted only a small portion of humanity. Yet progress would continue. "While we see the course of the final abolition of human slavery is onward, & ever give it the aid of our prayers & all justifiable means in our power, we must leave the progress as well as the result in his hands who sees the end, who chooses to work by slow influences; & with whom two thousand years are but as a single day."[20]

Lee looked to God, then, to end slavery, certainly not to the fanatical zealots in the North who sought instant righteousness. As early as 1844, he castigated recent "Anti-Slavery Society" resolutions that "contend for the ruin of the present American church & the destruction of the Union." These abolitionists had denounced the pulpit, which they saw (often with good reason) "as the great stronghold of slavery," and the republic's founders as "<u>swindlers</u>" for creating a republic "which after fifty years trial is found to be a <u>curse</u> not a <u>blessing</u>." Twelve years later, Lee's concerns remained. "Although the abolitionist" must know of God's slow but sure progress in ending slavery, "& must see that he has neither the right or power of operating except by moral means & suasion, & if he means well to the slave, he must not create angry feelings in the master; that although he may not approve the mode by which it pleases Providence to accomplish its purposes, the result will nevertheless be the same: that the reasons he gives for interference in what he has no concern, holds good for every kind of interference with our neighbours when we disapprove their conduct. Still I fear he will persevere in his evil course." Northern abolitionists reminded him of the New England Puritans who sought religious liberty for themselves only to deny it to those who disagreed with them. "Is it not strange that the descendants of those pilgrim fathers who crossed the Atlantic to preserve their own freedom of opinion, have always proved themselves intolerant of the spiritual liberty of others." Fearing for the Union, Lee agreed with President Pierce that "the systematic & progressive efforts of certain people of the North, to interfere with & change the domestic institutions of the South," are "both unlawful & entirely foreign to them & their duty; for which they are irresponsible & unaccountable; can only be accomplished by <u>them</u> through the agency of a civil & servile war."[21]

Ultimately, only divine action could resolve the problem, Lee believed, and God was fortuitously at work, however slowly. For human beings to force a solution constituted, to Lee, a futile and prideful interference with the heavenly plan. Instead, they should do what God had appointed them to do. In the Lees' case, Mary could attend to the spiritual needs of the "servants," and Robert could free them according to what his father-in-law specified. Beyond that, mortals could only pray and wait. Such was the inescapable demand of his providential theology.

The Problem of Providence

More than any other issue in Lee's day, the reality of slavery challenged the theology of providence as many, like Lee, sought to live it out. Lee agreed that the institution was wrong, but beyond what was in his own immediate power, he left its abolition to God in a process he believed would be inexorable, if long. But that was a conclusion fraught with difficulties.

It virtually ensured the status quo. Only God knew how long the divinely led process would take. While a thousand earthly ages are in God's sight like an evening gone, mortals might not see much change from one age to the next. Thus mortals can, and must, be patient. They should do what they can do and, beyond that, be "resigned" to the rest. Lee's was not totally a laissez-faire attitude, as some have suggested, but it came close.

Lee applied the same principle to Mary's worsening arthritis as he did to slavery. She should go to the spas to relieve her pain, but accept faithfully whatever might befall her. For her part, Mary tried to learn the lessons that God was trying to teach through her suffering. "Still painful in body," she wrote in her diary at the end of 1856; "oh may thy chastisement be improved for my soul's good." Only God could ultimately resolve her problem.[22]

But this perspective held two implications. First, as with slavery, Mary's healing lay ultimately beyond mortal power to accomplish. She could alleviate the symptoms but not cure the disease. Only God could do that. Second, human beings could and should do what they could, like visit the spas; but what they could do was truly limited. Likewise, what they could do about slavery was about as limited as what they could do regarding Mary's health. Mary could emancipate her maid and send her to Africa; Robert could free his father-in-law's slaves, as was his duty. But circumstances and God impeded how much they could accomplish: Mary's maid could have other ideas (and did); and realities (as he saw them) kept Robert from achieving his father-in-law's goal as soon as he wished. As for institutional slavery, in the end, only God could eliminate it. Until God chose the time to do so, people had to be resigned to its reality.

From that viewpoint, any kind of social action lay not only beyond their own personal control, but also beyond rightful human power, lest mortals try to force the hand of God. Both Lees condemned the abolitionists on that basis, while also deploring the political turmoil the antislavery movement was fomenting. The possibility that abolitionists might be in some way contributing to a work of God seems never to have occurred to either of them, for they had placed slavery beyond society's ability to resolve on its own. How God would resolve it, neither of them could say.

Yet evangelicals throughout the first half of the century had eagerly sought to improve society. They saw themselves as agents of God trying to make the world more godly. Robert guided young men's lives toward virtue, knowledge, and responsibility; he strove to free his father-in-law's slaves. Mary had promoted Sunday schools and worship for blacks. Both of them fervently supported their church and its work in a host of ways. But, other than participating in the Colonization Society, all their efforts aimed to improve society through improving *individuals*: better people would make a better world. That was the extent of their involvement in social reform. From that perspective, they could do no more. Anything further had to be left to providence.

CHAPTER 16

"Scatter Thou the Peoples That Delight in War"

Lee's First Great Decision

Both Lees watched the growing national conflict with ever-increasing alarm, which their religious convictions only intensified. They both were politically sophisticated. While Lee, as an army officer, had to maintain political neutrality, Mary did not. Like many evangelicals, she (and probably Robert) tended to favor Whigs over Democrats until that party dissolved in the 1850s. They worried, though, over the increasing factionalism besetting the country. "Mr. Buchanan it appears, is to be our next President," Lee observed to Mary after the 1856 election. "I hope he will be able to extinguish fanaticism North & South, & cultivate love for the country & Union, & restore harmony between the different sections." Having earlier singled out abolitionists for criticism, he here cited fanatics in the South as well. The situation was so complex, they each adjudged, that only God's providence could resolve it.[1]

The Growing Tension

Providence did not bestow harmony under Buchanan. Tensions only increased during his term of office, and exploded. On October 17, 1859, a young officer named James Ewell Brown Stuart hurried to Arlington to bring his former superintendent news that a huge mob had seized the federal arsenal at Harpers Ferry, Virginia. The secretary of war, he said, wanted to see Lee at once. Lee and Stuart went first to the War Office, then to the White House to meet with the president himself. Buchanan ordered Lee to lead troops to quell what seemed to be a slave insurgency. By 10 p.m., he was in command near the scene. He had not taken time even to change into uniform.

By the time Lee arrived, it had become clear that, far from the rumored thousands of insurgents, only a handful of men led by John Brown were involved. They had taken hostages (one a cousin of George Washington). After battling local citizens and hastily called militiamen, the few militants who remained had barricaded themselves inside a firehouse on the armory grounds. Under a flag of truce, Stuart delivered Lee's ultimatum to surrender. Brown refused. Soldiers stormed the firehouse, captured Brown and his men, and rescued the remaining hostages. The "Harpers Ferry conspiracy" was over. Six weeks later, as cadets from Virginia Military Institute guarded against disruption, "the old fellow mounted the gallows with a firm step and stood upon the platform without wavering," one cadet wrote his mother. Brown "shook hands with the sheriff as if he was going away for a day or two. After his head being covered he had to stand on the platform ten minutes and during the whole time did not say a word or show the slightest humor. At last the rope was out and only a spasmodic contraction of the arms took place and he hung perfectly still for half an hour." He added, "There was no disturbance."[2]

Five years later, Mary, by then an ardent Confederate, recalled the debacle as an unmistakable prelude to war. Then, at least, providence had intervened: "The infamous attempt of John Brown & his accomplices to incite our negroes to murder & insurrection though thro' the mercy of God a signal failure." The affair "should have opened our eyes to the machinations of the party of fanatical abolitionists, unprincipled & cruel who exalted this vile assassin into a hero & martyr."[3] Lee remained silent on the matter.

Brown's raid intensified talk of secession. Just as Lee held conflicted opinions about slavery, so he did on secession. He had long been familiar with the controversies over states' rights. Writing a friend in 1832 from Fort Monroe, he cited, without opining on, the wranglings that had pitted President Andrew Jackson against South Carolina over whether a state had the right to disregard a federal law, specifically a national tariff that some Southerners believed taxed them unjustly. "There is nothing new here or in these parts, Nullification! Nullification!! Nullification!!!"[4] The idea that a state could annul a federal statute foreshadowed the struggles that followed over slavery and states' rights.

Nearly three decades later, Abraham Lincoln was elected president of the United States. Lee, like the rest of his family, shared the gathering gloom over the nation's future. In mid-January 1861, back in Texas in command of the Second Cavalry, he shared his conflicted mind with his kinswoman Annette Carter, the daughter of a prominent Marylander. Lee made his fundamental loyalty clear. "If the Union is dissolved, I shall return to Virginia & share the fortune of my people." But secession would bode catastrophe. "Before so great a calamity befalls the Country, I hope all honourable means of maintaining the Constitution, & the equal rights of the people will be first exhausted." He suggested one effort she herself could make: "Tell your father he must not allow Maryland to be tacked on to S. Carolina before the just demands of the South have been fairly presented to the North & rejected. Then if the rights guaranteed by the Constitution are denied us, & the citizens of one portion of the Country are granted privileges not extended to the other, we can with a clear Conscience separate." He hoped that leaders in Washington would perceive the justice of the Southern position, reason would prevail, and the Union would survive. If they did not, separation would become warranted. Virginia, and Maryland, could justifiably secede. "I am for maintaining all our rights, not for abandoning all for the sake of one." But what rights were at stake? Lee did not specify. He knew full well, though, what would follow: "Fierce & bloody war." Secession "is revolution & war at last, and cannot be otherwise, so we might as well look at it in its true character."

Yet Lee, having spent his adult life serving the United States, professed his abiding dedication to the nation. "As an American citizen I prize my government & country highly, & there is no sacrifice I am not willing to make for their preservation save that of honour," he assured his cousin. "I trust there is wisdom, patriotism enough in the country to save them, for I cannot anticipate so great a calamity to the nation as a dissolution of the Union."[5]

Lee family letters reflected the growing tension. In January 1861, Mary informed Mildred, away at school, that she would postpone a trip to Baltimore and feared she would never go. "I do not feel much in heart w/o anywhere viewing constantly the sad state of my country, we must be more earnest in supplication to that Almighty Power who alone can save us. That is all we poor women can do." Lee's analysis resembled his wife's. "As far as I can judge from the papers we are between a state of anarchy & civil war. May God avert from us both." He continued, "It has been evident for years that the country was doomed to run the full length of democracy. To what a fearful pass it has brought us. I fear mankind for years will not be sufficiently christianized to bear the absence of restraint & force." By the time he wrote, four states had seceded and another three were poised to leave. "Then if the border States are dragged into the gulf of revolution," he warned, "one half of the Country will be arrayed against the other. I must try & be patient & await the end for I can do nothing to hasten or retard it."[6]

Six days later, Lee shared with Agnes his doubts that peace between the sections could long endure "unless the present hostile feelings could be allayed." He felt as powerless as Mary did, admitting that he could "do nothing but trust to the wisdom & patriotism of the nation & to the overruling providence of a merciful God." The actions of his home state were crucial to both the nation's future and his own. "I am particularly anxious that Virginia should keep right, & as she was chiefly instrumental in the formation & inauguration of the Constitution"—indeed, his own forebears, his father among them, had fought to create the nation that was in such jeopardy—"so I would wish that she might be able to maintain it & to save the union."[7]

Lee expanded his thought in a letter to Rooney. "The South in my opinion has been aggrieved by the acts of the North as you say. I feel the aggression, & am willing to take every proper step for redress. It is the principle I contend for, not individual or private benefit." Again, he did not explain precisely *how* the South was aggrieved. But he reaffirmed his patriotism: "As an American citizen I take great pride in my country, her prosperity & institutions & would defend any state if her rights were invaded." He could

anticipate no greater calamity for the country than a dissolution of the Union. It would be an accumulation of all the evils we complain of, & I am willing to sacrifice every thing but honour for its preservation. I hope therefore that all constitutional means will be exhausted, before there is a resort to force. Secession is nothing but revolution. The framers of our Constitution never exhausted so much labour, wisdom & forbearance[?] in its formation, & surrounded it with so many guards & securities, if it was intended to be broken by every member of the Confederacy at will. It was intended for perpetual union, so expressed in the preamble, & for the establishment of a government, not a compact, which can only be dissolved by resolution in the consent of all the people in convention assembled. It is idle to talk of secession. Anarchy would have been established & not a government, by Washington, Hamilton, Jefferson, Madison & the

other patriots of the Revolution. In 1808 secession was termed treason by Virg^a statesmen. What can it be now?

Lee was referring to the opposition of New England states to Jefferson's
embargo of 1808, then to the War of 1812, which led to the Hartford
Convention of 1814–1815 that threatened to dissolve the Union. Once
again, the very nature of the Union was at stake; "a union that can only
be maintained by swords & bayonets, & in which strife & civil war are to
take the place of brotherly love & kindness, has no charm for me," he
declared. "I shall mourn for my country, & for the welfare & progress of
mankind. If the Union is dissolved & the government disrupted, I shall
return to my native state & share the miseries of my people & save in her
defence will draw my sword no more."[8]

A month later, with "a sad heavy heart," Mary admitted to Annie
that she, too, was losing hope. "The prospects before us are sad indeed
& as I think both parties are in the wrong in this fratricidal war there is
nothing comforting even in the hope that God may prosper the right,
for I see no right in the matter. We can only pray that in his mercy he
will spare us." Five days later, she told Mildred that she was praying
"that the Almighty may listen to the prayers of the faithful in the land &
direct their counsels for good—& that the designs of ambitious & selfish
politicians who would dismember our glorious country may be frustrated—especially that our own state may act right & obtain the merit
promised in the Bible to the peacemakers."[9]

Lee himself had grown increasingly uncomfortable. Texas held a
convention that, on February 1, voted to secede from the Union. Suddenly Lee found himself an officer of an army stationed in a hostile
country. General Winfield Scott ordered him to Washington. Lee left
Fort Mason on February 13. By the time he reached San Antonio on
February 16, Texas Rangers had taken control. Lee's superior, David
Twiggs, had surrendered to the state militia. Lee immediately changed
into civilian clothes, spent several days in the city, and left for home.[10]

The Big Decision

How Lee responded to the crisis has been defined more by heroic imagination than contemporaneous accounts. A Baptist minister and "Lost
Cause" advocate, who knew Lee during his Lexington days, depicted

him struggling with his decision to resign his commission, dropping to his knees in prayer. Such stories surround Lee's decision with a religious aura.[11] Two descriptions written nearer the event by people close to Lee cast a less romantic light on it. One comes from his daughter Mary Custis, in an account she composed for a prospective biographer, discovered in 2002 in a trunk filled with Lee papers and left in an Alexandria bank. The other is a memorandum of conversations between General Lee, when he was president of Washington College, and William Allan, one of his professors. Allan immediately jotted down Lee's words. Each relies on personal, postwar memories, in one case seven years after the event, in the other case, nine years. Together they give a clearer picture of the events and motivations surrounding the major turning point of Lee's life.

Lee arrived home on March 1. On March 4, Lincoln became president. A day or two later, Lee went to visit Winfield Scott, he recalled to Allan, not knowing why the commanding general wanted to see him. Lee wondered if he might be offered command of the army, even over the heads of more senior officers, though he stressed that he could not "go on duty against the South." But Scott had a more pedestrian chore in mind for Lee: to help revise army regulations. Scott discounted the chances for war, showing Lee a sheaf of letters from Lincoln and Secretary of State William Seward. In what Lee termed a "very pacific . . . tone," Seward emphatically declared that he "would not remain in the cabinet if he thought any thing but peace [were] contemplated." For his own part, Lee reiterated that if he might "be placed on duty against the South he wanted to know so that he might at once resign" and thereby avoid the indignity of quitting the army after receiving orders. He returned to Arlington greatly relieved.[12]

Lee did not see Scott again until April 18. By then, a convention in Richmond on April 4 had refused to take Virginia out of the Union by a vote of 88 to 45. On April 12, however, Confederates fired on Fort Sumter. Two days later, when Mary Custis and her father went to the Sunday service in Alexandria, they heard of Sumter's surrender as they left Christ Church. Walking to their customary lunch at her aunt's home nearby, Lee muttered of his fellow officer who commanded the fort, "Poor General Anderson! He was a determined man, & I know held out to the last."[13]

On April 15, Lincoln called for seventy-five thousand troops to respond to the crisis. Two days later, Virginia's convention reconvened.

Citing "the oppression of the Southern slaveholding states," it reversed its earlier decision, voting 88 to 55 to secede.

Before this news reached Lee, Francis Blair, a force in Washington politics since Andrew Jackson's presidency, asked to see him. On April 18 they met at the home of Blair's son, Montgomery, postmaster general in Lincoln's cabinet, across the street from the War Department in what is now the President's Guest House. Blair revealed that Lincoln and his cabinet wanted Lee to become commander in chief of the Union forces—Scott was too old for the role—and "tried in every way to persuade" Lee to accept. Blair appealed to Lee's patriotism, to his ambition, and to his historic connections that caused the people of the country to look to him "as the representative of the Washington family." They "talked all over the secession question," which, Lee agreed, was "folly." Regarding slavery, Lee recalled to Allan that "as the negro was concerned he would willingly give up his own (400) for peace." Mary Custis quoted him saying to *Seward* (who in Allan's telling was not present) "that if he could give me the whole four millions of slaves into my own hands tomorrow, they would not weigh one moment in the balance against the union." Whether Lee claimed he would free *all* the slaves to save the Union or only those under his control, both accounts emphasize that Lee did not consider slavery as the reason for the decision he had to make.[14] Emancipation for him was a small, even welcomed, price to pay for union.

Having made his position clear, Lee walked across Pennsylvania Avenue to the War Department office, next to the White House. Winfield Scott, the army's commanding general, dropped what he was doing and "received him kindly." Lee summarized his conversation with Blair and repeated his decision and the reasons for it. Scott said he had expected as much, from their earlier meeting after Lee returned from Texas, but expressed his "deep regret." As Lee later told Allan, he returned to Arlington that night, concluded he ought to resign before receiving any orders that he could not in conscience obey, wrote out his resignation, then set it aside so he could reflect on his action before submitting it.[15] Even as Lee met with Blair and Scott, a visitor to Arlington was describing the Richmond convention to the family. Secession had not yet been announced. When Lee returned home, hearing the report, he remarked, "I presume the poor old State will go out. I d'ont think she need to do so, yet at least, but so many are trying to push her out that she will have to go I suppose."[16]

On Friday, April 19, Southern sympathizers in Baltimore mobbed Massachusetts troops marching through the city to defend Washington. In the melee, a friend of Mrs. Lee was killed. Hearing this news, Lee summoned his family into his office. Seated at his table, he read them his letter of resignation from the army. "This is a copy of the letter which I have sent to Gen. Scott," he told them. "I wrote it early in the morning when I first came down & dispatched 'Perry' [a slave who ran errands for the family] over to 'Washington' with it before breakfast." He added, "I mention this to show you that I was not at all influenced by the exciting news from 'Baltimore.'"

No one said a word. Lee broke the silence. "I suppose you all think I have done very wrong, but it had come to this, & after my last interview with Gen. Scott I felt that I ought to wait no longer." Mary Custis spoke up. "Indeed, Papa, I d'ont think you have done wrong at all." She knew that she alone in the family circle came closest to being "Secesh," a result, she said, from "living in the country" away from the influences of Washington. All others were "traditionally, my mother especially, a conservative, or 'Union' family."

Wider reaction was swift. Orton Williams, Markie's brother assigned to Scott's staff, told them at their midday dinner that Scott had already received and approved Lee's resignation but that "all in the Depart[ment] were in a stir over it." Mary Custis quoted Williams that "now that 'Cousin Robert' had resigned every one seemed to be doing so." Scott himself took to his office sofa, refused to see anyone, and "mourned as for a loss of a son," Williams reported. The old general demanded, emotionally, "d'ont mention Robert Lee's name to me again, I cannot bear it." Hearing this, Lee predicted, "Yes, he is going to hold on to the Union,—but I believe it will kill him; I don't think he can live through it all." (Scott did survive the war. He retired that fall, and died in 1866 of what Mary called "vanity," a trait for which the soldier nicknamed "Old Fuss 'n Feathers" had long been notorious.)

When Mary Custis and her father returned to Christ Church the following Sunday, April 21, they found "that really quiet little town in another great state of fermentation." News of Virginia's secession had spread. Crowds surrounded Lee "as if their faith was pinned to him alone." Rumors had circulated that he had been arrested as soon as he resigned. When the tale reached Rooney at his farm on the Pamunkey, he took captive the crews of two lumber schooners anchored on the river. On the trip home from church, Lee, unaware of his son's action, counseled caution: "You see how unfortunate it is to yield to <u>excitement</u>, let me beg of you all, whatever happens, & there are probably very trying times before you, when I may not be with you to advise you, that you will listen to your reason, not to your impulses. Try to keep cool in <u>all</u> circumstances."[17] It was advice Lee's own father might have given him.

The New Command

Meanwhile, Judge John Robertson traveled from Richmond at Governor John Letcher's behest, hoping to persuade Scott and Lee to side with Virginia against the Union. That Saturday, the day Lee submitted his resignation, Scott was in no mood to entertain such an idea. He dismissed Robertson abruptly. Lee by contrast proposed to meet with the judge after church the next day. It remains unclear whether Lee saw Robertson or his colleagues, but he did agree to accompany Robertson to Richmond. The next morning the two met in Alexandria and boarded the train for Richmond.[18]

Planning to spend the night in the capital and return to Arlington the next day, Lee checked in at the Spotswood Hotel, then called on the governor. Letcher minced no words. He asked Lee to take command of Virginia's forces as a major general.[19] Lee agreed.

Even then, was war inevitable? Some still hoped not. James May, a professor of ecclesiastical history and polity at Virginia Theological Seminary and an admirer of Lee, heard rumors of Lee's new position. While Lee and Robertson journeyed to Richmond, May hurriedly wrote to Lee's cousin Cassius suggesting that Robert use his position, "by God's blessing, [to] bring peace to our distracted country. O how my heart leaped at the thought!" May had learned of Lee's high regard as a soldier. More important still for May was Lee's faith. "It is sad that so few of our public men are Christians. Colonel Lee is the grand exception. I know, in an official post, which is not that of head of the government, he would find it difficult to follow the private promptings of his own Christian mind, for a soldier's business is not to advise his superior but to obey. But great respect would be shown to the judgment & Christian spirit of one so distinguished as he." May wondered, might Lee have a God-given mission to save the whole country? "Virginia gave us our original Independence through her Washington. She gave us our

National Constitution through Jefferson & Madison & others. Can she now," he asked, "while we are threatened with the immeasurable evils of Civil War, give us through Colonel Lee, peace?"[20]

Cassius immediately forwarded May's letter to Lee. He admitted that his own speculations had inspired May's suggestion. He too wished that Lee's rumored command "might lead to some peaceful settlement of our difficulties. I hoped this from the friendship between yrself & Gen Scott." He added his prayer to May's, "that God may make you instrumental in saving our land from this dreadful strife."[21]

Two days later, Lee was appointed general. Virginia had formally joined the Confederacy. After expressing his gratitude to Cassius and for May's thought, he wrote, "I fear it is now out of the power of man, & in God alone must be our trust." Lee anticipated adopting a defensive strategy that would "resist aggression & allow time to allay the passions & reason to resume her Sway." He hoped "that a merciful Providence will not turn his face entirely from us & dash us from the height to which his Smiles had raised us."[22]

Why?

Why did Lee refuse to command the army he had served for decades, resign his commission in the military of his nation, and agree to lead the forces of his state? Clearly, his decision carried weight. He was more respected in Virginia and beyond than he realized. James May heard that Lee's fellow officers "would unanimously declare him to be, in all military qualification, without a rival in the service." He was perhaps the only soldier in history to be offered the command of two opposing armies, and in one single week. Such was his reputation within the army that his resignation led to a surge of Southern soldiers following his example. As for civilians, Alexandria's townspeople, worried that he had been arrested, gathered around him, in Mary's phrase, "as if their faith was pinned to him alone." Their local newspaper opined that his "reputation, his acknowledged ability, his chivalric character, his probity, honor, and—may we add, to his eternal praise—his Christian life and conduct—make his very name a 'tower of strength.'"[23]

Lee based his decision not on how others would react, however, but rather on what he perceived as right. He hoped others would do the same, and make their own choices based on their own principles. What, then, were Lee's?

Lee did not side with Virginia to perpetuate slavery. The accounts of Mary Custis Lee and William Allan reiterate the position he outlined in letters to his family. He considered slavery to be an evil, a curse on white and black alike, that God, in due course, would bring to an end. Precisely how slavery would cease was best left to God and not to human intervention, which would inevitably be plagued by sin—as, in his eyes, Northern abolitionists amply proved. Although he never shared the Custis family's passion for colonizing freed slaves in Africa, he claimed, after the war, "always to have been in favor of emancipation—gradual emancipation."[24] However self-serving his perspective may have been, and however unrealistic it surely was, he nevertheless hoped for slavery to end.

On what basis, then, did Lee choose to fight for the South? He wrote that the Southern states had been "aggrieved" and had just complaints that the North needed to hear and address. Unfortunately for our understanding, he did not identify those grievances, though he did cite interference with the "domestic institutions" of the South—slavery, obviously—that "certain people of the North" wanted to impose, by civil war if necessary. Paradoxically, he agreed to lead the forces that would preserve the institution he opposed.[25]

Three observations may address the paradox. The first concerns his theology. As a providentialist, he left the solution to God. Humans should not force the divine hand even if they believe they are helping the divine plan. Of course, he heartily encouraged the very human endeavor of spreading the gospel—clearly a work of God. Evidently he distinguished between political and spiritual efforts, without seeing any connection between the two.

The second factor involved Lee's loyalty to his "country." Was that country Virginia, or was it the United States? Without question, he loved his home state. Returning from Missouri in 1840, he characterized the state as "a great country and will one day be a grand one." But despite Missouri's "life animation and prosperity," Lee preferred Virginia. "I felt so elated when I again found myself within the confines of the Ancient Dominion," he wrote a kinsman, "that I nodded to all the old trees as I passed, chatted with the drivers and stable boys, shook hands with the landlords, and in the fulness of my heart—don't tell Cousin Mary—wanted to kiss all the pretty girls I met."[26] In a word, Virginia was his home.

Lee's reference to Missouri as a "country" hints at another widely shared conception of his time. The United States was not yet a solidified nation. It lacked a truly national identity. Other than through its post offices, the federal government had little presence in the lives of most Americans. Rather, the state evoked a person's primary loyalty. One was a Virginian or a Georgian or a Minnesotan before one was an American. Indeed, a common name for the country was plural—*these* United States—rather than singular—*the* United States. It took a civil war to forge the thirty-two states into one nation. As a former Union general reminisced, "We must emphasize this one statement which was ever on the lips of many good men in 1860 and '61, to wit: 'My first allegiance is due to my State!'" Only after the country added the Fourteenth Amendment in 1868 did the Constitution affirm the preeminence of national over state citizenship.[27]

As a US Army officer, Lee visited and lived in more parts of the United States than most Americans of his era, giving him a broader perspective on the nation than others could have had. He complimented his brother-in-law Edward Childe, who, as an American in Paris writing in a French newspaper in 1857, "expose[d] the threatened evils" of events in his native land. Lee agreed, he wrote Childe, "that your country [the US] was the whole Country. That its limits contained no North, no South, no East, no West, but embraced the broad Union, in all its might & strength; present & future. On that subject my resolution is taken, & my mind fixed. I know no other Country, no other Government, than the United States & their Constitution."[28] Nevertheless, for Lee, "the United States" remained a plural noun.

Finally, especially between 1857 and 1861, Lee believed the Constitution itself was under attack. Forces outside of the South threatened intrusions into the sovereignty of states (specifically over slavery), thereby contradicting the philosophy of a federal union and undermining the very nature of the nation. Fanaticism on both sides had prevailed precisely as the Founders—and his own father—had dreaded. In the early days of the Revolution, Henry had grown skeptical of the people's ability to attain and then sustain the public virtue deemed essential to American independence. Republics of the past had foundered when a free people grew selfish, corrupt, or lazy in their vigilance of liberties, allowing tyranny to grow. Now, Lee feared, the country had run "the full length of democracy."[29]

The balance between federal and state governments was, in Lee's view, being upset by an ever more powerful central government that imperiled the sovereignty of the states, threatening the tyranny that his father's generation had feared. In the spring of 1861, that government threatened to invade his state. Suddenly an abstract possibility became an immediate prospect, forcing his personal decision to join one side or the other, or somehow to sit out the crisis. For some years he had pledged not to raise his sword against his native state, yet for far longer he had served what he called "Uncle Sam."[30]

Lee faced, then, an excruciating ethical dilemma. He wished slavery to end, but he opposed the means being used to abolish it. The end did not justify the means, especially because the means, he believed, would also destroy the very essence of the Union. Honor impelled him to rise to the defense of both his state and the Constitution of the United States that he had sworn to defend. After honor came duty. Both were principles he had known and pursued since birth. They were integral elements of his paternal inheritance.

Lee appears to have taken what ethicists call a nonconsequentialist approach, which is not concerned with the results of a decision so much as with the moral actor or action, that is, what makes a "good" person or a "good" action. An emphasis on the individual finds its origins in ancient Greek philosophy, particularly in the *Nichomachean Ethics*. In that work, which Lee may have read as a boy, Aristotle explores the role of virtue in developing a "good" life. Becoming a "virtuous" person, and thus seeking the highest good for human beings, was for Aristotle the surest means of attaining happiness. Somewhat different is the "deontological" theory of ethics proposed by Immanuel Kant, which makes duty (in Greek, *deon*) the most important criterion in moral action. The quality of what a person *does*, Kant believed, contributes most to the development of a moral person and a moral society. Fulfilling one's obligation, one's duty, regardless of the immediate outcome, takes on prime importance.[31]

The Enlightenment tradition took each of these theories seriously. Latitudinarian preachers and their followers who influenced colonial Virginia Anglicanism prized "happiness" and extolled "virtue." Kant was developing his principles of ethics as the new American nation was taking shape. At the same time, Jeremy Bentham, the English philosopher, expounded a "utilitarianism" that stresses neither the act nor the actor but the consequence; it seeks the best outcome. Lee apparently gave no consideration to the results of his decision;

indeed, what consequences he could foresee were bleak. Lee was no utilitarian.

Strikingly, his father's influence seemed to dominate his thinking to the virtual exclusion of his mother's. Given Ann Carter's evangelical perspective, he could well have embraced what ethicists call the divine command theory, in which a person seeks guidance from God or external revelation to make a decision.[32] He did not. In his explanations, he never mentions God. Despite the pious influences surrounding him, and regardless of his own providential convictions, no *theological* consideration seems to have shaped his decision. Given his evangelical bent, dropping to his knees to ask God's guidance would seem as natural as J. William Jones had depicted him doing;[33] but his daughter's account describes no such thing. There is no outward sign of religious searching, no evidence of inward contemplation of the divine will. Nor did Lee exhort others to decide as he decided, which he may have encouraged if he perceived himself acting at God's command.

Instead, Lee seems to have relied on the heritage of his father's ethical emphasis on virtue and duty. His letters indicate as much. What he penned to his cousin Roger Jones, an army lieutenant, typifies what he wrote to others: "Sympathizing with you in the troubles that are pressing so heavily upon our beloved country, & entirely agreeing with you in your notions of allegiance etc., I have been unable to make up my mind to raise my hand against my native state, my relatives, my children & my home. I have therefore resigned my commission in the Army & never desire again to draw my sword save in defence of my native state. I consider it useless to go into the reasons that influenced me. I can give you no advice. I merely tell you what I have done that you may do better."[34] Without specifying the "reasons that influenced me," Lee cited "notions of allegiance" to "my native state" as most important. This was the language of duty and honor, of what a virtuous man embodies, of what his father had sought to instill in his sons. Ethics of the Enlightenment prized above all else "doing the right thing." Lee knew better than anyone what secession would mean and what war would bring. He surely assumed that his wife's home would immediately fall into Federal hands, which it did. No matter; duty did not consider the consequences.

Honor and duty lay at the heart of Lee's personal code. But it was his *personal* code. He did not try to impose it on others. Indeed, many fellow Virginians who had served the national military, notably Winfield

174

Scott and the future general George Thomas, chose to remain loyal to the Union. Lee left to others, including his own children, freedom to reach their own conscientious conclusions. He never suggested, and indeed denied, that his was the only right decision. As well, he declined to exhort others to follow his lead. These factors imply an ethical rather than theological emphasis in his thought. Of course, the two can never be fully segregated. Still, had Lee based his decision on religious conviction, he might have suggested that God had led him to it. If his choice reflected the will of the Lord, then he would have held the evangelical responsibility to enjoin others to follow the same godly path. The absence of any such language, too, reflects a fundamentally ethical basis for his conclusion.[35]

His decision four years later would be quite different.

CHAPTER 17

"Who Teacheth My Hands to War"

~

The Years of Struggle

Three weeks before accepting command of Virginia's forces, Lee commented on an essay that his daughter Mildred had composed at her school in Winchester. Evidently she had written about three professions, one of them his own. Her penmanship drew a gentle paternal rebuke. So did her orthography, which evoked a light but telling comment on the eve of war: "I noticed that you spelt Saturday with two ts (Satturday). One is considered enough in the Army, but perhaps the fashion is to have two. I hope you did justice to the Farmer the Soldier & the Sailor. The first is the most useful citizen. The two last necessary evils, which will disappear when the world becomes sufficiently Christianized, I mean the military not the commercial Sailor."[1]

The outbreak of war represented, for both Robert and Mary Lee, the failure of, among others, Christians, especially leaders who claimed to be Christians. Before the war, each blamed politicians on both sides for the growing strife. After it, Mary blamed the "party of the fanatical abolitionists," holding Lincoln especially responsible. "Even after the election of Lincoln by this faction," she recalled in a postwar diary, "Peace might have been maintained if *they* had not *predetermined* to provoke the South to hostilities or if *their* chosen President had possessed the moral courage to resist the evil influences that were brought to bear upon him."[2] Now matters were in the hands of soldiers.

Neither Robert nor Mary thought war to be God's will. When it happened, each called on the Almighty to sustain the cause they each came to support. God, they prayed, was on their side. And they had at least one Episcopal theologian who agreed with them. "It would be impiety to doubt our triumph. We are working out a great thought of GOD—, namely the higher development of Humanity in its capacity for Constitutional Liberty."[3]

Lee's wartime career has been so well recorded that only a sketch is needed here. He took command of Virginia's military on April 22, 1861, leading it into battle for the first time on September 11 at Cheat Mountain, in what soon would become West Virginia. He then became military adviser to President Jefferson Davis in Richmond until June 1862, when he succeeded the wounded General Joseph E. Johnston as commander of the army on the Virginia peninsula. Lee renamed it the Army of Northern Virginia and remained its head through Second Manassas, Antietam, Fredericksburg, Chancellorsville, and Gettysburg, and until the end of the war. After the loss at Gettysburg, Lee tendered his resignation to Davis, who refused to accept it. Lee was promoted to general in chief of all Confederate forces in February 1865. On April 9, forced to retreat from Richmond, he surrendered to Union General Ulysses S. Grant at Appomattox.

After Lee left Arlington for Richmond in April 1861, he never again set foot in the house. Union troops occupied it. The family scattered, never fully to reunite. Each of his sons joined the Confederate army, Custis and Fitzhugh attaining the rank of general. Daughter Mary roamed the state. Annie withdrew to North Carolina, where she died in 1862, the only child to predecease Robert and Mary. The younger girls stayed in homes of friends and relatives, sometimes with their mother, who moved from place to place as the war progressed. The outbreak of war, then, sundered Lee not only from his home but also from his family. They encountered each other only as fortune (or, as Lee would have said, providence) allowed.

As always, letters poured forth as circumstances permitted. These document their understanding of God, and God's relationship to the war and to themselves. They indicate how their faith addressed their very changed world, filled as it was with death and sorrow, with the hope of victory and how to attain it, and the ultimate reality of defeat.

The End of the World as They Knew It

War ended the life the Lees had always known. The first casualty they faced was the loss of Arlington. In early May, Orton Williams rushed over from Washington to warn Mary that Federal troops would occupy the heights—and the house—the next day. They held off until May 23, but Mary had to leave. She escaped to Ravensworth.[4]

According to Daughter, Mary Lee had been inclined to support the Union, but that news reversed her sympathy. Before she fled, she wrote Mildred,

> The zealous patriots who are risking their lives to <u>preserve</u> the Union founded by Washington might come & take the grandaughter of his wife from her home & desecrate it, for whatever I have thought & even <u>now</u> think of the commencement of this horrible conflict <u>now</u> our duty is <u>plain</u>, to resist unto death. The government has proved itself so false & treacherous that we have nothing to hope. The men who are at the head of it seem to be without honour & without pity & I believe it would give them pleasure to lay waste our fair country. In God is our only hope.

Mary sent some heirlooms to Richmond and Ravensworth, and other items to Lexington, but she did not know what to do with the cats. "Pray for your country that it may yet be delivered," she advised. Her "country" had become Virginia. Soon it would be the South.[5]

Three days later, Lee tried to console Mary on her imminent loss. "I grieve at the necessity that drives you from your home," he began. "I can appreciate your feelings on the occasion & pray that you may receive comfort & strength in the difficulties that surround you." He then placed their concerns in a larger context. "When I reflect upon the calamity impending over the country, my own sorrows sink into insignificance." Still, they had urgent realities to face, such as where Mary and family could be safe. He suggested Fauquier County or Shenandoah County, somewhere removed from fighting. "Be content & resigned to God's will," he closed. "I shall be able to write seldom. Write to me as your letters will be my greatest comfort."[6]

Mary became increasingly apocalyptic. The day she read his letter, she awoke to a "lovely morning" at Arlington. "I never saw the country more beautiful, perfectly <u>radiant</u>[,] the yellow jessamine in full bloom & perfuming all the air but a deathlike stillness prevails everywhere," she wrote. "We may well exclaim, Can such things be? Can man thus trample upon all his Creator has lavished upon him of love & beauty?" She wondered if the end of the world were at hand. "I think the thousand years must be commencing when Satan is to be let loose upon earth, to blacken & mar its fair surface & while we must feel that our sins both personal & national merit the chastisement of the Almighty we may still implore him to spare us & with mercy not in wrath to visit us."[7]

Mary's world truly was ending. She was bolting the only life she really knew. But Robert failed to perceive her despair. "I am glad to hear that you are at peace, & enjoying the sweet weather & beautiful flowers," he replied, as if she wallowed amid the jessamine in ignorant bliss. He tried to wake her to reality. "You had better complete your arrangements & retire further from the scene of war. It may burst upon you at any time. It is sad to think of the devastation, if not ruin it may bring upon a spot so endeared to us. But God's will be done. We must be resigned." His closing became habitual: "May He guard & keep you all is my constant prayer."[8]

Mary answered, "I will write as often as I can but always fear you will be too much occupied to read any long epistle." Perhaps she suspected that he did not apprehend what she confided in him. Still, she added, "May God bless you." Was this war that "something more for the glory of God" that she wondered about when he was confirmed? "May God bless you & make you an instrument for the honour & salvation of your home & country."[9]

War marked a kind of eschaton for each of them. Mary's was obvious. She was losing her home, her way of life, and her heritage, and the physical associations of her past were rapidly coming to an end. She was among the first to face the dislocation that thousands of Southerners would endure over the next four years. Robert's world was ending as well. He had left the army to which he had devoted his career, and the house that for decades had been his home. He bade farewell to the United States of America. In time he would rejoin it, but the vision that he held of its nature was passing him by. In fighting for the Confederacy, he was struggling not just against Yankee armies, but also against a different concept of the Constitution and Union.

But was he also contending against the will of God?

Defending the Family While Defending the State

"All is gloom & uncertainty & I see nothing before me but war," Mary wrote Mildred before fleeing to Ravensworth. "I look to God, alone to preserve us." Mildred might not be able to return to her school. Mary also worried about Robert. She had not heard from him in a week and feared "he is quite worn out with business." Mary repeated to Precious Life the comment she had made to her husband: "God grant that he may successfully & honourably defend his state & family."[10]

While striving to bolster the army, Lee strained to buck up his family, especially his wife. Like countless Southerners (and Northerners too), he looked upon war as a punishment for sins, with individual ramifications, which he took personally: such were the ways of providence. "I fear we have not been grateful enough for the happiness there within our reach, & our heavenly father has found it necessary to deprive us of what He had given us," he confessed. "I acknowledge my ingratitude, my transgressions & my unworthiness, & submit with resignation to what He thinks proper to inflict upon me." True to the old Virginia theme of cooperating with God's providence, and of suffering the consequences of not doing so, Lee deemed himself complicit in their loss of Arlington—though he drew no connection between losing Arlington and his joining the Confederacy, much less showed any guilt about it. They had to move on. "We must trust all [in Arlington] to Him." Mary had to flee Ravensworth, which was becoming too dangerous. Distressing as it was, he admitted, "it cannot be helped, & we must bear our trials like Christians."[11]

Apparently Lee's suggesting that they had not appreciated their blessings failed to comfort Mary. Two weeks later, he wrote, "I am sorry to learn that you are so anxious & uneasy about pressing events." He tried a different approach, urging acceptance in the spirit of Bishop Wilson. "We cannot change or hinder" events, "& it is not the part of wisdom to be annoyed by them. In this time of great suffering to the state & country our private distresses we must bear with resignation like Christians & not aggravate them by repining, trusting to a kind & merciful God to overrule them for our good." By then Mary had retreated west to Kinloch, the home of cousins in Fauquier County. "I hope you may secure a safe & quiet retreat & make yourself contented with our lot," he wrote, "which I feel as well as yourself, & which with my other anxieties press heavily upon me." In truth, other anxieties prevented him from giving her much support. Agnes and Rob were in Richmond, and, he admonished her, "You must all endeavour to take care of yourselves, do what is needful & necessary & not care whether it is agreeable."[12] They were all on their own.

Mary was already striving to resign herself. The same day that Robert wrote, she declared to Mildred, "We look to God alone for help in the troubles which environ us. He seems so far to have protected us signally." As proof, she cited a skirmish in Fairfax County that had gone well for the Virginians, just as other Southerners, at that same moment, perceived God's blessing their cause in a clash near Hampton Roads. They all came to the same conclusion: that only through God could the South triumph, but, by God, it could. On her thirtieth wedding anniversary, Mary professed to Agnes, "We should all unite night & day in the most earnest cries to the Almighty to bless our cause. We are the weaker & it is only by his help that we can prevail. It is fearful to think of the overwhelming force arrayed against us but if God be on our side we will not we will not [*sic*] fear. He has promised to protect the weak & bring down the pride of the oppressor."[13]

Mary's hopes remained unrealistically high. She repeated rumors to Agnes of a coup against the government in Washington that of course were false. A month later, after their army had done so well at the First Battle of Manassas, she dared to hope that they "may possibly get to Arlington sooner than we expect." The "hand of God has been so <u>manifest</u>" in that victory, she exulted. "Shall we not unceasingly pray that he will guide us to the end & deliver us from our enemies." She then quickly reverted to the humility her husband advised. "May we never become vainglorious or think we are to conquer in our own thoughts." Lee took a more realistic view. Men had died in battle. More would. "Sorrow for those they left behind, friends, relatives & families," just as he had done when burying the children in the Texas prairie. "The former are at rest. The latter must suffer. The battle will be repeated there in greater force." Still, he rejoiced with her in the victory. "I hope God will again smile on us & strengthen our hearts & arms."[14]

Faith in the Time of War

The Lees' early wartime letters revealed the theological themes that guided them throughout the conflict, consistent with what they had already come to understand. As the war progressed, their beliefs became the more intense as they were tested under dreadful conditions.

Above all was the "Great God who rideth in the heavens," as Lee described to Agnes in 1863 from Orange County. God's goodness can be seen first in creation. "What a beautiful world God in his loving kindness to his creatures has given us," he marveled to Mary that summer, "notwithstanding the ravages of war" in which mortals "mar his gifts." Nothing can erase or eclipse the benevolence of God, who created nature for human welfare even in wartime. Complaining of a lack of fruit in the summer of 1864, he wrote Mary, "The drought & heat still continues & the dust is almost intolerable to man & beast. But God will send us a sweet rain in time, to refresh us & save the vegetables, corn, &c."[15]

The Lees perceived God's benevolence for mortals, both generally and personally. Mary's prayers for the country acknowledged the supreme Governor, who, as her ancestor George Washington had believed, guided nations along the course of history. They also trusted in God to care no less for individuals. Lee encouraged Agnes to pray to the God who creates all things "to give us strength & courage to do the work he has set before us, & to him be all the praise!" They were each reiterating the dual concept of general and particular providence in a God from whom all blessings flow. Thus in 1862 Lee told Annie and Agnes, "I heartily join you in sincere gratitude to Almighty God for gra[n]ting such success as he has seen fit to our arms, and pray and trust that his blessings and favor may be continued until an honorable peace is accomplished, and the whole country instead of being joined in struggle with each other should be united in praise & serving him." But Lee himself did not write the letter; Custis did it for him, for he had hurt his hand in a riding accident. Still, in God's providence, all worked for good. "You are right in supposing the great inconvenience I suffer in being disabled in both hands. It has been a great affliction and hindrance to me. But when I think of how much others have suffered, and how I and mine have been preserved amid the terrible dangers which have surrounded us, I am filled with thankfulness to the Gracious Giver of all Good for his mercies, and try to express my gratitude in adoration. You must help me with your pure prayers, and on your part do all that is becoming and proper." For Lee, the Almighty was the source of all hope. After Gettysburg, he shared with Mary his prayer "that our merciful father in heaven may grant us yet, the days he has allotted us on earth, much health & peace."[16]

Not all his hopes were realized, though, so Lee had to apply his providential convictions to the setbacks his army endured. After Union forces under George Meade escaped a trap Lee had set for them at Mine Run in Orange County, he jotted, "I am greatly disappointed at his getting off with so little damage, but we do not know what is best for us, & I believe a kind God has ordered all things for our good." But when things went well, he declared his thanks. In April 1864, a week before the bloody Wilderness campaign, he wrote, "I have been very grateful for the victories our merciful Father has given us. I pray they may continue!"[17]

Continued success, though, depended upon a force greater than Southern arms. As much as anyone, Lee knew the disadvantages the South faced in fighting the North. The "enemy" had more men, more money, more munitions, and more factories to make whatever they needed. The South had only God, or so Lee believed; he told Agnes that she "must pray to the great God . . . to give us strength & courage to do the work he has set before us."[18] He expressed the old colonial Virginian conviction that providence will bless God's people when they cooperate with the divine will, and punish them when they do not. As his father had put it, God rewards virtue and punishes vice.

This placed a burden on all Southerners devoted to the cause (though Northerners felt it too). A righteous cause demanded righteous soldiers in its service. One of Stonewall Jackson's chaplains warned that "pride and resentment, ambition and animosity" might well undermine the efficacy of prayers. This truth applied not only to fighting men but also to civilians. Providence required them to live up to their faith, to act in godly ways in order to be worthy of godly grace. Lee said as much to his family even before the war. He desired Mildred to live productively, enjoy doing good, win respect, and make "some amends to her Creator."[19] Lee stopped short of claiming that she, or anyone, could *earn* divine favor; that would fall into the ancient Pelagian heresy that human actions can merit God's grace. It was a tenet rejected by Augustine, by Protestants in the Reformation, and by Virginians under Bishop Meade. But during the war, Lee came close to it. He was not alone in showing touches of Arminianism, the seventeenth-century concept that had influenced his Anglican forebears; one could rely on God's grace while also cooperating with the grace that God offered. By Lee's day Arminianism had taken root in American Protestantism, thanks largely to the Methodists. Following John Wesley's lead, Arminians preached that God freely provided his "prevenient grace" to mortals that allowed them to choose God's salvation, and then, with the help of the Holy Spirit, to pursue "perfection," defined as freedom from willful sin. As the fastest-growing denomination in the country, Methodism influenced prewar Protestantism so broadly that even some Presbyterians strayed from Calvinism to adopt elements of its theology.[20]

Lee drew a corollary to the popular notion that one could willingly seek sinlessness: that a person, or a people, could choose *not* to try—and thus face dire consequences. He lamented to Annie in March 1862 that "it is plain we have not suffered enough, labored enough, repented enough, to deserve success."

> I trust that a merciful God will arouse us to a sense of our danger, bless our honest efforts, & drive back our enemies to their homes. Our people have not been earnest enough, have thought too much of themselves & their ease, & instead of turning out to a man, have been content to nurse themselves & their dimes, & leave the protection of themselves & families to others. To satisfy their consciences, they have been clamorous in criticising what others have done, & endeavoured to prove that they ought to do nothing. This is no way to accomplish our independence.[21]

In 1857 Robert had reminded Mary that "Providence requires us to use the means he has put under our control."[22] In 1862 he warned that through idleness, complacency, and faultfinding, Southerners were not acting to deserve God's favor. They were not cooperating with God.

After Gettysburg, Lee proclaimed as much to his army. President Davis had set aside August 21, 1863, "as a day of humiliation, fasting and prayer." Lee wanted a "Strict observance" of the day, suspended all but the most necessary military operations, and asked his men to conduct "divine services suitable to the occasion." He then exhorted his troops, "Soldiers! We have sinned Against Almighty God, We have forgotten His signal Mercies and have Cultivated a vengeful, haughty and boastful spirit. We have not remembered that the defenders of a just cause should be pure in his eyes; that our lives are in His hand and we have relied too much on our own arms for the achievement of our independence." His whole army was failing to do its part. It was not meriting God's favor. Lee did not allege that their willful sinfulness cost them victory at Gettysburg, but implied that, to win again, they must mend their lives in ways more than military alone. "God is our only refuge and our strength. Let us humble ourselves before Him. Let us confess our many sins and beseech Him to give us a higher Courage, a purer patriotism and more determined will that He will convert the hearts of our enemies; that He will hasten the time when war with its sorrows and sufferings shall cease, and that He will give us a name and place among the Nations of the earth."[23] Lee had criticized Puritans of colonial New England for not extending to others the religious liberty that they themselves enjoyed. But no New England preacher could have issued a more powerful jeremiad to warn his people of their collective responsibility before a providential God. Lee was no more defeatist than the Puritans who proclaimed that God disciplined those he loved, and God's chastisement evidenced in setbacks signified not divine desertion but rather divine concern. God would not abandon the South, so long as Southerners did not abandon their cause but instead lived in a manner worthy of it.[24]

When the appointed fast day came, all normal military activities ceased in Lee's army, then camped near Orange, Virginia. Just before noon, every unit that could find a chaplain or clergyman held a service. Captain Benjamin W. Justice of North Carolina went to one in town. He found St. Thomas Episcopal Church filled to capacity, with William Nelson Pendleton, by then Lee's commander of artillery, in the pulpit. "His text was the familiar passage from James; 'The effectual fervent prayer of the righteous availeth much' [5:16]. He in pointing out of national and individual sins was searching, eloquent, and just."[25]

The year before, a revival had swept the Confederate forces. This "day of humiliation" prompted a resurgence of fervor in Lee's army in what became the "Great Revival" of 1863-1864. Along with widespread religious interest and personal conversion—a tenth or more of Lee's forces made public confessions of faith—the revival conveyed, as Lee did, the conviction that soldiers had to observe divine commandments and be worthy to receive divine favor. Newspapers and even state legislatures repeated the same idea. On November 17, 1863, Georgia's general assembly passed a measure urging its people "to humble themselves before God, and with penitence for our past sins, national, social, and individual; and with an honest, earnest desire to obey His laws; implore through the merits of our Saviour, His forgiveness, and plead for wisdom to guide us."[26]

Lee endorsed the revival and would occasionally appear at its gatherings, to his men's gratification. He had long supported religious activity in his army and the chaplains who led it. As early as 1861, he had ordered enlisted men to attend Sabbath services "not only as a moral and religious duty"—even in wartime, one must keep God's commandments—but also for "the personal health and well-being of the troops." When chaplains found that some officers scheduled drills at the same time services were held, they complained to Lee, who said nothing at the time but later quietly resolved their concerns. He encouraged religious practices whenever possible, but limited them if military necessity precluded it, and on that basis he delicately declined an ardently Confederate rabbi's request for Jewish soldiers to take leave for high holy days.[27]

Lee followed his own principle whenever he could. When the war began, he attended Virginia's diocesan convention, at which Bishop Meade, in a "most impressive" sermon, meditated on his fifty years of ministry and on the South's situation, which the bishop had come to support fully. During the revival of the winter and spring of 1863–1864, he often attended St. Thomas Church in Orange, two miles from his headquarters along the Rapidan. Sometimes he brought others, such as A. P. Hill, Jeb Stuart, and even Jefferson Davis; his presence served as a magnet for his men. Captain Justice came to St. Thomas on November 22, 1863, specifically to see Lee and Davis. The president, he wrote his wife, "reminds one so forcibly of a postage stamp as to excite a smile." Lee, by contrast, was dressed in "a very plain uniform," and seemed "burly & 'beefy' & fat." Justice sat close enough "to see that a bunch of coarse, bristly black hair grows seemin[g]ly out of the orifice of each ear."[28]

Lee asked no more of others than he demanded of himself. What he asked of himself was great, perhaps greater than any mortal could attain. Early in the war, he told Annie, "I have been doing all that I can, with our small means & slow workmen, to defend the cities & coast here" in Savannah. Yet, striving as always to set an example, he did not hold himself up as a paragon. After all, modesty, in his father's tradition, was a virtue; and the humility enjoined in his mother's evangelicalism never left "sinful Robert." When one friend paid him a compliment, he responded, "While I know that the sentiments you express towards me are dictated alone by your kindness & charity of heart, aware how little they are merited, I feel humbled in reading them." He ascribed his successes to God: "For your prayers I am truly grateful, for in God alone do I look for a happy issue out of all our . . . troubles, & trust that out of the calamity of war which he has seen fit to visit upon us, he will bring great good." He made the same point to Mary. "I tremble for my country when I hear of confidence expressed in me. I know too well my weakness & that our only trust is in God." More fitting than praise of him was prayer to God. "My trust is in our Heavenly Father to whom my supplications continually ascend for you, my children & my country! I know if uttered in faith & truth they will be heard, & oh I pray they may be answered."[29]

Lee expected equal commitment from his family, constantly exhorting them to prayer and to behavior fitting their cause. When Lee heard that Daughter, Mary Custis, had visited Manassas a month before the first battle there, he pointedly asked her why she went—"for some good object I trust." He did not want her gallivanting around a country in crisis. "In times like these, the advancement of some praiseworthy object should be our only claim," he opined. "The practice of self denial & self sacrifice even was never more urgently demanded."[30] He had similarly advised cadets at West Point. Now the very cause for which he fought depended upon it. When Mildred pondered what she should do as she turned seventeen, he exclaimed to Mary, "I suppose she thinks she ought to do what is most agreeable to her present feelings as every body else does. I cannot concur with her! If she was <u>usefully</u> employed, I would not care how. But a life of idleness in times like these is sinful."[31]

Indeed, Lee insisted, the entire South must learn to sacrifice. Early in the war, while inspecting fortifications in Savannah, he heard discouraging news from Tennessee and Kentucky. "I hope God will at last crown our efforts with success," he told Mary. "But the contest must be long & severe, & the whole country has to go through much suffering. It is necessary we should be humbled & taught to be less boastful, less selfish, & more devoted to right & justice to all the world." It was a point many a Southern preacher was making, with limited success.[32]

Lee knew the South's weaknesses. But the God who gave David victory over Goliath could cause the Confederacy to prevail.[33] For God to be on their side, all of them—Lee, Mary, his children, the entire South—must uphold their end of the bargain with God.

The God of Battle

Lee adopted a virtual Old Testament perspective, by which God's specific providence gave or denied victory to armies and nations. He never quoted the Hebrew Scriptures in that regard, nor considered the Confederacy a new Israel. Still, as he assessed the region's strengths and weaknesses, he believed that the Confederacy could prevail only if God willed it. "I pray that our merciful father in heaven may protect & direct us," he wrote Mary as the rival armies maneuvered outside Fredericksburg in 1863. "In that case I fear no odds & no numbers." When uncertainty hung over the outcome at Vicksburg, he added, "May God bless us with a victory there too!"[34]

In the letter that implored God's help at Fredericksburg, Lee begged divine grace for Mary's health, "for which I shall be fervently thankful to our Heavenly Father." He prayed to a God whom he considered just as intimately involved with military maneuvers as with his family. "The enemy seems steadily to advance & apparently with his whole army," he noted in 1862. "I pray that the God of battle may be with us!" Days later, he was more specific. Not knowing what "the enemy" would do next, Lee admitted, "I pray God that he will confuse their counsels & return them to their own country. Our only trust & safety is in him."[35]

When his army succeeded, Lee credited God. In the Seven Days campaign of June 1862, when his troops drove the Yankees away from Richmond, Lee was "filled with gratitude to our heavenly father for all the mercies he has extended to us." The victory could have been more total, he knew; but he remained, if not philosophical, then theological. "Our success has not been as great or complete as I could have desired; but God knows what is best for us."[36]

Unlike many in the Confederacy, Lee did not blame military defeats upon specifically sinful behavior. In this he resembled Lincoln, who believed that the struggle "depended on Divine interposition and favor." General attitudes, the sort he bemoaned on Davis's fast day: these more than playing cards or cursing would discourage God's blessing.[37]

Lee hoped that God would look after the innocents caught in the maelstrom of war. After watching Fredericksburg's women and children evacuate the town to avoid Federal bombardment, he wrote Mary, "It was a piteous sight. But they have brave hearts. What is to become of them God only knows. I pray he may have mercy on them." When the enemy refused to show mercy, he invoked a different side of God. In 1864, hearing of the "havoc & devastation" that Federal troops wrought on women and children in the Middle Peninsula, Lee called for human resignation and divine retribution: "We must make up our minds to bear it all, until a Just & merciful God avenges us."[38]

Dealing with Death

A just God had plenty to avenge, if the Almighty were so inclined. Along with the suffering of civilians, Lee contended with the sickness and death of many friends and thousands of his troops. The loss of Arlington and the separation of his family weighed upon him. His son Fitzhugh, as he had come to call Rooney, had been captured. His daughter Annie had died. Amidst these burdens, he reminded Mary not to "repine at the will of God. It will eventuate in some good that we know not of now."[39]

Lee had always accepted the Protestant idea of inherent human evil. War caused him to perceive it intensely in "the enemy." Early in the war, when Lee was campaigning in what is now West Virginia with Fitzhugh and Colonel John A. Washington, Union snipers killed Washington and wounded Fitzhugh's horse. Lee wrote in fury, "Our enemy's have stamped their attack upon our rights, with additional infamy, by killing the lineal descendant and representative of him who under the guidance of Almighty God established them & by his virtues rendered our Republic immortal." He was even more infuriated by Yankee mistreatment of Middle Peninsula civilians in 1864. "That is their delight. It is a safe pleasure too to frighten & distress women & children, which is much to their taste."[40]

After the First Battle of Manassas, Lee cautioned Mary not to gloat over Confederate victories, but to remember the cost in lives, and to mourn not so much for the dead but to sorrow for those who loved them. This became a constant theme in his letters. "I grieve over our noble dead!" he exclaimed to Carter in 1863. He acutely felt the loss of those he knew personally. "I do not know how I can replace the gallant Pelham," he continued, praising the brilliant twenty-four-year-old artillery commander killed at Kelly's Ford. "So young so true so brave." But nearly always he placed death into the context either of duty well done or the will of providence: "Though stricken down in the dawn of manhood," he wrote of John Pelham, "his is the glory of duty done!"[41] He commiserated with a friend whose relative, a general, had been killed. "May God in his mercy mitigate [his wife's] sufferings!" he wrote. As for the friend, "he has the consolation of knowing that what is done by our Heavenly father, is done for our good, that his noble brother died the death of the patriot soldier, & is now at rest."[42]

Both the hope of eternity and the virtue of duty done mitigated, for Lee, the reality of death. It may suggest too how he bore the responsibility of ordering thousands of men into battles that resulted in so many deaths; indeed, Lee's army suffered astonishing casualties, perhaps three-quarters of his infantry. Such was God's providential will; as a South Carolina preacher declared, "not one of these brave men has fallen without His permission."[43] That may have been small consolation for the grieving, but it was some.

For Lee, as for Jeremy Taylor, death was inevitable, but heaven—and apparently not hell—awaited; the key was how one prepared throughout life for that event. Whether death came as a result of a summer virus on the frontier or a bullet in battle was of less consequence; providence dictated it, so one should animate oneself for whatever God willed, whenever that might be. If a soldier's death came honorably on the field of battle, he died doing his duty according to the will of God. Hosts of soldiers, especially those touched by the revival, adopted a similar perspective. With even greater bravery, they marched into battle ready to die. Many a soldier was convinced that "he was assisting at his own funeral."[44]

Lee, then, did not pity men who died in battle nearly so much as he lamented for their survivors. They faced the grief of loss and the difficulties that loss produced. They were the ones who suffered the sting of death.

Lee's response to the death of Stonewall Jackson reflected that sensibility. When notified of Jackson's severe injuries after the stunning Confederate victory at Chancellorsville, he refused to listen; "it is too painful a subject." On learning that doctors amputated Jackson's arm, he declared, "He has lost his left arm, but I have lost my right arm." Then, when Jackson died, he was more philosophical. "In addition to the death of friends & officers consequent upon the late battles, you will see we have to mourn the loss of the good & great Jackson. Any victory would be dear at such a price," he admitted to Mary. "I know not how to replace him. But God's will be done! I trust he will raise some one in his place."[45] Lee concerned himself more about the future of his military than about the future of Jackson's soul.

Lee showed even greater sorrow at the death of the young cousin he called "Hilly" Carter. "I can well imagine the grief at Shirly upon the arrival of the lifeless body of its gallant Son. He was a noble youth, as faithful to his God as to his country. Would that we had a thousand like him! But his Father in Heaven has taken him to himself. I know it was done in mercy & kindness to him & we should rejoice. . . . Still the pang of parting is bitter, & the loss of such a one to the country is great."[46]

The closer the person, the greater the grief. Fitzhugh's family seemed especially hard hit: first his son's death, then his own capture, finally the death of his wife, Charlotte Wickham. "God knows how I loved your dear dear wife," Lee wrote his son, "how sweet her memory is to me, & how I mourn her loss," a loss as great as if she were his daughter. "But my grief is not for her, but for ourselves. She is brighter & happier than ever, safe from all evil & awaiting us in her Heavenly abode. May God in his mercy make us to join her in eternal praise to our Lord & Saviour. Let us humbly bow ourselves before Him, & offer perpetual prayers for pardon & forgiveness!" But personal grief, however acute, must not distract from the ever-present challenge of duty. "We cannot indulge in grief however mournful yet pleasing," he went on. "Our country demands all our thoughts, all our energies. To resist the powerful combination now forming against us, will require every man at his place. If victorious we have everything to hope for in the future. If defeated nothing will be left us to live for." He was advising Fitzhugh to return to work. Duty demanded it, and he probably needed it. "We have no time to wait & you had better join your brigade. This week will in all probability bring us active work, & we must strike fast & strong." Lee's closing, though, struck a note of uncertainty. "My whole trust is in God, & I am ready for whatever he may ordain. May he guide, guard & strengthen us is my constant prayer."[47] What might God be ordaining?

When Annie died, two years earlier, Lee could hardly be consoled. In May 1862, Mary, Annie, and Mildred had been held captive near Fitzhugh's farm, the White House, which the Yankees burned. After Lee arranged with General George McClellan for their release, Annie, Agnes, Mildred, and Charlotte with her son Robert found refuge at a resort in Jones Springs, North Carolina, northeast of Raleigh. A month later, young Robert died. Then in October, Annie took ill. Mary rushed to join Agnes to care for her. When Daughter offered to come to help, Mary declined, but acknowledged Annie's poor condition. "She is in the hands of God who will do all things well for her." Annie, as she failed, never spoke of death, which Agnes decided was "conclusive proof that a deathbed is not the time to prepare for Heaven." One Sunday, the Lord's Day, Annie asked for a hymnbook—Mary thought her hand fell on a hymn entitled "In extremity"—but slept most of the day, as Agnes kept vigil. "Presently she said 'Lay me down, lay me down,'" Agnes recalled, "& afterwards 'I am ready to rise' which I feel now referred to what was to come." The Lees' second daughter died about seven the next morning.[48]

"My darling Annie[,] I never had expected to weave a funeral wreath for her," Mary wrote Daughter. In his grief, Lee responded in his customary way.

I cannot express my dear Mary the anguish I feel at the death of our sweet Annie. To know that I shall never see her again on earth, that her place in our circle which I always hope one day to rejoin is forever vacant, is agonizing in the extreme. But God in this as in all things has mingled mercy with the blow in selecting that one best prepared to leave us. He has taken the purest & best. May you be able to join me in saying His will be done! When I reflect on all she will escape in life, brief & painful at the best, & all we may hope she will enjoy with her sainted Gr[an]dmother, I cannot wish her back. I know how much you will grieve & how much she will be mourned by Agnes & the rest, & wish I could give you & them any comfort. But beyond our hope in the great mercy of God, & the belief that he takes us at the time & place when it is best for us to go, there is none. May that same mercy be extended to us all & may we be prepared for his summons![49]

Lee ascribed Annie's death to God's will. But there was one difference. Unlike his reaction to the boys' deaths in Texas, he made no mention of divine admonishment. He drew no lesson for the living, except to "be prepared" for God's "summons."

Annie's coffin, covered with flowers by kind neighbors, was interred in Warren County. Right after the war, Confederate veterans placed an obelisk at her tomb, and there her father and Agnes laid white hyacinths when they visited it on March 29, 1870.[50] In 1994, Annie's remains were reinterred in the family crypt beneath the chapel that Lee had built in Lexington at the school he served as president.

As Hope Faded

On July 12, 1863, Lee wrote Mary from Hagerstown, Maryland, a burdened man. His army was retreating from its defeat at Gettysburg. His last chance for military triumph on Northern soil, enough to turn Northern opinion against the war and coax out a negotiated peace, had failed. A week before the battle, Fitzhugh had been captured in Virginia by Federal troops. "We must expect to endure every injury that our enemies can inflict upon us & be resigned to it. Their conduct is not dictated by kindness or love, & therefore we should not expect them to behave otherwise than they do. But I do not think that we should follow their example. The consequences of war is horrid enough at best, surrounded by all the amelioration of civilization & Christianity. Why should we aggravate them?"[51]

Lee's view of Gettysburg was remarkably sanguine. Having advised Jefferson Davis that, "though reduced in numbers," the army's "condition is good and its confidence unimpaired," he conceded to Mary that "our success . . . was not as great as reported." He had expected to defeat the Yankees, "but God in His all wise Providence willed otherwise." He added, "I trust that our merciful God, our only help & refuge, will not desert us in this our hour of need, but will deliver us by his almighty hand" and show forth his glory.[52]

Lee still went to church when he could. In the spring of 1864, he made his way to St. Paul's, Richmond, hoping to find Mary present; she was not, but he heard a "very good sermon on the subject of the forgiveness of our enemies. It is a hard lesson to learn now," he allowed, "but still it is true & requires corresponding efforts." During the siege of Petersburg, he often attended St. Paul's Church there, coming to know its rector, the Reverend William Platt.[53]

The war was not kind to churches. A priest from Culpeper told Lee that "there is not a church standing in all that country" that the "enemy" controlled. "All are razed to the ground & the materials used often for the vilest purposes," even—Meade would have rolled over in his grave— pews transformed into seating for a "theatre."[54]

God seemed increasingly unwilling to grant the South victory. By 1863, the dark possibility of defeat dimmed a letter Lee wrote to Carter bemoaning the imminent loss of Charleston. "When it falls it will be heavy, but if we do our duty I trust we shall not be crushed; 'through God we shall do great acts; & it is He that shall tread down our enemies.'" The city did not fall until Sherman took it from the rear. Still, the Confederacy was treading down its enemies less and less. "It is evident that great danger is impending over us," he confided in mid-1864, but "I trust & believe he [God] will save us in his own good time."[55]

In the midst of war, personal joys still brightened his life. On his wedding anniversary in 1864, he asked Mary, "Do you recollect what a happy day thirty three years ago this was—How many hopes & pleasures it gave birth to? God has been very merciful and kind to us," despite Lee's thankless and sinful ways. He looked for "a little peace & rest together in this world & finally gather us & all he has given us around his throne in the world to come!"[56]

By the summer of 1864, Lee had been forced into fortifications around Petersburg. He knew he could not hold out much longer. News from the south and west was hardly better. On February 21, 1865, Lee informed his wife, then living in Richmond, "Sherman & Schofield are both advancing & seem to have every thing their own way, but trusting in a merciful God, who does not always give the battle to the strong, I pray we may not be overwhelmed." He alluded to the same passage from Ecclesiastes that he had cited before leaving for the Mexican War. This time, the odds were different, and his was definitely the weaker side. Yet, he wrote, "I shall . . . endeavour to do my duty & fight to the last." He had not lost heart, but did ask how she would cope if his army had to evacuate the city. "It is a fearful condition & we must rely for guidance & protection upon a kind providence. May it guard & comfort you." God's protection would be all the more imperative, he warned, if the city where she was living fell to the invader.[57]

Lee refused to give up. Providence, as he understood it, required him to hope, even as defeats increased. If with God all things are possible, if God chastens those he loves, if David has one last stone to fling at Goliath, then the chance always remained that the South could prevail. Lee had maintained from the first that victory could only come if God willed it. As long as they were not totally vanquished, as Washington had realized in the darkest days of the Revolution, he could hope.[58]

In the final months before Appomattox, Lee's letters become more terse, less frequent, and increasingly devoid of allusions to anything but the most pressing matters. Fearing that Agnes might get caught in the midst of battle, he warned her against trying to visit him, as much as he desired it; but, oddly, he offered none of his usual benedictions and invocations.

On Sunday, April 2, Jefferson Davis sat in his customary pew at St. Paul's Church in Richmond. Shortly after Minnigerode began his sermon, a sexton handed the president a telegram. Lee had written, "I think it will be necessary to move tonight." Davis quietly departed, soon followed by other officials and officers and then, despite the rector's pleas, the whole congregation.[59] Grant's troops had defeated Lee's army at Five Forks. Lee could hold the lines no longer. Richmond had to be abandoned. David had flung his final stone, and missed his target. Goliath lived.

Nearly a half-century later, Kate Pleasants, then an eight-year-old sitting with her mother in a pew at St. Paul's, recalled Davis's quick departure. "I can see him now—tall, gaunt, ashy pale[,] composed as a man would be who had nerved himself to die, and with his gray shawl over his shoulders he walked out of the Church into what he knew was the end of all his hopes."[60]

It marked the end of Lee's hopes as well. His army struggled to Appomattox. Lee faced few options, all of them so dire that death held its attractions. Lee reportedly told an aide "how easily I could get rid of all this and be at rest. I have only to ride along the lines and all will be over." He sighed. "But it is our duty to live. What will become of the women and children of the South, if we are not here to protect them?" Then, when Grant wrote suggesting that he surrender, one of his generals, Edward Porter Alexander, approached Lee with the basic idea of waging guerrilla warfare. "We would scatter like rabbits & partridges in the woods, & [Yankee forces] could not scatter so to catch us." Lee patiently explained the notion to be physically unworkable and practically unrealistic: "We have now simply to look the fact in the face that the Confederacy has failed." It was also morally impeachable. "As Christian men, Gen. Alexander, you & I have no right to think for one moment of our personal feelings or affairs. We must consider only the effect which our actions will have upon the country at large." Those consequences, he feared, would include "lawless bands" evoking harsh reprisals, all ensuring "fresh rapine & destruction." However, "if the men can be quietly & quickly returned to their homes there is time to plant crops & begin to repair the ravages of the war. That is what I must now try to bring about."[61]

With that, Lee surrendered, on gracious terms offered by Grant. Confederate soldiers could return home with their sidearms, baggage, and horses to start plowing their fields once again. They went with Lee's blessing for "the satisfaction that proceeds from the consciousness of duty faithfully performed" and his prayers to "a merciful God."[62] For Lee, on the battered horizon, a new purpose appeared. It was Palm Sunday.

As he rode back to Richmond, he faced endless uncertainties. What would he find in the capital? How fared his family? What would they do? He had a parole in his pocket, but would the government respect it? Would he be hanged for treason? What happens to David after Goliath has won? Or, even more deeply, was David truly the beloved of God?

If nothing else, Lee retained the love of his troops, and the respect even of his erstwhile foe. Grant had doffed his cap to honor him. Years later, a Virginian in the ranks recalled a conversation among Confederate soldiers. The idea of Darwinism had begun to excite controversy about human evolution from apes. One of the group ended the conversation: "Well, boys, the rest of us may be descended from monkeys, but one thing I am sure of: the Lord made 'Marse Robert.'"[63]

CHAPTER 18

"In the Bond of Peace, and in Righteousness of Life"

~

Lee's Second Great Decision

Lee straggled glumly from Appomattox to a Richmond in ruins. Block upon ravaged block in the business district, blackened hulks of once-thriving warehouses, factories, banks and offices, all gave horrific evidence of Virginia's devastation. Lee knew, too, that the fire was his own side's doing. Retreating Confederate soldiers had set it to keep supplies from Union hands. Like so many aspects of the war, it burst way out of control, destroying vastly more than anyone ever expected. Yet, the capitol and the steeple of St. Paul's Episcopal Church still dominated the hilltop above the desolation, offering perhaps the only glimmer of hope in a future beset with seemingly limitless problems.

When Lee surrendered, he and his army became prisoners of the Union. But General Ulysses Grant paroled them all, allowing the defeated soldiers to go home. That included Lee, who returned unmolested to Richmond. He rejoined his wife at their borrowed home at 707 East Franklin Street near St. Paul's, their refuge as the borrowed house on Oronoco Street near Christ Church had been for his mother after storms of her own. Not that they had much peace; the family posted doorkeepers to guarantee them some privacy from well-wishers. Only at night did Lee feel comfortable walking outdoors to get some exercise.[1]

That Richmonders relied on Federal supplies to survive only deepened the mortification of their defeat. Since pride filled Lee stomachs no more than anyone else's, the Confederacy's most famous general joined the ration line. One day, when he did, he encountered a friend, the Union general who oversaw the city's provisions. Marsena Patrick, the Federal provost marshal, had developed a mutual esteem with "Bob Lee" from their soldiering together in Mexico and Florida. The two gen-

197

erals clasped hands and chatted for an hour or more. Lee reportedly told him, "Patrick, the only question on which we ever differed, has been settled, and the Lord has decided against me."[2]

The story may not be true. Patrick's son recalled his father telling it, but his father's journal does not quote Lee directly. However, Lee expressed a strikingly similar sentiment to a priest friend at about the same time he would have spoken to Patrick. "God has thought fit to afflict us most deeply & his chastening hand is not yet stayed," he wrote to William Platt, whose church he attended during the siege of Petersburg. "How great must be our sins & how unrelenting our obduracy." What those sins were, and what sins he may have abetted or committed, Lee did not specify. But he did draw a conclusion: "We have only to submit to his gracious will & pray for his healing mercy." That homiletic point demanded an immediate application. "Now that the South is willing to have peace, I hope it may be accorded on a permanent basis; that the afflictions & interests of the country may be united and not a forced & hollow truce formed, to be broken at the first convenient opportunity. To this end all good men should labour."[3]

Both comments show all the marks of Lee's providential theology. He responded to defeat precisely as he reacted to other reverses in life, whether the death of a soldier's child in Texas, a battlefield victory not fully realized, Mary's woes, or Annie's death: things happen according to the will of an all-knowing, all-powerful God. Mortals must not repine but instead resign themselves by learning from setbacks and actively striving to do better in a manner consistent with what appears to be divine will. Such is one's duty and, indeed, one's responsibility to God. Yet to Platt he adds an astonishing admission, that God's "chastening hand" had been set against the South for "our sins" and "unrelenting . . . obduracy." The South had not only failed to merit the grace of God, it had actively offended the Almighty, who, out of divine justice, "afflict[s] us most deeply"—and, it would seem, deservedly.[4]

In that sense, Lee's perspective agreed with Lincoln's in his second inaugural address. Both sides had read from the same Bible, prayed to the same God, and "invoked His aid against the other." Both stood before an Almighty who "has His own purposes." And while "that of neither ha[d] been answered fully," those of the South were answered far less than those of the North.[5] Yet, as Lincoln avoided triumphalism, Lee avoided despair: the prayers of neither had been *denied* fully. Some modicum of hope abided. Such also was providence.

What, then, does one do? Lee, like "all good men," had an enormous "labour" ahead. His attitude allowed him to adjust to the South's loss to a degree that many of his fellow soldiers, and even his wife, could not. It also explains why he came to Washington College to promote rebuilding and reconciliation. In so doing, the defeated leader of war became a leader in promoting peace.

It was a daunting prospect. Many a Southerner could not even conceive of defeat. Mary Lee refused to believe it. On hearing the news from Appomattox, she reportedly declared, "General Lee is not the Confederacy, there is life in the old land yet." Days later, her son Custis arrived to correct her. Already, Lee had disabused President Davis's fantasy that "partisan war" by guerrillas would do anything more than devastate the country. "To save useless effusion of blood," he had urged "suspension of hostilities and the restoration of peace."[6] Lee knew the South had lost and needed to accept its collapse.

It had lost more than the war; it had also lost two-thirds of the assessed value of its wealth, two-fifths of its livestock, half of its farm machinery. Most devastating of all, a quarter of the Southern white male population of military age had died.[7]

A spiritual crisis inevitably gripped many in the South. Had not God been on their side? Three days after Lee's surrender, George Richard Browder, a Kentucky Methodist circuit rider and Southern sympathizer, exclaimed in his diary, "Rain! wind! thunder! What a storm last night! . . . Cousin Rose says the Heavens are weeping over Lee's surrender." Confederates who had pursued the war convinced of divine favor had to deal with the reality that, if God wills what happens in the world, they had been wrong. As the Confederate from Maryland had written his mother, "I did not believe God would allow us to be crushed." In May, a leading Richmond Presbyterian minister, Moses Hoge, who had run the Union blockade to procure Bibles for Confederate soldiers, lamented only slightly more theologically: "God's dark providence enwraps me like a pall."[8]

Lee did not concur with Cousin Rose. He never saw the war as many did, North and South: a holy crusade mandated by God Almighty.[9] Yes, he understood that only by heaven's grace could the South win—or could the North. Yes, he looked for the help of God and sought to perceive the Lord's hand at work in his side's favor. From the day that he resigned his US Army commission, his perspective always left room for the possibility that he could be wrong: for him it was a corollary to the evangelical belief in human sinfulness—including his own. His reported comment to Patrick expressed his fundamental conviction. The Lord had decided. Because of that he could accept, though not like, the result. The South had lost. He could only bow, obey, and move on.

Even so, Lee could not escape the pall of what providence had evidently ordained. From late winter into the summer of 1865, his personal letters reflected a striking change in language. Before then, he usually concluded with a prayer for God's grace or an assurance of his intercessions for the recipient. After Appomattox—nothing. Except in letters of condolence, or to clergymen or Markie Williams, months pass before Lee even mentioned God in correspondence. It was as if he silently assimilated the magnitude of having pursued an effort contrary to God's will.

Of course, that spring the people with whom he most freely shared his convictions, Mary above all, were mostly present with him. For the first time in four years, they did not need letters to communicate their thoughts. His prayer to be reunited with his family had been granted, if not in the way Lee had in mind.

Whether or not he was uncertain of God, he was assuredly uncertain of worldly prospects. Lee stood accused of treason. Many a Northern voice called for his execution, and though Lincoln and Grant seemed to preclude reprisals, Lincoln was dead. He had no home of his own, no employment, and questionable resources. After a life of near-constant work, he had nothing to do. Nor did Custis. His other sons, Fitzhugh and Rob, each had a farm to tend, bequeathed by Mary's father. But Custis's inheritance, the Arlington estate, had become a Union cemetery, so by midsummer he was looking for a position at Virginia Military Institute. If he could not teach, he could help Fitzhugh farm.[10]

That, at least, was productive. Lee rejoiced in Fitzhugh's "good prospects for corn" and his "cheerful prospects of the future. God grant they may be realized, which I am sure they will be if you will unite sound judgement to your usual energy in your operations": by summer, Lee began to use religious language again, typically recommending striving actively to achieve what God desired. "We must be patient," he advised his son, and let matters "take their course." For himself, Lee craved "some humble but quiet abode for your mother & sisters, where I hope they can be happy," preferably in "some grass country where the natural product of the land will do much for my subsistence." Despite his age, health, and inexperience, he planned to be a farmer.[11]

One person with whom he shared his soul was Markie Williams.

Though ever a loyal Yankee, she never severed ties with her Lee cousins. Unlike Lee's sister Anne Marshall, who cut him cold once he sided with Virginia, Markie sent him a sympathetic note after Appomattox. "You must not be too much distressed," Lee responded. "We must be resigned to necessity, & commit ourselves in adversity to the will of a merciful God as cheerfully as in prosperity. All is done for our good & our faith must continue unshaken."[12]

Ever so slowly, Lee reverted to his familiar theological formulations. "We have much to be thankful for," he wrote Markie in June. Encouraging her to "make herself useful to others," he conceded that he could "do little but am resigned to what is ordered by our Merciful God, who will I know do all that is good for us."[13] But what might that be?

The Second Great Decision

The war was over. With the capture of Davis on May 10 and the surrender on May 26 in Texas of Edmund Kirby Smith and his forces, the Confederacy ceased to exist. But hatreds and even violence persisted. Lincoln's death on April 15, the day before Easter, the very day Lee returned to Richmond, fanned the fury. Many a Northerner called for blood, notably Lee's. Many a Southerner craved revenge against the occupying foe. Former Confederates had lost their civil rights. Some threatened to leave the country altogether.

As he began making his peace with God, Lee began seeking peace with the newly reunited nation. Through a general amnesty, President Andrew Johnson restored rights to all Confederates except those on a list that included generals and ranking civilians—Lee definitely among them—and these he permitted to apply to him for clemency, which would be "liberally extended." On June 7, Lee did just that, even though an indictment had already been issued against him for treason. He also notified Grant that he was "ready to meet any charges that may be preferred against me, and [did] not wish to avoid trial."[14] Whether his letter to Johnson was lost or ignored, it was not acted on until August 5, 1975, when President Gerald Ford made his pardon official.

To his son Custis, Lee explained that by submitting to authorities, he was setting an example for all former Confederates to follow. To John Letcher, the Virginia governor who offered him command of the state's military in 1861, he expounded on the "duty of its citizens" to return to their homes and strive to rebuild their states. "All should unite in honest efforts to obliterate the effects of the war and to restore the blessings of peace. They should remain, if possible, in the country; promote harmony and good feeling; qualify themselves to vote" and elect able state and federal legislators. "I have invariably recommended this course since the cessation of hostilities and have endeavoured to practise it myself."[15]

Some Confederates, from privates to generals, chose a different route. They went abroad. Brigadier General Edward Porter Alexander, still convinced in the "Lost Cause's" righteousness, signed up with the army of Brazil. Others considered an invitation to emigrate to the short-lived Empire of Mexico, an offer Matthew Fontaine Maury accepted. A naval officer and scientist, Maury was called "pathfinder of the seas" for his pioneering studies in oceanography; before the war, he headed the US Naval Observatory in Washington, DC. When Virginia seceded, Maury, like Lee, resigned his commission. He served Confederate missions on both sides of the Atlantic. The war's end found his family in England and Maury in Cuba. Since the general amnesty President Johnson extended did not apply to those overseas, the potential of arrest made returning to Virginia imprudent. Even Lee agreed with that. So Maury made his way to Mexico. Its new emperor, Maximilian, an Austrian archduke who had once awarded Maury a medal for his accomplishments, welcomed him with a gala ball. He hoped that such a distinguished former Confederate would entice other former Confederates to create a colony where they and their "domestics"—former slaves—would create farms in sparsely populated parts of the country. Maury set about the goal of attracting as many as two hundred thousand Southerners to Mexico. He also began building an observatory.[16]

Maury excitedly wrote Lee about this colony. Convinced that "our Republican form of Government" in the United States "is a proved failure," he committed himself to building "here in Mexico a good and stable Empire which . . . may serve both as a light and as a beacon to our noble old state." Maximilian "is most anxious to introduce the immigration" of Virginian whites, together with their "emancipated negros" who would serve as "apprentices" until they could learn the language and ways of Mexico. Maury called this "the only bright spot that I can see with the future of our people."[17]

Lee took a different view altogether. In early September he responded to Maury, concurring with Maury's rationale but disagreeing, gently but insistently, with Maury's position:

We have certainly not found our form of Gov't all that was anticipated by its original founders. But that may be partly our fault, in expecting too much, partly to the absence of virtue in the people. As long as virtue was dominant in the Republic, so long was the happiness of the people secure. I cannot however despair of it yet. I look forward to better days, & trust that time and experience, the great teachers of men, under the guidance of an ever merciful God, may save us from destruction, & restore us the bright hopes and prospects of the past. The thought of abandoning the country & all that must be left in it, is abhorrent to my feelings; & I prefer to struggle for its restoration, and share its fate, than to give up all as lost.

Lee then drew the inevitable conclusion.

To remove our people with their domestics, to a portion of Mexico which would be favourable to them, would be a work of much difficulty. Did they possess the means, & could the system of apprenticeship you suggest, be established, the U.S. Gov't I think would interpose obstacles; & under the circumstances there would be difficulty in persuading the freedmen to emigrate. The citizens who can leave the country, & others who may be compelled to do so, will reap the fruits of your considerate labour; but I shall be very sorry if your presence be lost to Virginia. She has now need for all her sons, and can ill afford to spare you.[18]

Word of Lee's position had already spread. One twenty-seven-year-old veteran pondered following Maury's example. As a soldier, he had believed that his officers, "even Jackson—are only men, but Lee plans like God." So when he heard that Lee disapproved of leaving the country, he gave up on the idea. Lee wrote to another, "I do not know how far their emigration to another land will conduce to their prosperity." Barring necessity, "it would be better for them and their country if they remained at their homes and shared the fate of their respective States."[19]

Lee was employing the reasoned words and ethical thinking he had used to explain why he resigned his commission in 1861. In 1865, he counseled reconciling with the very nation he had rejected. How could he reverse himself so completely? He explained to General P. G. T. Beauregard, then contemplating offers from the armies of Brazil, Romania, and Egypt:

> I need not tell you, that true patriotism requires of men sometimes, to act exactly contrary at one period, to that which it does at another; & that the motive which impels them, viz. the desire to do right, is precisely the same. The circumstances which govern their actions undergo change, & their conduct must conform to the new order of things. History is full of illustrations of this. Washington himself is an example, at one time he fought against the French, under Braddock, in the service of the King of Great Britain; at another he fought with the French at Yorktown . . . against him. He has not been branded by the world with reproach for this, but his course has been applauded.

"New occasions teach new duties," the poet James Russell Lowell had written to protest the Mexican War.[20] Lee, ever conscious of duty, made the same point.

The ethical considerations that underlay his letter to Beauregard reflected Kant's concept of duty that had been so important to Lee for so long. When duty calls, one must not worry about consequences. If he had to swallow his pride and repress his resentment, so be it. And if it were God's will that he stay and rebuild the South, then such was his duty.

Lee had already paid a colossal price for doing what he deemed to be his duty. Fighting for the South meant losing his wife's home and jeopardizing their not inconsiderable resources, not to mention the hundreds of thousands dead and wounded and a devastated state and region. He never doubted the rightness of that duty even as he willingly bore its consequences. "I am aware of having done nothing wrong & cannot flee." He declined to join Markie on a trip to Europe so as to "avoid no prosecution the Gov^t thinks proper to institute."[21] Still, though he had thought his cause was right, God dictated otherwise. Duty now called him to do something else.

Moreover, the *ethical* basis of his decision to side with the South made pursuing a way of peace less onerous for Lee than it did for those who fought the war thinking heaven was on their side. Lee had made a primarily intellectual choice, not a leap of faith based on what he determined the Lord God of Hosts demanded. His perspective differed from that of the more theologically minded E. P. Alexander, who, just weeks after the surrender, wrote of "our cause" that "my faith in its righteousness is not for one moment shaken—and I feel confident that the dispensation is from above and that the precious blood that has been shed so freely will surely work out some good end."[22] Lee agreed about the dispensation from above and the hope for "some good end." But the subtle but vital distinction in going to war because he thought that it was right, rather than because God demanded it, made shifting to peace somewhat easier.

But there was another element. If ethical considerations guided his decision of 1861, by 1865 Lee approached decisions in a profoundly different—a profoundly *theological*—way. He began to discern a divine call, and with it, a clearly religious dimension to his duty. His new perception combined the philosophical emphasis of his father with the evangelical dimension of his mother. Lee discovered a new purpose for his life. He discerned a mission.

Little did Maury realize that Lee was following for himself the very advice he was proffering. At that moment, Lee was preparing to assume a new duty that, he came to believe, emanated from God. As it happened, Maury eventually joined him.

A New Cause

Just when the Lees needed to get out of Richmond, an old family friend, Elizabeth R. P. Cocke, lent them her farm, "Derwent," near Cartersville on the border between Powhatan and Cumberland Counties. Lee described it to Rob as "a comfortable but small house in a grove of oaks," and to Fitzhugh as "small and excessively hot." His more anxious wife pined for a permanent home, but foresaw a future "so dark now, that we are almost tempted to think God has forsaken us."[23] They spent a quiet summer there, Lee visiting neighbors and contemplating writing his memoirs, Mary complaining. Agnes and Mildred stayed with their parents. The younger brothers worked to revive Fitzhugh's farm at White House before Rob attended to his own inheritance, Romancoke, nearby. Custis awaited word on his appointment to the VMI faculty, which he eventually received. Mary Custis began her long career of visiting friends around the country and, eventually, the world.

Markie's was but one of many invitations for the Lees to venture abroad. A member of Parliament offered them his London home, which stood vacant except when the House of Commons met. An earl invited them to visit "for any length of time you may find it convenient to live in England." A vicar, F. W. Tremlett, who housed "victims of the war," bade Robert and Mary to share his "quiet parsonage" with his mother and sister. Tremlett and his parishioners had organized a pro-Confederate lobby, and the vicar had befriended and financially aided Maury, whom he guided into the Anglican faith. But living with a quirky cleric, a widow, and a spinster would not strike Lee's fancy. Nor would violating his own advice to stay in the country.[24]

But what would he do? As a boy saying his catechism, Lee had pledged "to get mine own living." He needed, and wanted, to support himself and his family. However, as Mary Custis complained, "the people of the South are offering my father everything but work; and work is the only thing he will accept at their hands."[25]

That was not altogether true. In fact, word spread around the country that Lee was looking for gainful employment. When a friend in Albemarle County, William Cabell, got wind of Lee's interest in farming *and* in education, he proposed that Lee open a school and live on a vacant farm he owned. When publishers learned that Lee pondered writing a history of the war, his memoirs, or both, they peppered him with requests to produce anything he composed. Some predicted six-figure sales, promising remuneration to him upwards of $50,000. Money aside, his nephew, Smith's son Fitzhugh, urged him to tell his story lest "our posterity have to depend upon biased northern text books for their knowledge of the history of 'the great rebellion.'" Lee gathered papers for the project, but once a new commitment arose, nothing came of it.[26]

Businesses clamored for Lee to serve on their boards or at least lend his name to their letterheads. One clergyman assured him, "There is not a businessman in any commercial city that could not abundantly afford to give you $20,000 pr. an. [per annum] merely for the use of yr name." Lee politely declined all offers then and after. An insurance company asked him to become managing director of a branch office it wanted to open in Richmond. He refused, pleading his inability to fulfill the task and unwillingness to leave what had become his new calling.[27]

Educational institutions also sought him out. The University of the South in Sewanee, Tennessee, asked him to lead the school. Lee refused because it was denominational (even though his own). He squelched talk of a position at the University of Virginia because he wanted to avoid a state school.[28] Then came an audacious inquiry from Lexington, Virginia. The trustees of Washington College sent their rector, Judge John W. Brockenbrough, to ask Lee to become their president.

The college traced its roots to 1749 as Liberty Hall Academy. It had come to the attention of George Washington when he received a gift from the Commonwealth of Virginia of a hundred shares of stock in the James River Company, a builder of canals. Valued at $50,000, it was a munificent sum but one Washington, one of the nation's wealthiest men, was unwilling to accept. He decided instead to give it to an educational institution. In 1796, the little school near Lexington received the gift and gratefully changed its name to Washington College.[29]

Lee had personal connections with the college. It bore the name of his wife's admired ancestor. Lee's father, Henry Lee III, Virginia's governor at the time of the gift, advised Washington to direct it to the Lexington-Staunton region. His half brother, Henry Lee IV, attended the school for a year to prepare for studies at William and Mary.[30]

The Civil War had not been kind to the college. Though Federal troops did not burn the school as they had its neighbor, VMI, they stole its books, smashed its scientific equipment, commandeered its main building for housing and left it a mess. Its students were few, its resources even fewer. In Rob's view, the college "was very poor, indifferently equipped with buildings, and with no means in sight to improve its condition."[31]

Then the trustees decided to ask Lee to lead it, hoping he would save it. They developed a plan to woo Lee to Lexington. Brockenbrough, a trustee, a former US and Confederate judge and Confederate congressman, would visit Lee in person. Friends would prepare Brockenbrough's way with encouraging letters to Lee. John Letcher began the assault on August 2, addressing Lee's concerns over his notoriety. As wartime governor, Letcher bore his share of infamy and paid for it. After Yankees burned VMI, they destroyed his home. Six weeks after Appomattox, they arrested him and "hurried [him] off to Washington." But there, he wrote Lee, he received such "great kindness and consideration" from his jailers, former congressional colleagues, and even President Johnson, that he determined, like Lee, to "exhibit no sullen and dissatisfied spirit" but rather to "encourage harmony and conciliation." In conversations with Union officers and other Northerners, he assured Lee, "not an unkind expression towards you, was used by any one." Concern for adverse public reaction should not deter him.[32]

Then Brockenbrough wrote a more positive argument: Lee could make a difference. "While so many other literary institutions of our beloved State lie crushed & bleeding under the iron hoof of war, Washington College, though a great deal suffers from the havoc & desolation everywhere left in its train, is still blessed with a vigorous vitality and needs only the aid of your illustrious character & attainments to reanimate her drooping fortunes & restore her to more than her pristine usefulness & prosperity."[33]

Letcher wrote again to stress the good Lee could do "in building up this institution, and disseminating the blessings of education amongst our people." Then William Nelson Pendleton fired forth. A West Pointer who became an Episcopal priest and served Grace Church in Lexington, Pendleton went to war with his local unit and rose to command all of Lee's artillery. He knew what would appeal to his former chieftain. "The destiny of our State & Country depends so greatly upon the right training of our young men," he wrote, adding that the college, which adjoined his church, was of all Virginia's schools of higher education "perhaps at present [the] most promising."[34]

Brockenbrough lacked the funds to travel to Derwent and a suit in which to look respectable. Trustees borrowed what he needed. Adequately attired, he arrived at Derwent to press his cause. Lee demurred. From his time serving as West Point's superintendent, he knew the burdens of leading an academic institution. So on the way home, Brockenbrough sent another letter, this time extolling what Lee could offer the struggling college: "You alone can fill its halls, by attracting to them not the youth of Virginia alone but of all the Southern & some even of the Northern States."[35]

The offer inspired Lee to seek godly counsel in the person of a nearby Episcopal priest. Joseph Pere Bell Wilmer, who the next year became bishop of Louisiana, was as much a product of the Diocese of Virginia as Lee: a graduate of the University of Virginia and Virginia Theological Seminary, ordained by Bishop Moore, priest in several parishes in the Old Dominion. His uncle William, a close associate of William Meade in reviving the diocese, was president of William and Mary, and his cousin was consecrated bishop of Alabama in the last public event of Meade's life. Lee rode over to Wilmer's home to discuss the college's offer. Wilmer suggested that other, "more conspicuous" schools would welcome him, but soon "discovered that [Lee's] mind towered above these earthly distinctions" and that "the *cause* gave dignity to the institution." Lee argued that "this door and not another was opened to him by Providence" and wanted reassurance that he was competent to do the job, so that his remaining years would be "a comfort and a blessing to his suffering country." Wilmer, emphasizing "the importance of

Christian education" at colleges, heartily encouraged him and, as he did, Lee's "whole countenance glowed with animation."[36]

Lee responded candidly to the trustees. He was daunted by the prospect; his strength was limited; he could not teach the courses in religion that the college's previous presidents—all ordained—had done. He knew full well that many a Northerner longed to see him with a rope around his neck, not as president of a college. On the other hand, he allowed, "I think it the duty of every citizen, in the present condition of the country, to do all in his power to aid in the restoration of peace and harmony, and in no way to oppose the policy of the State or general government directed to that object." Those who instructed the young held a special obligation to exemplify "submission to authority." If the trustees thought he would not bring disgrace upon the school and that his services might "be advantageous to the college and country," he would accept.[37]

The trustees, of course, jumped eagerly at his opening, and with "unanimity and enthusiasm" voted him president on August 31. The Lees would move to Lexington.

In Lee, the trustees were receiving more than a famous, if defeated, general. Lee did have some experience in higher education. He had done so well as a student that West Point retained him after graduation to teach mathematics. The army tried to assign him to teach at the academy in 1839. He quashed that idea and only reluctantly became superintendent in 1852, and proved himself to be an educational innovator. This new occasion, in 1865, taught a new duty that, Rob believed, compelled his father "by the great need of education in his State and in the South." Washington College provided an opportunity "for starting almost from the beginning, and for helping, by his experience and example, the youth of his country to become good and useful citizens." Lee had a purpose, a mission, a means to "do something more for the glory of God," precisely as Mary had hoped twelve years before when he was confirmed.[38]

Lee left Derwent on September 14. Four days later, he rode unannounced into Lexington. Before he reached the local hotel, a professor spotted Lee and, after two veterans assisted him down from Traveller, insisted that he stay at the home of his father-in-law, Colonel Samuel McDowell Reid, the oldest of the college trustees, about two blocks from the college. After several days, not wanting to inconvenience the family by staying longer, he moved to a hotel.[39]

Lee's first meeting with the trustees, on September 20, proved who was now in charge. They had envisioned a fancy inauguration with brass band, young white-robed girls welcoming dignitaries from hither and yon, and an impressive ceremony. Lee wanted none of it. Accordingly, on October 2 in his office in Payne Hall, he took the oath as president and received the keys to the college.[40] General Lee became President Lee. In an isolated town in western Virginia, Lee's last mission had begun.

Four years later, Lee reflected on the war and its aftermath. "We failed," he wrote, "but in the good Providence of God apparent failure often proves a blessing."[41]

CHAPTER 19

"To Put Away the Leaven of Malice"

~

Pursuing Reconciliation

In September 1865, Robert Edward Lee began a new life. For the first time since he had entered West Point four decades earlier, he had nothing to do with the army. "Home" was no longer Arlington or a military post or an army tent. Far from the seats of power in Washington and Richmond, he found himself in the Valley of Virginia in an isolated town at a tiny college on the brink of extinction. There he came to terms with a new reality. He prospered.

All these changes had transmogrified the setting of his life. Inwardly, matters had also changed. He had a new cause, a new purpose, a mission that he perceived had been sent from heaven. Unlike his four years of commitment to a cause that entailed the destructiveness of war, his new commitment meant building up, both by restoring old edifices scarred by conflict, and also, more importantly, by edifying young minds, an endeavor that included instilling the knowledge and service of God. The work was new, and it gave Lee the opportunity to follow two abiding loyalties: to his "country" now redefined as state, region, *and* nation; and to his God. If he had attended church the previous April 23, which he probably did, he heard the officiant beg God "to put away the leaven of malice and wickedness, that we may always serve thee in pureness of living and truth." In good Episcopal fashion, he would have responded, "Amen." Five months later, he had begun to live out that prayer in a new home, a new position, and a new church.

Settling In

Lee needed, first, a home for himself and his family. After the war, he and Mary lived essentially on the kindness of others. Never in his life had he owned his residence. In Lexington, a house came with the job, but at least he could make it their home for life. The president's residence, brick with white columns overlooking the outskirts of a tiny town, provided a poor comparison with the size of Arlington or its grand view of the nation's capital. But it held a special connection for Lee. After the previous president's daughter, Elinor Junkin, married a little-known VMI instructor, the newlyweds occupied two rooms in a wing on the right side of the house. Now the Lees lived in the same home once inhabited by Thomas Jonathan—"Stonewall"—Jackson.

Lee had to wait to move in. The house, having been rented to a local physician during the war, needed serious repair. While workmen rendered the place habitable, Lee stayed in a hotel and kept Mary apprised of progress. He was beginning to relax and look forward to the future. "I think we should enjoy all the amenities of life, that are within our reach, & which have been provided for us by our Heavenly Father."[1]

Lee escaped the hotel as often as he could to enjoy the beauties of his new area. For about a week he visited Rockbridge Baths, twelve miles north of town. He rode to the top of Jump Mountain, a prominent peak where, he told Mary, "we had one of the most beautiful views I ever saw." A month later he remarked that "nothing can be more beautiful than the mts."[2]

Custis still awaited word of his faculty appointment to the Virginia Military Institute. No one was more anxious that he should get the job than his father. Custis, also a general in the Confederate army, received the post by a unanimous vote of the trustees. Having Custis at the campus next door would alleviate Lee's loneliness, for he had confessed to missing his family "dreadfully." He had told Mildred, "Traveller is my only companion; I may also say my pleasure."[3]

Nonetheless, he had a job to do. "For myself I am content in the position in which events have placed me," he wrote in declining yet another job offer, "& trust yet to see the restoration of the South in prosperity & influence." That was his goal. "For this all must work in their respective spheres." He had found his sphere, and said as much to those outside the family. But to Mary he confided his anxiety. "Life is indeed gliding away, & I have nothing of good to shew for mine that is past.

I pray that I may be spared to accomplish something for the benefit of mankind & the honour of my God."[4]

With work lagging on the house, Lee and his family could not move in. First, the doctor and his family had trouble moving out. Then, shortages in materials to repair roof, fences, and stables delayed the start of seriously needed renovations until October 16, which a storm then interrupted. The house "is in wretched condition," Lee advised Mary three days later. He gently suggested that she contact her first cousin, who had cared for some of Arlington's household goods, as, he gently mentioned, "their use where originally intended is very uncertain." Mary still harbored hope of returning to her longtime home, hope that Lee knew was in vain.[5]

The family, meanwhile, remained in borrowed housing in central Virginia. After Lee left Derwent, they moved to a house in Bremo in Albemarle County for several weeks. Finally, in November, Mary, Agnes, Mildred, and Rob began their slow journey to Lexington. The canal company president provided a private barge, complete with dining room and cook. Mrs. Lee's arthritis had become so severe that she had to be lifted on and off the boat.

Meanwhile, Lexingtonians joined in preparing the house for their arrival. Ladies of the town had tried their best to furnish the house. With the help of Pendleton, back at his post at Grace Church, Francis Smith arranged for the piano on which Lee jokingly insisted that Mildred would "practice seven hours a day" so she could play it "promptly & gracefully whenever invited"—by her father, no doubt. By late November, Mrs. Lee's room had been readied under the careful attention of the ladies of Lexington. The rest of the house remained rather bare. But carpets from Arlington warmed the rooms, and a storeroom burst with pickles, preserves, game, and supplies provided by new neighbors in town and county.

Finally the family arrived, greeted with a breakfast prepared by a faculty wife. "We were all very grateful and happy—glad to get home," recalled Rob, "the only one we had had for four long years." They began making the house their home. By good fortune (or providence?), the Lees had sent the family's silver to Lexington before the war. Rob retrieved it, and, while the tableware was being restored, they used the contents of Lee's camp chest. In the spring, Lee set out a vegetable garden, planted roses and fruit trees, planned walks, and repaired the stable. "He at last had a home of his own, with his wife and daughters around him," Rob recalled, "and though it was not the little farm in the quiet country for which he had so longed, it was very near to it, and it gave rest to himself and those he loved most dearly."[6]

At last a semblance of civilian life surrounded them. They savored Christmas together and in peace. Mary Custis had not joined them, so Lee reported, "The young people have been enjoying themselves as usual at this season, & the holy days have given rise to several parties which seem to have produced much pleasure among them. The smiling faces of the girls from Staunton, occasioned by their Xmas visit to their homes, have added much to our enjoyment."[7]

President Lee

Meanwhile, Lee began work at his new job. He got to know the faculty and students, repaired damaged or decrepit buildings, and upgraded the grounds, which had not been maintained for years.[8] He daily faced stacks of letters that had to be answered. He also looked ahead to the college's future and ways it could assist in rebuilding the South and reconciling the nation. In the process, Lee not only saved the institution, he transformed it—or at least he tried.

Rebuilding the college demanded action on nearly every front. The school needed students. Fortunately, as Brockenbrough had predicted, interest abounded among young men who wanted to attend a college led by General Lee. Parents or siblings inquired about their sons or brothers, many writing from Virginia, some from the South, a few from the North.[9] Many had little knowledge of where the school was or what it was like. One inquirer thought Lee administered the University of Virginia. Another placed the school in Lynchburg. Quite a few presumed that a school headed by a general must be a military college.[10] A different motive drew former soldiers, one a Virginian who wished "to become (or remain) a member of your family." A veteran who had lost his right arm at Vicksburg scribbled an explanation to Lee with his left hand: "I have neather farther nor mother living so I have no body to recommend me but my self so you must excuse me for this time. I have nobody nearer than a granmother and she says that she will give me a good education. And I am not fit for this life without I have a good education. . . . I am 20 years old. I am indited for treason. . . . So if you will attend to this for me I will thank you verry much."[11] Lee answered all the letters, but sadly, his response to the young veteran was lost.

The faculty needed expanding, and prospective teachers were as interested as prospective students were in coming to General Lee's college. One was an English-born bandleader who served the Confederate army and styled himself "Single and an Episcopalian." Lee took a particular interest in filling the professorship of "Mental & Moral Philosophy." Whoever occupied that chair, Lee wrote to the Reverend Churchill Gibson of Petersburg, "should not only be a man of true piety, learning, & science; but should be so thoroughly imbued with the Heavenly principles of the blessed Gospel of Christ; as to make His Holy religion attractive to the young, to impress it upon their hearts, & to make them humble Christians. He should not only be free from bigotry, but clear of Sectarianism, & not a participator in Controversy; having for his whole object the teaching of wisdom, & the conversion of all the students from sin to the religion of Christ, of whatever sect or denomination."[12]

Meanwhile, Lee was putting his educational philosophy into practice. As his letter to Gibson indicates, Lee sought to apply at Washington College a perspective that embraced a strong spiritual component but also a profoundly practical element. For Lee, neither aspect was new. He had grown up in an environment that stressed both the moral and the pragmatic value of education. His values mirrored those expounded by educators within his own church, including William Augustus Muhlenberg and William Nelson Pendleton, who, before coming to Lexington, had founded Episcopal High School in Alexandria. These leaders sought to inculcate Christian moral development while utilizing "preventive moral discipline."[13]

At West Point, Lee had responsibility over the moral as well as the military and academic development of cadets. He also instituted practical reforms, such as redesigning the uniform and revising the curriculum. He applied the same principles—minus the military element—to the men at Washington College. His responsibility, he presumed, involved the totality of the student, including the spiritual component.

Lee found a similar philosophy already present at Washington College—to a point. Henry Ruffner, the college's president from 1836 to 1848, had declared it his "indispensable duty to teach the Christian religion to all who may be committed to my charge. By the Christian religion I do not mean the peculiar dogmas of any sect or school of theology. In the religious exercises of this college we use no sectarian creed, catechism, or formulary. We offer up our prayers to the Divine Father of our race in terms common to all Christian worshippers. We teach our students to read, and to understand for themselves the sacred records to which all protestants resort for instruction." In Ruffner's eyes, all Christian worshipers would be Protestants, at least at Washington College. During his presidency, from 1848 to 1861, Ruffner's successor, George Junkin, agreed, even as he placed the role of religion in a wider perspective. In his inaugural address, "Christianity, the Patron of Literature and Science," Junkin argued that schools are religious, not civil, institutions, stirringly concluding that his college must be "[t]he sword of the Lord and . . . Washington."[14]

That was the theory. In practice the school was not specifically sectarian, but from its start Presbyterians dominated it. All of Lee's predecessors had been ordained Presbyterians. When Lee arrived, Brockenbrough was the sole Episcopalian among the trustees. After Lee's death, parochial partisans debated whether the college had become too "Episcopalian" or too sectarian. No one dared raise that question while Lee was alive. He was comfortable, then, with the religious element of the college, so long as it was not specifically sectarian. "The object of a college is to secure the education of the mind, not a training in denominational religion," Lee noted to himself.

A second element, however, took him—and the school—into new territory, philosophically and practically. Lee's note to himself continued: the best means of achieving "the education of the mind" was by "bringing the greatest views[?] of intellectual influences to bear upon the mind" through a broad education.[15] The college had long held to the classical curriculum built upon the study of ancient languages and literature, supplemented to an extent with that of natural sciences. Lee immediately widened the courses his college offered. He proposed a professorship of modern languages, the study of which would provide more immediate and practical use than the traditional classics. He increased the place of English and history in the curriculum. He incorporated the law school founded by Brockenbrough in 1849 into the college. He sought to add the study of civil and mining engineering, business, journalism, and agriculture, though not all (notably agriculture) took root.[16]

He did so with a clear purpose: the college should help to prepare young men for lifelong usefulness to society, which would prosper as a result. To a Lynchburg cleric, he observed, "Nothing will compensate us for the depression of the standard of our moral and intellectual culture, and each State should take the most energetic measures to revive its schools and colleges; and if possible, to increase the facilities of instruction, and to elevate the standards of learning." In a note found on his desk after his death, Lee had written,

> The fundamental principle of the Collegiate System should be to give to the commercial, agricultural & mechanical classes the advantages of an education best adapted to their wants; the study of the classics being made optional with those desiring an education other than for professional purposes. All classes of the community are alike entitled to the benefits of high education; and if unable to find in the college the education they need, the productive classes will establish institutions for themselves, to which the body of the young will be attracted & but few will avail themselves of the instruction of the college. Every student should be allowed to pursue the study of his choice & the instructor should not be compelled to cool the ardour of those who wish to leave in order to accomodate the indolent & unfaithful.[17]

If students did not find at Washington College the kind of education they sought, he knew they would go elsewhere. The future of his society *and* his college was at stake.

Just as crucial for Lee was the moral element to education. "Physical united with intellectual education, but without moral training, produces a still more dangerous character," he wrote. "It is persons so educated who compose a large section of clever & designing criminals, also ambitious & unprincipled men in different ranks of society." He assured parents that their sons would experience a religious, though not sectarian, atmosphere at Washington College. Then he made sure their sons would find what he promised. In 1867 he proposed starting a Young Men's Christian Association (YMCA). Founded in 1845 in England, the YMCA first appeared in America in 1851. Lee knew of it as early as 1865; when Mary had wondered what to do with a $200 gift, he suggested that the YMCA could use it to help soldiers in need.[18] In Lexington it would be open to all church members in the student body and "all moral young men who are disposed to take part of it." By the winter of 1868 it boasted fifty members who assisted in the weekday chapel services and Sunday afternoon prayer meetings. They organized a library, even daring to ask General Lee for a donation; he gave $50 and graced its meetings with his presence. The YMCA coordinated all religious activities at the college. Its members volunteered as Sunday school teachers in "destitute points in the vicinity" and invited local clergy to address their interdenominational services.[19]

Lee revised the college's rules on formal religious services. When he arrived, daily services took place in a room on the colonnade. Regulations required students to be present, and most faculty attended voluntarily. Local clergy took turns in leading the services, which, Lee told the faculty, made the rites "more interesting and impressive." He added that clergy were involved in other ways; Pendleton, for instance, taught a required class in "declamation." The faculty concurred that the system was working.[20]

Lee himself attended chapel services each day. For that reason, as much as the requirement to attend, so did the students. Milton W. Humphreys recalled walking from the home where he boarded one and a half miles each morning to arrive in time for chapel. A "pious friend" accused him of "worshipping Lee rather than Jehovah." Humphreys replied, "I was."[21]

The new president wanted to place even more emphasis on religion. For a time, he considered creating the position of college chaplain. Presumably this person would coordinate if not replace the local clergy in presiding over services. Because no Methodists were members of the faculty or trustees, Lee suggested that a Methodist minister be the first chaplain. Lee received letters of inquiry or application, but the idea went no further.[22]

By 1866, an even larger project had captured Lee's imagination. The growing number of students could no longer fit into the chapel room. At the end of his first year, Lee proposed constructing a discrete chapel and converting the old one into a much-needed lecture space. For Lee, a proper chapel ranked ahead of the trustees' offer to build a larger home for him and his family.[23] The trustees entrusted the concept to a committee, which endorsed "the original idea of President Lee" to create "a separate building of characteristic architecture, devoted exclusively to religious worship and instruction." As Lee recommended, it would be placed in front of the college, cost an estimated $12,000, and be ready, at least in the shell of the building, to accommodate the entire student body when it returned just months later. It was a bold plan, perhaps too bold. That same week, Richard S. McCulloch, the college's professor of sciences, while visiting New York City, called on an architect, who proposed "a perfectly plain Gothic chapel of rubble masonry, suitable for College purposes." Its cruciform shape and exposed rafters would resemble an English parish church, a design then popular, especially among Episcopalians. But such a chapel would cost, in "New York City prices," $16,500 to seat five hundred people, $18,500 for a hundred more—architect fees not included.[24]

Fortunately for the college, professional services were right at hand, for free. Thomas H. Williamson, a VMI professor of civil and military engineering, taught a course in architecture for which he wrote the country's first textbook on the subject.[25] Custis taught in the same department. Architecture interested him, too, and he owned several books on the topic. Suddenly, three Episcopalians were designing a chapel for the traditionally Presbyterian school.

Custis had seen a "book of Churches" that struck his eye. It may have been not of churches but of the Smithsonian Institution, which John Renwick had recently designed as the first major building of Norman-style architecture in the country. Robert Dale Owen, a congressman who chaired the Smithsonian's building committee, published a monograph not only to justify the unique design but even more to recommend it as prototypically "American." It suited the new nation even better than the classical style, as it could more easily accommodate chimneys, stairs, and windows; adapt itself better to varying purposes and climates; and be cheaper to build. In a time when most building designs were copied from publications, his copious illustrations made the Smithsonian easy to emulate. Moreover, Lexingtonians had recently begun using a Gothic mode. VMI was the first major neo-Gothic academic campus in America. Homeowners were building houses in the style.[26]

Williamson drew up two floor plans, both in the neo-Gothic style. One called for amphitheater-like seating in a semicircle around a dais. The other proposed a platform at one end of the building with pews extending back to a vestibule, divided by two aisles. The latter design was adopted.[27]

Both its placement and its exterior set the chapel apart from the college's academic buildings. With their triangular pediments and white columns in a vaguely classical style, they evoke a federalist-era sense of classical learning, as if to declare the virtues and priorities of the Enlightenment. Like them, the chapel was built with brick, but there the similarities ended. It stands by itself, Romanesque in design and Romantic in spirit. Set more into the landscape than atop it, the chapel provides an architectural counterpoint to the academic classrooms. It also copies the Norman-inspired Smithsonian—a tower resembling a flared turret of a "castle," semicircular arches over doors and diagonally mullioned windows, and decorative details. Its interior of pews and balcony, with windows of clear glass, resembles the Presbyterian mode, such as New Providence Church, built in 1857 in the nearby village of Raphine, rather than the more "Episcopal" style that featured one center aisle, stained wood, and colored glass.

In September, about the time students were returning to school, the trustees signed a contract with Pole and Shields, a local building firm, which appointed George W. Pettigrew as superintendent of works. (He joined the college staff soon after.) A year and a half later, two years after Lee first suggested the idea, the building was finished. The satisfied president praised the edifice as a "pleasing as well [as] a useful addition to the College buildings."[28]

The new chapel stood ready to house that year's commencement exercises, which included its dedication. "Quite a large audience" gathered at 9 a.m. on Sunday, June 8, for an ecumenical celebration involving local clergy. The Presbyterian pastor, Dr. William White, gave the invocation and benediction; his choir led the music. A Methodist, the Reverend Samuel Rogers, read the Scriptures; the Reverend J. William Jones of the Baptist church gave the prayer of dedication; and Pendleton gave the address, which the local newspaper called "as entertaining as it was profound and well considered." Many in the congregation then walked to the Presbyterian church for the baccalaureate sermon given by an Episcopalian, Lee's former pastor in Richmond, Dr. Minnigerode. That night, a preacher from Fincastle lectured to the YMCA.[29]

To this new house of God, when school resumed that fall, students came every weekday, and no longer because they were required to do so. In 1868, probably at Lee's urging and surely with his concurrence, the faculty revoked the requirement that students attend service and adjusted the hours to make worship more convenient. The trustees grudgingly adopted the changes, one of the few issues on which they disagreed with Lee.[30] He set the example, sitting each day in the first pew to the far left of the dais. A plaque now marks the spot.

Thereafter, six days a week during school terms, local clergy officiated at morning services. Having clerics from the town's churches allowed each student to worship according to his own denomination, so long as that was Baptist, Episcopal, Methodist, or Presbyterian. Students often chipped in a dollar or two each year to defray the expenses of the visiting clergy.[31] The college held no service on Sundays so that students could attend local churches with the families with whom they boarded (the few dormitories, which Lee considered veritable classrooms for vice, were limited to upperclassmen).

In time, students became less diligent in attending. Lee resorted to every ploy he could think of to inspire them to come. The day he suffered his ultimately fatal attack, he had hurried through breakfast to shoo his daughters off to chapel, which, Mary wrote the next day to Carter, "has been his fancy lately thinking if the ladies would patronise it that the students would be more interested in going there."[32]

The new chapel housed other activities as well. It served as a gathering place for lectures, concerts, and other campus meetings such as the festive anniversaries of the two student literary societies. The YMCA met in its basement rooms. The college treasurer's office was there, as was Lee's, adding to the importance of the place.[33]

In his policies and practice of religion on campus, Lee exemplified more than the importance of daily worship. In the old Virginia tradition of denominational expansiveness, he welcomed clergy of every Protestant denomination in Lexington[34] to lead services. That the chapel was "dedicated" but not "consecrated" in a particular denomination made it open to all traditions. Lee gave religion an important physical presence on the campus in the form of a distinctive and significant edifice, in a style and location that set it uniquely apart from the college's other buildings. Then he used that building in ways that drew together the campus community for services, lectures, and concerts in the main body of the chapel. In the basement, the business of the college was conducted, the activities of the YMCA were held, and students met with the president himself—which for some became itself a spiritual experience. The chapel represented Lee's principles on religion and its place in education.

Lee expressed those principles in other ways, ways that students and faculty cherished for life. He took a personal interest in each one in the college. He learned each student's name and addressed him as "Mister." He noted when any student—or faculty member—did not attend class without adequate excuse. When he reported students' deficiencies to their parents, he did so with the same tact that he employed at West Point, assuring one father that his son "is careful not to injure his health by too much study."[35]

The former General Lee avoided military-style discipline at the college, choosing instead to emphasize personal duty and responsibility over rules and regulations. One of his erstwhile artillery generals, A. L. Long, explained that Lee sought to prepare his students for civilian life, "and that the rigors of military methods was not here desirable." He reduced the number of penalties, extended the benefit of the doubt, expected students to strive for high standards inside and outside the classroom, and punished or expelled students as he had to. When a student from Kentucky appeared before Lee to answer for his bad behavior, he was chewing tobacco, a habit Lee detested. He ordered the young man, "Go out and remove that quid, and never appear before me again chewing tobacco." The student withdrew, then returned, the wad still in his cheek. After one look, Lee wrote out a statement that he had the Kentuckian read: he was "dismissed from Washington College for disrespect to the president."[36]

Lee could be firm, but he sought also to be fair. One cold morning, the potbellied stove in the room of Edward Joynes, the professor of modern languages, exploded and nearly killed him. Joynes suspected that a disgruntled student had tried to assassinate him by means of an explosive hidden in a log. Just before the next chapel service, Lee delicately suggested that anyone with information call at his office before noon. By 11 a.m., two trembling freshmen appeared to explain that someone had been taking wood from a study room they had rented. To expose the culprit, one of them bored a hole in a hickory stick, loaded it with gunpowder, sealed it with clay, and told his roommates never to use that log. A janitor assigned to haul wood from a pile some two hundred yards away was instead taking logs from the students and placing them by the professors' doors, the charged stick being one. Lee laughed. He told the student, "Your plan to find out who was taking your wood was a good one, but your powder charge was too heavy. The next time use less powder."[37]

Speaking at chapel that day, Lee reiterated his philosophy of personal conduct. He reminded the students, an alumnus recalled, "that the faculty had issued no rules for student government, that each and every one was presumed to be a gentleman and that by tacit agreement the control of the students was left to the student body and the individual sense of honor of each student." When a new student asked for a copy of the college's regulations, Lee responded, "We have no printed rules. We have but one rule here, and it is that every student must be a gentleman." The student later realized "the comprehensiveness of his remark, and how completely it covered every essential rule that should govern the conduct and intercourse of men."[38] His guidance of individuals, as well as of the institution, demonstrated what he believed.

Success soon showed. By the end of Lee's third academic year, the chapel had been dedicated, but not before a gallery had been added, late, to the plans, to house a growing student body. The 1867–1868 academic year saw the largest enrollment ever at the college, 410. Suddenly the school ranked as the second largest in the South, behind only the University of Virginia with its 475 students. By comparison with other private institutions, at about the same time Yale College enrolled 505 undergraduates and Harvard, 529. To "General Lee's College" came students from every state of the old Confederacy and every border state but Delaware; one or more students came from New Jersey, New York, Massachusetts, Illinois, California, and—making the student body truly international—Mexico. Such numbers were not exceeded until 1907.[39]

They had more disciplines to study than ever before: journalism, mining, civil engineering, expanded courses in the sciences and humanities. Brockenbrough's law school had been incorporated into the college. To teach these diverse courses and the growing number of students who took them, the senior faculty more than doubled in size from just three years earlier, from four to ten, with additional men teaching in lower-ranked positions. The quality of the faculty grew, too; college presidents were willing to leave their positions to teach under General Lee. At least one did. Another faculty recruit, William Preston Johnston, son of General Albert Sidney Johnston, eventually became president first of Louisiana State University and then of the new Tulane University.[40]

Lee and the faculty held even higher aspirations. They sought to "meet the wants of the country and lead in Southern Education" by trying "to give the broadest and most thorough development to the practical and industrial sciences of the age." Even its expanded curriculum could not meet the needs of Southerners seeking an intensely scientific curriculum; for that, they had to go north. So the faculty proposed creating the first scientific school in the South, comparable to what West Point, Yale, and Harvard already had, at a cost of $200,000.[41]

Under Lee, Washington College had become more vigorous and more studious. It was raising its academic standards and, if Lee had his way, the standards of its students' characters and religious commitments. "If I could only know that all the young men in the college were good Christians I should have nothing more to desire," he reportedly stated. "I dread the thought of any student going away from the college without becoming a sincere Christian."[42] Meanwhile, he set them an example of regular worship, both daily in chapel and on Sundays at Grace Episcopal Church.

Grace Church

When Pendleton urged Lee to take the presidency of Washington College, he probably figured he would pick up a parishioner. During the war years, the two had formed a close bond. Afterward, Lee had congratulated Pendleton on resuming "the exercise of your sacred profession, for there is no labour so beneficent, so elevated and so sublime, as the teaching of salvation to every man. I hope your career on earth may be crowned with success, and everlasting peace and happiness your portion in Heaven." Pendleton presumed correctly. Lee became active in Grace Church and its governance. Within eight days of his arriving in Lexington, its vestry unanimously elected him as a member.[43]

He joined Grace Church at a hard moment in its history. Their rector, the former Confederate brigadier general, took his bishop's instructions to intercede as he wished for rulers and all in authority, in accordance with Episcopal custom, as permission not to mention the president of the United States. Federal authorities insisted that he do so. Pendleton had refused to swear the postwar oath of allegiance. The previous July, he had been arrested after what US officials deemed an inflammatory sermon. Despite President Andrew Johnson's forbidding the military from interfering with religious services, they closed his church. Pendleton held Sunday services in the rectory, located about two blocks away. Worship in the church did not resume until January 1866.[44]

Both the church and its rectory suffered badly from wartime neglect. The church roof leaked. Windows, blinds, the vestibule, and fences all needed repair. The congregants needed stoves to warm them and lamps to light their way, but they could not even pay their rector. The vestry put Lee on a committee to confront the congregation's needs. Then, numbers began to swell with the revival of the two schools. Enrollment at VMI grew to nearly three hundred, and Washington College to more than four hundred. Many students from each school, and some professors, were Episcopalians. Latimer Parish (its formal name), started in 1840 by Smith and Williamson specifically to minister to the students of the two colleges, found its reason for being renewed. By 1866, so many young men crowded every pew that more had to be added, to the evident jealousy of Presbyterians who, Williamson wrote his daughter, "do not rejoice so much at the College prosperity as they would do if it were not accompanied by the strong Episcopal influences, which the new President and some of his Professors have brought into the community with them." In 1869 Bishop Johns confirmed sixty-six souls, including forty-nine VMI cadets, four members of the VMI staff, eight Washington College students, and William Preston Johnston.[45]

Obviously the parish needed a larger church. In 1868, Pendleton proposed enlarging or rebuilding it. Typically, his daughter recalled, "Some of the old church members were opposed to both schemes." Her father countered with the idea of expanding facilities just for a Sunday school and a "lecture-room." But a parish unable to pay its priest could hardly afford any construction. The South faced the same problem, so Pendleton went north for help for his ministry, which was growing especially with the young. He returned with several thousand dollars, including a gift from the famous preacher Henry Ward Beecher, and also some funds for the college.[46]

Lee remained constantly active in Grace Church and, through it, the Diocese of Virginia. Each year, the pewholders reelected him to the parish vestry, which from 1867 to 1870 unanimously chose him as a delegate to the annual diocesan councils. Some at the 1868 council wanted to send both Lee and Pendleton as deputies to that year's General Convention. First Pendleton and then Lee declined, lest the presence of two Confederate generals disrupt the amicable relations among sections that the Episcopal Church was striving to restore.[47]

Like all vestry members, Lee signed the oath of conformity required by the diocese: "I do believe the Holy Scriptures of the Old and New Testament to be the Word of God, and to contain all things necessary to salvation; and I do yield my hearty assent and approbation to the doctrines and worship of the Protestant Episcopal Church in these United States. And I promise that I will faithfully execute the office of a vestryman of Latimer Parish in Rockbridge County, without prejudice, favor, or affection, according to the best of my skill and knowledge." In signing, he was joined by such estimable souls as Smith, Johnston, Williamson—and by Charles L. Figgatt, a cashier at the Bank of Lexington who a quarter-century later disappeared with the funds that the church, VMI, the county, and depositors had entrusted to the bank.[48]

In the 1860s, Lexington hardly had money for anyone to embezzle, least of all Grace Church. Lee chaired the vestry's committee on finances. It was a fruitless task. Even with outside help, the parish could not raise sufficient funds to pay the rector, much less increase his salary, as Lee urged. He noted dryly to Mildred, "the Episcopalians are few in number & light of purse." So the Lee family pitched in to help. Lee told Mildred of an Advent supper to raise funds to repair the building. "Your mother & sisters are busy with their contributions"—ice cream from Agnes, a fruitcake from Mary—"& your brother, cousins & father are expected to attend." The next evening the Presbyterians held a benefit to purchase an organ. If nothing else, the events raised spirits; as Agnes exclaimed to her sister, in "these Christmas times Lexington has been so unusually gay"; and Grace Church received new paint.[49]

The next August, Lee was visiting the spa at White Sulphur Springs when a concert there benefited Grace Church. He happily reported to Mary that the proceeds totaled $605. Two magnates, William W. Corcoran and George Peabody, enhanced the sum with another $100 each, "For all of which," Lee wrote, "I am extremely grateful."[50]

Lee himself was not too shy to ask for help. In contributing to another church's organ fund, he enclosed an appeal for Grace Church that he asked the recipients to circulate. The flyer stressed the opportunities for "distributing the blessings of the Gospel" especially to the young men at the colleges who could "become greatly useful in the Lord's service, as Ministers, and as efficient laymen."[51]

Lee remained in touch with the churches and clergy to which he had ties. As weather allowed an aging man to do, he attended St. Paul's when he was in Richmond. During the summer of 1865, he reconnected with his cousin Cassius and met with Bishop Johns at Virginia Seminary, which Cassius had tried to protect during the war. Lee also welcomed the return of the *Southern Churchman* into print, hoping his five-dollar gift would help it "ever prosper, & continue to dispence good to the state & country."[52] Some things were returning to normal.

Soon Grace Church had won a place in his heart. In thanking a friend for her gift to the church, he indicated that "there are three or four churches in Va. in which I take particular interest. Grace Church in Lexington & St. Peters Church in New Kent are two of them." He valued Grace Church "for the opportunity it possesses of advancing the cause of religion among the young," and St. Peter's "second for its association with the recollections of Genl Washington," who was married there.[53] One symbolized the past. The other looked toward the future, and that was the one he valued the more.

That typified Lee's outlook in general. After four years of destruction and death, he sought to build up the South and reconcile the country as he could, and to move forward into a new day of peace and prosperity. His efforts showed significant success. But the peace that followed proved to be more uneasy than he had hoped.

CHAPTER 20

"The Mouth of the Deceitful Is Opened upon Me"

~

The Uneasy Peace

L ee was able to make the transition from war to peace to a degree that others, in the North as well as the South, could not. Unlike some of his officers, he remained in his state, region, and nation, striving to do precisely what he advised others to do.[1] Unlike his wife, he mostly surmounted his rancor over the recent past. Unlike many in the South, he accepted the new order of things, at least in the war's immediate aftermath. To the degree he was able to do so, his faith was one reason why he could.

Although he could find a measure of peace in his new role, mission, and home, troubles of the wider world intruded into the relative calm of Lexington, sometimes enticing or even demanding responses from Lee. Divine providence may have brought a new reality, and to be faithful Lee would have to resign himself to it. But faithfulness did not require Lee to agree with every aspect of what mortals made of this new day, nor to like what they did.

The Problem at Home

Robert Lee had committed himself to a course of reconciliation. Mary had not. Lee had a job to do. Mary did not. Lee had never personally owned a home. Nor had Mary, but other than her relatively brief stints on army posts, she had always lived in the house where she was born; and though her father had left Arlington House and its estate to their son Custis, she retained lifetime use of it. Arlington was effectively hers. It remained "a place dearer to me than my life, the scene of every memory of that life whether for joy or sorrow, the birth place of my children, where I was wedded, & where I hoped to die & be laid under those noble oaks by the side of my parents to whom as an only child I had been an object of absorbing & tender love." Her husband's decision to side with Virginia changed everything. The estate was too vulnerable, too tempting, too strategically important for the defense of Washington for Federal troops not to occupy it. Still, she recalled four years after the occupation, "the idea of leaving this home could scarcely be endured."[2] But she had to flee. With that, and Arlington's occupation by Yankee forces, she left behind any lingering Unionist sympathies.

In 1862 Congress enacted a law requiring property owners in "insurrectionary districts" to pay their taxes in person. Mary Lee owed $92.07. She asked her cousin Philip Fendell to pay the bill in Alexandria, but the authorities insisted that she, and no one else, had to appear. Since that was impossible, the Arlington estate was auctioned, and the sole bidder, the US government, paid $26,800, a quarter of its assessed value. With ownership vested in Federal hands, *de jure* as well as *de facto*, troops under Brigadier General Montgomery Meigs, the army's quartermaster general, who detested the Confederacy, denuded the forests surrounding the house, built cabins for the soldiers, and in time created freedmen's villages for emancipated slaves. In 1864 interments of the Federal dead began, with graves dug close to the house. Meigs achieved his goal that no Lee would ever inhabit the mansion again.[3]

Mary took its loss bitterly. Her husband advised her to resign herself to the reality, but she would not. She had held as providential a view of God and world as her husband did. Soon after leaving her home she wrote to a friend, "While we can trace the hand of God stretched out for our protection let us not provoke him to withdraw it by undue exultation but go on in an humble trust upon Divine Providence to defend ourselves."[4] But losing Arlington especially festered, her bile breaking into the open in letters to friends. "My heart will never know rest or peace while my dear home is . . . used" as a cemetery, she wrote in the spring of 1866, "& I am almost *maddened* daily by the accounts I read in the paper of the number of interments continually placed there." She ascribed her loss to human sin. "My home was too beautiful stretched out before their eyes to escape their avarice & covetousness."[5]

Robert Lee had to deal somehow with his deeply resentful wife. He nudged her gently to give up her hope of regaining Arlington even as he tried to do what he could to recover it,[6] implored her to do what she could to preserve her health, and advised her to be resigned to God's will. He looked toward the future. She wallowed in her lost past. In their youth, she had been the one to exhort her fiancé Robert to come to Jesus. In their older years, he was the one who more obligingly accepted what he perceived to be the dictates of divine providence.

The Problem of Race

In the new order that the postwar period inaugurated, nothing was stranger to the Lees than the relationship between whites and blacks. Lee, typically, refused to comment publicly on the topic. Mary did not. Both found it challenging.

The war ended slavery. That much was obvious and of itself not a regret to Lee. He had no love for the institution, even less for it after trying to meet Mr. Custis's instructions to emancipate the enslaved workers who expected freedom earlier than probate proved possible. Lee had fantasized to Francis Blair about saving the Union by freeing the slaves. Toward the end of the war, he advised Jefferson Davis to end slavery and recruit the newly freed blacks for the Confederate army. He had also written state senator Andrew Hunter in early 1865, in which he began by saying slavery was "controlled by humane laws and influenced by Christianity and an enlightened public sentiment, as the best that can exist" between white and black races—"as at present." Since that could not continue, he suggested that the South utilize blacks as soldiers. He concluded by proposing "a well-digested plan of gradual and general emancipation." Even as a measure of desperation, Confederate politicians pilloried the idea. Appomattox made the issue moot.[7]

All along, Lee had foreseen the end to slavery as the will of God. It simply came sooner than he ever anticipated. Just before his death he reflected to John Leyburn, a Presbyterian minister in Baltimore, "So far from engaging in a war to perpetuate slavery, I am rejoiced that slavery is abolished. I believe it will be greatly for the interests of the South. So fully am I satisfied of this, as regards Virginia especially, that I would cheerfully have lost all I have lost by the war, and have suffered all I have suffered, to have this object attained."[8]

But the Lees' way of life had always relied upon servants. Before the war, most of them were enslaved. After it, the Lees had to start all over with a new staff who, of course, they would hire. Moving to Lexington, Lee had trouble finding satisfactory servants, regardless of race.

By then, too, Lee had developed a sour attitude about black workers and African Americans generally. In June 1865 he visited Thomas H. Carter, his first cousin's son and a veteran of Lee's artillery. Carter needed able-bodied laborers to restore his farm on the Pamunkey River, but he also had to care for ninety former slaves who had remained on his property, mostly women, children, and old men. Lee advised his cousin "to get rid" of them; "the government would provide for them," and Carter could "secure white labour" to replace them. Lee added, "I have always observed that wherever you find the negro, everything is going down around him, and wherever you find the white man, you see everything around him improving."[9] Three years later, Rob had the same need as Carter in reviving Romancoke, the farm his grandfather had bequeathed him. At the time, European immigration was increasing. Lee suggested that he hire German or Dutch laborers, or white Virginians—but not African Americans. "You will never prosper with the blacks, and it is abhorrent to a reflecting mind to be supporting and cherishing those who are plotting and working for your injury, and all of whose sympathies and associations are antagonistic to yours. I wish them no evil in the world—on the contrary, will do them every good in my power, and know that they are misled by those to whom they have given their confidence; but our material, social, and political interests are naturally with the whites."[10]

Mary wrote no less scathingly. "We are all here dreadfully plundered by the lazy idle negroes who are lounging about the streets doing nothing but looking what they may plunder during the night," she complained in 1866. "We have been raided on twice already but fortunately they did not get a great deal either time."[11]

Yet the family recognized exceptions to their generalization. Rob appreciatively described Milly Howard, a free black woman employed in Lexington as his mother's "faithful and capable servant" who "took great pride in dressing" Mrs. Lee "in becoming caps, etc., to receive her numerous visitors." She accompanied the family to the Greenbrier in White Sulphur Springs, where, during their three-week sojourn, she prepared her mistress to "appear at her best" to greet visitors to their cottage. Milly Howard and her husband Reuben, a farmer, were free residents of Rockbridge County in 1853, if not as early as 1819.[12]

Keeping private opinions of freedmen to himself, Lee chose his public words carefully. When a joint committee of Congress summoned him to Washington on February 17, 1866, legislators interrogated him on many topics, including race. On the proposed Fourteenth Amendment granting civil rights to freedmen, Lee opined that "at this time, they cannot vote intelligently." Asked if Virginia would be better off if the former slaves would leave the state, he responded, "I think it would be better for Virginia if she could get rid of them. That is no new opinion with me. I have always thought so, and have always been in favor of emancipation—gradual emancipation."[13]

Lee's racial views did not differ significantly from those of other prominent white men and women of his day. Very few saw blacks as even potentially equal to whites, and not even Lincoln foresaw a truly multiracial society. Even into his presidency, he held the fantasy that colonizing the black population would best resolve the country's problems. Harriet Beecher Stowe, whose depiction of slavery in *Uncle Tom's Cabin* had so offended Markie Williams, did not specifically endorse the idea, but she included an epilogue that argued for Northerners to prepare freedmen and freedwomen to "put in practice" in Liberia "the lessons they have learned in America"—an indication of how widespread the totally impracticable idea was.[14]

Lee never developed an enthusiasm for colonization comparable to Lincoln's (or, for that matter, to that of the women in his own family). His basic viewpoint did, however, resemble what Lincoln claimed in his 1854 debates with Stephen Douglas: "There is a physical difference between the white and black races which I believe will forever forbid the two races living together on terms of social and political equality." While avoiding the demeaning language of many whites, North and South, Lee went further than Lincoln in claiming the superiority of the white race over all others, whether Indian or Latino or black. He went further in another respect as well. He considered certain ethnicities among Caucasians to be preeminent. In 1866 Lee suggested to an English visitor to America that there may be differences among various populations, and "that to no race are we more indebted for the virtues and qualifications which constitute a great people, than to the Anglo Saxon."[15]

Still, for each, simple justice was quite another issue, even if that justice might be limited. Lincoln set aside his earlier prejudices to advocate rights for all men, especially the right to vote. Yet he preferred limiting suffrage to the better-educated blacks and those who served in the Union forces. Likewise, Lee favored "restricted suffrage" that would limit voting by most blacks and at least some whites, not because of race but because their lack of education would prevent them from voting intelligently and make them vulnerable to exploitation.[16] His objection arose not so much from racial views as from patriarchal paternalism, and it implied the possibility that at some point these groups could vote wisely.

Lee spent his entire life in a patriarchal, patrician environment, but one leavened by Christian conviction. His mentor, Bishop Meade, consistently taught that "servants" were people too. Lee may not have seen all people as inherently equal, but personal prejudice did not prevent him from promoting justice for all people, regardless of color. In Lexington, he faced numerous opportunities to do so. Halfway through Lee's tenure as president, word reached the college of a large gathering to be held on March 22, 1867, at the freedmen's school in Lexington. Five students decided to look in, literally, on the proceedings. As they peered through a window, a black man approached them. The men exchanged words, which turned to curses. Then one of the students, J. A. McNeill, drew his pistol and struck the man. He ran off just before the other four students were arrested and brought before the mayor. Three days later, the faculty apologized for the students' conduct and admonished the four. McNeill confessed his misconduct and was promptly expelled. When the assistant superintendent of the Freedmen's Bureau complained to Lee, he immediately gave an account of the event and the college's response. The matter ended there.[17] Two years later, faced with the potential of another such incident, Lee posted a notice warning students to "keep away from all such assemblies." Experience had shown, he said, "that should any disturbance occur, efforts will be made to put the blame on Washington College."[18] The students obliged.

White-black relations in Lexington remained, however, at the point of boiling throughout Lee's tenure. He faced another potentially deadly test on May 8, 1868. Francis H. Brockenbrough, the judge's youngest son, encountered a young black man named Caesar Griffin. The two started fighting, and Griffin shot Brockenbrough, wounding him seriously. Griffin was arrested, but before he could be taken to jail, some young men gathered and threatened to lynch him. Captain Harry Estill, an assistant professor at the college, dissuaded them. (In a more dramatic rendering, Lee is depicted as appearing to caution his students, "Young gentlemen," he said, "let the law take its course." According to local newspaper accounts, Estill did the job in Lee's spirit if not on his behalf.)[19]

Two days later, while Brockenbrough fought for his life, a rumor circulated that, if he died, students would storm the jail and kill Griffin. The military commissioner, Lieutenant Jacob Wagner, heard of it and apprised Lee, who immediately circulated word to the students "to abstain from any violation of the law, and to unite in preserving quiet and order on this and every occasion." The next day, the rumors were proven false, but Wagner, still alarmed, asked his superior, General Orlando B. Willcox, to reinforce his garrison to protect the peace. A company of soldiers arrived, but, fearing the worst, Wagner requested still more. Willcox wisely demurred until some incident warranted the additional troops; beyond some Lexingtonians shooting off their mouths or their pistols into the air, no further disruption developed. As Lee advised, the law took its course: Griffin was convicted and sentenced to two years in jail.[20]

Lee may have saved other lives too. In early 1866 a "highwayman" named Jonathan Hughes was hauled to the jail for stealing horses. Angry farmers gathered in front of the old brick building, restrained outside only by an elderly jailor. Students went to find out what the fuss was about. Then Lee moved quietly through the crowd urging that the law be allowed to deal with the matter. The crowd dispersed; Hughes was tried, convicted, and sentenced to eighteen years in prison.[21]

Lee knew more than anyone how, in such troubled times, news of his students lynching a black man, or sharing in the lynching of a white, would inflame public opinion and arouse political repercussions. Concern for his institution motivated Lee. But so did imperatives of human decency and justice, concerns which for Lee transcended racial divisions.

The Problem of Reconstruction

At the same time that these events disrupted the peace of Lexington, national trends veered away from the gentler reconstruction advocated by Presidents Lincoln and Johnson toward a more radical phase. The two presidents essentially sought to restore Southerners' civil and property rights. Congress, deeming that their policies had been too soft on the South, passed a series of measures over Johnson's veto that required former Confederate states to adopt new constitutions that extended the right to vote to all adult males. The legislation also obliged them to ratify the Fourteenth Amendment, which guaranteed civil rights to all freedmen and barred ex-Confederates from holding office. Until Southern states met these demands, they would not be readmitted to the Union but would be treated, instead, as military districts.[22]

It was Lee's worst nightmare. The mandates contradicted the gracious terms Grant had extended at Appomattox and Johnson had established for granting amnesty, as Lee understood them. They also represented the Federal government's enforcing union "by swords and bayonets," a fear that helped send Lee to war in the first place. For its part, though, the Southern establishment had used the more charitable provisions of 1865 and 1866 to reassert its control over state governments and of society, notably over the newly freed black minority.[23] That situation had become the congressional Republicans' worst nightmare.

As ever, Lee approached the situation discreetly, urging reconciliation, remaining out of the public eye, striving to rebuild his college and help his church, and thereby contributing his mite to reuniting the country. He believed he neither could nor should say or do anything. "I am not in a position to make it proper for me to take a public part in the affairs of the country," he wrote to John Brockenbrough, but instead do "all in my power to encourage our people to set manfully to work to restore the country, to rebuild their homes and churches, to educate their children, and to remain with their states, their friends and countrymen." He was, after all, a prisoner on parole.[24]

Mary, who rarely held her opinions to herself, was not so diplomatic. In her letter attacking the "lazy idle negroes," she added, "When we get rid of the freedmen's Bureau & can take the law in our hands we may perhaps do better. If they would only take all their pets north it would be a happy riddance."[25]

If Lee shared her passions, he was too discreet to say so outside of the family. However, his nephew Edward Lee Childe was part of the family circle, living safely in France, far from prying journalists or Radical Republican congressmen. Lee could be more open to him. "The South is to be placed under the dominion of the negroes," Lee predicted to his nephew in January 1868, "that their votes at the coming Presidential election may counterbalance the Conservative votes of the whites at the north." Using black suffrage for partisan gain was but the latest form of political manipulation that, both Robert and Mary argued, had brought on the war in the first place. "The war originated from a doubt-ful question of the Construction of the Constitution, about which our forefathers differed at the time of framing it," he continued. "The South recognized its settlement by the arbitrament of arms; but the purpose for which the south went to war has been perverted by the radical party. Had the present policy been then announced I cannot believe that it would have been tolerated by the country."[26]

Lee often reiterated his prewar argument about the nature of the Constitution. The problem he saw after the war was the same he had seen before it: the failure to live up to the founding vision of the na-tion. In 1869 he complained to Childe about the disenfranchisement of former Confederates and the confiscation of their property (not men-tioning that the loss of Arlington was one result of the policy). Still, he reaffirmed his fundamental faith: "Although Republican forms of Govt: are not now in good repute they still have my preference over all oth-ers. . . . [I]t was not the form of Government that was at fault, but its administration, not the Constitution but the people." He reverted to the ideals of the previous century and generation: "The former was too pure for the latter. It requires a virtuous people to support a republican government & the world has not yet I fear reached the proper standard of morality & integrity to live under the rule of religion and reason. But the time I believe will come, though I shall never see it."[27] Lee was in fact declaring his own purpose in life. In his mission from God, his goal was both religious and secular; the two merged in his striving to build up a "virtuous people." He was bringing his mother's evangelical passion to his father's enlightened objectives.

Lee revealed to Childe another reason that he could simultaneously chafe under acts of Congress yet strive for reconciliation and reunion: politicians were to blame, not the vision. He pinned on them, as he had on abolitionists before the war, the troubles of the nation and its failure to embrace the promises of peace that augured so much good for the country after Appomattox.

Lee seethed, too, over what he considered the needless death of his cousin Orton Williams, Markie's brother. Orton had joined the Con-federate army and commanded an artillery unit under Lee. In 1863 he had been captured behind Yankee lines wearing civilian clothes, sum-marily tried as a spy, and hanged six hours later. Lee took the news hard when he first heard it. In 1866 he still seethed. "My blood boils at the thought of the atrocious outrage, against every manly & christian sentiment which the Great God alone is able to forgive," he fumed to Markie. "I cannot trust my pen or tongue to utter my feelings. He alone can give us resignation."[28]

How was this different from the thousands upon thousands of other deaths during the war, many the result of Lee's orders? To Lee, Williams's execution was willingly performed by men in a miscarriage of justice; it was an act of sin, not of war. Deaths on the battlefield were acts of providence. Never mind that Williams had acted foolishly.

Lee purposefully kept his profile low. "*I have thought, from the time of cessation of hostilities*," he wrote to Varina Davis, the former Confederate first lady, "*that silence and patience on the part of the South was the true course*, and I think so still." Except when he had to testify before Congress, he avoided public statements. His work in remote Lexington allowed him to avoid major public appearances and commitments. He declined the pleas of Robert Ould, a state senator, to run as a candidate for governor in 1867. Excusing himself on the basis of his advancing age, inadequate experience, and preference to serve Virginia where he was, Lee also explained that his election "would be used to excite hostility toward the State, and to injure the people in the eyes of the country by the dominant party; and I therefore can not consent to become the instrument of bringing distress upon those whose prosperity and happiness are so dear to me." For him, that happiness remained paramount. "If my disfranchisement and privation of civil rights, would secure to the citizens of the State the enjoyment of civil liberty and equal rights under the Constitution, I would willingly accept them in their stead."[29]

On one occasion, he broke his pattern in a way that showed his anger over Reconstruction. The Lees spent much of the summer of 1868 at the Greenbrier in White Sulphur Springs, where the baths provided Mary relief from pain. In August, Lee was approached by a former foe, William S. Rosecrans, a Union general who had outfoxed Lee in western Virginia and later suffered an inglorious defeat at Chickamauga. Rosecrans was serving as US minister to Mexico. As a Democrat not eager to see Republicans (especially Grant, who had cashiered him after his loss) win that fall's elections, he wanted Lee to consult Southern leaders gathered at the Greenbrier and prepare a statement he could use to assist his party. Lee obliged, gathering together a large group that included the former Confederate vice president, Alexander Stephens, P. G. T. Beauregard, and John Letcher. They met with Rosecrans at Lee's cottage and produced a response that, as expected, "Old Rosy" published widely.

The "White Sulphur paper" purported to express "the sentiment of the Southern people," but, with Lee's name prominently first among the signers, it encapsulated his opinions. It accepted the fact that questions over slavery and secession "were decided by the war," and claimed that Southerners almost unanimously intended "in good faith to abide by that decision." As a result, the letter continued, "the Southern people laid down their arms and sought to resume their former relations with the United States Government" under terms that implied a return to the status quo antebellum, that is, the old social and political order minus slavery and secession. It was what Lee seemed to have thought Grant had promised at Appomattox.

In that spirit, the statement continued, Southern states abolished slavery, annulled their secession ordinances, and sought peacefully and sincerely "to fulfill all their duties under the Constitution of the United States, which they had sworn to protect." Then arose the major problem that caused Lee such unease. If the Southerners' "action in these particulars had been met in a spirit of frankness and cordiality, we believe that, ere this, old irritations would have passed away, and the wounds inflicted by the war would have been, in a great measure, healed." That is, Northerners failed to live up to their side of the bargain. This was *their* fault, for, "as far as we are advised, the people of the South entertain no unfriendly feeling towards the government of the United States, but they complain that their rights under the Constitution are withheld from them in the administration thereof."

The group then refuted allegations about poor race relations in the South. They denied any hostility (efforts to reestablish quasi slavery notwithstanding).[30] Instead, they asserted, oppressing the black population would be counterproductive to everyone's prosperity, if nothing else, because it constituted a major portion of the labor supply. White Southerners needed them to produce crops. Black Southerners needed jobs so they would not "become paupers, dependent on public bounty." Any problem, they contended, resulted from Reconstruction. "We believe that but for the influences exerted to stir up the passions of the negroes that the two races would soon adjust themselves on a basis of mutual kindness and advantage."

The writers then appealed to Northern prejudice. "It is true that the people of the South, together with the people of the North and West, are, for obvious reasons, opposed to any system of laws which will place the political power of the country in the hands of the negro race." They were correct; majorities in other sections feared the dominance of non-white races.[31] But, the Southern leaders asserted, they meant well: "This opposition springs from no feelings of enmity, but from a deep seated conviction that at present the negroes have neither the intelligence nor other qualifications which are necessary to make them safe depositories of political power. They would inevitably become the victims of demagogues, who for selfish purposes would mislead them, to the serious injury of the public." Lee's paternalism was clear, as was his fear of democracy and of troublemakers who would exploit the ignorance of the masses—especially the black masses—for their own selfish ends.

It is a revealing document. It places Lee's phobias in full view, along with his denials of historical and contemporaneous reality. In that sense the letter heralded fantasies of idyllic Dixie where old times should not be forgotten. It also expressed the complaints of Southern leaders about the direction of Reconstruction, which, they alleged, was not what they thought they had been promised nor what they expected. Yet it concluded by reasserting Lee's hopes for the future:

> The great want of the South is peace. The people earnestly desire tranquility and the restoration of the Union. They deprecate disorder and excitement as the most serious obstacle to their prosperity. They ask a restoration of their rights under the Constitution. They desire relief from oppressive misrule. Above all, they would appeal to their countrymen for the re-establishment in the Southern States of that which has justly been the right of every American—the right of self-government. Establish these on a firm basis, and we can safely promise on behalf of the Southern people that they will faithfully obey the Constitution and laws of the United States, treat the negro with kindness and humanity, and fulfill every duty incumbent on peaceful citizens loyal to the Constitution of the country.[32]

Lee's perception of the South, if indeed the statement embodied it, was naive at best and dishonest at worst. It also may have shown the depth of his fury at Reconstruction, which—perhaps—he expressed as the meeting of Southern leaders adjourned. According to Robert Louis Dabney, Fletcher S. Stockdale, who had briefly served as governor of Texas in 1865, attended the meeting with Rosecrans and had expressed some defiance. When he left the meeting, Lee thanked Stockdale for his "brave, true words." He explained that he had guarded his public words carefully, but then said, "Governor, if I had foreseen the use those people"—his frequent term for Northerners—"designed to make of their victory, there would have been no surrender at Appomattox Courthouse; no, sir, not by me." Then, Dabney wrote, "throwing back his head like an old war-horse," Lee added, "Had I foreseen these results of subjugation, I would have preferred to die at Appomattox with my brave men, my sword in this right hand." Asking Stockdale not to repeat his statement, Lee bade him good morning.[33]

The quotation is highly questionable on historical grounds. Its sentiment nevertheless resembles what Lee had written to his nephew earlier that year.[34] He was in fact angry. He believed that acts, policies, and events precipitated by radical Northerners gave him reason to be (even as he ignored provocations from radical Southerners). But in public, he held his tongue, and in word and deed pursued the mission he believed God had given him. When the organizer of the Gettysburg Battlefield Memorial Association invited Lee to join other leaders to mark sites for monuments, Lee declined, advising "not to keep open the sores of war, but to follow the example of those nations who endeavoured to obliterate the marks of civil strife and to commit to oblivion the feelings it engendered." His nephew Childe, in an early biography of his uncle, related the story of a mother who presented to him her two sons as she berated the North. Lee instructed her, "Madam, don't bring up your sons to detest the United States Government. Recollect that we form but one country *now*. Abandon all these local animosities, and make your sons Americans."[35] If the story is true, it arises from the same motive he sought to fulfill at Washington College and Grace Church, and, indeed, in the reunited nation.

These elements seem contradictory, even hypocritical: his private ire over the direction of the country, his public words and deeds aimed at reconciliation. Yet Lee's era held its share of contradictions. He faced the ever-present dichotomy between reality and ideals that would to some degree be true for anyone who holds a vision of the way things should be. Moreover, the vision he held was not always that of others, especially on what the postwar nation should aim to be. He sought reconciliation, but for him that meant *restoration*, returning to antebellum social norms with only the exclusion of slavery. Many Northerners, whether Grant in one way and Radical Republicans in others, held widely differing views.[36] Nevertheless, Lee's theology gave him a means of resolving these seemingly conflicting viewpoints, if only for himself.

He could deplore the political machinations of radical reconstruction while retaining his commitment to what he saw as the greater will of God. Human action would inevitably fall short of the divine intention; God's plan is greater and, by providence, someday will prevail. That remained the marrow of Lee's faith. He therefore could acquiesce, however grudgingly, to the reality of human failing while pursuing what he believed to be the divine plan, recognizing the reality of his own frailty. God's plan was clear. Providence had spoken through the North's victory and decided against Lee and the Confederacy. Lee had the responsibility to resign himself and submit, willingly and actively, to what the Almighty had ordained. Come what may, Lee could retain his hope and labor for what he saw as the will of the Lord.

CHAPTER 21

"Do Now Rest from Their Labors"

~

The Earthly End

Autumn in Lexington can be glorious: clear, warm days made all the brighter by the first golden tinges on the trees. September 28, 1870, did not dawn as one of those days: it was gray, wet, and cold. As a front moved in, the weather turned progressively worse.

Lee rose exceptionally early that morning. After breakfast, he hurried Agnes and Mildred off to the chapel service, in pursuit of his new theory that having young ladies in the congregation would inspire greater attendance among the young male students whose diligence was beginning to slip. If he followed his normal custom, he attended too. Afterward, in his office in the chapel basement, he busied himself with the endless stream of letters to read or write: prospective students inquiring about admission, bills requiring authorization for payment, parents craving reassurance or, more likely, receiving his warning of their sons' precarious standing. Writing his friend Samuel Tagart, whom he had visited in Baltimore the previous summer, provided a brief respite from college business. Tagart had recently asked about Lee's health. "In answer to your question," Lee responded, "I reply that I am much better."[1]

Lee's health had concerned more than just the Marylander. During the war, Lee had endured two broken wrists, a heart attack, and chronic rheumatism. In the autumn of 1869, Lee had suffered heart problems that, he confided to Custis and other intimates, he feared would kill him. He pondered resigning the presidency, which was the last thing the trustees and faculty wanted. They offered Lee a reprieve from his duties during the spring of 1870 so that he could take what they hoped would be a relaxing trip through the South.[2]

He found little relaxation. From the start, at every train stop along his way, crowds swarmed around him eager to catch a glimpse of, or, even better, shake the hand of or glean a word from, the Hero of the South whose exploits were already approaching the mythological. At least the trip allowed him to visit the grave of his beloved Annie in North Carolina.

Back in Virginia, Lee spent several weeks in Hot Springs in neighboring Bath County. He savored its warm waters and relished views of its gentle mountains. On Sundays he probably attended services at little Christ Church in Warm Springs. Mary disturbed his peace with some worries from home. They faced difficulties with servants, now hired rather than enslaved. A cow they owned was ill enough to require "very gentle treatment" from one of those servants. (To Lee's regret, the cow died, but, he wrote Agnes, "I am glad that she is out of misery.") Baths notwithstanding, physical weakness still plagued him, as did the attention his presence always drew. "It is very wearying being at these public places," he told Mary, "and the benefit hardly worth the cost." He added, portentously, "I do not think that I can even stand Lexington long." Evidently he hid his weariness well; William Preston Johnston, reported that Lee began the academic year with "that quiet zeal and noiseless energy that marked all his actions." His colleagues were relieved.[3] They should not have been.

At around 1:30 p.m., his morning's work completed, Lee walked home for dinner. He consumed his usual plate of grapes and then dined on "but a poor pair of chickens." As always, he took what he termed his postprandial "snooze" in an armchair in the dining room's bay window, placed so he could enjoy the view of hills and fields beyond the college. As he rested, Mildred practiced Felix Mendelssohn's *Songs without Words* on the piano. When she came to the movement called "Funeral March,"[4] Lee walked over to her and "in his playful way" said, "Life, that is a doleful piece you are playing."

Lee faced one more appointment that day. The vestry was meeting at Grace Church. As he gave Mildred his customary kiss upon leaving, he muttered, "I wish I did not have to go, & listen to all that powwow." For several moments he stood at the door, then walked down the hill to the church for his 4 p.m. appointment.[5]

Lee well knew the session would be tiresome. Grace Church faced two problems that simply had to be addressed. One was space. The congregation had outgrown its facilities. The other was money. The parish had deferred maintenance on the rectory where the Pendletons lived, and had failed to pay Pendleton's salary in full. As senior warden, Lee found himself in the midst of trying to resolve the predicaments. He, Francis Smith, Thomas Williamson, W. P. Johnston, and one other had been appointed in May 1869 to consider "the enlargement of the Church, the repair on the Parsonage; and the payment of the church debts; and to raise the necessary funds for these purposes." Three months later, the vestry had added Custis to the group. The following year, the same three who had overseen the construction of the college chapel—the two Lees and Williamson—were appointed "to proceed as they think proper in securing the needed increased accommodation for the congregation of Grace Church." But, as Robert had told Mary, "Resolutions will not build the church. It will require money."[6]

They faced a further complication at the meeting, for Pendleton had forced the issue. He formally recommended either enlarging or replacing the building, and offered to make another tour to raise funds to do so. He also complained that his salary of $1,000 was inadequate, asked for an increase if possible, and tendered his resignation if a younger, or at least different, pastor could in the vestry's opinion better serve Grace Church. The vestry had the delicate task of responding to their pastor and his mixed messages.[7] Lee knew a difficult meeting awaited him.

By the time Lee left home, a steady rain had thoroughly dampened the already chilly day. He took a seat in a pew in the unheated church, his military cape loosely covering his shoulders. As members gathered, they swapped stories of Bishop Meade and also of Chief Justice John Marshall, whose portrait had just arrived to grace the college walls and whose descendant had just arrived to join the student body.[8] Then Lee called the meeting to order.

For the next three hours, the vestry gradually ticked off its items of business. It appointed a committee of three to "raise funds for increasing Church accommodations." To head that daunting task they anointed the formidable Francis Smith, then prudently requested some of the congregation's leading ladies to help: the wife of Matthew Fontaine Maury, the VMI oceanographer already renowned as the "pathfinder of the seas"; a relative of former Governor Letcher; and "Mrs. Mary Lee."

To pay for this project, they agreed to Pendleton's idea of a fundraising tour if he thought it would be worthwhile. He would visit Richmond, Norfolk, and Baltimore to collect pledges, then proceed to Louisville, Mobile, and New Orleans to raise additional contributions.

As for the rector's pay, the treasurer reported that for six years Pendleton had received an average of only $764.16 per year. After voting to raise his salary to $1,200, the vestry appointed another committee to determine how to fulfill its commitment. According to Johnston, who was chosen to lead that effort, members went round and round trying to raise that amount among themselves, only to fall short by $55. Finally, Lee said in a low voice, "I will give that sum." With that, they adjourned. Johnston later thought that Lee "seemed tired toward the close of the meeting," and "showed an unusual flush, but at the time no apprehensions were felt."[9]

The meeting had been long, tedious, difficult, but ultimately productive. As Lee walked out into the chilly air, a fellow vestryman, the physician Robert L. Madison, remarked that it was too damp for either of them to be out. "Yes," said Lee, "but you see I am well wrapped up." In spite of all they had just been through, Lee appeared unusually cheerful as he chatted with his friends until they reached the gate of the president's house.[10]

The family had delayed their "tea," as they called their supper, until Lee arrived home at about 7:30. As he entered the dining room, Mary asked, "Where have you been all this time, we have been waiting for you." He took his customary place at the table, standing to say grace. Mary, Agnes, and Custis waited for words that he could not speak: "the lips could not utter the prayer of the heart." Lee sat down. Mary said that he looked tired and offered him a cup of tea, but he responded unintelligibly. They called Mildred from the parlor where she was laughing with two students. By then her father was "looking very strange & speaking incoherently," she recalled. The family immediately summoned Madison and the other physician, Howard Barton, who had also attended the vestry meeting, contacting both before they reached home. While waiting for the doctors, the family helped Lee into the same armchair he had occupied that afternoon. When the first doctor arrived, he ordered Lee into the "small, low, single bed," which they placed with the head facing the bay window so he could take in the scenery he admired.[11]

By then the afternoon rain had developed into a horrific downpour. It would flood the region so thoroughly that mail delivery stopped for eight days. In the president's house, Mildred recorded, "there was darkness in our hearts!"

Because her husband remained in the dining room, Mary, confined to her wheelchair on the main floor of the house, could come and go to tend to him as one day followed upon another. She kept vigil at his bedside by day, as Agnes did by night. Each morning Mildred relieved Agnes and gave her father his breakfast; he could still sit up to eat. Through the day, Custis sat with him for hours at a time, "& always one of the College Professors." Lee seemed to know what was happening around him, to understand what was said, and to respond, if only in monosyllables. Still, as Mildred recorded, "The silence was awful!"[12]

Lee lapsed in and out of consciousness. "I remember one day as I was stroking his hand," Mildred wrote later, "he took mine up & kissed it—& another time I heard him say 'precious baby'—& then again 'I am so weary'! Some one said, 'General, you will soon be able to take a ride on Traveller'—& he shook his head sadly." Agnes and Mildred sat by in silence, not even reading passages from the Bible or his favorite hymns. "Words seemed frozen in our mouths, he was speechless—so were we!" Custis came from VMI to relieve them, as Mary passively watched. Callers came by offering sympathy and help. Strangely, no one thought to contact Mary Custis, Fitzhugh, or Rob.

For two days Lee slept "almost continuously," Mary apprised Carter. Doctors thought that sleep might cure him. When rest alone availed nothing, they began treating him with medicines, even resorting to turpentine, which for centuries had been used as an inhalant, and more recently was being marketed across America as a veritable cure-all. Their concoctions "aroused" him and let him enjoy the food they provided. Mary held out hope that "a life so important to his family & country may be longer spared."[13]

A week passed. Suddenly, on Monday, October 10, Lee's condition deteriorated. Custis tried to buoy him with hopes of improvement, but Lee shook his head and pointed upward. Tuesday was worse still. "His face had an agonized expression," and he was more restless, though Mildred perceived "a light in his eyes as he saw me!" She went to bed, exhausted. Almost immediately, Agnes woke her. Entering the dining room, Mildred found doctors attending him and Pendleton reading the "prayers for the dead" from the Book of Common Prayer.[14] Mary sat in her wheelchair, their children kneeling around his bed. The family remained with him "through the dreadful hours of that long night."

By Wednesday morning, October weather had returned in all its glory. In the dining room of the president's house, Lee lingered. At 9 a.m. "he seemed to be struggling," so Mildred hurriedly summoned Dr. Madison. The physician came, looked at Lee, and walked away without a word. Lee died a moment later.

For two weeks, Mary had kept watch stoically or, as Lee would have advised, with "resignation." Now she succumbed to her emotions. In the privacy of her room, she put her arms around Precious Life and cried, "Do be kind to me now!"[15]

News spread quickly. The college promptly suspended all classes. Mourning had begun.

Agnes laid out clothes for his burial: a black suit, fit for a civilian. Mildred wondered if dressing him in his Confederate uniform might have been considered treasonous. Having been summoned at last, Rooney and Rob arrived. Dignitaries flowed into town. The faculty at once voted to urge the trustees to maintain Lee's office precisely as he left it, and also to rename the college. Meeting on the day of Lee's funeral, the trustees concurred on all counts. In adopting the name Washington and Lee University, the trustees sought to honor the first of its namesakes as "Founder," the other as the "Restorer of our beloved College"—while at the same time elevating the school's status to that of university. They also requested the family to allow his remains to "remain forever within the walls of this College" marked by a monument "which may stand as a perpetual memorial of his virtues."[16]

On Thursday, Lee's body was borne from the house to the chapel, both so recently completed. Students and cadets marched in solemn procession, gathering in the chapel as Lee's coffin, covered by a pall and adorned with boxwood, arborvitae, strawflowers, and scented geraniums, was arranged. Then Pendleton walked to the rostrum to lead a simple service. He asked the question, "Why did General Lee come here?" As a student, Charles Meriwether, reported later that day to his cousin, it was not for employment, Pendleton said, nor retirement. "To train and lead on the minds of the young men of the South in the Arts and literature" was one motive, the rector agreed, before telling of an incident that occurred in spring 1866. He had encountered Lee as he walked to chapel to lead the morning service. They continued together. "Just before getting to chapel, he stopped and there seemed to be something on his mind. I looked at him. The tears glistened in his eyes, and I asked him what it was. He answered, 'Unless we can induce all these young men to become honest, sincere Christians, we will have failed my object in coming here.'" The priest, an evangelical in the style of Meade, concluded with an exhortation to accomplish Lee's objectives. A prayer followed. Meriwether heard sobs, admitting that his own eyes "were wet with tears, but it was all I could do to restrain them."[17]

The body lay in state as students and cadets kept constant watch, until Saturday's funeral. Mary could not attend. She stayed at home reading letters he had written to her over the years. The crowd far exceeded the chapel's seating capacity. Inside, Pendleton read the simple burial office from the Book of Common Prayer, assisted by William White of the Presbyterian church and J. William Jones, the Baptist pastor. The rite consisted of readings from Scripture and of prayers, but traditionally did not include a sermon, much less a eulogy; nor had Lee wished to have any. The service itself was neither more nor less than any Episcopalian would have had.[18]

When the rite concluded, hundreds of mourners gathered on the bank in front of the chapel and sang the hymn that Mary had chosen for the occasion, Lee's favorite:[19]

> How firm a foundation, ye saints of the Lord,
> Is laid for your faith in his excellent word!
> What more can he say than to you he hath said,
> You who unto Jesus for refuge have fled?
>
> Fear not, I am with thee; O be not dismay'd,
> I, I am thy God, and will still give thee aid;
> I'll strengthen thee, help thee, and cause thee to stand,
> Upheld by my righteous, omnipotent hand.
>
> When through the deep waters I call thee to go,
> The rivers of woe shall not thee overflow;
> For I will be with thee, thy troubles to bless,
> And sanctify to thee thy deepest distress.
>
> When through fiery trials thy pathway shall lie,
> My grace, all-sufficient, shall be thy supply;
> The flame shall not hurt thee; I only design
> Thy dross to consume, and thy gold to refine.
>
> The soul that on Jesus hath leaned for repose,
> I will not, I will not desert to his foes;
> That soul, though all hell shall endeavour to shake,
> I'll never—no, never—no, never forsake.[20]

The Debated Legacy Begins

As Lexington mourned Lee, so did the South. The day after he died, activity in Richmond halted. Bells tolled from sunrise to sunset. That Saturday, as thousands gathered in Lexington for his funeral, ten thousand mourned him outside Atlanta's city hall. All businesses closed in Lynchburg, Richmond, Montgomery, Savannah, Atlanta, and countless towns throughout the South. Many of those cities held services to honor Lee.[21]

Yet appreciation for Lee, if not grief, spread beyond the region. The *Philadelphia Evening Telegraph* wrote that Lee's death "was received with regret throughout the country," and papers from "the North as well as the South, without distinction of party, have kindly articles, in which much is said of the purity and dignity of his character."[22]

That was not universally true. Two Ohio journals contrasted totally over Lee's memory. The *Stark County Democrat* of Canton declared that "here in the North, wherever justice has assumed the place of prejudice, the name of General Lee is the synonym for every virtue which mortal man possesses." Beyond his military proficiency, Lee's example to Southerners "was incalculable in its results, and it was upon such men that the South was wont to lean in this hour of her humiliation and woe." The *Tiffin Tribune* dissented. While his death will "be regretted by very many in the North, . . . those most true to his memory will regret that his death had not taken place ten years ago, before his previous fair fame had been stained with rebellion."[23]

Outside the South, disagreement pervaded the nation. Hearing that employees at the US customs house in Savannah lowered the Stars and Stripes to half-mast, superiors quickly raised it back; in Kansas the *Leavenworth Weekly Times* indignantly objected to honoring the man who had devoted "*his best powers, his mightiest energies*, to the organization, and the hurling of the *rebel* army against this grand temple of Freedom." Yet from the west, the *Washington Standard* in Olympia opined, "Whatever may be thought of the cause to which he pledged his life, fortune, and position, no liberal minded man will question the purity and sincerity of his motives. As a military man he had no peer; in his private character he had no superior."[24]

Personal opinions, too, remained divided, strong, and enduring, across race and time. As the war ended, an African American barber in Philadelphia told a Southern gentleman in his chair, "I wish I had

Jeff. Davis, or Beauregard, or Benjamin, or Wigfall where you are sitting, I would never let them leave this chair alive." "What would you do
to Lee?" asked the Southerner. The barber replied, "I would be proud
to shave him, sir. Such a good and great man ought never to die." The
customer persisted, "But he fought against you—he was your enemy as
well as the others." "Sir," said the barber, "all the harm he did us was
done like a man, and in the open field, and he believed he was doing
his duty." Frederick Douglass, though, the former slave and a leading
voice of black Americans, bemoaned "the *nauseating* flatteries of the
late Robert E. Lee" in newspapers that made it seem "that the soldier
who kills the most men in battle, even in a bad cause, is the greatest
Christian, and entitled to the highest place in heaven."[25]

What elevated Lee in the eyes of New York newspapers in particular,
even more than his military expertise, was his conduct after the war,
which they attributed to his character. The *Tribune* marveled "that a
man could be a traitor to his country and yet strictly honest toward his
fellow-men." Such was Lee. "Though guilty of weak and wicked acts,
it cannot be shown that he ever did a mean thing; and it was his mis-
fortune that he was less firm of purpose than by nature generous and
yielding," and thus "he was not wholly bad." The *New York Herald* took
a still more positive tone. "Many brighter intellects than Lee's were
misled by the dazzling will-o'-the-wisp of State rights," but he alone
among Southern leaders "fitly comprehended the magnanimity of the
Government" and, "confessing by all his acts that his own cause was lost
forever, deported himself with the modest dignity that becomes a fallen
chief." The fact that the South's most venerated hero would quietly take
on such a task in a humble college in a remote town in western Virginia,
far from vindictive antagonists and adulatory crowds alike, especially
impressed the *New York World*. Its editor noted that, to a greater degree
than many Union supporters, Lee contributed "to make our triumph
complete, noble, and assured," and that "must command the deliberate
admiration even of those who most earnestly condemned the course
upon which he decided."[26]

In short, Lee, the vanquished chieftain in war, had become a leader
in peace, esteemed by even some of his former foes. His character impelled him to move from one to the other, and his character was shaped
by his faith.

Non Incautus Futuri

~

A Personal Epilogue

To me, Lee's personal greatness emerges in the last years of his life. Having spent four years engaged in war and destruction, he devoted the next five to restoring and reclaiming what had been destroyed in Virginia, the South, and the nation. As much as his values reflected the past, he looked toward, and built for, the years to come. In so doing, he fulfilled the Lee family motto, *Non Incautus Futuri*, generally translated by the university that adopted Lee's name, "Not unmindful of the future."[1]

By looking to the future, Lee saved Washington College. He accepted the presidency of a school in shambles, resurrected it, and made it greater than it had ever been. He did so by directing its energies toward the immediate needs of the state, region, and country. His name and reputation attracted donors and students. His expectations helped motivate students to strive for serious learning and gentlemanly behavior. Once an ingenious military tactician, he proved himself an equally inventive, forward-looking, innovative educator who envisioned the future and sought to position his school to prepare for it. He brought the college into the late nineteenth century in ways that heralded the twentieth, and under his leadership, it reached its highest enrollment of the entire century.

Lee also saved Grace Church. When Lee arrived in town, the recalcitrant acts of its uncompromising rector, William Nelson Pendleton, had caused the church to be closed by federal dictate. Five years later, the congregation was thriving, in no small measure because the students and faculty Lee drew to the college were also drawn to the church he attended. Its building, suffering from wartime neglect, needed immediate repairs and, because of its growth, soon groaned under the happy burden of so many people, especially young people, attending its services. Like so many Southerners, Lexington's Episcopalians lacked resources to provide much beyond their bare necessities. Undeterred, the vestry, led quietly by Lee, managed at his last meeting on earth both to pay the rector and to envisage a larger church that could pursue and expand the congregation's mission and work. Ironically, Lee's death made building that church possible. At its first meeting after Lee died, the vestry elected Custis Lee to fill his father's place (as he would soon do at the college as well), then voted to proceed with the "improvement and enlargement" of the building. The next day the vestry authorized constructing a church seating twelve hundred people—later wisely scaling that back to eight hundred—with Sunday school and meeting rooms, bearing the name Grace Memorial Church in Lee's honor.[2] Responding to appeals that cited Lee's name and interest, donors over time made the new church a reality.

Similarly, Lee also helped to save the South. He tried to set it on a course that led to reunion, reconciliation, and recuperation, and provided an example of how that might be done. While never repudiating either the cause for which he fought or the constitutional principle that led him to fight, he understood what the South needed, which was a spirit of resignation—as his tradition defined the term—that not only accepted but also sought to restore union and work toward genuine progress and prosperity.

Progressive in so many ways, Lee did not offer similar leadership in matters of race. Lee accepted the racial assumptions that prevailed generally among whites of his day, fought a war that aimed to preserve the institution he rued, and extended those earlier racial assumptions after that effort had failed, even as the defeat of his troops brought what he considered the positive benefit of freeing all slaves. Then, he took a far rosier attitude toward the South's efforts toward Reconstruction and toward the freedmen than facts warranted.

At the same time, he avoided the blatant racism that came to pervade the South—and eventually the North. He had long recognized the humanity of African Americans, insisted on the need for justice for them as for all people, and welcomed the end of slavery.

No wonder, then, that Lee's heritage remains as complex and controversial as the age in which he lived. He seemed to know it would be, as he limited his public presence and resolutely declined to run for governor of Virginia. He shielded his name against political, sectional, or economic misuse. He actively discouraged memorializing Confederate battles. Nevertheless, at his death, "Lost Cause" impulses broke forth in full measure, waving the name of Lee the general alongside the rebel battle flag, even as Northern whites and Southern whites strove to reconcile the nation—a mission he sought—albeit with a reassertion, North and South, of segregation, white supremacy, and racism, trends contrary to his beliefs if not always to his actions. Or perhaps it was the other way around, as John McClure suggests in arguing that although he consistently denounced the intimidation of African Americans and their teachers in Lexington, his "boys" knew his political views—or thought they did—and behaved accordingly.[3]

Interpretations of the alleged incident at St. Paul's Church in Richmond, when Lee reportedly knelt next to a black man at the communion rail, illustrate the enigma of his heritage, and arguably his character. The first published account of it appeared only in 1905, related by a die-hard Confederate with racist views, named Thomas L. Broun. But the incident would have occurred in the late spring of 1865, at about the time Lee had spoken to Marsena Patrick and written of God's "chastening hand" to William Platt, precisely when Lee was dealing with the spiritual consequences of war, defeat, his role, and what—by God—lay ahead for him, the South, and the nation. Did Lee act to reassert Southern white status, or to signify healing and reconciliation? The historian Philip Schwarz, in exploring the purported event, suggests that more deeply understanding Lee's spirituality would assist in interpreting the event. "What might there have been in his religious convictions," he asked, "that would motivate him to act as he did in the June 1865 incident?"[4]

If the story is true, it suggests that Lee honestly believed that everyone had a place at God's table, regardless of human differentiation. Even so, a double tragedy abides: First, that in his last years such a principle did not extend even further, beyond his commitment to educating and evangelizing the young, rebuilding the South, and restoring the unity of the nation, to ensuring a place for all people at society's table as well as God's. Second, that this spirit that he sought to pursue—however incompletely—did not continue, and that he did not live longer to help it spread. However, examining Lee's ethnic attitudes alongside three other elements of his outlook helps to reveal both the limits and the expansiveness of his perspective on the world. Held together, these various temperaments also had the ironic effect of tempering the negative sides of each.

By twenty-first-century standards, Lee's racial positions are, to say the least, regressive. Yet by those of his own era, they were, if not progressive, then at the very least typical. The enlightened authors who permeated his childhood education were less than enlightened on matters of race; David Hume, the Scottish philosopher, opposed slavery but declared "the negroes to be naturally inferior to the whites. There scarcely ever was a civilized nation of that complexion, nor even any individual eminent either in action or speculation." Lee said virtually as much to his cousin, Thomas Carter. But whites were, to his eye, superior not only to blacks. Serving in the army widened his experience of other races, notably Indian and Latino, far more than that of most Americans. That experience confirmed—to him—the opinion of the vast majority of whites of his day, who considered themselves at the top of the evolutionary pyramid.[5]

Yet some, even among Caucasians, were closer to the top than others. In 1866 Lee suggested to an English correspondent that his "visit to America must have impressed upon [him] the fact, that though climate, government and circumstances have produced changes in the character of the people, yet in all essential qualities, they resemble the races from which they are sprung; and that to no race are we more indebted for the virtues and qualifications which constitute a great people, than to the Anglo Saxon."[6]

Whatever Lee's private opinions, however, he carefully upheld the laws and practices of his day for the benefit of all persons, regardless of race. He insisted on justice for everyone, black or white, as he did in confronting potential lynch mobs at the Lexington courthouse, or, earlier, in planning for the emancipation of the Custis slaves at a time certain. Moreover, his private views did not preclude his care and concern for individuals, regardless of race or station. As a young lieutenant, he took his late mother's slave Nat to Georgia to care for the old man's health. During the war Lee looked after the well-being of Perry and Meredith, two slaves who were with him. Of course, in so doing he may also have suffered the naïveté, or even outright self-deception, of many slaveholders that the institution was not as bad as it was.

Two other elements inherent in Lee's background moderated his ethnic views: his patrician class and the paternalist perspective that accompanied it. Lee spent his lifetime in the rarefied air of Virginia's elite.

He spent much of his life in one of the nation's most prominent mansions, placed upon such a height that its residents would look down on the rest of the world. Throughout his life, Lee held himself aloof from others; it should surprise no one that he avoided the Christmas eggnog festivities at West Point. But though later characterized as "the marble man," no one ever called him a snob. Moreover, with *noblesse* came the obligation of duty: to serve, to oversee, to seek the long view over society's well-being, following the example of such luminaries as Washington, Jefferson, Franklin, and the other founders who assumed a longtime perch above the madding crowd. It should also surprise no one that the Constitution they wrote provided for the people to elect directly only the House of Representatives; all others were indirectly chosen in order to promote what Jefferson called an "aristocracy of talent," theoretically open to anyone, but still an "aristocracy." Nevertheless, Lee spent most of his career as a soldier of middling rank, accepting without complaint whatever quarters were assigned him. He moved easily from the superintendent's house at West Point to a tent in the dusty Texas frontier, where he showed as much concern for soldiers grieving the death of their sons as he did for his social peers.

Arlington House stood, too, as a shrine to paternalism. This classical ideal held three characteristics. First, a relationship: the term derives from the Latin *pater*, "father." Second, a superiority: as the father heads the family, so the father figure oversees those dependent upon him. Third, an element of caring: it is the paternal responsibility to provide for dependents, helping them to grow and prosper. Though paternalism vests power in the father figure, it is to be used in the best interests of all.[7]

This had been a noble ideal of ancient Rome and prized in colonial Virginia. No home was more classical than Arlington, both outwardly with its columns and pediment placed high on a hill, and inwardly in the hierarchy of the estate over which its owner presided. Major Custis, the *pater*, lived with his wife off his lands, beneficently presiding over his world; following them were his daughter and her husband in the next tier, then their children, the males being the primary future heirs; the white overseers; finally, lowest, the enslaved population with their own hierarchy, the house servants in the lead.[8]

As an ideal, paternalism (or, more appropriately to include both genders, parentalism) justified slavery even as it also undermined it. Master and mistress looked after their slaves, providing the necessities of life, while slaves in turn obediently and loyally sustained the means for the master and family to live. In so doing, advocates insisted, everyone benefited. Yet it also presumed the very humanity of bondsmen, placing them within a family context so that they by definition differed from animals held as chattel. As well, paternal/maternal responsibility weighed especially heavily on Christian masters and mistresses who, at least in their own minds, had committed themselves to practice the Golden Rule and to teach the true faith to their slaves.[9] For that reason Bishop Meade had energetically advised slaveholders to do just that for the benefit of the souls of their "servants."

Thus, faith, the fourth critical characteristic of Lee's perspective, shows its effects. For Meade, the Custises, and the Lees to use the term "servants" rather than "slaves" reflected their paternalist attitudes, but it also coincided with their evangelical religion and created an innate disjuncture. The Bible may assume slavery as a given, but Jesus came as a "servant."[10]

So, then, blacks might be racially and socially inferior in the eyes of the masters and mistresses of Arlington, but both parentalism and faith required the patricians to care for them.

Mr. Custis built a structure for his "servants" to use as a schoolroom (even if they did not) and as a church (which they did, and he joined them). Mrs. Custis and Mary taught the rudiments of religion and of reading to help their servants prepare for eternity and Liberia at the same time. Robert cared, in personal ways, first for Nat, then later for Perry and Meredith. Of course, they all may have done so with the naïveté (or self-deception) of many slaveholders that the institution was not as bad as it was. In so doing, though, these assumptions also opened ways to refute antislavery claims. Markie, in her diary, denied Harriet Beecher Stowe's depiction of slavery in *Uncle Tom's Cabin* on the basis of the good treatment of Arlington's enslaved population and the care their benevolent master provided.[11] Her theory was, of course, belied by reality. Slaves rarely received remotely humane treatment.

Still, his relationship with Nat, Peter, and Meredith may point toward a respect that Lee offered to individuals regardless of their race. The historian Elizabeth Varon records another incident, potentially as ambiguous as the scene at St. Paul's but much better attested. When Lee entered the McLean house at Appomattox to surrender, Grant introduced him to his staff. That included his military secretary, Ely S. Parker, a Native American who was an Iroquois sachem. Another Grant aide,

Horace Porter, remembered Lee eyeing Parker's "swarthy features" as if to mistake Parker "for a negro, and was struck with astonishment to find that the commander of the Union armies had one of that race on his personal staff." Parker's memory differed. "After Lee had stared at me for a moment . . . he extended his hand and said, 'I am glad to see one real American here.' I shook his hand and said, 'We are all Americans.'"[12] Grace was met with grace.

If Parker more accurately depicted Lee's response to a person of color, that suggests an attitude by which Lee, though prone to stereotyping along ethnic and racial lines, nevertheless proffered his hand—in Parker's case literally—to individuals. This attitude carried over to political life. Though committed to the ideals of the American republic, Lee harbored his doubts about democracy. Demagogues and abolitionists could too easily sway the masses, causing Lee, as states started seceding, to conclude that "the country was doomed to run the full length of democracy." Then, after the war, uneducated and vulnerable freedmen, he alleged, were "misled by those to whom they have given their confidence." He wanted to discourage voting by African Americans, but also by those white Americans who he believed lacked sufficient education to use their franchise wisely.[13] At the least, he saw exceptions to the general rule he perceived. At best, he held out hope for those whom he considered lesser to rise to the highest attainments they were capable of attaining. If so, he extended generally the same aspirations he cherished for his students.

As Lee dealt with these aspects of his reality—a slave-owning, patriarchal, patrician way of life—his faith at once informed and mitigated his engagement with these conditions. On slavery, he absorbed the teaching of his mentor, Bishop Meade, that "servants" were people too. Meade's view itself deepened the fundamental paradox of slavery as an institution, that some people owned other people whom they treated as chattel, buying and selling, feeding and nurturing but also beating and even killing those whom Meade preached were children of God. Still, the Lee family pursued Meade's basic point, leading some of them to teach enslaved children and to seek to free and relocate others to Africa, but also providing a theological foundation to Lee's hope to end slavery.

Leaving matters in God's providential hands posed two related ethical problems, though. One thing the idea did not do was to challenge those who believed in it: God would take care of things. Along with that, it let people off the hook. Lee may well have washed his own hands of full responsibility for any role in bringing slavery to an end. Worse yet, it could even have allowed a rationalization for fighting for Southern independence designed to perpetuate the institution he heartily disliked. But the concept of providence also allowed him to accept emancipation and deal with the consequences; this too, after all, was God's will. Understanding providence allowed him to shift from war to peace, from leading armies in battle to leading young men to promote prosperity. He had won the hearts of Southerners—to such a degree that one Georgian feared that by idolizing Lee as the South had done Jackson, they had alienated the Almighty.

To the degree that Lee recognized his role, he aimed to use it for good: whether he succeeded or not remains an open question. So, though many, in the North and the South, saw him as a symbol of either treason or a righteous cause, others, in the North as well as the South, considered him a moral force for progress. One who perceived him in that light was the Ohio newspaperman in the *Stark County Democrat* who considered his death "a great calamity to the people of the South"—and, one might add, the entire nation.[14]

The *Stark County Democrat*'s admiration would not have been possible without the most remarkable feature of Lee's character: his ability to turn from leading in war to leading in peace. He had fought courageously for a cause that ended in utter defeat. In so doing he and his family lost nearly all they had, and his region and country vastly more. Yet almost immediately he committed himself to repairing the physical destruction and, even more challengingly, the deep emotional and spiritual wounds the war inflicted. He did not come to Lexington an utterly transformed man, but he came a very different one. As a person of faith, convinced of God's providence, he had had to wrestle with what seemed to be the will of God, and how he had been on the wrong side of it: the Lord had "decided against" him and his cause. What, then, does one do? If God's "chastening hand" were raised against the South and thus Lee himself, he too had to make amends. His answer was to turn toward what God favored, and to a new cause to which he believed God called him.

This "turning" did not constitute a thoroughgoing conversion regarding his faith, his constitutional convictions, or his service to the Confederacy. A brilliant student, Milton Humphreys, who had attended Washington College just before the war and returned after serving in the military, threw himself so thoroughly into his studies that Lee expressed concern for the young man's health. "I am so impatient to make up for the time I lost in the army," he pleaded. Lee responded, almost in anger: "Mr. Humphreys! However long you live and whatever you accomplish, you will find that the time you spent in the Confederate army was the most profitably spent portion of your life. Never again speak of having lost time in the army." Humphreys added, "And I never again did."[15]

Yet Lee did show a turning. The biblical term *metanoia*, translated as "repentance," often describes a change of mind or of life, sometimes with regret or remorse and always with a sense of surrender. Beyond mere submission, *metanoia* involves actively engaging in ways that exhibit that change of mind—what Lee would call "resignation." This concept underlies his thought in a letter to his closest postwar confidante, Markie Williams, at the end of 1865. "In looking back upon the calamities that have befallen us," he wrote, "I cannot trust my hand to write the feelings of my heart; but bow in humble submission to His will, who never afflicts us unnecessarily, or punishes us without a merciful purpose. His will be done! I have endeavoured to do what is right, & in his eyes, it never can be made wrong."[16]

His last phrase may err too much on the side of self-justification. Nevertheless, as Lee confronted the tremendous decisions and tribulations of his tumultuous era, he sought consciously to hold his faith through the "fiery trials" and "deep waters" that the congregation sang about at his funeral. He grew in that faith steadily, reaching a culmination in his years of seeking, if not altogether finding, peace.

Acknowledgments

R obert E. Lee may never have quoted Ecclesiastes 12:12: "Of making many books there is no end." The passage applies nonetheless to Lee as a subject. My daring to add one more book to the endless stream has been made possible only by the contributions and support of a great many people.

Librarians and archivists are a rare and blessed breed. I could not have functioned without them. Those at Virginia Theological Seminary, with its wealth of resources, helped immensely, notably Julia Randle, with her long insight into Virginia Episcopal history (first as VTS archivist and now as historiographer of the Diocese of Virginia), and more recently Christopher Pote, who aided with illustrations from the VTS collection. Judy Hynson graciously welcomed me to the duPont Memorial Library at Stratford Hall and plied me with valuable materials, as did John Coski, together with subsequent advice, at the Museum of the Confederacy, and also in Richmond, the staff of the Library of Virginia. Mary O. Klein, archivist of the Diocese of Maryland, graciously advised me on the Lee family churchgoing in Baltimore.

Letters of the Lee family lie scattered across the nation, but they landed in abundance in three notable libraries. To their staffs I am immeasurably grateful. The Library of Congress holds the collections of several authors, notably Ethel Armes. Vastly more reside in two collections; and without them, and the people who provided them for me, this work would simply not have been possible. The Virginia Historical Society in Richmond is one. For over a dozen years, Lee Shepard, Frances Pollard, John McClure, and their always helpful staff cheerfully and unstintingly assisted me by bringing forth, and sometimes deciphering, countless documents from the collection. The Leyburn Library at Washington and Lee University is the other. Many of its staff provided unstinting help, above all the denizens of Special Collections. Led first by Vaughan Stanley, and then Thomas Camden, who with Seth McCormick-Goodhart, Lisa McCown, and Byron Faidley, they became genuine partners in research.

To supplement illustrations from W&L Special Collections, Patricia Hobbs and her staff provided other resources from the University collection, as did Col. Keith Gibson from VMI and Kimberly Robinson from Arlington House, all with the most gracious of help.

Historians of Lee were generous in their encouragement and guidance, notably Prof. Gary Gallagher and the late Elizabeth Brown Pryor.

Robert Rhode shared his enthusiasm for Lee and his knowledge of Petersburg, and Sam Gwynne the comfort of a successful author.

For over a decade, my friend of even longer a time, Andrew Wolfe, offered counsel and reinforcement on publishing and publicizing this book and, at points, simply in getting it done. Additionally, two long-time friends all too familiar with the vagaries of publishing, Spencer and Beverly Tucker, calmed fears and raised spirits by their support.

Colleagues at Southern Virginia University have been genuinely collegial. Fellow denizens of Durham 3 graciously abided my nabbing them for the odd question on some arcane bit of knowledge, which they readily provided according to their expertise: William Silverman and Scott Dransfield on literature, Ryan Johnston on economics, and on matters philosophical, Jan-Erik Jones, aided by his wife, Kristen. I am grateful to fellow historians Lora Knight and Virginia Mosser, and especially to Francis MacDonnell, who became not just a guide but also a cheerleader. All these along with Madison Sowell and SVU as a whole welcomed me with gracious warmth, making possible a second vocation that I cherish.

A variety of people read some or all of the manuscript in various stages, and offered helpful suggestions: Prof. Stephen Cushman of the University of Virginia; the Reverend Jackson Hershbell; the Very Reverend Gary Kriss, formerly of Nashotah House, on Anglicanism; Dr. Alexandra Brown of W&L on several points of biblical scholarship; and Dr. Caleb Dance on the Lee motto. Among those reading various drafts were a trio in Richmond, Harry F. Byrd IV, the Reverend Wallace Adams-Riley of St. Paul's Church, and my son, Trevor, who read it once with the group, then again on the prepublication draft when he caught what slipped by others, including me. My student Wright Noel gave insightful advice on one chapter I inflicted on his class. The sharp eye of Pamela Minkler, MD, caught all too many errors in the penultimate draft. Two longtime friends from the W&L Department of History, now retired, took particular interest in the project. Dr. Taylor Sanders gave a thorough and helpful reading. Dr. J. Holt Merchant championed this project, scrutinized the manuscript multiple times, offered innumerable suggestions, and guided me constantly. Another friend and onetime parishioner, Evelyn Bence, edited the text with grace and understanding. To the William B. Eerdmans Publishing Company and especially to Mark Noll, editor of the Library of Religious Biography; David Bratt, editor; Kelsey Kaemingk, project editor; and Tom Raabe, who skillfully edited the manuscript, I am deeply grateful for their confidence in this project.

Two teachers from my student days indirectly but constantly influenced my research and writing by their scholarship, standards, and example: the late Sydney Ahlstrom, and Harry Stout.

I am grateful to the parish that first piqued my interest in what Robert E. Lee actually believed. It called my family and me to Virginia nearly thirty years ago and has challenged and sustained me ever since.

From the time this project began, my children have graduated from colleges and professional schools; two entered into matrimony and one into parenthood. Throughout, they accorded me their patience, hospitality on still yet another research trip, and always their love. I am grateful to Andrew, to Trevor and Kristin, and to Meredith and Scott.

All of that, and more—and especially patience—can be said of Melissa, not only over the last dozen years, but for well over forty.

During those four decades and counting, I have been the beneficiary of the love and support of her parents, Don and Billie McCoy. Don was one of the first enthusiasts of this project. He read an early draft and responded with his customary candor that I needed to hear. Billie provided frequent hospitality of her home during research and writing. I regret that Don is not around to read the final product. I offer it in thanksgiving for them both.

Select Bibliography

Manuscript Collections

The College of William and Mary, Swem Library: William Meade Papers
Harvard University, Houghton Library: Gamaliel Bradford Papers
Library of Congress, Manuscript Division
  Beverly Middleton Papers
  Custis-Lee Family Papers
  Ethel Armes Collection of Lee Family Papers
Library of Virginia
Museum of the Confederacy*
Stratford Hall
University of Virginia, Special Collections
University of Virginia, the Albert and Shirley Small Special Collections
  Library
Virginia Historical Society
  Lee Family Papers
  George Bolling Lee Papers
  Mary Custis Lee Papers
Virginia Military Institute, Preston Library, Archives
Washington and Lee University, James G. Leyburn Library, Special Collections and Archives
  James Lewis Howe Papers
  Robert E. Lee Papers
  Schoenbrun Papers

  * The Museum of the Confederacy in Richmond merged in 2013 with the American Civil War Center to form the American Civil War Museum, and transferred its archives to the Virginia Historical Society.

Primary Sources

Allan, William. "Memoranda of Conversations with General Lee." February 26 and March 10, 1868 (WLU 0064). Also in Gary Gallagher, ed. *Lee the Soldier.* Lincoln: University of Nebraska Press, 1996.

Andrews, Marietta Minnigerode. *Memoirs of a Poor Relation.* New York: Dutton, 1930.

Bedell, Gregory T. *"Pay Thy Vows": A Pastoral Address Subsequent to Confirmation.* New York: Stanford & Swords, 1853.

Calvert, Elizabeth Gibbon Randolph. "Childhood Days at Arlington Mixed with After Memories." Unpublished manuscript, circa 1870. Arlington House, #2541.

Craven, Avery, ed. *"To Markie": The Letters of Robert E. Lee to Martha Custis Williams.* Cambridge, MA: Harvard University Press, 1933.

Diocese of Virginia. *Journal of the Fifty-Fifth Annual Convention of the Protestant Episcopal Church in Virginia.* Baltimore: Joseph Robinson, 1850.

Grace Church (R. E. Lee Memorial), Lexington, VA. Vestry Minutes.

Hobart, John Henry. *The Candidate for Confirmation Instructed.* 1819. Reprint, Protestant Episcopal Tract Society, [1830].

Lee, Agnes. *Growing Up in the 1850s.* Edited by Mary Custis Lee deButts. Chapel Hill: UNC Press, 1984.

Lee, Charles Carter. "My Boyhood—II." Unpublished manuscript, UVa Mss 9934, Box 9.

Lee, Henry. *Memoirs of the War in the Southern Department of the United States.* With a biography of the author by Robert E. Lee. New York: University Publishing, 1869.

Lee, Mary Anna Randolph Custis. "My Reminiscences of the War." Derwent, September 186[5]. VHS L5144 a 1397–1472. Reprint, "Mary Custis Lee's Reminiscences of the War." Edited by Robert E. L. deButts Jr. *VMHB* 109, no. 3 (2001): 301–25.

Lee, Robert E. *The Wartime Papers of Robert E. Lee.* Edited by Clifford Dowdey and Louis H. Manarin. 1961. Reprint, New York: Da Capo Press, 1987.

Lee, Susan Pendleton. *Memoirs of William Nelson Pendleton, D.D.* 1893. Reprint, Harrisonburg, VA: Sprinkle Publications, 1991.

McDonald, Hunter. "General Robert E. Lee after Appomattox." Reprint, *Tennessee Historical Magazine* 9, no. 2 (July 1923): 87–101, in WLU/LP M135.

McIlvaine, Charles P. *Pastoral Letter to the Clergy and Laity of the Protestant Episcopal Church in the Diocese of Ohio, on the Subject of Confirmation and Church Music.* Columbus: Ohio State Journal Company, 1855.

Meade, William. *The Candidate for Confirmation Self-Examined.* New York: Protestant Episcopal Tract Society, [1841].

_____. *Conversations on the Catechism of the Protestant Episcopal Church.* New York: Protestant Episcopal Society for the Promotion of Evangelical Knowledge, 1857.

_____. *Explanation of the Church Catechism.* New York: Protestant Episcopal Society for the Promotion of Evangelical Knowledge, 1856.

_____. *Family Prayers.* Alexandria, VA: W. M. Morrison, 1834.

_____. *Old Churches, Ministers, and Families of Virginia.* 2 vols. Philadelphia, 1857. Reprint, Baltimore: Genealogical Publishing, 1995.

_____. "On the Duty of Affording Religious Instruction," in *Plain Sermons for Servants,* by T. T. Castleman and others. New York: Stanford & Swords, 1852.

_____. *Pastoral Letter of Bishop Meade, to the Congregations of the Protestant Episcopal Church of Virginia.* Richmond: H. K. Ellyson, 1847.

_____. *Pastoral Letter . . . on the Duty of Affording Religious Instruction to Those in Bondage.* 1834. Reprint, Richmond: H. K. Ellyson, 1853.

_____. *Remarks on a Pamphlet concerning the Canon on Lay Discipline.* Washington, DC: Gideon & Co., 1850.

_____. *Sermon Delivered . . . at the Opening of the Convention of the Diocese of Virginia.* N.p.: John Heiskell, 1818.

Muhlenberg, William Augustus. *The Application of Christianity to Education.* Jamaica, NY: Sleight & George, 1828.

Otey, James H. *Preparation of Candidates for Confirmation.* Nashville: Bang, Walker & Co., 1857.

Patrick, Marsena Rudolph. *Inside Lincoln's Army.* New York: T. Yoseloff, 1964.

Pryor, Elizabeth Brown. "'Thou Knowest Not the Time of Thy Visitation': A Newly Discovered Letter Reveals Robert E. Lee's Lonely Struggle with Disunion." *VMHB* 119, no. 3 (September 2011).

Riley, Franklin L., ed. *General Robert E. Lee after Appomattox.* New York: Macmillan, 1922.

Williams, Martha Custis. Transcript of Journals of Martha Custis Williams. Arlington House Archives.

Wilson, Thomas. *Sacra Privata.* 1781. London: J. G. & F. Rivington, 1837.

Select Bibliography

Secondary Sources

Ahlstrom, Sydney E. *A Religious History of the American People*. New Haven: YUP, 1972.

Ambrose, Stephen E. *Duty, Honor, Country: A History of West Point*. Baltimore: Johns Hopkins University Press, 1999.

Armes, Ethel. *Stratford Hall: The Great House of the Lees*. Richmond: Garrett and Massie, 1936.

Beringer, Richard E., et al. *Why the South Lost the Civil War*. Athens: University of Georgia Press, 1986.

Bond, Edward L. *Damned Souls in a Tobacco Colony: Religion in Seventeenth-Century Virginia*. Macon, GA: Mercer University Press, 2000.

The Book of Common Prayer [1789]. Philadelphia: Hall & Sellers, 1790.

The Book of Common Prayer [1979]. New York: Church Publishing Co., 1986.

Booty, John. *Mission and Ministry: A History of Virginia Theological Seminary*. Harrisburg, PA: Morehouse, 1995.

Brock, R. A., ed. *Gen. Robert Edward Lee: Soldier, Citizen, and Christian Patriot*. Richmond: Royal Publishing Co., 1897.

Brooke, George M., Jr. *General Lee's Church*. Lexington, VA: News-Gazette, 1984.

Brydon, G. Maclaren. *The Established Church in Virginia and the Revolution*. Richmond: Virginia Diocesan Library, 1930.

Butler, Diana Hochstedt. *Standing against the Whirlwind: Evangelical Episcopalians in Nineteenth Century America*. New York: OUP, 1995.

Childe, Edward Lee. *Life and Campaigns of General Lee*. Translated by George Litting. London: Chatto and Windus, 1875.

Coulling, Mary P. *The Lee Girls*. Winston-Salem, NC: J. F. Blair, 1987.

Cragg, Gerald R. *The Church and the Age of Reason, 1648–1789*. London: Penguin, 1970.

Crenshaw, Ollinger. *General Lee's College: The Rise and Growth of Washington and Lee University*. New York: Random House, 1968.

_____. "General Lee's College." Unpublished typescript. 2 vols. WLU Special Collections, 1973.

Davis, William C. *Crucible of Command*. Boston: Da Capo Press, 2014.

_____. *Jefferson Davis: The Man and His Hour*. New York: HarperCollins, 1991.

Donald, David Herbert. *Lincoln*. New York: Simon and Schuster, 1995.

Eisenhower, John S. D. *So Far from God: The U.S. War with Mexico, 1846–1848.* New York: Random House, 1989.

Ellis, Joseph. *His Excellency: George Washington.* New York: Knopf, 2004.

Fellman, Michael. *The Making of Robert E. Lee.* Baltimore: Johns Hopkins University Press, 2000.

Fisher, Lewis F. *Saint Mark's Episcopal Church: 150 Years of Ministry in Downtown San Antonio, 1858–2008.* San Antonio: Maverick Publishing, 2008.

Flood, Charles Bracelen. *Lee: The Last Years.* Boston: Houghton Mifflin, 1981.

Freeman, Douglas Southall. *R. E. Lee: A Biography.* 4 vols. New York: Charles Scribner's Sons, 1934.

Green, Wharton J. *Recollections and Reflections.* Raleigh, NC: Edwards and Broughton, 1906.

Greer, Rowan A. *Christian Hope and Christian Life: Raids on the Inarticulate.* New York: Crossroad, 2001.

Gwynne, Samuel C. *Rebel Yell: The Violence, Passion, and Redemption of Stonewall Jackson.* New York: Scribner, 2014.

Hatchett, Marion J. *Commentary on the American Prayer Book.* New York: Seabury, 1980.

Hendrick, Burton J. *The Lees of Virginia.* Boston: Little, Brown, 1935.

Hess, Earl J. *Lee's Tar Heels: The Pettigrew-Kirkland-MacRae Brigade.* Chapel Hill: UNC Press, 2002.

Holloway, Richard, ed. *The Anglican Tradition.* Wilton, CT: Morehouse-Barlow, 1984.

Holmes, David Lynn, Jr. *A Brief History of the Episcopal Church.* Valley Forge, PA: Trinity, 1993.

———. *The Faiths of the Founding Fathers.* Oxford: OUP, 2006.

———. "William Meade and the Church of Virginia, 1789–1829." PhD diss., Princeton University, 1971.

Horn, Jonathan. *The Man Who Would Not Be Washington.* New York: Scribner, 2015.

James, Molly Field. *With Joyful Acceptance, Maybe: Developing a Contemporary Theology of Suffering in Conversation with Five Christian Thinkers: Gregory the Great, Julian of Norwich, Jeremy Taylor, C. S. Lewis, and Ivone Gebara.* Eugene, OR: Wipf & Stock, 2013.

Johns, John. *A Memoir of the Life of the Right Rev. William Meade D.D.* Baltimore: Innes & Co., 1867.

Jones, J. William. *Life and Letters of Robert Edward Lee.* New York: Neale, 1906.

_____. *Personal Reminiscences . . . of Gen. Robert E. Lee.* New York: D. Appleton, 1874.

Korda, Michael. *Clouds of Glory: The Life and Legend of Robert E. Lee.* New York: Harper, 2014.

Lee, Edmund Jennings, ed. *Lee of Virginia, 1642–1892: Biographical and Genealogical Sketches of the Descendants of Colonel Richard Lee.* Philadelphia, 1895.

Lee, Robert E., Jr. *Recollections and Letters of General Robert E. Lee.* New York: Doubleday, Page, 1905.

Lengel, Edward G. *Inventing George Washington: America's Founder, in Myth and Memory.* New York: Harper, 2011.

Lewis, Charles Lee. *Matthew Fontaine Maury, the Pathfinder of the Seas.* Annapolis, MD: US Naval Institute, 1927.

Lyle, Royster, and Pamela Hemenway Simpson. *The Architecture of Historic Lexington.* Charlottesville: University Press of Virginia, 1977.

Magnusson, Kjartan. "The History of Washington College under Robert E. Lee, 1865–1870." EdD diss., Brigham Young University, 1989.

McCabe, James D. *Life and Campaigns of General Robert E. Lee.* Atlanta: National Publishing Co., 1866.

McCaslin, Richard B. *Lee in the Shadow of Washington.* Baton Rouge: Louisiana State University Press, 2001.

McGivigan, John R., and Mitchel Snay, eds. *Religion and the Antebellum Debate over Slavery.* Athens: University of Georgia Press, 1998.

Moorman, John R. H. *The Anglican Spiritual Tradition.* Springfield, IL: Templegate, 1983.

Morrison, Jeffry H. *John Witherspoon and the Founding of the American Republic.* Notre Dame: University of Notre Dame Press, 2005.

Nagle, Paul C. *The Lees of Virginia.* New York: OUP, 1990.

Nelson, John K. *A Blessed Company: Parishes, Parsons, and Parishioners in Anglican Virginia, 1690–1776.* Chapel Hill: UNC Press, 2001.

Nelson, Robert. *Reminiscences of the Right Rev. William Meade, D.D.* Shanghai: "Ching-Foong" General Printing Office, 1873.

Noll, Mark A. *America's God: From Jonathan Edwards to Abraham Lincoln.* Oxford: OUP, 2002.

_____. *The Civil War as a Theological Crisis.* Chapel Hill: UNC Press, 2006.

Oakes, James. *The Ruling Race: A History of American Slaveholders.* New York: Knopf, 1982.

Owen, Robert Dale. *Hints on Public Architecture*. New York: Putnam, 1849.

Pappas, George S. *To the Point: The United States Military Academy, 1802–1902*. Westport, CT: Praeger, 1993.

Penelhum, Terence. *Butler*. London: Routledge & Kegan Paul, 1985.

Prichard, Robert W. *A History of the Episcopal Church*. Harrisburg, PA: Morehouse, 1991.

_____. *The Nature of Salvation: Theological Consensus in the Episcopal Church, 1801–1873*. Urbana: University of Illinois Press, 1997.

Pryor, Elizabeth Brown. *Reading the Man: Robert E. Lee through His Private Letters*. New York: Viking, 2007.

Rable, George C. *God's Almost Chosen Peoples*. Chapel Hill: UNC Press, 2010.

Richardson, Heather Cox. *The Death of Reconstruction: Race, Labor, and Politics in the Post–Civil War North, 1865–1901*. Cambridge, MA: Harvard University Press, 2001.

Rister, Carl Coke. *Robert E. Lee in Texas*. 1946. Reprint, Norman: University of Oklahoma Press, 2004.

Rodgers, Eugene L. *And Then . . . a Cathedral: A History of Christ Church Cathedral, St. Louis, Missouri*. St. Louis: Christ Church Cathedral, 1970.

Rolle, Andrew F. *The Lost Cause: The Confederate Exodus to Mexico*. Norman: University of Oklahoma Press, 1965.

Romero, Sidney J. *Religion in the Rebel Ranks*. Lanham, MD: University Press of America, 1983.

Ruffin, J. Rixey. *A Paradise of Reason: William Bentley and Enlightenment Christianity in the Early Republic*. Oxford: OUP, 2008.

Sanborn, Margaret. *Robert E. Lee: A Portrait*. 2 vols. Moose, WY: Homestead Publishing, 1996.

Shattuck, Gardiner H. *A Shield and Hiding Place: The Religious Life of the Civil War Armies*. Macon, GA: Mercer University Press, 1987.

Slaughter, Philip. *Memoirs of the Life of the Rt. Rev. William Meade*. Richmond: Randolph and English, 1885.

Spellman, W. M. *The Latitudinarians and the Church of England, 1660–1700*. Athens: University of Georgia Press, 1993.

Sykes, Stephen, and John Booty, eds. *The Study of Anglicanism*. London: SPCK/Fortress, 1988.

Taylor, Walter H. *Four Years with General Lee*. New York: D. Appleton, 1877.

Thomas, Emory M. *Robert E. Lee: A Biography*. New York: Norton, 1995.

Thompson, Mary V. *"In the Hands of a Good Providence": Religion in the*

Life of George Washington. Charlottesville: University of Virginia Press, 2008.

Thornton, Martin. *English Spirituality*. Cambridge, MA: Cowley, [1963].

Timmons, Mark. *Moral Theory: An Introduction*. Lanham, MD: Rowman & Littlefield, 2002.

Wallenstein, Peter, and Bertram Wyatt-Brown, eds. *Virginia's Civil War*. Charlottesville: University of Virginia Press, 2005.

Wheelan, Joseph. *Invading Mexico: America's Continental Dream and the Mexican War, 1846–1848*. New York: Carroll & Graf Publishers, 2007.

Wilson, Charles Reagan. *Baptized in Blood: The Religion of the Lost Cause, 1865–1920*. 2nd ed. Athens: University of Georgia Press, 2009.

Wilson, Emily V. *Popular Life of Gen. Robert Edward Lee*. Baltimore: John Murphy & Co., 1872.

Winner, Lauren F. *A Cheerful and Comfortable Faith: Anglican Religious Practice in the Elite Households of Eighteenth-Century Virginia*. New Haven: YUP, 2010.

Woodworth, Steven E. *While God Is Marching On: The Religious World of Civil War Soldiers*. Lawrence: University Press of Kansas, 2001.

Wyatt-Brown, Bertram. *Southern Honor: Ethics and Behavior in the Old South*. New York: OUP, 1982.

Yarema, Allan. *The American Colonization Society: An Avenue to Freedom?* Lanham, MD: University Press of America, 2006.

Articles and Miscellaneous Items

Blosser, Jacob M. "Pursuing Happiness in Colonial Virginia." *VMHB* 118, no. 3 (2010): 211–45.

Bond, Edward L. "Lived Religion in Colonial Virginia." In *From Jamestown to Jefferson*, edited by Paul Rasor and Richard E. Bond, pp. 43–73. Charlottesville: University of Virginia Press, 2011.

Bond, Edward L., and Joan R. Gunderson. "The Episcopal Church in Virginia, 1607–2007." *VMHB* 115, no. 2 (2007): 163–344.

Byrne, Karen L. "Our Little Sanctuary in the Woods: Spiritual Life at Arlington Chapel." *Arlington Historical Magazine* 12, no. 2 (October 2002): 38–44.

DeButts, Robert E. L., Jr. "Lee in Love: Courtship and Correspondence in Antebellum Virginia." *VMHB* 115, no. 4 (2007): 487–575.

_____, ed. "Mary Custis Lee's 'Reminiscences of the War." *VMHB* 109, no. 3 (2001): 301–25.

Holmes, David L. "The Decline and Revival of the Church of Virginia." In *Up from Independence: The Episcopal Church in Virginia*, 51–109. N.p.: Interdiocesan Bicentennial Committee of the Virginias, 1976.

Lee, S. L. "War Time in Alexandria, Virginia." *South Atlantic Quarterly* 4, no. 3 (July 1905): 234–48.

"Memoir of Mrs. Harriotte Lee Taliaferro concerning Events in Virginia, April 11–21, 1861." *VMHB* 57, no. 4 (October 1949): 416–20.

"Negro Communed at St. Paul's Church." *Confederate Veteran* 13 (August 1905): 360.

Ruffner, William Henry. "The History of Washington College, 1830–1848." *Historical Papers* (Lexington: WLU), no. 6 (1904): 1–110.

Schwarz, Philip. "Robert E. Lee and the Black Man." Unpublished talk at St. Paul's Episcopal Church Adult Forum, January 13, 2002.

Tarter, Brent. "Reflections on the Church of England in Colonial Virginia." *VMHB* 112, no. 4 (2004): 338–71.

Abbreviations

ACL	Ann Hill Carter Lee
AH	Arlington House
BCP	Book of Common Prayer
BCP 1789	Book of Common Prayer (Philadelphia: Hall & Sellers, 1790)
CCL	Charles Carter Lee
CUP	Cambridge University Press
HL	Henry Lee III ("Light-Horse Harry")
LFDA	Lee Family Digital Archive (www.leefamilyarchive.org)
LOC	Library of Congress, Manuscript Division
LOC/BM	Library of Congress, Manuscript Division, Beverly Middleton Papers
LOC/CLFP	Library of Congress, Manuscript Division, Custis-Lee Family Papers
LOC/EA	Library of Congress, Manuscript Division, Ethel Armes Collection of Lee Family Papers
LVA	Library of Virginia
MARC	Mary Anna Randolph Custis (later Mrs. Robert E. Lee)
MCL/d	Mary Custis Lee (daughter)
MLFC	Mary Lee Fitzhugh Custis (mother-in-law)
OUP	Oxford University Press
REL	Robert E. Lee
REL Jr.	Robert E. Lee Jr.
SH	Stratford Hall
SSL	Sidney Smith Lee
UNC Press	University of North Carolina Press

UVa	University of Virginia, Albert and Shirley Small Special Collections Library
VHS	Virginia Historical Society
VHS/LFP	Virginia Historical Society, Lee Family Papers
VHS/GBLP	Virginia Historical Society, George Bolling Lee Papers
VHS/MCL/d/P	Virginia Historical Society, Mary Custis Lee Papers
VMHB	*Virginia Magazine of History and Biography*
VMI	Virginia Military Institute
VTS	Virginia Theological Seminary
W&M	College of William and Mary, Earl Gregg Swem Library
WHFL	William Henry Fitzhugh Lee (Rooney)
WLU	Washington and Lee University, James G. Leyburn Library, Special Collections and Archives
WLU/Howe	Washington and Lee University, James G. Leyburn Library, Special Collections and Archives, James Lewis Howe Papers
WLU/LP	Washington and Lee University, James G. Leyburn Library, Special Collections and Archives, Robert E. Lee Papers
YUP	Yale University Press

Notes

Notes to the Preface

1. William Meade, *Old Churches, Ministers, and Families of Virginia*, 2 vols. (Philadelphia, 1857; reprint, Baltimore: Genealogical Publishing, 1995), 2:231–32; William Meade, *Sermon Delivered . . . at the Opening of the Convention of the Diocese of Virginia* (n.p.: John Heiskell, 1818), pp. 22–23.

2. Charles Bracelen Flood, *Lee: The Last Years* (Boston: Houghton Mifflin, 1981), pp. 65–66. See "Negro Communed at St. Paul's Church," *Richmond Times-Dispatch*, April 16, 1905, p. 5; "Negro Communed at St. Paul's Church," *Confederate Veteran* 13 (August 1905): 360; Philip Schwarz, "Robert E. Lee and the Black Man" (unpublished talk at St. Paul's Episcopal Church Adult Forum, Richmond, January 13, 2002). No contemporaneous account of the story has been found. Compare the contrasting interpretations of Emory M. Thomas, Michael Fellman, and Bertram Wyatt-Brown in *Virginia's Civil War*, ed. Peter Wallenstein and Bertram Wyatt-Brown (Charlottesville: University of Virginia Press, 2005), pp. 16, 19–20, 35–36.

3. On "myth," see Northrop Frye, *Anatomy of Criticism* (Princeton: Princeton University Press, 1957), pp. 54–55, 64–65. Among Lee historians, Douglas Southall Freeman focuses primarily on Lee's military life and largely avoids addressing what he calls Lee's "simple soul" (*R. E. Lee: A Biography*, 4 vols. [New York: Charles Scribner's Sons, 1934], 1:ix). Michael Fellman, in *The Making of Robert E. Lee* (Baltimore: Johns Hopkins University Press, 2000), especially ch. 3, takes a psychoanalytical approach that stresses Lee's stoicism. Emory M. Thomas, *Robert E. Lee: A Biography* (New York: Norton, 1995), approaches his faith with matter-of-fact neutrality. By contrast, J. William Jones, *Personal Reminiscences . . . of Gen. Robert E. Lee* (New York: D. Appleton, 1874), and Robert R. Brown, *And One Was a Soldier: The Spiritual Pilgrimage of Robert E. Lee* (Shippensburg, PA: White Mane Books, 1998), amount to hagiographies.

4. The New Testament frequently refers to Christian believers as "saints." In his letters, Paul often extends greetings from the "saints" of one church or to the "saints" of another (e.g., Rom. 1:7; 2 Cor. 1:1; 13:12; Phil. 1:1; 4:22) or offers his personal greetings to individuals (Phil. 4:21).

Notes to Chapter 1

1. Hunter McDonald, "General Robert E. Lee after Appomattox," reprint, *Tennessee Historical Magazine* 9, no. 2 (July 1923): 87–101, in WLU/LP M135, p. 5.

2. Don Lipman, "April 1861: The War between the States Begins—What Was the Weather Like?," *Washington Post* (blog), April 11, 2011, accessed June 21, 2016, http://www.washingtonpost.com/blogs/capitalweathergang/post/april1861thewarbetween thestatesbeginswhatwastheweatherlike/2011/04/11/AFU3DxKD_blog.html.

3. A letter from Mary Custis Lee (his daughter) is printed in Elizabeth Brown Pryor, "'Thou Knowest Not the Time of Thy Visitation': A Newly Discovered Letter Reveals Robert E. Lee's Lonely Struggle with Disunion," *VMHB* 119, no. 3 (September 2011): 289. In a short memoir composed ten years after the incident, Lee's eldest daughter, Mary Custis, acknowledged the frailties of memory, and shows it here: as commander of Fort Sumter, Anderson then held the rank of major, though he received a promotion soon after.

4. Pryor, "Thou Knowest," p. 290.

5. "Memoir of Mrs. Harriotte Lee Taliaferro concerning Events in Virginia, April 11–21, 1861," *VMHB* 57, no. 4 (October 1949): 419; Collect for the Third Sunday after Easter, BCP 1789; 1 Pet. 2:13–14, Epistle for the Third Sunday after Easter.

6. "The Grace," BCP 1789, §9, the Order for Daily Morning Prayer; Pryor, "Thou Knowest," p. 291.

7. "Memoir of Mrs. Harriotte Lee Taliaferro," p. 419. She never saw Lee. See S. L. Lee, "War Time in Alexandria, Virginia," *South Atlantic Quarterly* 4, no. 3 (July 1905): 235. Susan Lee was another daughter of Robert's cousin Cassius.

8. Pryor, "Thou Knowest," p. 291.

9. Frank Marcon to his mother [Mrs. Matchill(?)], May 22, 1865, WLU, Schoenbrun Collection, #0349. Cf. Mark A. Noll, *The Civil War as a Theological Crisis* (Chapel Hill: UNC Press, 2006), ch. 18, especially pp. 75–81.

10. Franklin L. Riley, ed., *General Robert E. Lee after Appomattox* (New York: Macmillan, 1922), pp. 1–2.

11. Quoted in an address at Sewanee around 1870, in REL Jr., *Recollections and Letters of General Robert E. Lee* (New York: Doubleday, Page, 1905), pp. 182–83.

12. REL to Trustees, near Cartersville, VA, August 24, 1865, WLU/LP 0064; Trustees Minutes, August 31, 1865, WLU.

13. The words "Anglican" and "Episcopal" can be interchangeable. In this work, "Episcopal" will refer to the denomination that grew out of the Church of England in the United States after the American Revolution. "Anglican" implies the larger tradition, which the Episcopal Church in the United States, the Church of England, and sister churches in other areas of the Anglican Communion represent, and is the more appropriate term to describe the Church of England in colonial Virginia.

Notes to Chapter 2

1. BCP 1789, §17, the Catechism.

2. Paul C. Nagle, *The Lees of Virginia* (New York: OUP, 1990), pp. 56–57, 62.

3. Many of these ideas are expressed in the Articles of Religion, also called the

Thirty-Nine Articles, usually printed in the BCPs of the provinces of the Anglican Communion. For the US version, see The Book of Common Prayer (of the Episcopal Church) (New York: Church Publishing, 1986), pp. 867–76.

4. The first Virginians would have used the Book of Common Prayer of 1603. England produced another in 1662 that became the official liturgy until the first American edition of 1789.

5. The Book of Common Prayer of 1662, used by Virginians until after the Revolution, provided that those "ready and desirous to be confirmed" could partake of Holy Communion even without being confirmed by a bishop, a provision that the first American Book of Common Prayer retained (cf. concluding rubric of the confirmation rite in each book). See John K. Nelson, *A Blessed Company: Parishes, Parsons, and Parishioners in Anglican Virginia, 1690–1776* (Chapel Hill: UNC Press, 2001), p. 220; Edward L. Bond, "Lived Religion in Colonial Virginia," in *From Jamestown to Jefferson*, ed. Paul Rasor and Richard E. Bond (Charlottesville: University of Virginia Press, 2011), pp. 50–51.

6. Nelson, *A Blessed Company*, pp. 47, 53, 62.

7. Brent Tarter, "Reflections on the Church of England in Colonial Virginia," *VMHB* 112, no. 4 (2004): 347–48; Edward L. Bond and Joan R. Gunderson, "The Episcopal Church in Virginia, 1607–2007," *VMHB* 115, no. 2 (2007): 176, 181, 185; Nelson, *A Blessed Company*, pp. 244–52.

8. Lauren F. Winner, *A Cheerful and Comfortable Faith: Anglican Religious Practice in the Elite Households of Eighteenth-Century Virginia* (New Haven: YUP, 2010), p. 91. On books, see Edward L. Bond, *Damned Souls in a Tobacco Colony: Religion in Seventeenth-Century Virginia* (Macon, GA: Mercer University Press, 2000), pp. 264–68. The shelves of Mount Vernon included *A View of the Internal Evidences of the Christian Religion* by Soame Jenyns, an edition of 1789 that bore the name of Martha Washington and Mary Lee Fitzhugh Custis; see Mary V. Thompson, *"In the Hands of a Good Providence": Religion in the Life of George Washington* (Charlottesville: University of Virginia Press, 2008), p. 61 and n. 51.

9. Bond, *Damned Souls*, pp. 264, 277–80.

10. Winner, *Cheerful and Comfortable Faith*, ch. 4, passim; p. 36. See Nelson, *A Blessed Company*, p. 215, on Ann Carter Lee's kinsman defending the idea of home baptism. Journals of Martha Custis Williams (Arlington House Archives) (hereafter "Markie, Diary"), e.g., entries for October 30 and November 15, 1853, March 10 and 12, 1854, and September 12, 1857. Mount Vernon was an exception; instead of family prayers, Martha Washington withdrew for her own Bible reading and prayers (Markie, Diary, May 25, 1856, and September 12, 1857; see ch. 5 below).

11. BCP 1789, §17. Devereux Jarratt, a longtime parson of evangelical leanings, remembered the family teaching prayers and making "us very perfect in repeating the Catechism." See Nelson, *A Blessed Company*, p. 137; cf. Bond, "Lived Religion," p. 61.

12. Bond, *Damned Souls*, pp. 240–42, and Bond, "Lived Religion," p. 54; Bond and Gunderson, "The Episcopal Church," p. 192.

13. Nelson, *A Blessed Company*, pp. 65, 191–92. These can still be seen in colonial-era churches such as Bruton Parish in Williamsburg.

14. Bond and Gunderson, "The Episcopal Church," p. 188; Marion J. Hatchett, *Commentary on the American Prayer Book* (New York: Seabury, 1980), p. 151; Robert W.

Prichard, *A History of the Episcopal Church* (Harrisburg, PA: Morehouse, 1991), p. 122 (see n. 27); Bond, *Damned Souls*, p. 247, and Bond, "Lived Religion," p. 57.

15. John R. H. Moorman, *The Anglican Spiritual Tradition* (Springfield, IL: Templegate, 1983), p. 121; Bond and Gunderson, "The Episcopal Church," pp. 188–89; James Blair, quoted in Bond, *Damned Souls*, p. 250; Bond, "Lived Religion," p. 57.

16. Moorman, *The Anglican Spiritual Tradition*, pp. 116–18; Bond, "Lived Religion," pp. 64–66.

17. Isaac Barrow, quoted in Moorman, *The Anglican Spiritual Tradition*, p. 119; Moorman, p. 124; Gerald R. Cragg, *The Church and the Age of Reason, 1648–1789* (London: Penguin, 1970), pp. 68–69; W. M. Spellman, *The Latitudinarians and the Church of England, 1660–1700* (Athens: University of Georgia Press, 1993), pp. 13–14, 3–6, 133, 145; Bond, *Damned Souls*, pp. 258–60.

18. John Page, in Bond, *Damned Souls*, pp. 248–49.

19. On deism, see Terence Penelhum, *Butler* (London: Routledge & Kegan Paul, 1985), p. 100, and Sydney E. Ahlstrom, *A Religious History of the American People* (New Haven: YUP, 1972), pp. 357–58.

20. William Meade, *Old Churches, Ministers, and Families of Virginia*, 2 vols. (Philadelphia, 1857; reprint, Baltimore: Genealogical Publishing, 1995), 1:34 (see footnote); see David L. Holmes, "The Decline and Revival of the Church in Virginia," in *Up from Independence* (n.p.: Interdiocesan Bicentennial Commission, 1976), p. 89.

21. G. Maclaren Brydon, *The Established Church in Virginia and the Revolution* (Richmond: Virginia Diocesan Library, 1930), p. 10; cf. John Booty, *Mission and Ministry: A History of Virginia Theological Seminary* (Harrisburg, PA: Morehouse, 1995), p. 6; Bond and Gunderson, "The Episcopal Church," p. 192.

22. Bond, *Damned Souls*, pp. 243, 255; Jacob M. Blosser, "Pursuing Happiness in Colonial Virginia," *VMHB* 118, no. 3 (2010): 217–18, 230; see Spellman, *Latitudinarians*, p. 62.

23. See Bond, *Damned Souls*, pp. 247, 264, and ch. 12 below.

24. Joseph Ellis, *His Excellency: George Washington* (New York: Knopf, 2004), pp. 9, 45, 151, 269. Regarding *Rules*, Ellis wonders if Washington may have been performing an exercise in penmanship.

Notes to Chapter 3

1. Prov. 22:6 KJV (altered for the plural).

2. CCL, "My Boyhood—II," UVa Mss 9934, Box 9; William Meade, *Old Churches, Ministers, and Families of Virginia*, 2 vols. (Philadelphia, 1857; reprint, Baltimore: Genealogical Publishing, 1995), 1:19, 31, 18. See David L. Holmes, "The Decline and Revival of the Church in Virginia," in *Up from Independence* (n.p.: Interdiocesan Bicentennial Commission, 1976), p. 56.

3. Preface, BCP 1789, §2.

4. Marion J. Hatchett, *Commentary on the American Prayer Book* (New York: Seabury, 1980), p. 306.

5. Meade, *Old Churches*, 1:51; CCL, "My Boyhood," UVa Mss 9934, Box 9; REL to

Nathaniel Burwell, February 15, 1869, VHS Burwell Papers, Mss2 B95873 b 3; Journals of Martha Custis Williams, Arlington House Archives, March 11, 1854.

6. Jacob M. Blosser, "Pursuing Happiness in Colonial Virginia," *VMHB* 118, no. 3 (2010): 216.

7. John K. Nelson, *A Blessed Company: Parishes, Parsons, and Parishioners in Anglican Virginia, 1690–1776* (Chapel Hill: UNC Press, 2001), p. 193: a Chesterfield County grand jury in 1772 chastised the hymn singing in Dale Parish. On hymns: Robert W. Prichard, *A History of the Episcopal Church* (Harrisburg, PA: Morehouse, 1991), p. 65; Kenneth R. Long, *The Music of the English Church* (London: Hodder and Stoughton, 1971), pp. 331–32. Ironically, the Oxford movement, which Meade so vehemently opposed, "eventually broke down the prejudice against hymns" as a result of plumbing the depths of the ancient church.

8. See correspondence between Meade and MLFC, VHS/MCL/d/P Mss1 L5144 a, #395–405. The College of New Jersey formally changed its name to Princeton University in 1896.

9. *A Practical View of the Prevailing Religious Systems of Professed Christians in the Higher and Middle Classes of This Country Contrasted with Real Christianity* (1797).

10. David L. Holmes, *The Faiths of the Founding Fathers* (Oxford: OUP, 2006), pp. 110–11; Diana Hochstedt Butler, *Standing against the Whirlwind: Evangelical Episcopalians in Nineteenth Century America* (New York: OUP, 1995), pp. 12, 22–23n44.

11. George Dashiell, 1814, quoted in Butler, *Standing against the Whirlwind*, p. 12; Sydney E. Ahlstrom, *A Religious History of the American People* (New Haven: YUP, 1972), p. 263; McIlvaine, quoted from an 1851 address in Butler, p. 4.

12. See J. Rixey Ruffin, *A Paradise of Reason: William Bentley and Enlightenment Christianity in the Early Republic* (Oxford: OUP, 2008), p. 7; Butler, *Standing against the Whirlwind*, pp. 13–14.

13. Robert W. Prichard, *The Nature of Salvation: Theological Consensus in the Episcopal Church, 1801–1873* (Urbana: University of Illinois Press, 1997), pp. 19–20; see also pp. 24–29.

14. Edward L. Bond, *Damned Souls in a Tobacco Colony: Religion in Seventeenth-Century Virginia* (Macon, GA: Mercer University Press, 2000), pp. 220–21; Nelson, *A Blessed Company*, pp. 205–6; Butler, *Standing against the Whirlwind*, pp. 13–15.

15. ACL [to HL], Shirley, July 6, 1806, ACL Papers, 1805–1816, LOC/CLFP, Box 1; reprinted in Ethel Armes, *Stratford Hall: The Great House of the Lees* (Richmond: Garrett and Massie, 1936), pp. 306–7.

16. Charles Royster, *Light-Horse Harry Lee and the Legacy of the American Revolution* (New York: Knopf, 1981), pp. 77, 104–5; Emory M. Thomas, *Robert E. Lee: A Biography* (New York: Norton, 1995), p. 31 (also, Armes, *Stratford Hall*, p. 310).

17. REL, in HL, *Memoirs of the War in the Southern Department of the United States*, with a biography of the author by Robert E. Lee (New York: University Publishing, 1869), p. 53; ACL, quoted in Royster, *Light-Horse Harry Lee*, pp. 82–83.

18. See Thomas, *Robert E. Lee*, pp. 32–33; Elizabeth Brown Pryor, *Reading the Man: Robert E. Lee through His Private Letters* (New York: Viking, 2007), p. 16.

19. Donald R. Hickey, *The War of 1812: A Forgotten Conflict* (Urbana: University of Illinois Press, 1989), p. 201; see Douglas Southall Freeman, *R. E. Lee: A Biography*, 4 vols. (New York: Charles Scribner's Sons, 1934), 1:29–30.

20. ACL to CCL, Alexandria, July 17, 1816, LOC/EA, Box 2, original documents, 1809–1895, and Armes, *Stratford Hall*, p. 356.

21. HL to ACL, Caicos, August 29, 18??; Nassau, October 25, 18??, and December 27, 18?? (years not recorded), WLU, Schoenbrun Collection, #0394.

22. Thomas E. Templin, "Henry 'Light Horse Harry' Lee: A Biography" (PhD diss., University of Kentucky, 2 vols., 1975), 1:33–34; Mark A. Noll, *America's God: From Jonathan Edwards to Abraham Lincoln* (Oxford: OUP, 2002), pp. 105–6; Jeffry H. Morrison, *John Witherspoon and the Founding of the American Republic* (Notre Dame: University of Notre Dame Press, 2005), pp. 51–57.

23. CCL, "My Boyhood—II," UVa Mss 9934, Box 9.

24. HL to CCL, quoted in Armes, *Stratford Hall*, p. 325; ACL to Mrs. R. B. Lee, Stratford, VA, March 21, 1805, ACL Papers, 1805–1816, LOC/EA, Box 1; ACL to Berkeley, Stratford, VA, November 26, 1809, LOC/EA, Box 2, 1809–1895, also in Armes, pp. 323–24.

25. ACL to Dr. Robert Carter, Stratford, VA, October 1, 1805, LOC/CLFP, ACL Papers, 1805–1816; also in Armes, *Stratford Hall*, p. 305.

26. CCL, "My Boyhood—II," p. 19.

27. HL to ACL, Barbados, August 13, 1813, LOC/EA, Box 1, Henry Lee, 1779–1816, and Armes, *Stratford Hall*, p. 346; HL to CCL, Barbados, August 15, 1813, LOC/EA, Box 1, Henry Lee, 1779–1816, and Armes, *Stratford Hall*, p. 347. In his letter to Carter, Henry adds, "Hug my dear Robert for me & kiss little Mildred." Carter was actually Henry Lee's fourth child. He was preceded by a half sister and half brother, Lucy Grymes (1786–1860) and Henry (1787–1837), and a brother who died young.

28. HL to ACL, Barbados, September 13, 1813, LOC/CLFP (portions in Armes, *Stratford Hall*, p. 313). The quotation appears to be from Seneca, *Epistulae morales* 2.

29. Cf. Holmes, *Faiths*, ch. 8, especially pp. 83–84; and Richard B. McCaslin, *Lee in the Shadow of Washington* (Baton Rouge: Louisiana State University Press, 2001), p. 21, on Henry Lee commending to his children the works of John Locke and the example of Washington.

30. ACL to CCL at Harvard, Alexandria, July 17, 1816, LOC/EA, Box 2, 1809–1895, and Armes, *Stratford Hall*, p. 357.

31. F. L. Cross, ed., *Oxford Dictionary of the Christian Church* (Oxford: OUP, 1958), p. 1408, s.v. "Unitarianism"; cf. Ahlstrom, *Religious History*, ch. 24 (pp. 388–402). The epithet "Socinian" was applied to Unitarians in England and America. John Newton, author of the hymn "Amazing Grace," called the term "another word for infidelity": Herbert Schlossberg, *The Silent Revolution and the Making of Victorian England* (Columbus: Ohio State University Press, 2000), p. 26.

32. CCL to ACL, Cambridge, June 20, 1817 (or 1819), AH, #2549; CCL to ACL, Cambridge, January 31, 1819, AH, #2548. Robert may have harbored a rosier view of his father until late in his life, when he encountered a book critical of Light-Horse Harry. He had Mary write to his brother to ask about this work "containing a very circumstantial account of the last days of Gen. Henry Lee which differs so much & so painfully from what we know that Robert is much concerned to know its truth especially what relates to the great poverty & apparent destitution in which your father arrived at Cumberland, Md, his want of selfcontrol & great irritibility of temper." MARC to CCL, Lexington, August 1, 1870, LOC/EA, Box 2, MARC Papers, 1834–1871.

33. Quoted in Holmes, *Faiths*, p. 116.

Notes to Chapter 4

1. Walter H. Taylor, *Four Years with General Lee* (New York: D. Appleton, 1877), pp. 28, 30, 79.

2. Paul C. Nagle, *The Lees of Virginia* (New York: OUP, 1990), pp. 185–87.

3. Nagle, *The Lees of Virginia*, p. 188.

4. Edmund Jennings Lee, ed., *Lee of Virginia, 1642–1892: Biographical and Genealogical Sketches of the Descendants of Colonel Richard Lee* (Philadelphia, 1895), p. 374; William Meade, *Old Churches, Ministers, and Families of Virginia*, 2 vols. (Philadelphia, 1857; reprint, Baltimore: Genealogical Publishing, 1995), 2:269; Burton J. Hendrick, *The Lees of Virginia* (Boston: Little, Brown, 1935), p. 405.

5. Douglas Southall Freeman, *R. E. Lee: A Biography*, 4 vols. (New York: Charles Scribner's Sons, 1934), 1:34; 4:474; John Booty, *Mission and Ministry: A History of Virginia Theological Seminary* (Harrisburg, PA: Morehouse, 1995), p. 110.

6. Hendrick, *The Lees of Virginia*, p. 405.

7. CCL, "My Boyhood—II," UVa Mss 9934, Box 9, p. 19.

8. See Edward G. Lengel, *Inventing George Washington: America's Founder, in Myth and Memory* (New York: Harper, 2011), p. 34; Mary P. Coulling, *The Lee Girls* (Winston-Salem, NC: J. F. Blair, 1987), p. 5.

9. Journals of Martha Custis Williams, Arlington House Archives (hereafter "Markie, Diary"), September 12, 1857; December 12, 1857; January 8, 1855; May 25, 1856. She referred to the Book of Common Prayer (London: Charles Bill, 1722), now at VHS, Mss 6:4 C 969:1.

10. Elizabeth Gibbon Randolph Calvert, "Childhood Days at Arlington Mixed with After Memories" (unpublished manuscript, c. 1870, AH, #2541), p. 7; Markie, Diary, September 12, 1857.

11. Meade, *Old Churches*, 2:194–96. The Fitzhughs and Lees were connected through the marriage of Robert's great-grandfather's sister to William Fitzhugh, great-grandfather of Mary Lee Fitzhugh Custis. See the genealogical table in Hendrick, *The Lees of Virginia*.

12. Elizabeth Carter (Randolph) Turner to MLFC, Kinloch, VA, May 26, 1833, VHS/GBLP Mss1 L5114 b 49.

13. MLFC to MARC, Arlington, January 29, [1839], AH, #12643.

14. Cf. Meade to MLFC, Princeton, NJ, March 6, 1808, VHS/MCL/d/P Mss1 L5144 a, #395–405, and various letters in folders #426–439, 440–451, and 465–480.

15. CCL, "My Boyhood—II," p. 19.

Notes to Chapter 5

1. REL to MARC, Richmond, March 14, 1862, VHS Mss1 L51 c 346; *The Wartime Papers of Robert E. Lee*, ed. Clifford Dowdey and Louis H. Manarin (1961; reprint, New York: Da Capo Press, 1987), #124, p. 128; cf. REL to John Johns, Lexington, March 7, 1866, Letterbook, VHS/LFP Mss1 L51 c 737, pp. 98–99.

2. Douglas Southall Freeman, *R. E. Lee: A Biography*, 4 vols. (New York: Charles Scribner's Sons, 1934), 4:501; REL to MARC, March 14, 1862.

3. William Meade, *Old Churches, Ministers, and Families of Virginia*, 2 vols. (Philadelphia, 1857; reprint, Baltimore: Genealogical Publishing, 1995), 1:23–24, 26; David Lynn Holmes Jr., "William Meade and the Church of Virginia, 1789–1829" (PhD diss., Princeton University, 1971), p. 98.

4. BCP 1789, the Ministration of Private Baptism of Children in Houses (§15); Meade, *Old Churches*, 1:31–32, 58.

5. Meade, *Old Churches*, 1:45–46.

6. Meade, *Old Churches*, 1:32–33.

7. Meade, *Old Churches*, 1:34, 30. Marshall gave "with liberality" to create Virginia Theological Seminary.

8. Diana Hochstedt Butler, *Standing against the Whirlwind: Evangelical Episcopalians in Nineteenth Century America* (New York: OUP, 1995), pp. 27, 43.

9. John Booty, *Mission and Ministry: A History of Virginia Theological Seminary* (Harrisburg, PA: Morehouse, 1995), p. 27; Meade, *Old Churches*, 1:38; Moore to Edmund J. Lee, February 17, 1814, W&M, Swem Library, Meade Papers, Box 1, Folder 1.

10. *Washington Theological Repertory* 1, no. 1 (August 1819): 1, 3; see Butler, *Standing against the Whirlwind*, pp. 28–29, 32.

11. See ch. 8, n. 27 below.

12. Meade, *Old Churches*, 1:40–41.

13. Meade, *Old Churches*, 1:42–43; Holmes, "Meade," p. 4; see Butler, *Standing against the Whirlwind*, p. 6, for diocesan conventions as parallels to Methodist revival meetings.

14. Meade, *Old Churches*, 1:213; Susan Pendleton Lee, *Memoirs of William Nelson Pendleton, D.D.* (1893; reprint, Harrisonburg, VA: Sprinkle Publications, 1991), pp. 7, 69–73; see Meade, 2:488–90.

15. George M. Brooke Jr., *General Lee's Church* (Lexington, VA: News-Gazette, 1984), pp. 3, 5, 14; see Meade, *Old Churches*, 2:66.

16. Collect for the Third Sunday after Easter, BCP 1789, §15; Butler, *Standing against the Whirlwind*, p. 33.

17. See William Meade, *Pastoral Letter of Bishop Meade, to the Congregations of the Protestant Episcopal Church of Virginia* (Richmond: H. K. Ellyson, 1847).

18. Robert Nelson, *Reminiscences of the Right Rev. William Meade, D.D.* (Shanghai: "Ching-Foong" General Printing Office, 1873), pp. 27–29; Meade to Gen. Cochran, January 18, 1845, W&M, Swem Library, Meade Papers, Box 1, Folder 5.

19. Meade, *Old Churches*, 1:39.

20. Meade, *Old Churches*, 1:44, 58.

21. Key, quoted in William Meade, *Remarks on a Pamphlet concerning the Canon on Lay Discipline* (Washington, DC: Gideon & Co., 1850), pp. 21–22; Diocese of Virginia, *Journal of the Fifty-Fifth Annual Convention of the Protestant Episcopal Church in Virginia* (Baltimore: Joseph Robinson, 1850), pp. 38–39.

22. George C. Rable, *God's Almost Chosen Peoples* (Chapel Hill: UNC Press, 2010), p. 12; Edward L. Bond and Joan R. Gunderson, "The Episcopal Church in Virginia, 1607–2007," *VMHB* 115, no. 2 (2007): 226–28.

23. John R. McGivigan and Mitchel Snay, eds., *Religion and the Antebellum Debate over Slavery* (Athens: University of Georgia Press, 1998), pp. 8, 15. On Hopkins, cf. Rable, *God's Almost Chosen Peoples*, p. 226. William Meade, *Pastoral Letter . . . on the*

Duty of Affording Religious Instruction to Those in Bondage (1834; reprint, Richmond: H. K. Ellyson, 1853). Meade's teaching follows that of the first prominent evangelical Anglican in Virginia, Devereaux Jarrett, a priest who condoned slavery and the need for "correction"—that is, whipping. Douglas Ambrose, "Of Stations and Relations," in McGivigan and Snay, p. 51.

24. Meade to Davis, Millwood, VA, January 21, 1862, LOC, Correspondence of William Meade (1789–1862).

25. Holmes, "William Meade," pp. 203, 206; Elizabeth R. Vason, "Evangelical Womanhood," in McGivigan and Snay, *Religion and the Antebellum Debate*, p. 174; Allan Yarema, *The American Colonization Society: An Avenue to Freedom?* (Lanham, MD: University Press of America, 2006), pp. 20–21.

26. Meade to MLFC, Millwood, VA, April 16, 1832, VHS Mss2 c 9695 b; also, Meade to MLFC, Millwood, VA, May 30, 1825, UVa Ms 8365; Yarema, *The American Colonization Society*, pp. 20–21; see Robert E. L. deButts Jr., "Lee in Love: Courtship and Correspondence in Antebellum Virginia," *VMHB* 115, no. 4 (2007): 522n118.

27. Meade to MLFC, Millwood, VA, April 9, 1833, May 30, 1835, VHS Mss2 c 9695 b; cf. John Johns, *A Memoir of the Life of the Right Rev. William Meade D.D.* (Baltimore: Innes & Co., 1867), pp. 476–77. However, Holmes ("William Meade," p. 206) observes, "Though Meade freed all but the most feeble of his slaves after 1825, freedom treated them so disastrously that he ceased urging others to follow his example." See Philip Slaughter, *Memoirs of the Life of the Rt. Rev. William Meade* (Richmond: Randolph and English, 1885), p. 18.

28. Butler, *Standing against the Whirlwind*, p. 148; Meade to Polk, Millwood, VA, December 10, 1854(?), LOC, Meade Correspondence. Cf. Holmes, "William Meade," p. 206.

29. For a brief survey of the increasing defense of slavery in Southern churches, see McGivigan and Snay, *Religion and the Antebellum Debate*, pp. 15–16.

30. Meade, address to 1861 convention, quoted in Johns, *Meade*, p. 497.

31. Meade to McIlvaine, Millwood, VA, December 15, 1860, quoted in Johns, *Meade*, p. 492; cf. Meade to Johns, undated [probably January 1861], quoted in Johns, p. 495. On the division of denominations, see Sydney E. Ahlstrom, *A Religious History of the American People* (New Haven: YUP, 1972), pp. 659–65.

32. Butler, *Standing against the Whirlwind*, pp. 152, 166.

33. Meade to McIlvaine, Richmond, May 8, 1861, quoted in Johns, *Meade*, p. 494; address to 1861 convention, quoted in Johns, p. 498. Other Southern bishops were making similar turnarounds, e.g., James Hervey Otey of Tennessee (Rable, *God's Almost Chosen Peoples*, p. 52).

34. Meade to Stewart, Millwood, VA, July 14, 1861, LOC, Meade Correspondence. Rable, *God's Almost Chosen Peoples*, pp. 59–60; Robert W. Prichard, *A History of the Episcopal Church* (Harrisburg, PA: Morehouse, 1991), p. 145.

35. Meade to Stewart, Millwood, VA, July 26 and August 1 and 12, 1861, LOC, Meade Correspondence.

36. Meade to Stewart, August 1, 1861.

37. Meade to Stewart, Millwood, VA, November 30, 1861, LOC, Meade Correspondence.

38. Quoted in Johns, *Meade*, p. 512, and Booty, *Mission and Ministry*, pp. 111–12.

39. REL to MARC, Richmond, March 14, 1862, VHS Mss1 L51 c 346; *Wartime Papers*, p. 128; see also REL to Johns, March 7, 1866.

40. REL to Revd. Wm. Norwood, Lexington, VA, May 19, 1869, VHS Mss1 N8394 a 3.

41. REL to Johns, March 7, 1866.

Notes to Chapter 6

1. No record has been found. The baptism is not recorded in Lee family Bibles at VHS, nor does the Stratford Hall library have information; the church where it may have been recorded ceased operation long ago. Baptism as an infant was the custom of the day—and at home, despite injunctions by the clergy to conduct baptisms at church (see BCP 1789, §15).

2. HL to ACL, Barbados, September 13, 1813, LOC/CLFP, and Ethel Armes, *Stratford Hall: The Great House of the Lees* (Richmond: Garrett and Massie, 1936), p. 313; REL to CCL, Mexico City, May 15, 1848, UVa Mss 990b.

3. Sarah Lee to MARC, Gordonsville, VA, November 10, 1870, VHS/LFP Mss1 L51 c 708; Douglas Southall Freeman, *R. E. Lee: A Biography*, 4 vols. (New York: Charles Scribner's Sons, 1934), 1:333, 36; REL Jr., *Recollections and Letters of General Robert E. Lee* (New York: Doubleday, Page, 1905), pp. 415, 417; ACL to CCL, Alexandria, May 8, 1816 (Armes, *Stratford Hall*, p. 355).

4. Cassius Francis Lee to MARC, Menokin, Fairfax Co., VA, November 8, 1870, VHS/LFP Mss1 L51 c 707.

5. CCL, "My Boyhood—II," UVa Mss 9934, Box 9, pp. 5, 16.

6. "[H]e had known me in childhood, when I recited to him the church catechism, taught me by my mother before I could read; that his affection and interest, begun at that time . . . had continued to the present." REL to John Johns, Lexington, March 7, 1866, Letterbook, VHS/LFP Mss1 L51 c 737, p. 98. (See ch. 3 above.)

7. William Meade, *Explanation of the Church Catechism* (1849; reprint, New York: Protestant Episcopal Society for the Promotion of Evangelical Knowledge, 1856), pp. v–vi.

8. E.g., Meade, *Catechism*, based on the 32nd edition of a work on the catechism by Jas. Stillingfleet, MA, of the Church of England; and Meade, *Conversations on the Catechism of the Protestant Episcopal Church* (New York: Protestant Episcopal Society for the Promotion of Evangelical Knowledge, 1857).

9. Cassius Francis Lee to MARC, November 8, 1870.

10. Sarah Lee to MARC, November 10, 1870; Freeman, *R. E. Lee*, 1:39, 40, 42, quoting W. H. Fitzhugh, Lee's teacher W. B. Leary, and his brother Carter; Armes, *Stratford Hall*, p. 388. Benjamin Hallowell, quoted in Edmund Jennings Lee, ed., *Lee of Virginia, 1642–1892: Biographical and Genealogical Sketches of the Descendants of Colonel Richard Lee* (Philadelphia, 1895), pp. 413–14, and Freeman, 1:46.

11. Elizabeth Brown Pryor, *Reading the Man: Robert E. Lee through His Private Letters* (New York: Viking, 2007), p. 48; Jonathan Horn, *The Man Who Would Not Be Washington* (New York: Scribner, 2015), pp. 33, 39 (see CCL to Henry Lee IV, April 20, 1831, LVA, CCL Papers).

12. Pryor suggests that he had removed himself to vomit (*Reading the Man*, p. 64).

Cf. William C. Davis, *Jefferson Davis: The Man and His Hour* (New York: HarperCollins, 1991), pp. 35–36.

13. See George S. Pappas, *To the Point: The United States Military Academy, 1802–1902* (Westport, CT: Praeger, 1993), pp. 169–72.

14. Diana Hochstedt Butler, *Standing against the Whirlwind: Evangelical Episcopalians in Nineteenth Century America* (New York: OUP, 1995), p. 39.

15. Freeman, *R. E. Lee*, 1:59.

16. Butler, *Standing against the Whirlwind*, p. 40.

17. Butler, *Standing against the Whirlwind*, p. 40 (see p. 57n102); *Episcopal Church Annual* (Harrisburg, PA: Morehouse Publishing, 2000), p. 363.

18. Pappas, *To the Point*, pp. 273–74.

19. Margaret Sanborn, *Robert E. Lee: A Portrait* (Moose, WY: Homestead Publishing, 1996), 1:44.

20. Edmund Jennings Lee, "The Character of General Lee," in *Gen. Robert Edward Lee: Soldier, Citizen, and Christian Patriot*, ed. R. A. Brock (Richmond: Royal Publishing, 1897), p. 383. Sources vary on her date of death. Some, like Lee (above), record June 29; Freeman (*R. E. Lee*, 1:87) and Pryor (*Reading the Man*, p. 72) cite July 10; Thomas (*Robert E. Lee: A Biography* [New York: Norton, 1995], p. 56) concurs with Nagle (*The Lees of Virginia* [New York: OUP, 1990], p. 200) on July 29. In 1913 her remains were moved from Annandale to the Lee family crypt in Lee Chapel at Washington and Lee University, as were her husband's from Georgia.

21. Freeman, *R. E. Lee*, 1:92 (see A. L. Long, *Memoirs of Robert E. Lee*, 7th ed. [Secaucus, NJ: Blue and Grey Press, 1983], p. 30).

22. See Walter H. Taylor, *Four Years with General Lee* (New York: D. Appleton, 1877), pp. 57–58; REL to MARC, Cockspur Island, GA, December 24, 1831, VHS/MCL/d/P Mss1 L5144 a, §12, #812. Spelling had not yet been standardized.

23. REL to MARC, Cockspur Island, GA, December 28, 1830; Robert E. L. deButts Jr., "Lee in Love: Courtship and Correspondence in Antebellum Virginia," *VMHB* 115, no. 4 (2007): #7, p. 525; REL to CCL, November 16, 1830, Cockspur, GA; see REL to CCL, February 27, 1831, Cockspur, GA (both UVa Mss 1085).

Notes to Chapter 7

1. REL to Andrew Talcott, Ravensworth, VA, July 13, 1831, LVA, Lee Letters 1831–1834, #23766. The schoolroom blackboard was introduced to the United States by a mathematician at West Point in 1801.

2. REL to MLFC, Old Point, VA, April 24, 1832, quoted in Elizabeth Brown Pryor, *Reading the Man: Robert E. Lee through His Private Letters* (New York: Viking, 2007), p. 45; Mary P. Coulling, *The Lee Girls* (Winston-Salem, NC: J. F. Blair, 1987), p. 5. There is some issue as to whether she was born in 1807 or 1808. Martha Washington's Prayer Book records family births, including "Mary Anna Randolph Custis. Born at Annefield[,] Clark County, Virginia," with a date of October 1, 1808, but the final "8" appears to overwrite a "7" (VHS Mss6:4 C 969:1).

3. Jonathan Horn, *The Man Who Would Not Be Washington* (New York: Scribner, 2015), p. 42.

4. Quoted in Robert E. L. deButts Jr., "Lee in Love: Courtship and Correspondence in Antebellum Virginia," *VMHB* 115, no. 4 (2007): 488; REL to MARC, Cockspur, GA, December 28, 1830; "Lee in Love," #7, p. 526; see p. 567n126. Tradition holds that Lee proposed over a slice of cake in the dining room in 1830, but this letter suggests an earlier incident of some sort (see deButts, pp. 491–92).

5. Emory M. Thomas, *Robert E. Lee: A Biography* (New York: Norton, 1995), p. 56. On Henry Lee IV ("Black-Horse Harry"), see Douglas Southall Freeman, *R. E. Lee: A Biography*, 4 vols. (New York: Charles Scribner's Sons, 1934), 1:97; Ethel Armes, *Stratford Hall: The Great House of the Lees* (Richmond: Garrett and Massie, 1936), pp. 392–98; Paul C. Nagle, *The Lees of Virginia* (New York: OUP, 1990), pp. 206–17.

6. Doubts surround the time and place. Freeman opines that "it is impossible to fix the date of the proposal with certainty" (*R. E. Lee*, 1:104). Taylor places it "some time during that summer of 1830" (*Four Years with General Lee* [New York: D. Appleton, 1877], p. 61), and Pryor "by September" (*Reading the Man*, p. 76). DeButts surmises that the engagement took place shortly before Robert wrote to her on September 11 ("Lee in Love," pp. 491, 494), a chronology supported by Robert's letter to Carter on September 22. But an entry in Mary's diary of July 10, 1830, implies that, if the engagement had not been set, her heart's desire certainly had been—whether on Robert or on Jesus is tantalizingly unclear.

7. See Coulling, *The Lee Girls*, pp. 5–6. See ch. 15, n. 12 below, regarding "servant/slave" terminology.

8. On church attendance, cf. MARC, Diary, July 11, August 8, September 19, 1830, VHS Mss1 L51 g 3; on ministers, see Diary, July 23 and 25, 1830. Easter 1830 was an exception, as she was ill (Diary, [March] 20, 1831). The book was probably *A Memoir of the Rev. Edward Payson: Late Pastor of the Second Church in Portland*, by Asa Cummings, published in 1830. MARC, Diary, July 19, 1830. On daily prayers and teaching, see Journals of Martha Custis Williams, Arlington House Archives (hereafter "Markie, Diary"), September 12, 1857.

9. MLFC to MARC, Arlington, January 29, [1839], AH, #12643. Ann Randolph Page to MLFC, April 17, 1830, cited in deButts, "Lee in Love," n. 104. Custis, quoted in Marie Tyler-McGraw, *An African Republic: Black & White Virginians in the Making of Liberia* (Chapel Hill: UNC Press, 2007), p. 119.

10. Agnes Lee, *Growing Up in the 1850s*, ed. Mary Custis Lee deButts (Chapel Hill: UNC Press, 1984), p. 15; Markie, Diary, June 3, 1856.

11. MARC, Diary, July 4, 1830. She often omits punctuation.

12. MARC, Diary, July 22, 1830.

13. MARC, Diary, July 8, 1830.

14. MARC, Diary, July 5 and 7, 1830.

15. MARC, Diary, July 8 and 16, 1830.

16. MARC, Diary, July 10, 1830.

17. REL to CCL, Arlington, September 22, 1830, UVa Mss 1085, CCL Papers; REL to CCL, Arlington, September 30, 1830, UVa Mss 1085. The nature of his "resignation" is unclear: Was he contemplating leaving the army, or, by another definition, refusing to submit himself (see ch. 13)?

18. See Nancy F. Cott, "Marriage and Women's Citizenship in the United States, 1830–1934," *American Historical Review* 103, no. 5 (December 1998): 1440–74.

19. MARC, Diary, [September] 19, 1830.

20. REL to MARC, Wood Stock, VA, September 11, 1830, in deButts, "Lee in Love,"
#1, p. 514; MARC, Diary, September 12, 1830.

21. MARC to REL, Arlington, September 20, [1830], in deButts, "Lee in Love,"
#2, pp. 515–16.

22. REL to MARC, September 11, 1830; MARC to REL, September 20, [1830], in
deButts, "Lee in Love," pp. 515–16.

23. REL to MARC, Baltimore, October 30, 1830, in deButts, "Lee in Love," #3,
p. 518.

24. REL to MARC, Cockspur Island, GA, November 11, 1830, in deButts, "Lee in
Love," #4, pp. 519–21.

25. MARC, Diary, October 31, 1830. John P. McGuire was briefly rector of Christ
Church (1829–1830).

26. Cf. John R. H. Moorman, *The Anglican Spiritual Tradition* (Springfield, IL:
Templegate, 1983), pp. 116–52; Martin Thornton, *English Spirituality* (Cambridge,
MA: Cowley, [1963]), pp. 240–41, 261–65.

27. REL to MARC, Cockspur Island, GA, November 19, 1830, in deButts, "Lee in
Love," #5, p. 521. Mary's letters to Robert from this period have apparently been lost.

28. MARC, Diary, November 21, 1830. REL to MARC, Cockspur Island, GA, December 1, 1830, in deButts, "Lee in Love," #6, p. 523.

29. MARC, Diary, December 12, 1830 (see Gen. 19); REL to MARC, Cockspur Island, GA, December 28, 1830, in deButts, "Lee in Love," #7, pp. 525–26.

30. MARC, Diary, January 30, 1831; REL to MARC, Cockspur Island, GA, January
10, 1831, in deButts, "Lee in Love," #9, p. 531.

31. REL to MARC, Cockspur Island, GA, February 1, 1831, VHS/MCL/d/P Mss1
L5144 a, §12, #824.

32. REL to MARC, Cockspur Island, GA, February 14, 1831, VHS/MCL/d/P Mss1
L5144 a, §12, #825.

33. REL to MARC, Cockspur Island, GA, February 1, 1831, VHS/MCL/d/P Mss1
L5144 a, §12, #811.

34. MARC, Diary, February 13, 16, and 21, 1830, quoting verse 2 of "Children of
the Heavenly King," by John Cennick, a colleague of John Wesley (1742).

35. REL to MARC, Cockspur Island, GA, March 8, 1831, in deButts, "Lee in Love,"
#9, p. 533.

36. CCL to Henry Lee IV, December 17(?), 1831, UVa CCL Papers; ACL to CCL,
July 17, 1816, LOC/EA, Box 2, original documents, 1809–1895.The term "blue lights"
probably derives from an evangelical revival in the British navy of 1775–1815, when
certain officers earned the nickname by insisting on holding religious services on
board ships. See Richard Blake, *Evangelicals in the Royal Navy, 1775–1815: Blue Lights
and Psalm-Singers* (Woodbridge, UK: Boydell and Brewer, 2008).

37. MARC, Diary, [March] 20, 1831.

38. REL to MARC, Cockspur Island, GA, May 3, 1831, in deButts, "Lee in Love,"
#10, pp. 535–36.

39. REL to MARC, May 3, 1831, in deButts, pp. 536–37.

40. REL to MARC, Cockspur Island, GA, April 11, 1831, VHS/MCL/d/P Mss1 L5144
a, §12, #817; MARC, Diary, [April] 4, [1831]. Lee may be alluding to James 5:16: "The

effectual fervent prayer of a righteous man availeth much" (KJV). If so, he seems to be thankful for the prayers and blessings, in this case, of a righteous woman, Mrs. Mackay. Unlike the KJV, Jewish tradition sometimes translates Prov. 24:25 as "Upon those who give rebuke shall be delight, upon them shall come the blessing of the good" (see *Literature of the Synagogue*, ed. Joseph Heinemann and Jacob Petuchowski [Piscataway, NJ: Gorgias Press, 2006], p. 189). But the context seems not to fit, and, in any event, Lee would not likely have been aware of this reading.

41. REL to MARC, Cockspur Island, GA, April 20, 1831, VHS/MCL/d/P Mss1 L5144 a, §12, #818. In longtime English and apparently Episcopal custom, public weddings often occurred on Sundays within the context of the liturgy, in this case of Morning Prayer.

42. REL to MARC, n.p. [Fort Monroe, VA?], May 13, 1831, in deButts, "Lee in Love," #11, pp. 540–41.

43. MARC, Diary, May 17, 1831; REL to MARC, Old Point, VA, June 5, 1831, in deButts, "Lee in Love," #12, p. 542; MARC, Diary, June 5, 1831.

44. MLFC and MARC to REL, Arlington, June 11(?), 1831, in deButts, "Lee in Love," #13, p. 545.

45. MARC, Diary, June 12, 1831. The reference is to John 2:1-11.

46. MLFC and MARC to REL, June 11(?), 1831, in deButts, p. 544; REL to MARC, n.p., June 12, 1831, in deButts, "Lee in Love," #14, p. 546.

47. REL to MARC, June 12, 1831, in deButts, p. 548.

48. MARC, Diary, June 19, 1831.

49. REL to MARC, Old Point, VA, June 21, 1831, in deButts, "Lee in Love," #15, pp. 549, 550.

50. See REL to John ("Jack") Mackay, Washington, February 18, 1835, LOC/BM, for a description of a subsequent wedding that could have depicted his own.

51. MARC, Diary, July 3, 1831.

Notes to Chapter 8

1. [MARC], "Biography," p. 3, VHS Mss1 T2144 a 189-200; MARC and REL to MLFC, [Old Point Comfort, VA], [Sunday, August, 1831?], VHS/LFP Mss1 L51 c 5.

2. *The Chapel of the Centurion, Fort Monroe, Virginia*, FM Pamphlet 165-1 (September 18, 1965). Chevers enjoyed his military ministry and officially became chaplain when Congress created the post in 1838. He held the position for fifty years.

3. MARC to MLFC, Old Point Comfort, VA, [1831?], VHS/LFP Mss1 L51 c 14; Robert W. Prichard, *The Nature of Salvation: Theological Consensus in the Episcopal Church, 1801-1873* (Urbana: University of Illinois Press, 1997), pp. 19-24. This "high church" perspective draws on certain emphases of the English Reformation on apostolic succession, sacraments, ancient creeds, and external forms of worship, and is distinguished from the "catholic revival" that would soon follow. Wilmer, quoted in David L. Holmes, *A Brief History of the Episcopal Church* (Valley Forge, PA: Trinity, 1993), p. 71; see pp. 16-17, 61-62.

4. On Chevers, see http://orderofcenturions.org/chapel_of_the_centurion/index.html, accessed June 25, 2016; on Sunday schools, see Holmes, *Brief History*,

p. 103. Free public education in Virginia was not mandated until the Reconstruction-era constitution of 1869, a discussion to which Lee contributed (see ch. 18 below).

5. MARC to MLFC, Old Point Comfort, VA, [1831?], VHS/LFP Mss1 L51 c 5; see Sydney E. Ahlstrom, *A Religious History of the American People* (New Haven: YUP, 1972), p. 425, and Holmes, *Brief History*, pp. 68, 79. MARC to MLFC, [Old Point Comfort, VA], [1831?], VHS/LFP Mss1 L51 c 13.

6. MARC to MLFC, [Old Point Comfort, VA, 1831?], VHS/LFP Mss1 L51 c 14.

7. Elizabeth Gibbon Randolph Calvert, "Childhood Days at Arlington Mixed with After Memories" (unpublished manuscript, c. 1870, AH, #2541), p. 11. Markie Williams, during her stays at Arlington after MLFC's death, maintained the practice.

8. MARC to MLFC, Old Point Comfort, VA, [1833?], VHS/LFP Mss1 L 51 c 11; MARC to MLFC, Fort Monroe, VA, n.d., LVA, Custis-Lee-Mason Family Correspondence, 1756–1844, #20975, Folder 1. The Reverend Henry W. Ducachet (1796–1865) officiated for a time in Norfolk before becoming rector of St. Stephen's, Philadelphia, from1834 to his death. His text came from Prov. 26:13: "The slothful man saith, There is a lion in the way; a lion is in the streets."

9. MARC to MLFC, [Old Point Comfort, VA], April 23, [1833?], VHS/LFP Mss1 L51 c 4.

10. MARC to MLFC, [Old Point Comfort, VA], March 19, 1833, VHS/LFP Mss1 L51 c 15. *Bread of Deceit* is likely a publication for Sunday schools (Philadelphia: Latimer & Co., 1832).

11. MARC to MLFC, March 19, 1833; "I have been enabled," MARC to MLFC, Old Point Comfort, VA, [1831], VHS/LFP Mss1 L51 c 5.

12. REL to Andrew Talcott, Fort Monroe, VA, April 10, 1834, LOV, Lee Papers, 1831–1834, #23766 (quoting Matt. 26:41).

13. MARC to MLFC, April 11, [1834], quoted in Elizabeth Brown Pryor, *Reading the Man: Robert E. Lee through His Private Letters* (New York: Viking, 2007), p. 81; Mary alludes to Luke 10:42, in which Jesus says to the overly busy housekeeper Martha, "One thing is needful: and Mary hath chosen that good part, which shall not be taken away from her."

14. REL to MARC, Old Point Comfort, VA, April 24, 1832, VHS/LFP Mss1 L51 c 7; REL to Mackay, Fort Monroe, VA, June 26, 1834, LOC/BM.

15. REL to Mackay, Washington, February 18, 1835, LOC/BM.

16. REL to CCL, Fort Monroe, VA, December 6, 1833, UVA Mss 1085; also REL to Talcott, Fort Monroe, VA, November 22, 1833, LOV, Lee Papers, 1831–1834, #23766. On Meade, see Mary Meade to MARC, Mountain View, VA, April 28, 1853, VHS/LFP Mss1 L51 c 116.

17. REL to CCL, Old Point, VA, September 28, 1832, UVa Mss 1085; quotation source unknown.

18. REL to MARC, St. Louis, July 26, 1839, VHS/LFP Mss1 L51 c 21, quoting Prov. 22:6; quoted in Mary P. Coulling, *The Lee Girls* (Winston-Salem, NC: J. F. Blair, 1987), p. 13.

19. See Coulling, *The Lee Girls*, p. 14.

20. See Mark A. Noll, *America's God: From Jonathan Edwards to Abraham Lincoln* (Oxford: OUP, 2002), pp. 166–69.

21. Coulling, *The Lee Girls*, pp. 24–25 (see Marietta Minnigerode Andrews, *Mem-*

oirs of a Poor Relation [New York: Dutton, 1930], p. 91); REL to [Custis], Baltimore, May 23, 1847, LOC/BM.

22. REL to MARC, Fort Hamilton, NY, April 18–19, 1841, UVa Mss 990b.

23. *Southern Churchman*, all citations from vol. 5, 1839.

24. MARC to MLFC, Fort Hamilton, NY, January 6, 1841, VHS Mss1 L5144 a, §11:726–273.

25. On Cassius (January 4, 1839, p. 3); on renewals, see, e.g., "Mrs. Custis" of Alexandria and "Lt. R. E. Lee" of St. Louis (May 3, 1839, p. 71); MARC from Arlington in 1851 (January 17, 1851, p. 3); REL from Baltimore (January 8, 1852, p. 208); and MARC from West Point (February 3, 1853, p. 15).

26. REL to MARC, Fort Brown, TX, December 13, 1856, VHS Mss1 L51 c 179; REL to MARC, Camp Fredericksburg, VA, March 9, 1863, VHS/LFP Mss1 L51 c 437; REL to Rev. Francis Sprigg, Lexington, October 21, 1865, UVa Mss 4703, "Lee Family Mss 1814–1865," Box 28.

27. *Southern Churchman*, April 5, 1839, p. 55.

28. REL to CCL, St. Louis, August 15, 1837; REL to MARC, St. Louis, August 21, 1837; REL to CCL, St. Louis, October 8, 1837 (all UVa Mss 1085).

29. MARC to MLFC, St. Louis[?], July 4–5, [1838?], AH, #12640.

30. Eugene L. Rodgers, *And Then . . . a Cathedral: A History of Christ Church Cathedral, St. Louis, Missouri* (St. Louis: Christ Church Cathedral, 1970), pp. 7–8, 54, 62. This account differs somewhat from that of Greenough White, *An Apostle of the Western Church: Memoir of the Right Reverend Jackson Kemper* (New York: Thomas Whittaker, 1899).

31. REL to MARC, St. Louis, November 3, 1839, AH, #3700.

32. REL to MARC, St. Louis, September 4, 1840, VHS/LFP Mss1 L51 c 27. Peak was assistant to the rector from November 1839 to May 1840, when he became rector, serving until October 1842 (Rodgers, *And Then*, pp. 7–8).

33. Coulling, *The Lee Girls*, p. 17.

34. John Henry Newman, one of the leaders of the Oxford movement, was novel in decorating the church he served (and built) outside Oxford with flowers for Easter (see Newman to Mrs. J. Mozley, April 18, 1840, in *Letters and Correspondence of John Henry Newman*, ed. Anne Mozley, 2 vols. [London, 1891], 2:304); MARC to MLFC, [Fort Hamilton, NY], December 25, [1845], VHS/LFP Mss1 L51 c 37; Susan Pendleton Lee, *Memoirs of William Nelson Pendleton, D.D.* (1893; reprint, Harrisonburg, VA: Sprinkle Publications, 1991), pp. 468–69.

35. Meade to Rt. Rev. W. R. Whittingham, Richmond, October 14, 1840, W&M, Swem Library, Meade Papers, Box 1, Folder 4; Meade to Minister & Vestry of the Episcopal Church in Suffolk, Suffolk, April 25, 1845, Meade Papers, Box 1, Folder 5. On "honest tables," see Marion J. Hatchett, *Commentary on the American Prayer Book* (New York: Seabury, 1980), p. 301, and rubric in BCP 1552 ("Administracion of the Lordes Supper").

36. MARC to MLFC, Fort Hamilton, NY, September 10, 18[43?], LOV, Custis-Lee-Mason Family Correspondence, 1756–1844, #20975, Folder 1. Carey died in 1844 at age twenty-one.

37. A. L. Long, *Memoirs of Robert E. Lee*, 7th ed. (Secaucus, NJ: Blue and Grey Press, 1983), pp. 67–68, 70.

38. William Meade, *Sermon Delivered . . . at the Opening of the Convention of the Diocese of Virginia* (n.p.: John Heiskell, 1818), p. 17.

39. REL to MARC, Newport, RI, August 18, 1849, VHS/LFP Mss1 L51 c 98.

Notes to Chapter 9

1. William Meade, *Family Prayers* (Alexandria, VA: W. M. Morrison, 1834), p. 28.

2. REL to Martha Custis Williams, Governors Island, NY, June 7, 1846, in *"To Markie": The Letters of Robert E. Lee to Martha Custis Williams*, ed. Avery Craven (Cambridge, MA: Harvard University Press, 1933), pp. 18, 17.

3. REL to MARC, Fort Hamilton, NY, May 12, 1846, VHS/LFP Mss1 L51 c 47. Lee cites Eccles. 9:11: "I returned, and saw under the sun, that the race is not to the swift, nor the battle to the strong . . . ; but time and chance happeneth to them all."

4. Joseph Wheelan, *Invading Mexico: America's Continental Dream and the Mexican War, 1846–1848* (New York: Carroll & Graf Publishers, 2007), pp. 402–3; Grant, quoted from his memoirs in John S. D. Eisenhower, *So Far from God: The U.S. War with Mexico, 1846–1848* (New York: Random House, 1989), p. xvii.

5. Cf. Wheelan, *Invading Mexico*, pp. xix, 5–7, ch. 34; Diana Hochstedt Butler, *Standing against the Whirlwind: Evangelical Episcopalians in Nineteenth Century America* (New York: OUP, 1995), p. 22n44.

6. REL to CCL, Fort Hamilton, NY, July 13, 1846, Lee Papers, UVa Mss 990b/LFDA (Floyd County lies in southwestern Virginia, south of modern-day Blacksburg); REL to CCL, Arlington, September 1, 1846, UVa Mss 990b/LFDA.

7. Jesse Ames Spencer, *The United States: Its Beginnings, Progress, and Modern Development*, 10 vols. (New York: American Educational Alliance, 1912), 9:223.

8. REL to WHFL, Fort Hamilton, NY, March 31, 1846, VHS/LFP Mss1 L51 c 45.

9. REL to MARC, on a steamboat from New Orleans to Lavaca, TX, August 13, 1846, VHS/LFP Mss1 L51 c 50; Mary P. Coulling, *The Lee Girls* (Winston-Salem, NC: J. F. Blair, 1987), p. 17.

10. Michael Haines, "Fertility and Mortality in the United States," EH.net, accessed June 27, 2016, https://eh.net/encyclopedia/fertility-and-mortality-in-the -united-states/.

11. REL to CCL, September 1, 1846; REL to MARC, on steamship from Charleston to Savannah, September 4, 1846, VHS/LFP Mss1 L51 c 51.

12. REL to MARC, camp near Alamos River, Mexico, October 19, 1846, VHS/LFP Mss1 L51 c 57.

13. REL to MARC, camp near Monclova, Mexico, November 4, 1846, VHS Mss1 L51 c 58.

14. REL to MARC, camp near Monclova, Mexico, November 20, 1846, VHS Mss1 L51 c 61; REL to MARC, camp near Salitto, [Mexico], December 25, 1846, VHS Mss1 L51 c 67.

15. REL to MARC, on ship *Massachusetts*, off Lobos Island, February 22, 1847, VHS Mss1 L51 c 68.

16. REL to "my dear boys," on ship *Massachusetts*, off Lobos, February 27, 1847, VHS Mss1 L51 c 69.

17. REL to Custis, Veracruz, Mexico, April 11, 1847, VHS/LFP Mss1 L51 c 71; BCP 1789, §15, Administration of Public Baptism.

18. REL to Agnes, Mexico City, February 12, 1848, VHS Mss1 L51 c 75. The Reverend John D. McCarty of New York was the only Episcopal chaplain at the front; he became a noted missionary to the Pacific Northwest.

19. Emory M. Thomas, *Robert E. Lee: A Biography* (New York: Norton, 1995), p. 121.

20. Douglas Southall Freeman, *R. E. Lee: A Biography*, 4 vols. (New York: Charles Scribner's Sons, 1934), 1:239–41; Eisenhower, *So Far from God*, pp. 277–78.

21. Quoted in Thomas, *Robert E. Lee*, p. 133; see chs. 9–10 on Lee in the Mexican War.

22. REL to CCL, Mexico City, March 18, 1848, UVa Mss 990b; on duty being commended by his father, see HL to SSL, n.p., n.d., VHS/GBLP Mss1 L5114 b 25.

23. REL to CCL, March 3, 1848, UVa Mss 990b.

24. Quoted in Edmund Jennings Lee, "The Character of General Lee," in *Gen. Robert Edward Lee: Soldier, Citizen, and Christian Patriot*, ed. R. A. Brock (Richmond, 1897), p. 384.

25. REL to MARC, Mexico City, February 13, 1848, VHS/LFP Mss1 L51 c 76.

26. MARC to Mrs. Wm. Henry Stiles, Arlington, January 14, 1847, SH M2009.207.

27. REL to CCL, March 18, 1848.

Notes to Chapter 10

1. REL Jr., *Recollections and Letters of General Robert E. Lee* (New York: Doubleday, Page, 1905), pp. 3–4, 8.

2. Emory M. Thomas, *Robert E. Lee: A Biography* (New York: Norton, 1995), pp. 147–48.

3. REL to Martha Custis Williams, Baltimore, May 10, 1851, in *"To Markie": The Letters of Robert E. Lee to Martha Custis Williams*, ed. Avery Craven (Cambridge, MA: Harvard University Press, 1933), #10, p. 26.

4. John D. Kilbourne, "A Brief Sketch of Mount Calvary's History" (n.d.); "Mount Calvary Church" (n.d., c. 1968), both in the archives of the Diocese of Maryland; Meade to Whittingham, Richmond, October 14, 1840, W&M, Swem Library, Meade Papers, Box 1, Folder 4.

5. REL to Anna Maria Sarah (Goldsborough) Fitzhugh, Baltimore, March 30, 1850, VHS/LFP Mss1 L51 c 105.

6. *Laws of Maryland*, vol. 203, ch. 9, p. 207 (Diocese of Maryland archives).

7. REL Jr., *Recollections*, pp. 10–11.

8. Journals of Martha Custis Williams, Arlington House Archives, April 6, 1856, September 12, 1857; REL Jr., *Recollections*, p. 11; Mary P. Coulling, *The Lee Girls* (Winston-Salem, NC: J. F. Blair, 1987), p. 19.

9. REL to MARC, Fort Hamilton, NY, March 24, 1846, VHS/LFP Mss1 L51 c 44.

10. REL to Custis and WHFL, December 24, 1846, VHS/LFP Mss1 L51 c 66.

11. REL to Custis, Baltimore, January 12, 1852, LOC/BM.

12. REL to Custis, Fort Hamilton, NY, November 30, 1845, VHS/LFP Mss1 L51 c 35; REL to Custis, Fort Hamilton, NY, December 18, 1845, UVa Mss 38–462.

13. Thomas, *Robert E. Lee*, p. 105; REL to MARC, Fort Hamilton, NY, April 18, 1841, UVa Mss 990b; REL to MARC, March 24, 1846; REL to MARC, on steamboat from New Orleans to Lavaca, TX, August 13, 1846, VHS/LFP Mss1 L51 c 50; REL Jr., *Recollections*, p. 9.

14. J. A. James, *The Young Man's Friend and Guide through Life to Immortality* (London: Hamilton, Adams, & Co., 1851), pp. 227, 235; Custis to MARC, West Point, NY, March 19, 1853, VHS/LFP Mss1 L51 c 115. John Angell James (1785–1859), who published a counterpart for girls in 1853, was an English nonconformist preacher, evangelical, and slavery abolitionist.

15. MCL/d to MARC, May 20, 1853, Pelham Priory, New York, NY, VHS/LFP Mss1 L51 c 126. The book was most likely *The Life and Letters of Henry Venn*, first published in 1834. Venn had been a founder of the evangelical Clapham Sect in England that included William Wilberforce and John Newton, author of the hymn "Amazing Grace"; his son, John, and grandson, Henry, both led the Church Missionary Society.

16. MARC to "Abbey," Baltimore, August 22, [c. 1851], LFDA; MARC to Custis, Baltimore, February 15, 1852, LOC/BM/LFDA.

17. Custis to MARC, Fort Clinch, Amelia Island, FL, July 26, 1855, VHS/LFP Mss1 L51 c 143.

18. REL to MARC, San Antonio, September 13, 1856, VHS/LFP Mss1 L51 c 168; REL to WHFL, West Point, NY, June 15, 1853, UVa Mss 990b; Henry Adams, *The Education of Henry Adams* (Boston: Houghton Mifflin, 1961), pp. 59–60.

19. REL to Totten, St. Louis, July 9, 1839; REL to Fred. A. Smith, St. Louis, August 12, 1839 (both in Letterbook, VHS/LFP Mss1 L51 c 734, pp. 46, 47).

20. REL to Totten, Fort Carroll, MD, May 28, 1852, VHS/LFP Mss1 L51 c 735, p. 302; REL to Totten, Fort Carroll, MD, July 1, 1852, VHS/LFP Mss1 L51 c 735, p. 303; REL to Totten, Baltimore, July 25, 1852, VHS/LFP Mss1 L51 c 734, p. 178; REL to Totten, West Point, NY, September 1, 1852, WLU/LP/LFDA.

21. Wharton J. Green, *Recollections and Reflections* (Raleigh, NC: Edwards and Broughton, 1906), p. 69.

22. Edward L. Hartz, November 18, 1852, in Stephen E. Ambrose, *Duty, Honor, Country: A History of West Point* (Baltimore: Johns Hopkins University Press, 1999), p. 126; Green, *Recollections and Reflections*, p. 86.

23. Ambrose, *Duty, Honor, Country*, pp. 129, 141, 151, quoting REL to Totten, March 15, 1855.

24. REL Jr., *Recollections*, p. 18; Agnes Lee, *Growing Up in the 1850s*, ed. Mary Custis Lee deButts (Chapel Hill: UNC Press, 1984), pp. 32, 46, 47.

25. Ambrose, *Duty, Honor, Country*, pp. 166, 161; Douglas Southall Freeman, *R. E. Lee: A Biography*, 4 vols. (New York: Charles Scribner's Sons, 1934), 1:337–38. Green, *Recollections and Reflections*, pp. 88–90. Green adds that during the siege of Petersburg in 1864–1865, Gracie, by then a general, called to Lee, standing on the parapet, "For God's sake, General Lee, come down!" Lee ordered, "Back to the trenches, General Gracie!" His former cadet replied, "After you, General Lee." They both tumbled down into the trench (pp. 90–91).

26. O. O. Howard, "The Character and Campaigns of General Lee," in *Gen. Robert*

Edward Lee: Soldier, Citizen, and Christian Patriot, ed. R. A. Brock (Richmond, 1897), p. 351.

27. REL to Mr. Hlasko, West Point, NY, January 22, 1853, Letterbook, LVA #28045/LFDA; REL to Archibald Gracie, West Point, NY, October 6, 1852, LFDA.

28. REL to J. C. VanCamp, West Point, NY, December 14, 1852, LFDA.

29. REL to Edw. Knisley, West Point, NY, February 26, 1853, Letterbook, LVA #28045.

30. REL to Ira M. Harrison, J. C. Johnson, John B. Campfield, West Point, NY, December 22, 1852; REL to J. Faison, West Point, NY, January 22, 1853; REL to Rodman M. Price, West Point, NY, January 25, 1853 (all LFDA).

31. REL to B. O'Conner, West Point, NY, December 17, 1852, LFDA; REL to Mrs. Adele Fowler, West Point, NY, November 9, 1853; REL to W. C. Warren, West Point, NY, December 15, 1853 (all in Letterbook, LVA #28045).

32. REL to O'Conner, December 17, 1852; REL to Warren, December 15, 1853; REL to J. R. Torbert, West Point, NY, October 6, 1852, LFDA, in Letterbook, LVA #28045.

33. REL to Totten, West Point, NY, November 30, 1852, Letterbook, LVA #28045.

34. REL Jr., *Recollections*, p. 12; Agnes Lee, *Growing Up*, pp. 49, 35.

35. REL Jr., *Recollections*, p. 12; Agnes Lee, *Growing Up*, pp. 28, 30, 55.

36. Agnes Lee, *Growing Up*, pp. 45, 55.

Notes to Chapter 11

1. BCP 1789, §19. For background, see W. K. Lowther Clarke, *Liturgy and Worship* (London: SPCK, 1932), pp. 443–57; Charles U. Harris, "The Anglican Understanding of Confirmation," in *Confirmation: History, Doctrine, and Practice*, ed. Kendig Brubaker Cully (Greenwich, CT: Seabury, 1962), pp. 17–32.

2. John Henry Hobart, *The Candidate for Confirmation Instructed* (1819; reprint, Protestant Episcopal Tract Society, 1830), p. 11; Luke 22:19; 1 Cor. 11:24–25 (emphasis added). See ch. 2, n. 5 above, for the rubric in the BCP 1662.

3. Hobart, *Candidate*, p. 20.

4. Gregory T. Bedell, *"Pay Thy Vows": A Pastoral Address Subsequent to Confirmation* (New York: Stanford & Swords, 1853), pp. 9–10.

5. Charles P. McIlvaine, *Pastoral Letter to the Clergy and Laity of the Protestant Episcopal Church in the Diocese of Ohio, on the Subject of Confirmation and Church Music* (Columbus: Ohio State Journal Company, 1855), pp. 3–4; James H. Otey, *Preparation of Candidates for Confirmation* (Nashville: Bang, Walker & Co., 1857), p. 3 (cf. p. 13).

6. William Meade, *The Candidate for Confirmation Self-Examined* (New York: Protestant Episcopal Tract Society, [1841]), pp. 9–12, 26–27.

7. Cf. Diocese of Virginia, *Journal* (1850), pp. 38–39, 55 (see ch. 5 above).

8. BCP 1789, §15, Holy Baptism.

9. REL to MARC, San Antonio, June 18, 1860, VHS/LFP Mss1 L51 c 255.

10. Agnes Lee, *Growing Up in the 1850s*, ed. Mary Custis Lee deButts (Chapel Hill: UNC Press, 1984), p. 13.

11. REL to MCL/d, West Point, NY, April 25, 1853, VHS/MCL/d/P Mss1 L5144 a, §12, #844–858.

. comply

12. REL to MARC, West Point, NY, April 27, 1853, VHS Mss1 L51 c 117.

13. REL to MCL/d, West Point, NY, May 21, 1853, VHS/MCL/d/P Mss1 L5144 a, §23, #1323-1333. Lee alludes to Hagar in the wilderness (Gen. 16:13 KJV, though the word "should" is not part of the verse).

14. WHFL to MARC, n.p., April 29, 1853, VHS/MCL/d/P Mss1 L5144 a, §23, #1323-1333.

15. REL to MARC, West Point, NY, May 2, 1853, VHS Mss1 L51 c 118. The phrase "too wise to err" was often quoted at that time in sermons, including those by the popular evangelical English preacher Charles Spurgeon (Sermon #607), in devotional materials, and possibly in hymns. Its attribution to the English priest and poet John East is questionable, and in any event, the phrase may be older still (see *The Ladies' Repository* 22, no. 2 [February 1862]: 119).

16. Meade, *Candidate for Confirmation*, p. 10.

17. MARC, Diary, July 7, 1853, VHS Mss1 L51 g 4; Agnes Lee, *Growing Up*, pp. 18-19. Mary's date seems off by a month: Douglas Southall Freeman, *R. E. Lee: A Biography*, 4 vols. (New York: Charles Scribner's Sons, 1934), 1:330, indicates that the event occurred on July 17, which would correspond with Agnes's entry of July 20. Mary also referred to receiving Communion with Robert, usually administered on a Sunday, on which August 7 but not July 7 fell.

18. MARC to MCL/d, Arlington, June 15, 1853, VHS/MCL/d/P Mss1 L5144 a, §23, #1323-1333.

19. MARC, Diary, July 7, 1853.

Notes to Chapter 12

1. Mary V. Thompson, *"In the Hands of a Good Providence": Religion in the Life of George Washington* (Charlottesville: University of Virginia Press, 2008), p. 101.

2. REL to MARC, Camp Cooper, TX, June 9, 1857, VHS Mss1 L51 c 209; BCP 1789, §22.

3. Martin Thornton, "The Anglican Spiritual Tradition," in *The Anglican Tradition*, ed. Richard Holloway (Wilton, CT: Morehouse-Barlow, 1984), p. 86; see A. M. Allchin, "Anglican Spirituality," in *The Study of Anglicanism*, ed. Stephen Sykes and John Booty (London: SPCK/Fortress, 1988), p. 315; John R. H. Moorman, *The Anglican Spiritual Tradition* (Springfield, IL: Templegate, 1983), pp. 130-31. WLU, list of books in Lee's office, April 10, 2015.

4. MARC to MLFC, Old Point Comfort, VA, 1831, VHS/LFP Mss1 L51 c 5.

5. MARC to Custis, Baltimore, February 15, 1852, LOC/BM/LFDA; MARC to Mildred, Arlington, November 25, 1860, VHS/LFP Mss1 L51 c 266, alluding to Ps. 119:105 (see MARC to Mildred, Arlington, December 4, 1860, VHS/LFP Mss1 L51 c 265).

6. Journals of Martha Custis Williams, Arlington House Archives, March 19, 1854; REL to MCL/d, August 11, 1864, VHS/MCL/d/P Mss1 L5144 a, §14, #896-912. The edition he requested is now in the Special Collections of Leyburn Library at Washington and Lee; it had been smuggled from England to the Confederacy by the pastor of Second Presbyterian Church in Richmond, Moses Hoge. In thanking Hoge from his camp in Orange County, Lee prayed "that I may be able to practice its holy teachings" (REL

to Hoge, Orange Co., VA, March 10, 1864, in Peyton Harrison Hoge, *Moses Drury Hoge: Life and Letters* [Richmond: Presbyterian Committee of Publication, 1899], p. 196). The edition he received from Mary Custis is at the Museum of the Confederacy.

7. REL to MARC, Fort Brown, TX, December 27, 1856, VHS/LFP Mss1 L51 c 181.

8. REL to MARC, Culpeper, VA, June 14, 1863, VHS/LFP Mss1 L51 c 459.

9. REL to Col. F. R. Farrar, Lexington, September 19, 1866, Letterbook, VHS/LFP Mss1 L51 c 737, p. 200; Franklin L. Riley, ed., *General Robert E. Lee after Appomattox* (New York: Macmillan, 1922), pp. 28, 178, 188.

10. David Lynn Holmes Jr., *The Faiths of the Founding Fathers* (Oxford: OUP, 2006), pp. 83–84.

11. See Gabriel Gohau, *History of Geology*, rev. and trans. Albert V. Carozzi and Marguerite Carozzi (New Brunswick, NJ: Rutgers University Press, 1991), pp. 165–74 (on fossils, pp. 125–37); Sydney E. Ahlstrom, *A Religious History of the American People* (New Haven: YUP, 1972), pp. 766–67; Leonard G. Wilson, *Lyell in America: Transatlantic Geology, 1841–1853* (Baltimore: Johns Hopkins University Press, 1998), pp. 334, 160, 264–65, 173, 175.

12. Lee kept a diary (Memorandum Book #5, VHS Mss1 L51 b 52) in Texas from 1855 to early 1861, filling about half of a bound notebook. Then, in the very back of this book, he wrote on education and other topics, including one entry marked "Geology" (his underlining). Though his remarks are not dated, his educational ideas resemble what he expressed in early 1867 to a committee on which he served of Virginia's Education Society, suggesting that these were sketches for the report he submitted. If so, they probably date from late 1866. (Cf. REL to John B. Minor, Lexington, January 17, 1867, Letterbook, VHS/LFP Mss1 L51 c 738, pp. 15–18.)

13. REL, Memorandum Book #5. Pages are unnumbered.

14. Michael Hinton, *The Anglican Parochial Clergy* (London: SCM, 1994), p. 103.

15. HL to CCL, Nassau, November 20, 1817, quoted by REL in HL, *Memoirs of the War in the Southern Department of the United States*, with a biography of the author by Robert E. Lee (New York: University Publishing, 1869), p. 74; cf. Jeffry H. Morrison, *John Witherspoon and the Founding of the American Republic* (Notre Dame: University of Notre Dame Press, 2005), pp. 55–56.

16. CCL to REL, Powhatan County, VA, July 25, 1866 (HL, *Memoirs*, p. 56). REL, Memorandum Book #5.

17. J. R. H. Moorman, *A History of the Church in England* (London: Adam & Charles Black, 1953), pp. 379–80; Kenneth Hylson-Smith, *Evangelicals in the Church of England* (Edinburgh: T. & T. Clark, 1989), pp. 133–41; Ahlstrom, *Religious History*, pp. 766–67. On the challenge to Mosaic authorship of the Pentateuch, see Richard Elliott Friedman, *Who Wrote the Bible?* (Englewood Cliffs, NJ: Prentice-Hall, 1987), pp. 17–27; Jonathan Sheehan, *The Enlightenment Bible: Translation, Scholarship, Culture* (Princeton: Princeton University Press, 2005), pp. 247–53.

18. A. S. McGrade, "Reason," in Sykes and Booty, *The Study of Anglicanism*, p. 112; Ollinger Crenshaw, *General Lee's College: The Rise and Growth of Washington and Lee University* (New York: Random House, 1968), p. 162.

19. Collect for the Second Sunday in Advent, BCP 1789, §12.

20. John Macquarrie, "The Anglican Theological Tradition," in Holloway, *The Anglican Tradition*, p. 28.

21. The Apostles' and Nicene Creeds, BCP 1789, §9 & 10, Morning and Evening Prayer; REL to MARC, Culpeper, VA, June 9, 1863, VHS/LFP Mss1 L51 c 457; *The War-time Papers of Robert E. Lee*, ed. Clifford Dowdey and Louis H. Manarin (1961; reprint, New York: Da Capo Press, 1987), p. 507; Allchin, "Anglican Spirituality," p. 316. On Paley, see William H. Peterson, "On the Pattern and in the Power: A Historical Essay of Anglican Pastoral Care," in *Anglican Theology and Pastoral Care*, ed. James E. Griffiss (Wilton, CT: Morehouse-Barlow, 1985), p. 32.

22. REL to MARC, San Antonio, July 1, 1860, VHS/LFP Mss1 L51 c 257 (see MARC to Mildred, Hot Springs, VA, September 21–22, 1861, VHS/LFP Mss1 L51 c 320); REL to Annie, San Antonio, August 27, 1860, VHS/LFP Mss1 L51 c 260. The quotation from Thomas à Kempis comes from *The Imitation of Christ* (1.19) from circa 1425, which is the second most widely read devotional work after the Bible. Whether the Lees read it is not known.

23. REL to Annie, August 27, 1860. Lee cites the three young men delivered by God from the fiery furnace (Dan. 3).

24. REL to MARC, Lexington, October 27, 1865, VHS/LFP Mss1 L51 c 605.

25. REL to Markie, West Point, NY, June 29, 1854, in *"To Markie": The Letters of Robert E. Lee to Martha Custis Williams*, ed. Avery Craven (Cambridge, MA: Harvard University Press, 1933), #20, p. 48, quoting Rom. 7:19.

26. "Homely": Thornton, "The Anglican Spiritual Tradition," p. 84, and *English Spirituality* (Cambridge, MA: Cowley, [1963]), pp. 20, 215. REL to MARC, Lexington, November 20, 1865, VHS/LFP Mss1 L51 c 610; REL to MARC, Cockspur Island, GA, January 10, 1831, in Robert E. L. deButts Jr., "Lee in Love: Courtship and Correspondence in Antebellum Virginia," *VMHB* 115, no. 4 (2007): #8, p. 529; REL to MARC, April 25, 1847 (quoted in William C. Davis, *Crucible of Command* [Boston: Da Capo Press, 2014], p. 65); REL to Markie, West Point, NY, May 26, 1854 (*To Markie*, #19, p. 46). REL to MARC, San Antonio, June 2, 1860, quoted in J. William Jones, *Life and Letters of Robert Edward Lee* (New York: Neale, 1906), p. 113.

27. Mark A. Noll, *America's God: From Jonathan Edwards to Abraham Lincoln* (Oxford: OUP, 2002), p. 335; Ahlstrom, *Religious History*, pp. 420, 611.

28. BCP 1789, Morning Prayer, §9; Evening Prayer (also the Great Litany), §10. What became known as "the prayer of humble access" was first included in the order for the consecration of bishops and later attached to Holy Communion: see BCP 1789 (1845 ed., 564); Marion J. Hatchett, *Commentary on the American Prayer Book* (New York: Seabury, 1980), p. 382. William Meade, *Family Prayers* (Alexandria, VA: W. M. Morrison, 1834), pp. 36 (quoting Wilson), 72, especially 104–20.

29. BCP 1789, Morning Prayer, §9; Evening Prayer, §10; Holy Communion, §13; on thanksgivings, e.g., §11, "Prayers and Thanksgivings upon Several Occasions"; §26, "Prayer and Thanksgiving to Almighty God for the Fruits of the Earth." REL to Markie, West Point, NY, March 11, 1854 (*To Markie*, #16, p. 41).

30. Meade, *Family Prayers*, pp. 105–19.

31. F. L. Cross, ed., *Oxford Dictionary of the Christian Church* (Oxford: OUP, 1958), p. 1343, s.v. "Jeremy Taylor"; Molly Field James, *With Joyful Acceptance, Maybe: Developing a Contemporary Theology of Suffering in Conversation with Five Christian Thinkers: Gregory the Great, Julian of Norwich, Jeremy Taylor, C. S. Lewis, and Ivone Gebara* (Eugene, OR: Wipf & Stock, 2013), pp. 79–80.

32. Rowan A. Greer, *Christian Hope and Christian Life: Raids on the Inarticulate* (New York: Crossroad, 2001), pp. 210–11; James, *With Joyful Acceptance, Maybe*, pp. 79–82.

33. Greer, *Christian Hope*, p. 223, quoting Taylor, *Holy Living*, 6.3.

34. James, *With Joyful Acceptance, Maybe*, pp. 91, 99, 83; Greer, *Christian Hope*, pp. 227, 229, 234, quoting *Discourse VII, Of Faith*.

35. Annie to REL, Staunton, VA, April 9, 1857, VHS/LFP Mss1 L51 c 198; Agnes Lee, *Growing Up in the 1850s*, ed. Mary Custis Lee deButts (Chapel Hill: UNC Press, 1984), p. 19.

36. Quoted in Greer, *Christian Hope*, p. 238, from Taylor, *Unum Necessarium*, 1.2.36.

37. BCP 1789, from the "Prayer for the Whole State of Christ's Church," Holy Communion, §13; quoted in James, *With Joyful Acceptance, Maybe*, pp. 80–81.

38. Quoted in James, *With Joyful Acceptance, Maybe*, p. 91.

39. James, *With Joyful Acceptance, Maybe*, pp. 88, 81, 90.

40. Quoted in James, *With Joyful Acceptance, Maybe*, p. 91.

41. Wilson, quoted in Allchin, "Anglican Spirituality," p. 317.

42. William Law, *A Serious Call to a Devout and Holy Life*, ed. John W. Meister (Philadelphia: Westminster, 1955), pp. 118–19.

Notes to Chapter 13

1. REL to MARC, Camp Cooper, TX, April 19, 1857, VHS/LFP Mss1 L51 c 201.

2. Mark A. Noll, *America's God: From Jonathan Edwards to Abraham Lincoln* (Oxford: OUP, 2002), pp. 430–35; George C. Rable, *God's Almost Chosen Peoples* (Chapel Hill: UNC Press, 2010), pp. 2, 24–25; Samuel C. Gwynne, *Rebel Yell: The Violence, Passion, and Redemption of Stonewall Jackson* (New York: Scribner, 2014), pp. 50, 79, 103, 333, 446.

3. Gen. 22:1–14 KJV, note verses 8, 14. The Hebrew *raah* means "to see, perceive, regard," hence, "God will see to the sheep": cf. E. A. Speiser, *Genesis*, Anchor Bible (Garden City, NY: Doubleday, 1964), p. 161; Nahum M. Sarna, *The JPS Torah Commentaries* (Philadelphia: Jewish Publication Society, 1989), p. 152. Speiser suggests for verse 14, "God will see for himself" (p. 163). While agreeing that the verse could read "God will see to it, my son," Bill T. Arnold (*Genesis* [Cambridge: CUP, 2009], p. 206) indicates that a secondary translation of *raah* can be to "provide" or "furnish"—thus the usual English translation for Gen. 22:8.

4. Greek *pronoia*. See Wisd. of Sol. 17:2; 3 Macc. 4:21; 5:30; 4 Macc. 9:4; 13:19; 17:22; cf. C. F. D. Moule, *Interpreter's Dictionary of the Bible*, 4 vols. (New York: Abingdon, 1962), 3:941, s.v. "providence." On Lee's use of "providence" as a sustaining force, in addition to above, see, e.g., REL to Agnes, Fort Mason, TX, January 29, 1861, VHS Mss1 L51 c 272; REL to Mrs. [Stephen] Elliott, Lexington, February 27, 1867, Letterbook, VHS/LFP Mss1 L51 c 738, p. 21; and as a name for God, REL to Agnes, December 26, 1862, VHS/LFP Mss1 L51 c 421; *The Wartime Papers of Robert E. Lee*, ed. Clifford Dowdey and Louis H. Manarin (1961; reprint, New York: Da Capo Press, 1987), p. 354; REL to MARC, Camp Fredericksburg, VA, June 3, 1863, VHS/LFP Mss1 L51 c 56; *Wartime Papers*, #458, p. 500.

5. Quotations from Benjamin Wirt Farley, *The Providence of God* (Grand Rapids: Baker, 1988): Augustine (*City of God* 5.8), p. 104; Zwingli (*On Providence* 137), p. 144; Calvin (*Institutes* 1.16.3), p. 151.

6. Articles of Religion 17, "Of Predestination and Election," BCP 1928, p. 606, or 1979, p. 871. The Episcopal Church revised and adapted the Articles, adding them to the Prayer Book in 1801 (Marion J. Hatchett, *Commentary on the American Prayer Book* [New York: Seabury, 1980], p. 583).

7. See W. M. Spellman, *The Latitudinarians and the Church of England, 1660–1700* (Athens: University of Georgia Press, 1993), pp. 105–11.

8. Nicholas Guyatt, *Providence and the Invention of the United States, 1607–1876* (Cambridge: CUP, 2007), p. 58. Price's thinking resembles that of Joseph Butler and Immanuel Kant, and also of Benjamin Franklin, Thomas Jefferson, and John Adams (whom he met).

9. John F. Berens, *Providence and Patriotism in Early America, 1640–1815* (Charlottesville: University Press of Virginia, 1978), p. 157.

10. BCP 1789, §11, Prayers and Thanksgivings, for rain, for "those who are to be admitted into Holy Orders," "for a safe return from sea," "for deliverance from the plague"; and §23, "The Churching of Women."

11. REL to MARC, Fort Monroe, VA, June 2, 1832, quoted in Thomas L. Connelly, *The Marble Man: Robert E. Lee and His Image in American Society* (Baton Rouge: Louisiana State University Press, 1978), pp. 166–67; MARC to Mrs. Dickins, Kinloch, VA, June, 18, 18[??], AH, #2445; REL to MARC, Camp Cooper, TX, June 5, 1857, VHS/LFP Mss1 L51 c 215.

12. REL to MARC, June 5, 1857.

13. MARC to CCL, Arlington, June 17, [1856?], LOC/EA, Box 2, Mary Custis Lee, 1834–1871. REL to MCL/d, Arlington, August 8, 1858, VHS/MCL/d/P Mss1 L5144 a, #859–872.

14. BCP 1789, §10, Evening Prayer and Litany. I am not aware of any reference by Lee to the devil (in any term). On "the craft and subtilty of the devil or man," cf. the Litany.

15. REL to MARC, San Antonio, June 25, 1860, VHS Mss1 L51 c 256.

16. Thomas Wilson, *Sacra Privata* (1781; London: J. G. & F. Rivington, 1837), pp. 58, 52, 46; William Meade, *Family Prayers* (Alexandria, VA: W. M. Morrison, 1834), p. 96.

17. Wilson, *Sacra Privata*, pp. 74 (emphasis added) (see pp. 51–52), 49.

18. MARC, Diary, October 17, 1830, VHS Mss1 L51; see May 10, 1831, March 27, 1836. REL to Wm.[?] H. Cunningham, Esq., West Point, NY, November 8, 1853, Letterbook, LVA, #28045. REL to MARC, San Antonio, July 27, 1857, VHS/LFP Mss1 L51 c 219.

19. *Oxford English Dictionary*, s.vv. "repine" and "resign" (especially definitions 3b and 3c; n.b. "to resign our own and seek our Maker's will," William Cowper). For one contemporary explanation of a similar idea of providence, see Keith Ward, *Divine Action* (London: Collins, 1990), especially ch. 8.

20. REL to CCL, Old Point, VA, October 15, 1831, UVa Mss 1085/LFDA, quoting Corporal Nym in *Henry V*, act 2, scene 1. Lee mistakenly adds the second part, which comes in an earlier line.

21. MARC, Diary, February 14, 1836; see Elizabeth Brown Pryor, *Reading the Man: Robert E. Lee through His Private Letters* (New York: Viking, 2007), p. 102.

22. REL to MARC, Fort Hamilton, NY, January 11, 1846, VHS Mss1 L51 c 38; "For all conditions of men," BCP 1789 §9, Morning Prayer; Rom. 8:28 KJV.

23. E.g., Emory M. Thomas, *Robert E. Lee: A Biography* (New York: Norton, 1995), p. 253; Noah Andre Trudeau, *Robert E. Lee* (New York: Palgrave Macmillan, 2009), p. 175; Richard B. McCaslin, *Lee in the Shadow of Washington* (Baton Rouge: Louisiana State University Press, 2001), p. 232 (though he cites Connelly in *The Marble Man* as saying that "the key to Lee was his religious fatalism," a word Connelly does not use).

24. See Edward Craig, "Fatalism," in *Routledge Encyclopedia of Philosophy* (London: Routledge, 1998), pp. 564–65. Ideas of "determinism" grew during the Enlightenment era partially as a result of scientific advances, such as Newtonian physics, which provided explanations of concrete examples of events in the physical world (e.g., what goes up must come down): see Jeremy Butterfield, "Determinism and Indeterminism," in *Routledge Encyclopedia of Philosophy*, 3:33–39.

25. See Craig, "Fatalism," pp. 564–65; Butterfield, "Determinism and Indeterminism," 3:33–39.

26. On Lee's "stoic virtue," see Walter H. Taylor, *Four Years with General Lee* (New York: D. Appleton, 1877), p. 192; cp. Lee's "stoic resolve to accept whatever was and make the best of it": Thomas, *Robert E. Lee*, p. 196.

27. Michael Fellman, *The Making of Robert E. Lee* (Baltimore: Johns Hopkins University Press, 2000), e.g., pp. xv, 76, 209, 294 ("the old-fashioned Virginia gentleman-Roman of Stoic and Christian resignation"; see his index, p. 353); quotation, p. 7. McCaslin, *Lee in the Shadow*, p. 21; Charles Joyner, "A Man of Constant Sorrow," in *Virginia's Civil War*, ed. Peter Wallenstein and Bertram Wyatt-Brown (Charlottesville: University of Virginia Press, 2005), p. 52; Edward Valentine, "Reminiscences of General Lee," in Franklin L. Riley, ed., *General Robert E. Lee after Appomattox* (New York: Macmillan, 1922), p. 147; cf. Douglas Southall Freeman, *R. E. Lee: A Biography*, 4 vols. (New York: Charles Scribner's Sons, 1934), 4:464. On Stoicism, see "Stoicism," in *Cambridge Dictionary of Philosophy*, ed. Robert Audi, 2nd ed. (Cambridge: CUP, 1999), p. 879; Philip P. Hallie, "Stoicism," in *Routledge Encyclopedia of Philosophy*, 8:22 (article, pp. 19–22).

28. Valentine, "Reminiscences of General Lee," p. 148; Fellman, *Making*, p. xv. Fellman relies on McCaslin, who asserts that a "tattered copy" was on Lee's desk, a copy given to him by a recent translator (who had compared Lee to the emperor) published several years after the war—hardly time for it to become "tattered." Washington and Lee University, which sought to retain as much as possible from Lee's office when he died, has no such volume in its possession either in special collections or elsewhere (see list of books in Lee's office, W&L, April 10, 2015; Kyra Swanson, email to the author, April 10, 2015). See McCaslin, *Lee in the Shadow*, p. 218n52.

29. John Sellars, *Stoicism* (Berkeley: University of California Press, 2006), pp. 39–40.

30. Sellars, *Stoicism*, p. 156; Randolph H. McKim, *The Soul of Lee* (New York: Longmans, Green, 1918), pp. 204, 206.

31. Augustine (*City of God* 5.9), quoted in Jaroslav Pelikan, *The Christian Tradition*, 5 vols. (Chicago: University of Chicago Press, 1971), 1:282.

32. Among the first to reject the idea of Lee as Stoic was an early Northern admirer, Charles Francis Adams. Speaking at Lee's hundredth birthday celebration at Washington and Lee, Adams dismissed the notion that Lee was a Stoic and asserted that he was a Christian who, in hope, sought to reconcile North and South after the

war. Adams, "The Lee Centennial, January 7, 1907," *Washington and Lee University Bulletin* 6, no. 3 (July 1907): 33–34.

Notes to Chapter 14

1. Emory M. Thomas, *Robert E. Lee: A Biography* (New York: Norton, 1995), pp. 161–65.

2. REL, Memorandum Book #5, October 27, 1855, VHS Mss1 L51 b 52.

3. Cf. Carl Coke Rister, *Robert E. Lee in Texas* (1946; reprint, Norman: University of Oklahoma Press, 2004), pp. 19–52.

4. REL to MARC, Camp Cooper, TX, April 12, 1856, VHS Mss1 L51 c 154.

5. Quoted in Rister, *Lee in Texas*, p. 56.

6. REL to MARC, Fort Brown, TX, December 5, 1856, VHS/LFP Mss1 L51 c 178.

7. REL to MARC, Camp Cooper, TX, June 5, 1857, VHS/LFP Mss1 L51 c 215.

8. REL to MARC, San Antonio, June 18, 1860, VHS/LFP Mss1 L51 c 255.

9. REL to MARC, San Antonio, June 25, 1860, VHS/LFP Mss1 L51 c 256.

10. REL to MARC, Fort Brown, TX, February 16, 1857, VHS/LFP Mss1 L51 c 188.

11. REL, Diary, November 25, 1855, November 8, 1857, VHS Mss1 L51 b 52. Joseph Cruikshank Talbot, rector of Christ Church, Indianapolis, from 1853 to 1860, became "Missionary Bishop of the Northwest," serving areas from the Rio Grande to the Canadian border until 1865, when he was elected a bishop of Indiana. "Mr. Spencer" is unknown.

12. REL to MARC, Jefferson Barracks, MO, July 1, 1855, VHS/LFP Mss1 L51 c 141; see also REL to MARC, Jefferson Barracks, MO, August 26, 1855, VHS/LFP Mss1 L51 c 145.

13. REL, Diary, March 2, 1856. He refers to Trinity Church and its Gothic-style building completed in 1857 (see http://www.trinitygalv.org/history/, accessed April 14, 2015). The rector who founded the church, Benjamin Eaton, was actually Irish. Lee imprecisely quotes Hag. 2:7 ("I will shake all nations").

14. REL to MARC, Fort Brown, TX, November 15, 1856, VHS/LFP Mss1 L51 c 175. William Passmore was the first rector of the Church of the Advent, established 1851. REL to MARC, Fort Brown, TX, November 19, 1856, VHS/LFP Mss1 L51 c 176. Hab. 2:20 serves as an optional opening sentence in both Morning and Evening Prayer in the BCP.

15. REL to MARC, Fort Brown, TX, November 26, 1856, VHS/LFP Mss1 L51 c 177, quoting Isa. 42:3; REL to MARC, Fort Brown, TX, December 13, 1856, VHS Mss1 L51 c 179.

16. REL to MARC, November 15, 1856, quoting John 4:24 and alluding to Ps. 96:9; REL to MARC, December 13, 1856.

17. REL to MARC, June 18, 1860; REL to MARC, Fort Brown, TX, December 27, 1856, VHS/LFP Mss1 L51 c 181 (see ch. 12 above).

18. REL to MARC, Fort Mason, TX, April 12, 1857, VHS/LFP Mss1 L51 c 200.

19. REL, Diary, June 29, 1856 (see May 22, July 6, 13, 20).

20. REL to Honorable John Dick (House of Representatives), Camp Cooper, TX, August 2, 1856, Letterbook, VHS/LFP Mss1 L51 c 737.

21. REL to Dick, Camp Cooper, TX, May 6, 1857, Letterbook, VHS/LFP Mss1 L51 c 737.

22. REL to MARC, Camp Cooper, TX, June 9, 1857, VHS/LFP Mss1 L51 c 209.

23. REL to MARC, Camp Cooper, TX, June 22, 1857, VHS/LFP Mss1 L51 c 212.

24. Walter H. Taylor, *Four Years with General Lee* (New York: D. Appleton, 1877), p. 159. Though computing relative values over 150 years depends upon many variables and definitions, Lee's investments may be comparable to more than $1.5 million today. See MeasuringWorth.com, accessed June 29, 2016, https://www.measuringworth.com/uscompare/.

25. REL to MARC, February 16, 1857.

26. REL to Annie, San Antonio, August 27, 1860, VHS/LFP Mss1 L51 c 260; Dana to REL, Alexandria, May 12, 1859; E. C. Fletcher to REL, Alexandria, April 27, 1858, VHS/MCL/d/P Mss1 L5144 a, §16, #982–989. Why they did not earlier own a pew is unclear.

27. REL to Annie, August 27, 1860; REL to MARC, San Antonio, July 15, 1860, VHS/LFP Mss1 L51 c 258; see REL Jr., *Recollections and Letters of General Robert E. Lee* (New York: Doubleday, Page, 1905), p. 23; Lewis F. Fisher, *Saint Mark's Episcopal Church: 150 Years of Ministry in Downtown San Antonio, 1858-2008* (San Antonio: Maverick Publishing, 2008), pp. 8–14. After interruptions from war and economic depression, the building was finished in 1875. Texas tradition holds that Lee was elected to the vestry, taught Sunday school, and laid foundation stones for the new church, but no documentation supports such claims (Fisher, p. 14).

28. Karen L. Byrne, "Our Little Sanctuary in the Woods: Spiritual Life at Arlington Chapel," *Arlington Historical Magazine* 12, no. 2 (October 2002): 38–44. The chapel provided the basis for Trinity Episcopal Church in south Arlington.

29. REL to WHFL, Ringgold Barracks, TX, November 1, 1856; REL to Wickham, San Antonio, October 10, 1857, both in Letterbook, VHS/LFP Mss1 L51 c 734; REL to MARC, August 26, 1855.

30. REL to MARC, Jefferson Barracks, MO, July 9, 1855, VHS/LFP Mss1 L51 c 142.

31. Diocese of Virginia, *Journal* (1850), p. 62. The academy still abides as Stuart Hall, named for a subsequent headmistress, the widow of Confederate General J. E. B. Stuart.

32. Agnes Lee, *Growing Up in the 1850s*, ed. Mary Custis Lee deButts (Chapel Hill: UNC Press, 1984), pp. 96–97; Agnes to MARC, April 2, [1857], VHS/LFP Mss1 L51 c 25.

33. REL to MARC, June 18, 1860; REL to MARC, San Antonio, July 1, 1860, VHS/LFP Mss1 L51 c 257; REL Jr. to Mildred, University of Virginia, January 10, 1861, VHS/LFP Mss1 L51 c 269.

34. MARC to Mildred, Arlington, November 25, 1860, VHS/LFP Mss1 L51 c 266. Mary quotes from the Isaac Watts hymn, "Alas! And Did My Saviour Bleed." MARC to Mildred, Arlington, December 4, 1860, VHS/LFP Mss1 L51 c 265; MARC to Mildred[?], Arlington, April 10, 1861[?], VHS/LFP Mss1 L51 c 248.

35. REL to MARC, June 18, 1860.

Notes to Chapter 15

1. Emory M. Thomas, *Robert E. Lee: A Biography* (New York: Norton, 1995), p. 72. The precise number has never been clear.

2. HL, quoted in Charles Royster, *Light-Horse Harry Lee and the Legacy of the American Revolution* (New York: Knopf, 1981), p. 126; James Oakes, *The Ruling Race: A History of American Slaveholders* (New York: Knopf, 1982), pp. 191, 115; see Robert P. Forbes, "Slavery and the Evangelical Enlightenment," in *Religion and the Antebellum Debate over Slavery*, ed. John R. McGivigan and Mitchel Snay (Athens: University of Georgia Press, 1998), pp. 68–106.

3. William Meade, "Religious Instruction to Those in Bondage," in T. T. Castleman and others, *Plain Sermons for Servants* (New York: Stanford & Swords, 1852); Journals of Martha Custis Williams, Arlington House Archives (hereafter "Markie, Diary"), e.g., Wednesday [November 2, 1853]; November 6, 1853; April 6, 1856.

4. MARC to MLFC, [Old Point Comfort, VA], April 11, [1833?], VHS/LFP Mss1 L51 c 3.

5. David Lynn Holmes Jr., "William Meade and the Church of Virginia, 1789–1829" (PhD diss., Princeton University, 1971), pp. 203–5; Meade to MLFC, Millwood, VA, April 9, 1833, VHS Mss2 C9695 b 2–4.

6. Holmes, "William Meade," p. 206. Lincoln held onto the fantasy of colonization well into his presidency (David Herbert Donald, *Lincoln* [New York: Simon & Schuster, 1995], pp. 166–67).

7. MARC, Diary (1852–1858), May 20 and June 9, 1853, VHS Mss1 L51 g 4.

8. Holmes, "William Meade," p. 206.

9. MARC, Diary, July 30, 1854. On racial superiority within the context of paternalism, see Oakes, *The Ruling Race*, p. 194.

10. Markie, Diary, November 2, 1853.

11. REL to White, Washington, February 21, 1845, Letterbook, LVA #28045. Almost always, the KJV translates the Greek word *doulos* "servant" rather than "slave," as many modern versions do. Only once in the KJV does the word "slave" appear, and then regarding a different word than *doulos*.

12. REL to Hill Carter, Arlington, January 25, 1840, LOC/EA, REL, 1849–1865.

13. REL to Col. L. Thomas, Arlington, June 16, 1859, WLU, https://repository.wlu .edu/handle/11021/18694, accessed June 30, 2016.

14. Elizabeth Brown Pryor, *Reading the Man: Robert E. Lee through His Private Letters* (New York: Viking, 2007), p. 261; Thomas, *Robert E. Lee*, pp. 144, 175–76.

15. Oakes, *The Ruling Race*, p. 167; Markie, Diary, February 27, 1855.

16. Markie, Diary, November 1, 1853; Thomas, *Robert E. Lee*, pp. 176–78; MARC, Diary, May 11 and August 8, 1858.

17. Markie, Diary, November 18, 1853; REL to WHFL, Arlington, May 30, 1858, VHS/GBLP Mss1 L5114 c 26; Thomas, *Robert E. Lee*, p. 176; MARC to "Abby," [Arlington], February 10 and May 7, 1858, Museum of the Confederacy archives, Box 3. See Oakes, *The Ruling Race*, p. 180, on slave resistance.

18. Thomas, *Robert E. Lee*, p. 178; Michael Fellman, *The Making of Robert E. Lee* (Baltimore: Johns Hopkins University Press, 2000), pp. 65–67; Michael Korda, *Clouds of Glory: The Life and Legend of Robert E. Lee* (New York: Harper, 2014), pp. 205–9. For

a critical view of Lee as slave owner, see Pryor, *Reading the Man*, pp. 262–67. These charges were renewed with vigor soon after the war. See Elizabeth Varon, *Appomattox: Victory, Defeat, and Freedom at the End of the Civil War* (New York: OUP, 2014), pp. 232–33.

19. George C. Rable, *God's Almost Chosen Peoples* (Chapel Hill: UNC Press, 2010), p. 24; Mark A. Noll, *America's God: From Jonathan Edwards to Abraham Lincoln* (Oxford: OUP, 2002), p. 228.

20. REL to MARC, Fort Brown, TX, December 27, 1856, VHS/LFP Mss1 L51 c 181.

21. REL to MARC, Fort Hamilton, NY, April 13, [1844], VHS/GBLP Mss1 L5114 c 6; REL to MARC, December 27, 1856.

22. MARC, Diary, December 12, 1856; cf. REL to MARC, Fort Brown, TX, January 9, 1857, VHS/LFP Mss1 L51 c 184; REL to MARC, San Antonio, July 27, 1857, VHS/LFP Mss1 L51 c 219.

Notes to Chapter 16

1. On Whigs, see Mark A. Noll, *America's God: From Jonathan Edwards to Abraham Lincoln* (Oxford: OUP, 2002), pp. 312–19; Emory M. Thomas, *Robert E. Lee: A Biography* (New York: Norton, 1995), p. 79. REL to MARC, Fort Brown, TX, December 13, 1856, VHS/LFP Mss1 L51 c 179.

2. Cf. REL to Col. J. Cooper, Arlington, December 24, 1859, Letterbook, VHS/LFP Mss1 L51 c 737, his official report; Thomas, *Robert E. Lee*, pp. 179–83; see Jonathan Horn, *The Man Who Would Not Be Washington* (New York: Scribner, 2015), ch. 5, who says there were ten hostages, and Walter H. Taylor, *Four Years with General Lee* (New York: D. Appleton, 1877), pp. 179–82, who sets the number at thirteen. On the hanging, see Charles A. Davidson to his mother, Charlestown, VA, December 2, 1859, WLU, Schoenbrun Collection, #0394.

3. MARC, "My Reminiscences of the War," Derwent, VA, September 186[5], VHS L5144 a 1397–1472, reprinted as "Mary Custis Lee's Reminiscences of the War," *VMHB* 109, no. 3 (2001): 312.

4. REL to Captain Andrew Talcott, Old Point Comfort, VA, December 7, 1832, VHS Mss1 T 1434 b 139.

5. REL to Annette Carter, Fort Mason, TX, January 16, 1861, LFDA. Annette Carter's father, Charles Henry, was Lee's first cousin (REL Jr., *Recollections and Letters of General Robert E. Lee* [New York: Doubleday, Page, 1905], p. 307).

6. MARC to Mildred, Arlington, January 17, 1861, VHS/LFP Mss1 L51 c 270; REL to MARC, Fort Mason, TX, January 23, 1861, VHS/LFP Mss1 L51 c 271.

7. REL to Agnes, Fort Mason, TX, January 29, 1861, VHS/LFP Mss1 L51 c 272.

8. REL to WHFL, Fort Mason, TX, January 29, 1861, VHS/GBLP Mss1 L5114 c 41.

9. MARC to Annie, Arlington, February 19, 1861, VHS/LFP Mss1 L51 c 275; MARC to Mildred, Arlington, February 24, 1861, VHS/LFP Mss1 L51 c 276.

10. Thomas, *Robert E. Lee*, pp. 186–87.

11. Previously published accounts told a different story of Lee's decision to resign. One of the earliest described him pacing the floor in his bedroom all night; another, by a minister, depicted Lee dropping to his knees in prayer; and still another portrayed

him dramatically descending the stairs to announce his resignation, which he held in his hand. Though Mary Custis's account relies on a ten-year-old memory of conversations and events, it does coincide with verifiable facts; and she was there. Elizabeth Brown Pryor, "'Thou Knowest Not the Time of Thy Visitation': A Newly Discovered Letter Reveals Robert E. Lee's Lonely Struggle with Disunion," *VMHB* 119, no. 3 (September 2011): 279–80, 278. Pryor cites accounts of George Upshur, William Jones, and Thomas Nelson Page, some of which she had relied on in *Reading the Man: Robert E. Lee through His Private Letters* (New York: Viking, 2007), pp. 291–92.

12. William Allan, "Memoranda of Conversations with General Lee," February 26 and March 10, 1868, WLU 0064, also in Gary Gallagher, ed., *Lee the Soldier* (Lincoln: University of Nebraska Press, 1996), pp. 7–24.

13. Pryor, "Thou Knowest," p. 289. At the time, Anderson's rank was major.

14. Allan, "Memoranda," pp. 9–10; Pryor, "Thou Knowest," p. 289. Mary Custis's statement is the more likely, as slaves that Lee controlled were not technically his but belonged to the Custis estate, which was bequeathed not to him but to his family; and they probably numbered fewer than four hundred.

15. Allan, "Memoranda," pp. 10–11. The War Department stood on the site now occupied by the Eisenhower Executive Office Building.

16. Pryor, "Thou Knowest," p. 290, punctuation in original.

17. Allan, "Memoranda," pp. 10–11; Pryor, "Thou Knowest," pp. 289–91. Fitzhugh (Rooney) contacted Governor John Letcher, who advised releasing the men but keeping the stores.

18. Taylor, *Four Years*, pp. 188–89; Pryor, "Thou Knowest," p. 282; Pryor, *Reading the Man*, p. 294.

19. Taylor, *Four Years*, pp. 188–89.

20. John Booty, *Mission and Ministry: A History of Virginia Theological Seminary* (Harrisburg, PA: Morehouse, 1995), pp. 96–97; May to Cassius Lee, VTS, April 22, 1861, SH M2009.251.

21. Cassius Lee to REL, Alexandria, April 23, 1861, SH M2009.252.

22. REL to Cassius Lee, Richmond, April 25, 1861, SH M2009.253.

23. May to Cassius Lee, April 22, 1861. May cited positive comments about Lee from his brother-in-law, Major A. H. Bowman, who then served at West Point. *Alexandria Gazette*, April 20, 1861, quoted in Douglas Southall Freeman, *R. E. Lee: A Biography*, 4 vols. (New York: Charles Scribner's Sons, 1934), 1:445.

24. Thomas, *Robert E. Lee*, p. 382, quoting Lee's congressional testimony, February 17, 1866.

25. REL to MARC, Fort Brown, TX, December 27, 1856, VHS/LFP Mss1 L51 c 181. "Aggrieved": REL to WHFL, January 29, 1861.

26. REL to Hill Carter, Arlington, January 25, 1840, LOC/EA, Box 2, REL, 1849–1865.

27. O. O. Howard, "The Character and Campaigns of General Lee," in *Gen. Robert Edward Lee: Soldier, Citizen, and Christian Patriot*, ed. R. A. Brock (Richmond, 1897), p. 353; Lee Epstein and Thomas G. Walk, *Constitutional Law: Rights, Liberties, and Justice*, 8th ed. (Washington, DC: Sage, 2014), p. 604. Howard had been a cadet under Lee's superintendency (see above, p. 105).

28. REL to Childe, Fort Brown, TX, January 9, 1857, SH 2009.234.

29. REL to MARC, January 23, 1861; e.g., Madison's mistrust of passion inher-

ent in the "mob," *The Federalist*, #55 (cf. also #6). Charles Royster, *Light-Horse Harry Lee and the Legacy of the American Revolution* (New York: Knopf, 1981), pp. 31, 67. The centrality of virtue was stressed by, among others, Montesquieu (*The Spirit of the Laws* 3.3 and 4.5).

30. REL to MARC, [Fort Monroe, VA?], May 13, 1831, in Robert E. L. deButts Jr., "Lee in Love: Courtship and Correspondence in Antebellum Virginia," *VMHB* 115, no. 4 (2007): #11, pp. 540–41.

31. Cf. Mark Timmons, *Moral Theory: An Introduction* (Lanham, MD: Rowman & Littlefield, 2002), chs. 7; 9.

32. Timmons, *Moral Theory*, ch. 2.

33. See J. William Jones, *Life and Letters of Robert Edward Lee* (New York: Neale, 1906), p. 132 (cf. Freeman, *R. E. Lee*, 1:442), who based his information on a purported conversation with Mrs. Lee. Doubts of Jones's reliability emerged in the early 1900s: see George Hutcheson Denny (president of Washington and Lee) to Charles Francis Adams, October 26, 1906, Massachusetts Historical Society, Charles Francis Adams Papers, Box 14, Folder 10, and Adams to Denny, November 3, 1906, Charles Francis Adams Papers, Box 14, Folder 11. Jones, a Confederate chaplain who became pastor of the Baptist church in Lexington, became an apologist for the Lost Cause, writing several books on Lee, serving as secretary-treasurer of the Southern Historical Society, and editing fourteen volumes of the society's papers.

34. REL to Jones, Arlington, April 20, 1861, LOC/CLFP, Box 2, File "REL."

35. See George C. Rable, *God's Almost Chosen Peoples* (Chapel Hill: UNC Press, 2010), p. 137: "Even [Lee's] prayerful agonizing over whether to follow Virginia out of the union carried with it a kind of stoic sadness rather than any particular biblical or theological content." It may not have been as prayerful as earlier thought, but I concur with Rable about its content.

Notes to Chapter 17

1. REL to Mildred, Arlington, April 1, 1861, VHS/LFP Mss1 L51 c 278.

2. MARC, "Reminiscences," VHS/MCL/d/P Mss1 L5144 a, #1397–1472.

3. James Warley Miles of South Carolina, quoted in George C. Rable, *God's Almost Chosen Peoples* (Chapel Hill: UNC Press, 2010), pp. 54–55.

4. Mary P. Coulling, *The Lee Girls* (Winston-Salem, NC: J. F. Blair, 1987), pp. 86–88.

5. MARC to Mildred, Arlington, May 5, 1861, VHS/LFP Mss1 L51 c 284.

6. REL to MARC, Richmond, May 8, 1861, VHS/LFP Mss1 L 51 c 287.

7. MARC to REL, Arlington, May 9, 1861, VHS/LFP Mss1 L51 c 289, alluding to Rev. 20:6–7. Though common in American Protestantism of that era, millennialism—expectations of the imminent return of Christ in judgment—did not figure much in the Episcopal Church nor in Mary Lee's letters, though clearly she is aware of the idea invigorated with the onset of war. Whereas Julia Ward Howe welcomed it in writing "The Battle Hymn of the Republic" six months later, Mary feared the start of the tribulations that (for some schools of millennialist thought) preceded the second coming. See Rable, *God's Almost Chosen Peoples*, pp. 3, 24, 88.

8. REL to MARC, Richmond, May 11, 1861, VHS/LFP Mss1 L51 c 290; *The Wartime*

Papers of Robert E. Lee, ed. Clifford Dowdey and Louis H. Manarin (1961; reprint, New York: Da Capo Press, 1987), #27, pp. 25-26.

9. MARC, Diary, July 7, 1853, VHS Mss1 L51 g 3; see ch. 9 above; MARC to REL, Arlington, May 12, 1861, VHS/LFP Mss1 L51 c 291.

10. MARC to Mildred, Arlington, May 11, 1861, VHS Mss1 L51 c 292.

11. Rable, *God's Almost Chosen Peoples*, p. 54; REL to MARC, Richmond, May 25, 1861, VHS/LFP Mss1 L51 c 295; *Wartime Papers*, #43, pp. 36-37.

12. REL to MARC, Richmond, June 11, 1861, VHS/LFP Mss1 L51 c 298; *Wartime Papers*, #55, pp. 47-48.

13. MARC to Mildred, Chantilly and Kinloch, VA, June 11-12, 1861, VHS/LFP Mss1 L51 c 299; MARC to Agnes, n.p., June 30, 1861, VHS/LFP Mss1 L51 c 302. (Were the repeated "we will nots" an error, or an oblique reference to Robert's beloved hymn "How Firm a Foundation"?) Mary is probably referring to a skirmish at Fairfax Courthouse on June 1; on June 10 at Big Bethel, on the Virginia Peninsula, outnumbered Confederates held off a larger Union force (Rable, *God's Almost Chosen Peoples*, p. 74).

14. REL to MARC, Richmond, July 27, 1861, VHS/LFP Mss1 L51 c 307.

15. REL to Agnes, Camp Rapidan, VA, November 13, 1863, VHS/LFP Mss1 L51 c 488; *Wartime Papers*, #579, p. 623, slightly paraphrasing Ps. 68:4 and 33 (BCP and KJV); REL to MARC, Culpeper, VA, June 9, 1863, VHS/LFP Mss1 L51 c 457; *Wartime Papers*, #466, p. 507; REL to MARC, Camp Petersburg, VA, July 7, 1864, VHS/LFP Mss1 L51 c 533; *Wartime Papers*, #828, p. 817.

16. REL to Agnes, November 13, 1863; REL to Annie and Agnes, Washington's Run, VA, September 30, 1862, VHS/LFP Mss1 L51 c 387; REL to MARC, Rappahannock River, VA, October 19, 1863, VHS/LFP Mss1 L51 c 481; *Wartime Papers*, #567, p. 610.

17. REL to MARC, Camp Rapidan, VA, December 4, 1863, VHS/LFP Mss1 L51 c 493; *Wartime Papers*, #592, p. 631; see Emory M. Thomas, *Robert E. Lee: A Biography* (New York: Norton, 1995), pp. 311-12. REL to MARC, Orange Co., VA, April 27, 1864, VHS/LFP Mss1 L51 c 515.

18. REL to Agnes, November 13, 1863, VHS/LFP Mss1 L51 c 488; *Wartime Papers*, #579, p. 610.

19. Robert Louis Dabney, quoted in Rable, *God's Almost Chosen Peoples*, p. 73; Richard E. Beringer et al., *Why the South Lost the Civil War* (Athens: University of Georgia Press, 1986), pp. 271-72, 353-54. REL to MARC, San Antonio, June 18, 1860, VHS/LFP Mss1 L51 c 255.

20. Sydney E. Ahlstrom, *A Religious History of the American People* (New Haven: YUP, 1972), pp. 199, 372-73, 444; Mark A. Noll, *America's God: From Jonathan Edwards to Abraham Lincoln* (Oxford: OUP, 2002), pp. 27, 139, 341, 563.

21. REL to Annie, Savannah, March 2, 1862, VHS/LFP Mss1 L51 c 345; *Wartime Papers*, #121, pp. 121-22.

22. REL to MARC, Camp Cooper, TX, April 19, 1857, VHS Mss1 L51 c 201.

23. REL, General Orders #83, August 13, 1863, SH M2009.304. The biblical reference of "name and place" most likely is to Isa. 56:5, in which the Lord through the prophet promises to "eunuchs that keep my Sabbaths, and choose the things that please me, and take hold of my covenant," that they will have "a place and a name better than of sons and daughters" that "shall not be cut off." That oddly characterizes the status of Southerners, though.

24. REL to MARC, Fort Brown, TX, December 27, 1856, VHS/LFP Mss1 L51 c 181; on "jeremiad," see Harry S. Stout, *The New England Soul: Preaching and Religious Culture in Colonial New England* (New York: OUP, 1986), pp. 62–63. On the fast day as observed elsewhere in the Confederacy, see Rable, *God's Almost Chosen Peoples*, p. 275.

25. Justice to "My Sweet Darling Wife," Orange Courthouse, VA, August 21, 1863, quoted in Earl J. Hess, *Lee's Tar Heels: The Pettigrew-Kirkland-MacRae Brigade* (Chapel Hill: UNC Press, 2002), p. 196.

26. Rable, *God's Almost Chosen Peoples*, p. 306; Gardiner H. Shattuck, *A Shield and Hiding Place: The Religious Life of the Civil War Armies* (Macon, GA: Mercer University Press, 1987), pp. 99, 106; cf. J. William Jones, *Christ in the Camp* (Richmond: B. F. Johnson, 1888), p. 318; Georgia resolution quoted in Beringer, *Why the South Lost*, p. 270.

27. Sidney J. Romero, *Religion in the Rebel Ranks* (Lanham, MD: University Press of America, 1983), pp. 21, 86; REL, quoted in Steven E. Woodworth, *While God Is Marching On: The Religious World of Civil War Soldiers* (Lawrence: University Press of Kansas, 2001), p. 83; REL to Rabbi M. J. Michelbacher, Valley Mountain, VA, August 29, 1861, LVA #23003a. On Michelbacher, and on Southern Sabbath keeping in general, see Rable, *God's Almost Chosen Peoples*, pp. 253, 97, respectively.

28. REL to MARC, Richmond, May 16, 1861; *Wartime Papers*, #34, p. 31. Joseph Y. Rowe, *Saint Thomas Church: A History* (2008), p. 137: the church retains the pew where Lee sat, and the black locust tree where he tied Traveller stands in front of the church. Justice to his wife, Orange, VA, November 22, 1863, quoted in Hess, *Lee's Tar Heels*, p. 196. That Jones does not cite any connection of Lee with the revival in *Christ in the Camp* is telling, as it was always in Jones's interest to stress Lee's religiosity.

29. REL to Annie, March 2, 1862; *Wartime Papers*, #121, pp. 121–23; REL to Mrs. Sarah A. Lawton, Camp Fredericksburg, VA, January 8, 1863, LOC/CLFP; REL to MARC, Camp Fredericksburg, VA, November 22, 1862, VHS/LFP Mss1 L51 c 411; REL to MARC, Culpeper, VA, June 11, 1863, VHS Mss1 L51 c 458; *Wartime Papers*, #471, p. 511. On "sinful Robert," see above, p. 65.

30. REL to MARC, Richmond, June 24, 1861; *Wartime Papers*, #61, p. 53.

31. REL to MARC, Camp Fredericksburg, VA, May 14, 1863, VHS/LFP Mss1 L51 c 451.

32. REL to MARC, Savannah, February 8, 1862, VHS/LFP Mss1 L51 c 341; *Wartime Papers*, #109, pp. 111–12; Rable, *God's Almost Chosen Peoples*, p. 250.

33. 1 Sam. 17; cf. Beringer, *Why the South Lost*, p. 270; Rable, *God's Almost Chosen Peoples*, p. 63.

34. REL to MARC, Camp Fredericksburg, VA, May 31, 1863, VHS/LFP Mss1 L51 c 455; *Wartime Papers*, #456, p. 499; Rable, *God's Almost Chosen Peoples*, p. 152.

35. REL to MARC, May 31, 1863; REL to MARC, Camp near Culpeper Courthouse, VA, November 6, 1862, VHS/LFP Mss1 L51 c 401; REL to MARC, Camp near Culpeper Courthouse, VA, November 13, 1862, VHS/LFP Mss1 L51 c 403. Jackson held essentially the same attitude: Samuel C. Gwynne, *Rebel Yell: The Violence, Passion, and Redemption of Stonewall Jackson* (New York: Scribner, 2014), pp. 333, 407.

36. REL to MARC, Dabbs Farm, Henrico Co., VA, June 9, 1862, VHS Mss1 L51 c 356; *Wartime Papers*, #231, pp. 231–32, which corrects Lee's dating to July. In his official report, Lee declared that "the Federal army should have been destroyed." He continued, "Our enemy has met with a heavy loss from which he must take some time to recover & thus inconvenience his operations" (quoted in Thomas, *Robert E. Lee*, p. 243).

37. See Rable, *God's Almost Chosen Peoples*, p. 260.

38. REL to MARC, Camp Fredericksburg, VA, November 22, 1862, VHS/LFP Mss1 L51 c 407; *Wartime Papers*, #324, p. 343; REL to MARC, Camp Orange County, VA, April 3, 1864, VHS/LFP Mss1 c 511.

39. REL to MARC, Williamsport, PA, July 7, 1863, VHS/LFP Mss1 L51 c 462; *Wartime Papers*, #508, p. 542.

40. REL to Edward C. Turner, Camp at Valley River, VA, September 14, 1861, UVa Mss 11576; REL to MARC, April 3, 1864. Some have alleged that Lee avoided terming his opponents "the enemy"; not so.

41. REL to CCL, Camp Fredericksburg, VA, March 24, 1863, UVa Mss 990b.

42. REL to Lawton, January 8, 1863.

43. Casualties: Joseph Glatthaar, *General Lee's Army: From Victory to Collapse* (New York: Free Press, 2008), p. 490. The Reverend Edward Reed, quoted in Rable, *God's Almost Chosen Peoples*, p. 76.

44. Shattuck, *Shield and Hiding Place*, p. 100, quoting George Cary Eggleston, *Rebel's Recollections*.

45. Quoted in Thomas, *Robert E. Lee*, p. 287; REL to MARC, Camp Fredericksburg, VA, May 11, 1863, VHS/LFP Mss1 L51 c 450.

46. REL to MARC, May 14, 1863.

47. REL to WHFL, Camp Orange County, VA, April 24, 1864, LVA #19742d.

48. Coulling, *The Lee Girls*, pp. 103–4, 109–10; MARC to MCL/d, Jones Springs, Warren County, NC, October 18–19, 1862, VHS/LFP Mss1 L51 c 390; Agnes to MCL/d, Petersburg, VA, November 7, 1862, VHS/LFP Mss1 L51 c 400.

49. REL to MARC, camp near Winchester, VA, October 26, 1862, VHS/LFP Mss1 L51 c 396.

50. Thomas, *Robert E. Lee*, p. 407.

51. Elizabeth Varon, *Appomattox: Victory, Defeat, and Freedom at the End of the Civil War* (New York: OUP, 2014), p. 26; REL to MARC, camp near Hagerstown, MD, July 12, 1863, VHS Mss1 L51 c 463; *Wartime Papers*, #516, 547.

52. REL to Davis, headquarters near Hagerstown, MD, July 8, 1863, *Wartime Papers*, #510, p. 543; REL to MARC, July 12, 1863; *Wartime Papers*, #516, p. 547.

53. REL to MARC, Richmond, October 25, 1864, *Wartime Papers*, #908, p. 865.

54. REL to MARC, Camp Petersburg, VA, August 14, 1864, VHS/LFP Mss1 L51 c 542; *Wartime Papers*, #858, p. 837. For the fate of Southern churches more generally, see Rable, *God's Almost Chosen Peoples*, pp. 246, 318–19, 326–29.

55. REL to CCL, Camp Fredericksburg, VA, March 24, 1863, UVa Mss 990b, quoting Pss. 108:13 and 60:12; REL to MARC, Gaines' Mill, VA, June 4, 1864, VHS/LFP Mss1 L51 c 522; *Wartime Papers*, #753, p. 765.

56. REL to MARC, Camp Petersburg, VA, June 30, 1864, VHS/LFP Mss1 L51 c 531; *Wartime Papers*, #822, p. 812.

57. REL to MARC, Petersburg, VA, February 21, 1865, VHS Mss1 L51 c 572; *Wartime Papers*, #957, p. 907, quoting Eccles. 9:11 (cf. ch. 9 above, n. 3).

58. Matt. 19:26; Luke 1:37; Heb. 12:6. For a wider reaction in the Confederacy, see Rable, *God's Almost Chosen Peoples*, pp. 346–50, 363.

59. REL to Davis, Petersburg, VA, April 2, 1865, *Wartime Papers*, #990, p. 928; see William C. Davis, *Jefferson Davis: The Man and His Hour* (New York: HarperCollins, 1991), p. 605, and Rable, *God's Almost Chosen Peoples*, p. 8.

60. Kate Pleasants (Mrs. E. C.) Minor to Gamaliel Bradford, Richmond, January 21, 1911, Bradford Papers. She was responding to allegations that Davis tried to elude capture by wearing women's clothes, saying that he, like many men of the era, wore shawls to ward off the chill, as Davis did that fateful Sunday.

61. Emily V. Wilson, *Popular Life of Gen. Robert Edward Lee* (Baltimore: John Murphy & Co., 1872), p. 314; Gary W. Gallagher, ed., *Fighting for the Confederacy: The Personal Recollections of General Edward Porter Alexander* (Chapel Hill: UNC Press, 1989), pp. 532–33. This account differs in language and length from that in Alexander's book, *The American Civil War* (London: Siegle, Hill & Co., 1908), p. 605. The Gallagher volume comes from Alexander's manuscript memoir, so it may be more authoritative as well as more extensive. On the moral question other commanders faced in surrendering their armies, despite Jefferson Davis's entreaties to continue fighting, see Beringer, *Why the South Lost*, pp. 342–47. Also see Varon, *Appomattox*, p. 42, though she omits the reference to "Christian men."

62. Varon, *Appomattox*, pp. 57–58, 69 (quoting Lee's General Orders, No. 9).

63. C. S. S. Scott to Gamaliel Bradford, Staunton, VA, October 23, 1911, Harvard University, Houghton Library, Bradford Papers.

Notes to Chapter 18

1. Emory M. Thomas, *Robert E. Lee: A Biography* (New York: Norton, 1995), p. 369.

2. J. M. Patrick to Gamaliel Bradford, Coronado, CA, November 6, 1914, also October 19, 1914, and December 5, 1915, all Harvard University, Bradford Papers. Patrick resigned his command on June 12, 1865. Lee used similar language in writing John Letcher, though without the theological content: "The questions which for years were in dispute between the State and the Genl. Govts., and which unhappily were not decided by the dictates of reason, but referred to the decision of war, *having been decided against us*, it is the part of wisdom to acquiesce in the result, and of candor to recognize the fact." REL to Letcher, near Cartersville, VA, August 28, 1865, Letterbook, VHS/LFP Mss1 L51 c 737, pp. 22–23 (emphasis added).

3. Marsena Rudolph Patrick, *Inside Lincoln's Army* (New York: T. Yoseloff, 1964); REL to Platt, Richmond, May 16, 1865, VHS Microfilm Mss10 no. 242:39.

4. REL to Platt, May 16, 1865. Cf. Meade to John Stewart, [August?] 12, 1861, LOC, Meade Correspondence: "God is doubtless punishing both sides for their sins. . . ." See Elizabeth Varon, *Appomattox: Victory, Defeat, and Freedom at the End of the Civil War* (New York: OUP, 2014), pp. 102, 158–59.

5. On Lincoln, see George C. Rable, *God's Almost Chosen Peoples* (Chapel Hill: UNC Press, 2010), pp. 371–72.

6. Mary P. Coulling, *The Lee Girls* (Winston-Salem, NC: J. F. Blair, 1987), pp. 147–48; REL to Davis, Richmond, April 20, 1865; *The Wartime Papers of Robert E. Lee*, ed. Clifford Dowdey and Louis H. Manarin (1961; reprint, New York: Da Capo Press, 1987), #1006, p. 936.

7. James McPherson, *Ordeal by Fire* (New York: Knopf, 1981), p. 476.

8. Richard L. Troutman, ed., *The Heavens Are Weeping: The Diaries of George Richard Browder, 1852–1886* (Grand Rapids: Zondervan, 1987), p. 196; Frank Marcon to

his mother, Mrs. Matchill(?), Toronto, May 22, 1865, WLU, Schoenbrun Collection, #0349 (see p. 6 above). Hoge, quoted in Charles Reagan Wilson, *Baptized in Blood: The Religion of the Lost Cause, 1865–1920*, 2nd ed. (Athens: University of Georgia Press, 2009), p. 22. On a spiritual crisis in general, see Richard E. Beringer et al., *Why the South Lost the Civil War* (Athens: University of Georgia Press, 1986), pp. 351–54, which includes Bishop Johns's comment that, given their sins, he wondered why God had not punished Southerners even sooner and more harshly (pp. 352–53); and Mark A. Noll, *The Civil War as a Theological Crisis* (Chapel Hill: UNC Press, 2006), pp. 75–81.

9. See Varon, *Appomattox*, p. 84.

10. See Varon, *Appomattox*, pp. 51–52.

11. REL to WHFL, near Cartersville, VA, July 29, 1865, VHS/GBLP Mss1 L5114 c 62.

12. REL to Martha Custis Williams (hereafter Markie), Richmond, May 2, 1865, in *"To Markie": The Letters of Robert E. Lee to Martha Custis Williams*, ed. Avery Craven (Cambridge, MA: Harvard University Press, 1933), p. 61.

13. REL to Markie, Richmond, June 20, 1865, in *"To Markie,"* #27, p. 62.

14. Johnson, Amnesty Proclamation, May 29, 1865; REL to Grant, Richmond, June 13, 1865, in REL Jr., *Recollections and Letters of General Robert E. Lee* (New York: Doubleday, Page, 1905), p. 164. With Grant's insistence, charges were dropped on June 20, 1867. See Varon, *Appomattox*, pp. 197–202.

15. REL Jr., *Recollections*, pp. 163–65.

16. On Alexander: Frederick M. Colston to Gamaliel Bradford, Baltimore, October 9, 1911, Harvard University, Bradford Papers; Andrew F. Rolle, *The Lost Cause: The Confederate Exodus to Mexico* (Norman: University of Oklahoma Press, 1965), pp. 132, 136–37; REL to Richard S. Maury, near Cartersville, VA, July 31, 1865, and September 11, 1865, WLU Special Collection, 0064; Charles Lee Lewis, *Matthew Fontaine Maury, the Pathfinder of the Seas* (Annapolis, MD: US Naval Institute, 1927), pp. 188–95.

17. Maury to REL, Mexico, August 8, 1865, VHS Mss2 L515 a 33.

18. REL to Maury, near Cartersville, VA, September 8, 1865, WLU/LP 0064.

19. Quoted in REL Jr., *Recollections*, p. 163.

20. REL to Beauregard, Lexington, October 3, 1865, Letterbook, VHS/LFP Mss1 L51 c 737, pp. 22–23. Lowell, "The Present Crisis" (1845): see *The Hymnal 1940 Companion* (New York: Church Pension Fund, 1951), p. 312. A portion of Lowell's long poem, including these lines, entered the Episcopal Church's hymnal, though after Lee's death.

21. REL to Markie, June 20, 1865.

22. Quoted from a letter from Alexander to his father, Joseph Colston, April 22, 1865, in Colston to Bradford, Baltimore, October 9, 1911, Harvard University, Bradford Papers.

23. All quoted in Thomas, *Robert E. Lee*, p. 373.

24. Thomas Connolly to REL, New York, May 17, 1865; Lord Abinger [Lt.-Gen. William Frederick Scarlett, Third Baron Abinger] to REL, London, April 24, 1865; Tremlett to REL, St. Peter's, Belsize Park, NW (London), May 25, 1865 (all VHS/MCL/d/P Mss1 L5144 a, §14, #913–933); see Lewis, *Matthew Fontaine Maury*, pp. 185, 233, 237–38.

25. Quoted in Elizabeth Brown Pryor, *Reading the Man: Robert E. Lee through His Private Letters* (New York: Viking, 2007), p. 436.

26. Cabell to REL, Norwood, VA, August 20, 1865, VHS/MCL/d/P Mss1 L5144 a, §14, #913–933; Joseph L. Topham to REL, Cincinnati, August 17, 1865; also W. S. Williams & Co., Hartford, CT, September 5, 1865; C. R. Richardson to REL, New York, September 7, 1865, and others; William Fitzhugh Lee to REL, Richmond, September 7, 1865 (all WLU/LP, Letters to and about Lee); REL to Topham, Lexington, October 6, 1865, WLU/LP/LFDA.

27. Edward Payson Walton to REL, New Orleans, April 13, 1866, WLU/LP/LFDA; REL to Henry I. Furber, Lexington, December 23, 1868, and February 8, 1869, WLU/LP.

28. W. M. Green to REL, University Place, TN, August 20, 1868, VHS/MCL/d/P Mss1 L5144 a, #1019; REL Jr., *Recollections*, p. 179 (Green was chancellor of the University of the South).

29. Ollinger Crenshaw, *General Lee's College: The Rise and Growth of Washington and Lee University* (New York: Random House, 1968), pp. 26–28.

30. Ethel Armes, *Stratford Hall: The Great House of the Lees* (Richmond: Garrett and Massie, 1936), pp. 315, 366.

31. REL Jr., *Recollections*, p. 180.

32. Letcher to REL, Lexington, August 2, 1865, WLU/LP.

33. Trustees to REL, Lexington, August 5, 1865, WLU/LP.

34. Letcher to REL, Lexington, August 5, 1865, WLU/LP; Pendleton to REL, Lexington, August 5, 1865, WLU/LP.

35. Crenshaw, *General Lee's College*, pp. 146–47; Brockenbrough to REL, on board packet *Jefferson*, August 10, 1865, WLU/LP.

36. Quoted from an address at Sewanee circa 1870, in REL Jr., *Recollections*, pp. 182–83.

37. REL to Trustees, August 24, 1865, WLU/LP, and quoted in REL Jr., *Recollections*, p. 181.

38. REL Jr., *Recollections*, p. 183; MARC, Diary, July 7, 1853, VHS Mss1 L51 g 3.

39. REL to MARC, Lexington, September 19, 1865, VHS Mss1 L51 c 595 (in REL Jr., *Recollections*, p. 184); REL to G. A. White, September 18, 1865, WLU/LP.

40. Crenshaw, *General Lee's College*, pp. 148–49; REL Jr., *Recollections*, p. 187; William [A. Anderson?] to Paul M. Penick, Clarendon, VA, May 6, 1935, WLU Special Collections, Treasurer's files, Series 1, Box 1, Folder 34.

41. REL to George W. Jones, March 22, 1869, quoted in Richard B. McCaslin, *Lee in the Shadow of Washington* (Baton Rouge: Louisiana State University Press, 2001), p. 192.

Notes to Chapter 19

1. R. H. Phillips to Francis Smith, Staunton, VA, August 11, 1865; William Nelson Pendleton to Smith, Lexington, October 14, 1865, WLU/LP; REL to MARC, Lexington, November 20, 1865, VHS/LFP Mss1 L51 c 610.

2. REL to MARC, Rockbridge Baths, VA, September 25, 1865, VHS/LFP Mss1 L51 c 596; REL to MARC, Lexington, October 27, 1865, VHS/LFP Mss1 L51 c 605; REL to MARC, Lexington, October 3, 1865, VHS/LFP Mss1 L51 c 597.

3. REL to MARC, September 25, 1865; REL to MARC, October 3, 1865 (both quoted in REL Jr., *Recollections and Letters of General Robert E. Lee* [New York: Doubleday, Page,

1905], pp. 186–87); REL to Mildred, Lexington, October 29, 1865, quoted in REL Jr., p. 193.

4. REL to E. M. Bruce, Lexington, September 25, 1865, WLU/LP, Copy Letterbook (LFDA); REL to MARC, Lexington, October 9, 1865, VHS/LFP Mss1 L51 c 598.

5. REL to MARC, Lexington, October 19, 1865, VHS/LFP Mss1 L51 c 602.

6. REL Jr., *Recollections*, pp. 196–99, 203–5.

7. REL to MCL/d, [Lexington], postmarked December 31, [1865], VHS/MCL/d/P Mss1 L5144 a, §14.

8. See REL Jr., *Recollections*, p. 205.

9. E.g., Edmund Berkely to REL, Prince William County, VA, September 18, 1865; Mrs. C. T. Nash to REL, New Orleans, September 26, 1865; Gen. A. R. Wright to REL, Augusta, GA, September 27, 1865; John Wm. McGriffey to REL, Columbus, OH, September 30, 1865 (all in WLU/LP, Letters to and about Lee).

10. E.g., C. G. Fruman to REL, Eminence, KY, March 13, 1866; Meade Woodson to REL, Fincastle, VA, March 15, 1866; Geo. A. B. Hays to REL, Fair View, LA, May 23, 1866; Alf. Ronan to REL, St. James, LA, May 24, 1866; J. B. Lamb to REL, Fayetteville, TN, June 8, 1866 (all WLU/LP, Letters to and about Lee); Ollinger Crenshaw, *General Lee's College: The Rise and Growth of Washington and Lee University* (New York: Random House, 1968), p. 150.

11. A. C. Penn to REL, Mayo Forge, Patrick County, VA, November 1, 1865; John H. Finley to REL, Knoxville, TN, November 5, 1865 (both in WLU/LP).

12. William J. Eldeston to REL, Russellville, KY, November 14, 1865, WLU/LP; REL to Gibson, Lexington, January 24, 1866, WLU/LP/LDFA; Gibson to REL, Petersburg, VA, December 24, 1865, WLU/LP; Crenshaw, *General Lee's College*, p. 196. Gibson, of Grace Episcopal Church in downtown Petersburg, had delicately proposed for the post his brother-in-law, the president of Hampden-Sydney College—whose brother, awkwardly enough, was also being considered. The chair went to someone else altogether, John L. Kirkpatrick, the Presbyterian president of Davidson College. At least Gibson received a donation from Lee to help build his church, construction having halted during the siege.

13. William Augustus Muhlenberg, *The Application of Christianity to Education*. (Jamaica, NY: Sleight & George, 1828). In charging Pendleton with creating a high school in Alexandria, Meade instructed Pendleton to seek out Muhlenberg's ideas. Susan Pendleton Lee, *Memoirs of William Nelson Pendleton* (Philadelphia: J. B. Lippincott, 1893; Harrisonburg, VA: Sprinkle Publications, 1991), pp. 72, 74

14. William Henry Ruffner, "The History of Washington College, 1830–1848," *Historical Papers* (Lexington: WLU), no. 6, 1904, pp. 33–34; Kjartan Theodore Magnusson, "The History of Washington College under Robert E. Lee, 1865–1870" (EdD diss., Brigham Young University, 1989), pp. 44–45, 49. Junkin paraphrase: Judg. 7:20.

15. REL, Memorandum Book #5, VHS Mss1 L51 b 52.

16. Crenshaw, *General Lee's College*, pp. 160–65.

17. REL to Rev. G. W. Leyburn, Lexington, March 20, 1866, Letterbook, VHS/LFP Mss1 L51 c 737, p. 108; note in Lee's hand left in his "Memorandum Book Oct '65," on his office desk at the time of his death. Whether this is his thought or copied from another is not clear.

18. REL, Memorandum Book #5, VHS Mss1 L51 b 52; Crenshaw, *General Lee's*

College, pp. 196–202; Wm. Hunter to REL, Savannah, March 9, 1866, WLU/LP; REL to MARC, Petersburg, VA, February 23, 1865, VHS Mss1 L51 c 573.

19. Crenshaw, *General Lee's College*, p. 212; Magnusson, "History," p. 125; "The Y. M. C. Association," *Southern Collegian*, October 9, 1869, p. 5.

20. REL, report to Trustees, June, 1866; Faculty Minutes, June 26, 1866, WLU, Trustees Papers, Folder 163; see REL to clergy, September 12, 1870, WLU/LP, Lee Copy Letterbook.

21. M. W. Humphreys, "Reminiscences of General Lee as President," in *General Robert E. Lee after Appomattox*, ed. Franklin L. Riley (New York: Macmillan, 1922), p. 34. The able Humphreys remained at the college to teach classics under Lee.

22. REL to Col. Wm. Allan, Staunton, VA, Rockbridge Baths, VA, July 27, 1866, Letterbook, VHS/LFP L51 c 737, pp. 186–87; Jno. Echols to REL, Staunton, VA, July 31, 1866, WLU/LP.

23. REL, handwritten notes and formal report to Trustees, June 1866, WLU, Trustees Papers, Folder 163; Royster Lyle and Pamela Hemenway Simpson, *The Architecture of Historic Lexington* (Charlottesville: University Press of Virginia, 1977), p. 158; Magnusson, "History," p. 125.

24. Grounds & Building Committee report, July 26, 1866, WLU, Trustees Papers, Folder 163; McCulloch to REL, New York, July 24, 1866, WLU/LP. Lee's original plan has been lost.

25. Williamson, "Engineering Dept. Annual Report 1848," VMI Archives, Williamson Papers, Folder 2; *An Elementary Course of Architecture and Civil Engineering, Compiled from the Most Approved Authors for the Use of the Cadets of the Virginia Military Institute* (Lexington: Samuel Gillock, 1850); Lyle and Simpson, *Architecture of Historic Lexington*, pp. 279–80.

26. Robert Dale Owen, *Hints on Public Architecture* (New York: Putnam, 1849), pp. 8, 10, 12–13, 35–37, 98, 104–9; Lyle and Simpson, *Architecture of Historic Lexington*, pp. 27–32

27. Lyle and Simpson, *Architecture of Historic Lexington*, pp. 158–60; McCulloch to REL, New York, July 24, 1866, WLU/LP.

28. Simpson, "Lee Chapel," WLU; Faculty Minutes, January 14, 1867, WLU.

29. *Gazette & Banner*, June 10, 1868, p. 3; June 14, 1868, p. 3.

30. Faculty Minutes, September 16, 1868, WLU, Faculty Minutes; Simpson, "Lee Chapel"; Magnusson, "History," p. 125. The trustees also wanted to provide Lee with a handsome residence and a large annuity, which Lee vetoed; the house, built under his supervision at much reduced cost, is still used by the college's presidents. A. L. Long, *Memoirs of Robert E. Lee*, 7th ed. (Secaucus, NJ: Blue and Grey Press, 1983), p. 453.

31. Long, *Memoirs*, p. 451; ledger, Edward C. Gordon Papers, VHS, Mss1 G 6546 a 225.

32. MARC to CCL, Lexington, October 7, [1870], LOC/EA, MCL Papers, Box 2, 1834–1872.

33. *The Lee Museum*, undated pamphlet (William M. Brown, 1928 [WLU]); see "Anniversary Celebration of the Graham P. Society," *Collegian*, January 22, 1870, p. 5, and "Anniversary Celebration of the Washington L. Society," *Collegian*, February 26, 1870, p. 5.

34. The first St. Patrick's Catholic Church was not built until 1874 (Lyle and Simpson, *Architecture of Historic Lexington*, p. 31).

35. Douglas Southall Freeman, *R. E. Lee: A Biography*, 4 vols. (New York: Charles Scribner's Sons, 1934), 4:275; R. W. Rogers, "Reminiscences of General Lee and Washington College," in Riley, *Lee after Appomattox*, p. 60 (Rogers was that student); see Long, *Memoirs*, p. 448.

36. Freeman, *R. E. Lee*, 4:288.

37. J. W. Ewing, "An Incident in the Life of General R. E. Lee," in Riley, *Lee after Appomattox*, pp. 70–72.

38. Ewing, "An Incident," p. 71; John B. Collyar, "A College Boy's Observation of General Lee," in Riley, *Lee after Appomattox*, p. 66; Matt. 22:35–40. The "Summary of the Law" was appointed as an optional addition to the Decalogue; see BCP 1789, §13, Holy Communion. Freeman declares that "Lee initiated the honor system" that guides Washington and Lee University to this day (*R. E. Lee*, 4:278). As much as Lee prized honor and sought to instill it in others (see Long, *Memoir*, p. 447), Freeman's source (Collyar, p. 66) does not support this assertion; and apparently no documentary evidence links Lee directly with the system.

39. WLU/Howe 0080, Folder 170; George W. Pierson, *A Yale Book of Numbers* (New Haven: Yale University, 1983), p. A-1.3; Samuel Eliot Morison, *The Development of Harvard University, 1869–1929* (Cambridge, MA: Harvard University Press, 1930), p. xc (figure for the 1868–1869 term). Harvard and Yale figures reflect only their colleges and not their scientific schools. For the 1907 figure, see Crenshaw, *General Lee's College*, p. 274.

40. WLU/Howe 0080, Folder 170.

41. Faculty Minutes, [undated] 1868, WLU SC Trustees Papers, Coll. 0028, Folder 172.

42. C. A. Graves, "General Lee at Lexington," in Riley, *Lee after Appomattox*, p. 25. Graves, a student under Lee, does not cite the time or context of Lee's statement. Jones quotes a similar statement in such a way that Freeman doubts its authenticity (*R. E. Lee*, 4:283n45).

43. REL to Pendleton, near Cartersville, VA, August 28, 1865, WLU/LP. On the bond with Pendleton, see Ewing, "An Incident," p. 73. Regarding the vestry, see Minutes, Grace Church, Lexington, September 28, 1865 (parish archives).

44. Lee, *Memoirs of Pendleton*, pp. 422–24, 428. On praying for the president, see, e.g., "A Prayer for the President of the United States, and of All in Civil Authority," BCP 1789, §29, Morning Prayer.

45. Vestry Minutes, October 11, 1866; Lee, *Memoirs of Pendleton*, pp. 435, 447; Williamson to "Nannie," October 12, 1866, WLU/Howe, Box 10, Folder 182; George M. Brooke Jr., *General Lee's Church* (Lexington, VA: News-Gazette, 1984), p. 24.

46. Lee, *Memoirs of Pendleton*, pp. 445–46, 449.

47. Vestry Minutes, May 10, 1867, May 14, 1868, May 19, 1869, May 11, 1870; Lee, *Memoirs of Pendleton*, p. 433. On the postwar church, see David Lynn Holmes Jr., *A Brief History of the Episcopal Church* (Valley Forge, PA: Trinity, 1993), p. 82.

48. Vestry Minutes, February 19, 1868, May 19, 1869; Brooke, *General Lee's Church*, p. 40.

49. Lee, *Memoirs of Pendleton*, p. 447; Brooke, *General Lee's Church*, p. 24; Vestry Minutes, November 19, 1868; REL to Mildred, Lexington, December 21–22, 1866, VHS/LFP Mss1 L51 c 678; see also, REL Jr., *Recollections*, p. 248; Agnes to Mildred, Lexington, January 6, 1866, VHS/LFP Mss1 L51 c 616.

50. REL to MARC, White Sulphur Springs, WV, August 10, 1867, VHS/LFP Mss1 L51 c 675; see also, REL Jr., *Recollections*, p. 366; and REL to MARC, White Sulphur Springs, WV, August 14, 1867, VHS/LFP Mss1 L51 c 676; also in REL Jr., p. 367; Vestry Minutes, September 8, 1869.

51. Enclosed in a letter of REL to the Misses Fontaine, September 16, 1869, LVA #23784.

52. REL to MARC, Richmond, March 29, 1870, VHS/LFP Mss1 L51 c 683, see also, REL Jr., *Recollections*, p. 389; REL to MARC, Alexandria, July 15, 1870, VHS/LFP Mss1 L51 c 694; REL to Rev. Francis Sprigg, Lexington, October 21, 1865, VHS Mss2 L515 a 141.

53. REL to Miss Virginia Ritchie, Lexington, October 23, 1869, VHS Mss2 L515 a 82.

Notes to Chapter 20

1. See letters quoted in REL Jr., *Recollections and Letters of General Robert E. Lee* (New York: Doubleday, Page, 1905), pp. 163–65.

2. MARC, "Reminiscences," VHS L5144 a 1397–1472, also in *VMHB* 109, no. 3 (2001): 315.

3. Robert M. Poole, "How Arlington National Cemetery Came to Be," *Smithsonian*, November 2009, http://www.smithsonianmag.com/history/how-arlington-national -cemetery-came-to-be-145147007, accessed January 19, 2016.

4. MARC to Mrs. Francis Asbury Dickins, Kinloch, VA, June 18, [1861], AH, #2445. No year is written, but Mary Lee stayed at Kinloch only in 1861. Margaret Randolph Dickins came from the prominent Randolph family of Tuckahoe plantation in Goochland. She and her husband, a Washington attorney, retreated to Ossian Hall in Fairfax County during the war years, though he was detained several times as a Confederate sympathizer.

5. MARC to Emily Mason, Lexington, April 20, 1866, quoted in Emory M. Thomas, *Robert E. Lee: A Biography* (New York: Norton, 1995), p. 383.

6. Cf. Douglas Southall Freeman, *R. E. Lee: A Biography*, 4 vols. (New York: Charles Scribner's Sons, 1934), 4:385–90.

7. REL to Hunter, Richmond, January 11, 1865, http://www.civilwar.org/ education/history/primarysources/robert-e-lee-to-andrew.html, accessed July 5, 2016. On Jefferson Davis and efforts to enlist blacks in the Confederate cause, see William C. Davis, *Jefferson Davis: The Man and His Hour* (New York: HarperCollins, 1991), pp. 541, 597–99.

8. William Allan, "Memoranda of Conversations with General Lee," February 26 and March 10, 1868, WLU 0064, also in Gary Gallagher, ed., *Lee the Soldier* (Lincoln: University of Nebraska Press, 1996), p. 12. Lee quoted in Freeman, *R. E. Lee*, 4:401 (see caveat in n. 15).

9. REL Jr., *Recollections*, pp. 199, 166–68. Difficulties with servants (race not mentioned) continued to plague the Lees: see REL to Agnes, March 12, 1868, VHS/LFP Mss1 L51 c 653; see also REL Jr., p. 308.

10. REL to REL Jr., Lexington, March 12, 1868, in REL Jr., *Recollections*, p. 306. On

the general impetus to find and employ European immigrants in the postwar country, see Heather Cox Richardson, *The Death of Reconstruction: Race, Labor, and Politics in the Post–Civil War North, 1865–1901* (Cambridge, MA: Harvard University Press, 2001), p. 30.

11. MARC to Emily Mason, Lexington, May 20, 1866, quoted in Thomas, *Robert E. Lee*, p. 383.

12. REL Jr., *Recollections*, p. 275. Three children are listed as born to the couple, Martha Elizabeth (b. 1853), Marsellus (b. 1858), and an unnamed child who died two weeks after birth (1855). *Rockbridge County Births, 1853–1877* (Athens, GA: Iberian Publishing, 1988), 1:295; *Rockbridge County, Virginia Death Register, 1853–1870* (Athens, GA: Iberian Publishing, 1991), p. 37. Another son, William O., a twenty-two-year-old laborer, married Elizabeth C. Hilley on June 18, 1863 (Louise M. Perkins, *Rockbridge County Marriages, 1851–1885* [Signal Mountain, TN: Mountain Press, 1989], p. 184). The Howards' names vary in spelling. A "Reuben Howard" is listed as a "Free Negro" in county tax records as early as 1819, suggesting that the Howards could have been a longtime, well-established family within Rockbridge's free black community. *Rockbridge County Personal Property Tax Lists, 1782–1821* (LVA).

13. Quoted in Thomas, *Robert E. Lee*, p. 382.

14. Elizabeth Varon, *Appomattox: Victory, Defeat, and Freedom at the End of the Civil War* (New York: OUP, 2014), p. 222; David Herbert Donald, *Lincoln* (New York: Simon and Schuster, 1995), pp. 166–67; Harriet Beecher Stowe, *Uncle Tom's Cabin* (Boston: John P. Jewett, 1852), p. 318.

15. Quoted in Donald, *Lincoln*, p. 221 (for a fuller discussion, see note on pp. 633–34). On racism in the North, see Richardson, *The Death of Reconstruction*, pp. 11–14. REL to W. H. Nettleton, Lexington, May 21, 1866, Letterbook, VHS/LFP Mss1 L51 c 737, p. 145.

16. William Preston Johnston, "Memorandum," in Gallagher, *Lee the Soldier*, p. 30.

17. Freeman, *R. E. Lee*, 4:316–17; John M. McClure, "The Freedmen's Bureau School in Lexington versus 'General Lee's Boys,'" in *Virginia's Civil War*, ed. Peter Wallenstein and Bertram Wyatt-Brown (Charlottesville: University of Virginia Press, 2005), pp. 193–94; Thomas, *Robert E. Lee*, p. 386; see REL to J. W. Sharp, April 13, 1867, WLU/LP, Lee Copy Letterbook II. Students had also disrupted the post office and delayed mails, so Lee admonished the student body accordingly (Minutes, March 25, 1867, and notice of March 26, 1867, Faculty Minutes, WLU Special Collections).

18. Varon, *Appomattox*, p. 223; Thomas, *Robert E. Lee*, p. 386; see REL to Jno. W. Jordon, Nov. 20, 1868, Letter Book II, 209; and Lee Notice, WLU/LP, Lee Copy Letterbook II, pp. 209, 208, and A. L. Long, *Memoirs of Robert E. Lee*, 7th ed. (Secaucus, NJ: Blue and Grey Press, 1983), p. 449. On race relations in Lexington, see McClure, "Freedmen's Bureau," pp. 189–200.

19. Contrast Freeman, *R. E. Lee*, 4:358–59, and Franklin L. Riley, ed., *General Robert E. Lee after Appomattox* (New York: Macmillan, 1922), pp. 129–30, with the *Lexington Gazette and Banner*, May 27, 1868, p. 3 (and May 13, 1868, p. e), and Ollinger Crenshaw, *General Lee's College: The Rise and Growth of Washington and Lee University* (New York: Random House, 1968), p. 151, and his typescript, "General Lee's College" (unpublished typescript, 2 vols., WLU Special Collections, 1973), p. 564.

20. Freeman, *R. E. Lee*, 4:358–59. Griffin's trial was marked by procedural ma-

neuverings finally resolved by the chief justice of the United States, Salmon Chase. See REL to Strickler, May 10, 1868; REL to Wagner, May 11, 1868 (WLU/LP); Riley, *Lee after Appomattox*, pp. 129–30; REL Jr., *Recollections*, p. 300.

21. *Staunton Spectator*, January 30, 1866, p. 3; May 1, 1866, p. 3; C. A. Graves, "General Lee at Lexington," in Riley, *Lee after Appomattox*, pp. 28–30. (Since Hughes had served with notable lack of distinction in the Confederate army, and accounts do not identify him otherwise, presumably he was white.)

22. See Lincoln's address to Congress, December 1863 (cf. Donald, *Lincoln*, pp. 469–74) and in 1865 (Donald, pp. 562–65), and Richardson, *The Death of Reconstruction*, pp. 20–21, for a summary of Johnson's vision.

23. Cf. Thomas, *Robert E. Lee*, p. 385 (see ch. 16, n. 10 above). See Freeman, *R. E. Lee*, 4:251–52, on Lee's view of Johnson's policies.

24. REL to Brockenbrough, January 23, 1866, WLU/LP, Correspondence from Lee, Box 3.

25. MARC to Mason, May 20, 1866.

26. Elizabeth Brown Pryor, *Reading the Man: Robert E. Lee through His Private Letters* (New York: Viking, 2007), p. 449; REL to Childe, Lexington, January 16, 1868, SH M2009.355.

27. REL to Childe, Lexington, February 16, 1869, SH M2009.370. Intriguingly, he then adds praise of Spain for creating a constitutional monarchy.

28. REL to Martha Custis Williams, Lexington, December 1, 1866, in *"To Markie": The Letters of Robert E. Lee to Martha Custis Williams*, ed. Avery Craven (Cambridge, MA: Harvard University Press, 1933), #31, pp. 71–72; see Pryor, *Reading the Man*, pp. 372–75. How Williams got himself into that predicament has never been clear.

29. Lee to Davis, February 23, 1866, quoted in REL Jr., *Recollections*, p. 223. On his silence, see Pryor, *Reading the Man*, p. 449. REL to Ould, Lexington, February 4, 1867, Letterbook 1866–1870, VHS/LFP Mss1 L51 c 738, pp. 18–20.

30. See Richardson, *The Death of Reconstruction*, p. 17: white gangs terrorized blacks, and organizations emerged to institutionalize harassment; some states enacted "black codes" limiting freedmen's rights; Texas and Mississippi rejected the Thirteenth Amendment; Southern states elected ex-Confederates to state and federal offices, such as former vice president Alexander Stephens to the US Senate from Georgia.

31. Richardson, *The Death of Reconstruction*, pp. 11–13.

32. REL to Rosecrans, White Sulphur Springs, WV, August 26, 1868, Letterbook, VHS/LFP Mss1 L51 c 738.

33. Thomas Cary Johnson, *Life and Letters of Robert Louis Dabney* (Richmond: Presbyterian Committee on Publications, 1903), pp. 497–500. Dabney, a Presbyterian minister and scholar who taught at Union Presbyterian Seminary in Richmond, had been a chaplain under Stonewall Jackson and published one of the first biographies of the general. In 1895 he related Stockdale's reminiscence of the Rosecrans meeting and Lee's comments, which he heard in 1883 just before (he said) Stockdale died. The account relies, then, on two reminiscences, each a dozen or more years old. At least two errors are clear: Stockdale said the meeting occurred in 1870 whereas documents place the statement two years earlier; and Stockdale died in 1890.

34. REL to Childe, January 16, 1868.

35. REL to David McConaughy, Lexington, August 9, 1869, WLU/LP; Edward Lee Childe, *Life and Campaigns of General Lee*, trans. George Litting (London: Chatto and Windus, 1875), p. 331; see also, Margaret Sanborn, *Robert E. Lee: A Portrait* (Moose, WY: Homestead Publishing, 1996), 2:308; Charles Bracelen Flood, *Lee: The Last Years* (Boston: Houghton Mifflin, 1981), p. 152.

36. Varon, *Appomattox*, pp. 39, 202–3, 220–21.

Notes to Chapter 21

1. Quoted in REL Jr., *Recollections and Letters of General Robert E. Lee* (New York: Doubleday, Page, 1905), p. 433.

2. Elizabeth Varon, *Appomattox: Victory, Defeat, and Freedom at the End of the Civil War* (New York: OUP, 2014), p. 24; Faculty Minutes, April 5, 1870; Trustee Minutes, April 19, 1870, WLU; Ollinger Crenshaw, *General Lee's College: The Rise and Growth of Washington and Lee University* (New York: Random House, 1968), p. 171.

3. REL to MARC, Hot Springs, WV, August 19, 1870, VHS/LFP Mss1 L51 c 700; REL to Agnes, Hot Springs, WV, August 23, 1870, VHS/LFP Mss1 L51 c 702; both quoted in REL Jr., *Recollections*, pp. 428, 430, 435.

4. Opus 62, no. 3 in E minor, *andante maestoso, "Trauermarsch"* (1844).

5. MARC to CCL, Lexington, October 7, 1870, quoted in Elizabeth Brown Pryor, *Reading the Man: Robert E. Lee through His Private Letters* (New York: Viking, 2007), p. 460; Mildred, "My Recollections of My Father's Death, August 21st 1888," VHS Mss5:1 L5114:1.

6. Vestry Minutes, May 9, 1869, July 6, 1870; REL to MARC, Ravensworth, VA, July 20, 1870, VHS Mss1 L51 c 695; REL Jr., *Recollections*, p. 418.

7. Pendleton to Grace Church Vestry, Vestry Minutes, September 28, 1870, pp. 66–67; Susan Pendleton Lee, *Memoirs of William Nelson Pendleton* (1893; reprint, Harrisonburg, VA: Sprinkle Publications, 1991), p. 454.

8. REL to Ann L. Jones, Lexington, September 23, 1870; abstract at W&L; LFDA #3021.

9. Grace Church/R. E. Lee Memorial Church, Vestry Minutes, September 28, 1870, pp. 65–66; Pendleton to Vestry, pp. 66–67; Johnson, quoted in REL Jr., *Recollections*, pp. 435–36.

10. James D. McCabe, *Life and Campaigns of General Robert E. Lee* (Atlanta: National Publishing Co., 1866), p. 647.

11. Mildred, "Recollections"; Johnston, in REL Jr., *Recollections*, p. 436.

12. Mildred, "Recollections"; Johnston, in REL Jr., *Recollections*, p. 437. The two accounts vary; Johnston wrote that Lee could answer questions orally though briefly, whereas Mildred recalled him "merely nodding & shaking his head if we asked him what he wanted."

13. MARC to CCL, October 7, 1870, quoted in Pryor, *Reading the Man*, p. 461. The turpentine-based elixir may have been Hamlin's Wizard Oil, first produced in 1861 in Chicago by a magician and his brother and advertised to cure ailments from toothaches to cancer and pneumonia.

14. "Prayers for the Dead" would have been premature. More likely, Pendleton

used portions of the "Visitation of the Sick," particularly those "for the dying" (BCP 1789, §20).

15. Mildred, "Recollections."

16. Minutes of the Trustees, October 15, 1870, pp. 340, 344, 348, 350, 352. About fifteen years later, the chapel was extended to house the recumbent statue of Lee by Edward Valentine on the main floor, with a crypt for Lee's remains and those of his family in the basement adjacent to Lee's office. Traveller's bones, having been displayed in the chapel museum for many years, were interred just outside in 1971.

17. Meriwether to "Cousin Jessie," W&L, October 15, 1870, WLU/LP, 0064. Similar quotes from Lee were cited by other local clergy: see ch. 19 above.

18. McCabe, *Life and Campaigns*, pp. 650–53; BCP 1789, §23, the Order for the Burial of the Dead.

19. Mildred, "Recollections."

20. *Hymnal and Canticles of the Protestant Episcopal Church*, ed. A. B. Goodrich and Walter B. Gilbert (New York: Dutton, 1888) [1874 ed.], #398. Some mystery surrounds which tunes and verses Lee used. Music was not included in old hymnals, including those associated with the Lee family. In *The Hymnal 1982*, the Episcopal Church sets these five verses to the tune "Foundation," which derives from a Southern melody of the "sacred harp" tradition, and "Lyons," attributed to Johann Michael Haydn. However, the 1874/1888 Episcopal hymnal suggests the tune "Datchet." Intriguingly, the newly renamed Washington and Lee University published a hymnal for use in its chapel the year after Lee died. It adds an additional verse:

E'en down to old age, all My people shall prove
My sovereign, eternal, unchangeable love;
And then when gray hairs shall their temples adorn,
Like lambs they shall still in My bosom be borne.

It also offers two options for tunes, "Goshen" and "Portuguese Hymn." The latter was also used in an 1885 hymnal of the evangelical breakaway group the Reformed Episcopal Church. "Portuguese Hymn" is better known as "*Adeste Fidelis.*" An 1894 edition of an Episcopal hymnal provides two tunes, "*Adeste Fidelis*" and "Foundation." It is quite possible that the voices outside the chapel at Lee's funeral sang forth, to different words, the hymn tune now best known as "O Come, All Ye Faithful."

21. "The Funeral of Gen. Lee," *Richmond Daily Dispatch*, October 17, 1870, p. 3.

22. "General Lee," *Philadelphia Evening Telegraph*, October 15, 1870, p. 1.

23. "Death of General Robert E. Lee," *Stark County (OH) Democrat*, October 27, 1870, p. 1. (It cites the "E" in his name as "Edmund," and lists its source as *Enquirer*.) "Death of General Robert E. Lee," *Tiffin (OH) Tribune*, October 20, 1870, p. 1.

24. "The Lowering of the Flag," *Leavenworth (KS) Weekly Times*, October 20, 1870, p. 2 (see "Honors to General Lee at a United States Custom House," *Philadelphia Evening Telegraph*, October 13, 1870, p. 8). "Death of Robert E. Lee," *Washington Standard*, October 15, 1870, p. 2.

25. McCabe, *Life and Campaigns*, pp. 642–43 (Judah Benjamin had served as Confederate attorney general, secretary of war, and secretary of state; Louis Wigfall was a Confederate general and senator); Douglass, quoted from an article of 1871 in David Blight, *Frederick Douglass's Civil War: Keeping Faith in Jubilee* (Baton Rouge: LSU Press, 1991), p. 229.

26. "Robert E. Lee," *New-York Daily Tribune*, October 13, 1870, p. 4; other quotations in this paragraph come from "Northern Papers," *Richmond Daily Dispatch*, October 15, 1870, p. 1.

Notes to the Epilogue

1. Though long identified as the Lee family motto, background information on its derivation is sparse. It may have first been adopted by the Lees of Shropshire as early as the thirteenth century, and probably derived from a phrase in one of Horace's *Satires*. A crest of uncertain vintage, used by the Lees of Coton, included the motto *Ne Incautus Futuri*, and provided the basis for Washington and Lee's combination of Lee and Washington heraldry. See William Blackstone Lee, "Lees of Langley and Coton," in *Lee of Virginia, 1642–1892: Biographical and Genealogical Sketches of the Descendants of Colonel Richard Lee*, ed. Edmund Jennings Lee (Philadelphia, 1895), p. 24.

2. *Virginia Gazette*, Lexington, October 21, 1870, p. 2; Vestry Minutes, October 18–19, 1870. The building was consecrated in 1886, and the parish's name was changed to R. E. Lee Memorial Church in 1903 (and to R. E. Lee Memorial Episcopal Church in 2015). George M. Brooke Jr., *General Lee's Church* (Lexington, VA: News-Gazette, 1984), p. 41; Vestry Minutes, April 24, 1903, and November 16, 2015.

3. John M. McClure, "The Freedmen's Bureau School in Lexington versus 'General Lee's Boys,'" in *Virginia's Civil War*, ed. Peter Wallenstein and Bertram Wyatt-Brown (Charlottesville: University of Virginia Press, 2005), p. 198.

4. On the "enigma" of Lee, see Charles Joyner, "A Man of Constant Sorrow," in Wallenstein and Wyatt-Brown, *Virginia's Civil War*, pp. 45–53. On St. Paul's, see Philip J. Schwarz, "General Lee and Visibility" (talk at Stratford Hall Plantation Seminar on Slavery, August 4, 2000, http://www.stratalum.org/leecommunion.htm, accessed July 6, 2016). Among Schwarz's observations is that though Broun was identified as a colonel in the 1903 newspaper accounts, his obituary in the *Confederate Veteran* cites him as a major.

5. Elizabeth Varon, *Appomattox: Victory, Defeat, and Freedom at the End of the Civil War* (New York: OUP, 2014), p. 222 (see above, pp. 230–34); David Hume, *Essays, Moral, Political, and Literary*, ed. Eugene F. Miller (Indianapolis: Liberty Fund, 1985), p. 208n10; REL, quoted in REL Jr., *Recollections and Letters of General Robert E. Lee* (New York: Doubleday, Page, 1905), p. 168. On racism in the North, see Heather Cox Richardson, *The Death of Reconstruction: Race, Labor, and Politics in the Post–Civil War North, 1865–1901* (Cambridge, MA: Harvard University Press, 2001), pp. 11–14.

6. REL to Mr. W. H. Nettleton, Lexington, May 21, 1866, Letterbook, VHS/LFP Mss1 L51 c 737, p. 145. David Hume had also implied a similar distinction among Caucasians (Hume, *Essays*).

7. See Peter Suber, "Paternalism," in *Philosophy of Law: An Encyclopedia*, ed. Christopher B. Gray (New York: Garland Publishing, 1999), 2:632–35.

8. Cf. Peter Garnsey and Richard Saller et al., *The Roman Empire: Economy, Society, and Culture*, 2nd ed. (Oakland: University of California Press, 2015), pp. 151–71. The Latin term *domus*, however, better applies as it extends the scope of *familia* to all in the household. Major Custis, though, hardly exerted the potentially oppressive power

of the ancient *patria potestas* over his slaves, much less his kin. Cf. Garnsey and Saller, "Patronal Power Relations," in *Paul and Empire: Religion and Power in Roman Imperial Society*, ed. Richard A. Horsley (Harrisburg, PA: Trinity, 1997), p. 96, especially regarding the ethics of reciprocity between benefactor and recipient.

9. Lacy D. Ford, *Deliver Us from Evil: The Slavery Question in the Old South* (Oxford: OUP, 2009), p. 147. He offers a somewhat different set of guiding principles of paternalism, and also concentrates on the lower South, especially the Lowcountry of South Carolina.

10. E.g., Phil. 2:7; see Ford, *Deliver Us from Evil*, pp. 150, 157, 160.

11. Journals of Martha Custis Williams, Arlington House Archives, November 2, 1853.

12. Varon, *Appomattox*, pp. 55, 64.

13. REL to MARC, Fort Mason, TX, January 23, 1861, VHS/LFP Mss1 L51 c 271; REL to REL Jr., Lexington, March 12, 1868, in REL Jr., *Recollections*, p. 306. See Elizabeth Brown Pryor, *Reading the Man: Robert E. Lee through His Private Letters* (New York: Viking, 2007), p. 451, regarding restrictions on whites as well as blacks (n. 38) and regarding governorship; REL to Ould, Lexington, February 4, 1867, Letterbook 1866–1870, VHS/LFP Mss1 L51 c 738, pp. 18–20.

14. George C. Rable, *God's Almost Chosen Peoples* (Chapel Hill: UNC Press, 2010), p. 389; "Death of General Robert E. Lee," *Stark County (OH) Democrat*, October 27, 1870.

15. Humphreys, "Reminiscences," in *General Robert E. Lee after Appomattox*, ed. Franklin L. Riley (New York: Macmillan, 1922), p. 39.

16. Cf. "μετανοέω," in *Theological Dictionary of the New Testament*, ed. Gerhard Kittel (Grand Rapids: Eerdmans, 1967), 4:975–1008, especially pp. 1007–8; Luke 17:3–4; 2 Cor. 7:9–10. REL to Martha Custis Williams, Lexington, December 20, 1865, in *"To Markie": The Letters of Robert E. Lee to Martha Custis Williams*, ed. Avery Craven (Cambridge, MA: Harvard University Press, 1933), #29, p. 66.

Index

Abolitionism, 157–60, 171, 176, 230
Adams, Charles Francis, 297n32
Adams, Henry, 102–3
Addison, Walter, 38, 43
African Americans: and evangelical
    Episcopalianism, 75–76; on Lee's
    legacy, 249–50; Lee's postwar views
    of, 230–34, 235–36, 238–39, 252–58;
    receipt of communion at St. Paul's
    Episcopal Church, x–xi, 253; Recon-
    struction and voting rights, 232–33,
    235–36, 257. *See also* Colonization
    movement; Lee, Robert E., racial
    views of; Racial views; Slavery
African Education Society, 44
"Agnes." *See* Lee, Eleanor Agnes ("Ag-
    nes") (daughter)
Alexander, Edward Porter, 195, 202,
    204, 307n61
Alexandria Academy, 50
Allan, William, 166, 167, 171
American Colonization Society. *See*
    Colonization movement
Anderson, Robert, 3–4
Anglicanism (Church of England),
    11–13, 20–22, 64, 273n13; the "catho-
    lic revival," 19, 83–85, 285n3; colonial
    Virginians' adaptation of, 11–19,
    20–22; link between God's grace and
    nature, 123; "low church" and "high
    church" differences, 25, 75, 83–85,
    98, 143–44, 285n3; rite of confirma-
    tion, 109; Taylor's understandings of
    life and death, 125–28, 133, 146, 190;

Thirty-Nine Articles, 130, 273–74n3,
    296n6; views of the Trinity, 122–23.
    See also Episcopalianism, Virginia
"Annie." *See* Lee, Anne Carter ("Annie")
    (daughter)
Aristotle, 173
Arlington House (Custis family estate),
    35–36, 56–58, 177–79, 228–30,
    255–57; Custis and Lee family slaves
    ("servants") at, 21, 76, 151, 153–56,
    167, 254, 255–57, 302n14; Federal
    troops' occupation during Civil War,
    177–79, 180, 189, 228–30; the Lees'
    family life at, 2, 79–80, 97–98, 139,
    147–48, 255; Markie Williams and
    Custis family at, 35, 147–48, 154,
    155–56; Mrs. Custis and, 35–36, 58;
    paternalism, 255–57; slaveholding at,
    76, 147–48, 153–56, 255–57, 302n14
Arminianism, 17, 131, 183
Arminius, Jacob, 131
Augustine of Hippo, 112, 130–31, 138,
    183

Bainbridge, Harry, 146
Baptism: and confirmation rites,
    109–10; evangelical Episcopalianism,
    24–25, 109–10; Lee's, 3, 10, 14, 49,
    281n1; Roman Catholic rite of, 141
Barton, Howard, 245
Battle of Bull Run, First, 181
Battle of Fredericksburg, 187–88
Battle of Gettysburg, 177, 192–93
Battle of Manassas, First, 187, 189

(mid-1850s), 148; Corps of Engineers, 54–55, 107, 113; during engagement to Mary, 62–70; at Fort Hamilton in New York, 79, 80, 82–83, 88–89, 100, 135; at Fort Monroe, 71, 73–79; guarding Texas frontier in command of the Second Calvary, 108, 118, 129, 139–47, 151, 163, 165; handling diseases and deaths of his officers, 144–46; Mexican War, 4, 5, 85, 88–96; resignation of commission and decision to lead Confederate Virginia, 4–6, 9, 165–75, 204, 229, 301–2n11; salary, finances, and investments, 146, 299n24; at St. Louis, 81–82; as superintendent of Military Academy at West Point, 5, 103–8, 113, 209, 215; as West Point cadet, 51–54, 103. *See also* Lee, Robert E., and Civil War

Lee, Robert E., and Civil War, 1–6, 176–96, 236; accepting command to lead Confederate Virginia's forces, 6, 9, 169–75, 177, 204; as advisor to Davis, 37, 177, 193, 230; allegiance and loyalty to state of Virginia, 171–72, 174; belief that state sovereignty and the Constitution were under attack, 172–73; call for Confederate army's "day of humiliation" and sacrifice, 184–86; call for sacrifice by the South, 184–87; dealing with Confederate defeat, 7, 192–96, 197–205, 241, 258, 307n2; dealing with deaths of soldiers and family, 188–92, 236–37; decision to resign military commission and to side with the Confederacy, 4–6, 9, 165–75, 204, 229, 301–2n11; and defeat of Richmond, 6, 193–94, 197; and doctrine of providence, 180, 182–85, 189–90, 193, 194, 198, 241, 258; and family, 176–82, 186–87, 190–92; on Gettysburg defeat, 192–93; lament for survivors and loved ones, 189, 190; promotion to chief of Confederate forces, 177; religious interpretations and religious faith, 176–77, 180, 181–93, 236, 304n23; response to outbreak of war, 176–77; response to the growing national conflict, 3–5, 161–75; and

slavery issue, 167, 171; surrender to Grant at Appomattox, x, 6, 177, 195, 240, 256–57

Lee, Robert E., during postwar period, 7, 197–210, 211–24, 228–41; correspondence with Markie Williams, 200–201, 259; dealing with the Confederate defeat, 7, 192–96, 197–205, 307n2; decision to remain in Virginia and work for reconciliation/restoration, 9, 201–5, 228, 240–41, 252, 258; doubts about democracy, 257; efforts to restrict black voting rights (suffrage), 232–33, 235–36, 257; family life, 200, 228–30; family residence at Derwent farm, 205, 208, 213; fury at Reconstruction, 234–41; and Grace Church in Lexington, 224–27; hope for return to antebellum social norms minus slavery, 238–41; parole and pardon for treason, 6, 195, 197, 201, 235; racial views and relationships between freed blacks and whites, 230–34, 235–36, 238–39, 252–58; return to Richmond, 6, 197, 201; searching for meaningful work, 7, 205–6; and the South's postwar spiritual crisis, 199–201; Washington College presidency, 211–24, 233–34, 251. *See also* Lee, Robert E., Washington College presidency of

Lee, Robert E., racial views of, xi, 151–60, 167, 171, 230–34, 252–58; and abolitionism/emancipation, 157–60, 171, 230, 258; advice to Confederate leaders, 230; Christian paternalism and racial hierarchies, 153–55, 233, 239, 254–58; decision to resign commission and fight for the South, 167, 171; efforts to restrict black voting rights (suffrage), 232–33, 235–36, 257; and family's slaveholding, 151, 153–56, 167, 230–31, 302n14; and father-in-law's slaves, 155–56, 254; and Fourteenth Amendment, 232; postwar racial views and race relations, 230–34, 235–36, 238–39, 252–58; on providence and slavery, 158–60, 171, 257–58; religious views of slavery, 157–60, 230; story of the